W9-CDV-274

Author's Route

Scale

| 0 | 30 | 60 | 90 | kilometers |

| 0 | 20 | 40 | 60 | miles |

Sept-Îles

Baie-Comeau
Haute Rive

Cap-Chat

Gaspé

St.-Nazaire
Ima
Chicoutimi

Matane

St. Lawrence R.

Saguenay R.

Rimouski

New Richmond
New Carlisle

Rivière-du-Loup

La Durantaye
St.-Raphaël

Séverin

oke
ville

Quebec:
The
People
Speak

Quebec: The People Speak

Rick Butler

Doubleday Canada Limited / *Toronto*
Doubleday & Company, Inc. / *New York*
1978

ISBN: 0-385-13496-7
Library of Congress Catalog Card Number: 77-15146

First Edition

Design by Robert Burgess Garbutt

Printed and bound in Canada by The Bryant Press Limited

All but three photos were taken by the author.
The photos of Jacques and Paul Rose are courtesy
of Rose Rose; the photo of Pauline Julien is by
Birgit of Paris.

Excerpts from this book first
appeared in *Weekend* Magazine.

To My Parents,
Canadians by choice via Ireland and America

Preface

This book grew from a spontaneous idea one February morning in 1977 to 7,000 miles of travelling, hundreds of interviews and photographs, months of translating, editing, and writing, and finally to the pages you read today. I decided to make the commitment to what became an exhilarating but often difficult task for a very straightforward reason: Canada is in real danger of breaking apart, largely, I think because of a profound and potentially tragic lack of understanding of the Quebec people by the rest of the country.

Politically, emotionally, and intellectually, Canadians were almost totally unprepared when the unthinkable began to happen in the early '60s: the FLQ bombings, demonstrations in the streets of Montreal, demands for special status, international diplomatic incidents, followed by the October Crisis of 1970 and, finally, the election of the PQ government in November of 1976. It is not surprising that the public reacted to these events with bewilderment ("What does Quebec really want anyway?"), defensiveness ("Why should Quebec be treated any differently from the other provinces?"), and often outright antagonism ("They can't break up this country and then expect us to shake hands and wave goodbye").

Over these past 15 years, radio, television, news agencies, and the press have given us a surplus of facts, crisis-oriented reporting, familiar politicians, detached journalists, and articulate and usually bilingual "official spokesmen," but somewhere in the journalistic gristmill Quebec's ordinary people have been forgotten—and we have all become the losers. I hope that *Quebec: The People Speak* will help to correct this situation by acting as a mirror reflecting that fundamental but often-ignored reality of Quebec life: its everyday people. In these pages you will find no politicians, only a few well-known Québécois, and 100 outspoken, thoughtful, often passionate, always honest, people from all parts of Quebec—taxi drivers, union organizers, professors, waitresses, housewives, the unemployed, students, businessmen, retired people, fishermen, newspapermen, farmers, pioneers, a cartoonist, and many, many others.

Since I explained the structure and research methods behind this book to each person interviewed, readers are also entitled to an explanation. I have used what is often termed the oral-history method, although the label is somewhat inaccurate in this case because the subject is highly contemporary. An important difference between this book and some others of the *genre* is that the interviewees here (with one exception) are identified by name, occupation, and place of residence. There are two reasons for doing this: first, it is a more precise and verifiable way of presenting information than using anonymous material. And second, the interviews take on a greater significance and impact when associated with real people from specific occupations and social classes, living in known places. Of all requests made for interviews only three were refused. The fact that people were required to give their names did not prevent them from being candid. One question I did have to confront from some of the more radical francophones was, "Are you getting any money from the federal government to do this book?" When I told them that I was not, they agreed to be interviewed.

After an informal chat, we began the taped interview, which was conducted in the person's mother tongue and usually lasted from 20 to 30 minutes. I asked certain standard questions, as can be inferred from the text, and in addition our conversation often ranged over territory of the person's own choosing. I may have selected the people, started the conversation, and steered it in serveral directions, but each interview soon took on a life of its own, often yielding real excitement and unexpected revelations.

I began the interviews with some nervousness, being a non-Quebecker and asking probing political questions in my second language. Happily though, any misgivings were soon swept away by the cooperation, openness, and candour of the people and their willingness to speak on the record. Time after time I was invited into their homes and made to feel welcome—it was almost as if they had been waiting for someone to listen.

The first interview was conducted in early May, 1977, and the last one six months later on October 29. Some of the interviewees were selected before my trip began, by preliminary research in the Quebec newspapers and through contacts in the regions; but the majority were chosen through hard work at the local level. I travelled by camper, working, eating, and sleeping on the road. It proved a very efficient way of working. A typical day began around 8:30 A.M. with conversations, phone calls, a visit to the local paper, one or more interviews during the day, and often an at-home interview that evening. From May to August, 1977, I worked virtually seven days a week, 16 hours a day in cities and towns, visiting factories, bars, garages, parks, union halls, newspapers, boards of trade, street corners, museums, households, universities, and numerous other places. Many people referred me to their friends, workmates, associates, or whatever, and so the chain grew.

The taped interviews were transcribed on paper, in the majority of cases translated, and then edited. The original language of the interview is indicated by the (F) or (E) immediately below the person's name. Editing reduced the interviews from one third to one half their original length as repetition, rambling, occasional dullness, and my questions were omitted. From time to time, a question has been rephrased in the words of the interviewee when it was essential for an understanding of the reply. However, nothing of substance has been changed or added.

There is also a personal approach or spirit that guided this work and if I can express it in one word it would be "fairness." I have tried to be fair and representative in the selection of interviewees, including people from all social classes, age groups, urban and rural areas (although the majority are from towns and cities), both language groups, radical and conservative elements, and those at all points in the federalist-*indépendantiste* spectrum. No one has been censored: from bank presidents to the most radical *indépendantistes*, you will meet them in the following pages just as I met them in person. If there is one personal quality the many Québécois I met said that they valued most highly it is honesty and frankness. I hope the people in this book will consider it an honest reflection of themselves and their home.

While the conversations with Quebeckers are the basis of this book, I enthusiastically recommend the appendixes — the summary of Bill 101, riding results of November 1976 election, the Quebec-Canada chronology, the statistical tables — and also the suggested reading list. I have compiled them in the hope that they will provide additional background for further discussion of many important issues in the Quebec-Canada debate.

A number of people who joined in the preparation of this book deserve special thanks: research assistant Pierre Louis Lapointe; Dawn Butt and Vala Monestime, who undertook the massive job of transcribing interviews and typing the final manuscript for an often-harried author; Paulette Cry and Gilles Laniel, who provided vital assistance in translating many of the French interviews; Crombie McNeill, for photo reproduction; Saint Paul University, which provided generous research support; my editor at Doubleday, Betty Jane Corson, for her immediate enthusiasm for the proposal of a first author and her editorial advice and personal support; and most important of all, of course, the people of Quebec who opened the doors of their homes, hearts, and minds to me with honesty, genuine hospitality, and good grace, and made this book possible—*du fond de mon coeur, merci beaucoup*.

Finally, to those in Canada and abroad who are reading these lines because they want to know what Quebeckers *really* want, *bienvenu*.

Rick Butler
Ottawa
November, 1977

Contents

Quebec:
The
People
Speak

Chapter 1

Montreal

I *started work on this book by making the two-hour drive from Ottawa to Montreal (population 2,757,132; 64% French★). Anyone who thinks Canada is the land where the bland lead the bland hasn't visited Montreal, the city that takes you by the senses and emotions and demands a reaction. The home of Expo and the Expos, Pauline Julien, Paul Rose, Jean Drapeau, the Olympic Stadium, art in the subways, the Bank of Montreal, St. Catherine Street, beautiful women, fine food, artists, street jugglers, and Pierre Trudeau, Montreal reaches out effortlessly to touch the most reserved of English souls, not to mention the thousands of new arrivals from around the world.*

Montrealers, like their mayor, are not renowned for their modesty and are fond of reminding visitors that this is the world's largest French-speaking city after Paris and North America's liveliest, most cosmopolitan city with possible competition from New York. And it is difficult not to agree. Any vision of a Canada without Montreal, let alone without Quebec, is a cultural as well as an economic nightmare.

In addition to being the country's largest film, television, and record production centre, Montreal is the artistic, literary, and theatrical capital of French Canada. There is also a great deal of money here. The city is a financial centre with the head offices of five federally chartered banks, some 70

★All population figures cited in this book are from Statistics Canada 1976. The French percentages refer to the language as a mother tongue and are based on 1971 data.

trust and insurance companies, and many large national corporations such as Bell Canada, Alcan Aluminum, Seagram's Distillers, STELCO, Domtar, Power Corporation, C.I.L., Steinberg's, Imperial Tobacco, Dupont, Molson's, and Canada Steamship Lines. Located on the St. Lawrence waterway midway between the Atlantic Ocean and the Great Lakes, Montreal is also the transportation and distribution centre of Canada. Two hundred and fifty trains and literally hundreds of jets and ships arrive and depart every day. Canadian National, Canadian Pacific, and Air Canada all maintain their head offices here. This city has attracted perhaps more than its share of post-Olympics, post-November 15, 1976 detractors, but never is Montreal dismissed as being small time.

First visited by Cartier in 1535 and then founded as a permanent settlement in 1642, complete with stockade to keep the previous residents at bay, Montreal grew and prospered with New France until 1759. La Conquête precipitated the abrupt return to France of most local merchants, administrators, and professionals, leaving the 60,000 French-speaking colonists in Quebec to the mercy of the English garrison and a small but powerful commercial clique.

By the time of Confederation 108 years later, Montreal had become a bicultural centre with a population that was fully 50 percent English speaking. Nineteenth-century Montreal was an even more bicultural centre than it is today and for several decades adopted the practice of alternately electing English- and French-speaking mayors. Today the language of business and opportunity is still largely English, a fact often ignored in English Canada but clearly perceived by the city's substantial immigrant community, which has overwhelmingly decided to educate its children in English.

In the November 1976 election, 25 of Montreal's 41 seats were won by the Parti Québécois. If Montreal opts for separation in the forthcoming referendum, the rest of Quebec will not be far behind. The PQ was born here in 1967 and its objective of independence for Quebec to a large extent rests in the hearts and minds of Montrealers. The people in this first chapter—French, English, Italian, German; radical, conservative; elated, apprehensive; rich, poor; taxi drivers, students, businessmen, housewives — are all living in Montreal by choice and filled with hope and concern for the future.

Mickey Fullerton
Taxi driver, Montreal
(E)
"No — not Toronto. No thanks."

Born and raised in Pointe St.-Charles — or "The Pointe" as he calls it —
Mickey Fullerton, a unilingual English Montrealer in his early 40s, is
intensely proud of his city. Clearly, his attachment to Montreal overrides any
language problems he may have. It is particularly interesting to learn his
feelings about Toronto. While Toronto-bashing has become almost a
Canadian national pastime, Mr. Fullerton displays none of the grudging
admiration that other Canadians often have for Toronto. The view from
Montreal is apparently less impressive.

I enjoy driving taxi. I meet terrific people and that's a fact. Plus you make
a decent living. I raised two kids on the strength of it—good, damn good
kids — and I have a good wife, a good home. I have lived a level-headed
life. I enjoy going to work and meeting the people and being in the
elements — you are outdoors and not confined to regulated hours, to a
factory or an office and you haven't got a boss over your head.

I love this whole town, I really do. I love what it's all about. It's
unique. It's very cosmopolitan, very continental. It's like being in
another country. I've been all over the North American continent. I've
been as far as Baffin Island and right down to the tip of the southern
United States. I've gone as far West as you can get, through many, many
states and I have discussed and debated and met a lot of people. I am not
knocking other places, but I am just saying that this place has got it all.

For one thing, you can get the best food in North America — and I
mean the *best* food — and you don't have to pay a lot for it. You've got
great people, with flair, a sense of humour. And you've got the best
hockey team in the world, that's for sure. The best football team — and
the Expos will come in someday, believe me!

And here in Montreal neighbours aren't just the people next door, the
people across the street, the people behind you. True neighbours are six,
seven, eight streets away too. You see it on summer days: people sit in
their undershirts on their galleries—you call them porches, we call them
galleries — and have a cold beer; they yell and roar at one another and at
cars going by. It's a lot of fun.

The French will yell at the English, *"Maudit bloke."* You haven't
heard that expression? We're also "square-heads." That's what

Englishmen are and of course "frogs" are what Frenchmen are. They all have nicknames, little jokes, about one another. This is the area of lower-income-bracket people. It is like — it is sort of the hard end of town, but it's a good area. The people who live here want to live here. If they had the option, most of them wouldn't get out. Yes, Pointe St.-Charles is like a town in itself. Pick it up and set it down anywhere in rural Canada and you've got yourself a small town.

The people in Montreal enjoy their city. When you go up St. Catherine Street, what are you going to find? Montrealers are using St. Catherine Street. Torontonians are not using Yonge Street. The transients, the misfits — they are making use of the centre of Toronto. But here you will find French Canadians living in their city. Now, I know Toronto quite well. I have been there and stayed there for months at different times in my life. I find it a big village; I find it very cold. It doesn't have a "Toronto" atmosphere. When I say that I mean Montreal has a "Montreal" atmosphere, I mean there is a feeling, there is a culture; not true in Toronto. They still have a Victorian mind in Toronto, you know, and that to me is repugnant. The middle-class Torontonian still spelling the word "pregnant" in front of his kids. That type of thing.

I am certainly not knocking all English because I am English, as you know. But people will still make a statement like: "He wouldn't serve me in English." And I say: "Why should he? This is a French province. If you go to England, are they going to talk Egyptian to you?"

I really think that Canadians outside Quebec don't understand the situation here at all. You read how horrible and how terrible things are. Well, that's just the media that serves that up. A businessman or a tourist who comes to Quebec changes his opinion if he stays here for any amount of time at all. He changes his opinion radically, he really does. My wife and I visited Scarborough a few months ago, and some people — supposedly level-headed, responsible people—were giving their opinion of what is going on here. Well, I didn't even know they were talking about Montreal! I work here, and I just don't go from my door to my little shop and back home again — I am all over this town and I didn't recognize Montreal in what they were saying.

One guy said to me, he said, "When I go to Montreal on business, I am afraid to be there." "You are afraid? Of what?" I said. He said, "I don't know, I am just afraid." So I said, "What in God's name are you afraid of, man?" You know, he was afraid because of everything he'd heard or read about — like the gangsterism that Montreal supposedly has, and the political situation. You'd think every French Canadian has got a baseball bat under his coat or something. I thought this guy was a clown, but there were quite a few people sort of nodding their heads in agreement, so it would seem the majority think the same way. I tried to persuade him—it was like trying to convert him. I said to him, "My God, it is the opposite. You go to Montreal and you're accepted beautifully. They are easy-going with you. It is a friendly city."

I'll tell you a surprising thing about the French people, the French fares, I've had since the election. This is a fact: they are more gentle with you. They are; they really are. I'm talking about 90 percent now. I don't know what it is. It's almost like an apologetic thing. But now they seem more sympathetic to you. It's sort of: "Look, we're not going to butcher you. I am a guy like you. I am not one of those government people who are ready to ram it down your throat." That type of feeling. Do you know what I mean? Now my French is just medium. Not half as good as I would like it, but I will improve on that and more so now because the old thumbscrews are on a bit. I should have done it anyway, let's face it.

Hindsight is perfect and what is going to happen I really don't know. Trudeau knows a hell of a lot more than I do—he is a pretty intelligent individual—and I think he is running the country as best as he can. You know, maybe somebody else could run it better but I don't know where they are! Or who they are! Joe Clark? He is not strong enough. It is a silly thing to say but he is not a good enough political animal. He is wishy-washy to me.

I think Quebec will make a damn good run at separation. But no, I don't think it will happen, definitely not. It just can't work because there is enough French Canadians that just don't want it, that are really frightened of it, especially with the economy going down now. Let's face it, eating comes first. Oh, language and all that fussing is fine, but average guys like me with a wife and two kids have got to worry about eating. And you can think about that in any language. You know?

If Quebec doesn't separate, there'll probably be a looser form of federation . . . could I live with that? I definitely could. Oh yeah, in fact, that's not all bad, if you think about it. You see, the whole country—never mind Quebec—the whole country from end to end is so different, so massive and so different in ways of life and peoples and everything else, a looser federalism wouldn't hurt at all.

When I look ahead a few years I feel that the rest of Canada and the rest of the world is going to get the idea that when you live in Ontario it is very, very logical to speak English and when you live in Quebec vice-versa. I think it is practically a natural route we are on. See, what they are trying to correct is 200 years in 10. There is a lot of frustration, you know, and a lot of people getting jilted and shuffled around, but I think in the future—I think eventually it will iron itself out and things will be more comfortable for both the French and English here.

Shirley McCaskill
Unemployed, Montreal
(E)

"I feel actually like a stranger in my own province now."

One of the most economically vulnerable and politically defensive groups in Quebec is the province's English-speaking working class. Faced with French language requirements in the labour market, together with persistently high unemployment levels, they are understandably anxious about their future in Quebec, and increasingly bitter at the prospect of economic and social changes apparently beyond their control. Also, there is evidence that the traditionally close-knit working-class English-French Montreal neighbourhoods are lately experiencing more overt racial tension. One alternative for the English like Shirley McCaskill and her husband Ken is to move West, but that decision does not come easily to people with deep roots in Montreal .

I've always felt attached to Congregation Street, but it's really changing. Our side of the railroad track was sort of English, Polish, Ukrainian, and Irish. Now it is predominantly French. Most of the English people have moved out of our neighbourhood.

We have spent 16 years now on Congregation Street and there still are a few elderly people around who have lived here for years. And I guess we will be here forever, but other than that it has changed immensely. I would say 80 percent. The families that have moved in are, I would say, mostly on welfare, and there is loud music blaring and beer drinking and that until two and three in the morning, and this goes on just about nightly. These are things that didn't happen before. It was sort of a working-class area and everybody was quiet and friendly and just did their own thing, you know.

Back even 10 years ago we all got along. I had two neighbours beside me at that time that were French, and I still to this day call one of them Ma because she became like a mother to me, almost. Today you don't have this type of neighbour. They are sort of sticking to themselves and they don't want to associate with you.

I've noticed a change for the worse here in the last few years. There are more fights between the two groups. You know, an English guy and a French guy get into a fight, go back to their friends, and the next thing you know two gangs are at it out in the street. And the bar just down the corner isn't the same anymore. Before, everyone used to mix together, but now it's the French at one end and the English at the other. Just last week a friend of my husband's came into the house white as a sheet. He'd been in the bar and some guy was waving a gun around in there. The guy didn't find who he was looking for but if he had, anybody in the place could have got it. That sort of thing scares you.

All this is too bad because my roots are in Montreal, you know. One set of grandparents came from England; the others were from Ireland. They came as young married couples and spent all of their lives in Canada. Most of them are in the Pointe now. I've got two sons who have gone to Vancouver to live. One has been gone a year and my other son left in June. They couldn't find work because they don't speak French. I sent my kids to English schools, and today I'm sorry I didn't put them into French schools.

Do I consider myself a Québécois? No, I consider myself a Canadian. I'd prefer to say Canadian. I am born in Quebec, raised in Quebec, and really I belong to Quebec, but I don't like really the feeling here right now. I get the feeling that I am getting pushed out of Quebec. You know, right now I am upset and I want to leave in the worst way and go and live in Vancouver. Even my husband Ken, who's in the CNR, is the only English chap left in the boiler room, and he can go back I think 10 years or less when they were pretty well all English in there.

He doesn't speak a word of French. Except to curse, that's about all! So it kind of gives you a funny feeling. Here on the street the kids will run by and call you *maudit Anglais* [damn English] or something. I guess they are being taught this by their parents, and I don't feel it is right. It is sometimes hard to figure out, hard to sort out your own feelings.

I know one thing though. I don't have any use for the PQ, and my husband feels the same way. And we don't believe that it began with the PQ—we feel it goes way back to when De Gaulle was here and that type of thing. It started right from there. Then we had the FLQ trouble and the whole bit. So we can't really blame René Lévesque for what is happening now. It just seems that once it gets started, it seems to snowball... Teaching the youngsters to hate the English or to hate the French, that snowballs too, and now they are in their teens and now they are dead against the English and this is not right. I would put all the English kids in French school and the French in English schools and let them all come out bilingual. I don't think that we'd have a problem then.

The English, you know, can leave, can go anywhere, do anything. But the poor little French guy is going to get kind of stuck in his own corner if he is not going to learn English at all and everything has to be kept French in Quebec. Where is he going to go? A lot of promises were made to the French people. Like jobs and that sort of thing. And now these promises are not coming through. There are no jobs and they are closing plants down.

Lévesque and all his Cabinet members and the media are spending far too much time on language issues and they are not worrying about the economy of Quebec. And what is going to happen, God knows. Maybe five years from now we will be back in the bush where the Indians were.

Unemployment is high here. Right here in my family there are three of us unemployed, myself and my two sons, and we are people who have always worked. You know, my husband has been 26 years in his job, so we are not people that quit a job and just keep going on unemployment. We have never been on welfare, but the majority of Pointe St.-Charles now are unemployed and on welfare or unemployment.

I have to report to my Canada Manpower officer and I do so quite frequently. He usually has a pile of jobs on his desk which he shows me and reads off to me, but it is a problem again of being fully bilingual. This seems to be my problem of getting employment. In my last job I was mostly in an office, I wasn't dealing with the public. A few years ago I was a saleslady and I always had someone else working alongside me that could take a French person if I was stuck. But today I don't think you'd even get an application made out for a sales job if you couldn't speak French. My boys had the same problem at Canada Manpower. My son asked his Manpower officer, "Why do I have to speak French to cut chesterfield patterns?" But still he has to be bilingual or he can't get a job.

Of course I will vote "No" in the referendum. But I don't feel that Trudeau is too worried about it and I don't feel he is too inclined to put too much of a stop to independence. Or try and help the English, who are having problems with the French.

What could he do? It's pretty hard to say. But I think he could get a little bit tougher with them. I feel that he is in cahoots with René Lévesque, and also with Bourassa when he was there. I feel we need somebody stronger, in English, in Ottawa. Most of Trudeau's Cabinet now are French; one by one he has gradually sort of squeezed out the English Cabinet ministers and put in French—I feel that maybe Canada one day will be strictly French and the English are going to have to run like hell to get out of here.

I feel more like a tourist here. I feel actually like a stranger in my own province now. If I go out shopping now and I ask a girl for something, she answers me only in French. I understand some, but I know a lot of people who do not. How are they to shop if people won't help them in English? Before, you didn't have this. I feel like an outsider now.

If the referendum passes, we'll move out of here with the rest of our friends. Twelve couples we know have gone now—to Calgary and Vancouver. So I think Ken and I will just pack up and go.

Alex Radmanovich
CP wire service editor, Montreal
(E)

**"To the French kids
I was a Polack."**

Alex Radmanovich immigrated with his parents to Canada from Yugoslavia in 1958. After attending public school in Rouyn-Noranda he studied at Bishop's University in Lennoxville and worked as a newspaper reporter and editor before joining the staff of Canadian Press in Montreal. Many French Quebeckers today often feel insulted and culturally threatened at the decision of most recent immigrants to send their children to English schools. However, according to Alex Radmanovich, when immigrants do enrol in the French school system, they are often not made to feel particularly welcome.

This is an exciting time to be in Quebec and to be reporting or channelling information from Quebec on the English CP wire. French Canadians are more emotional, more hot-blooded, than Anglo-Saxons; they are not reserved, they are not restrained, and for that reason alone I guess you get all kinds of things happening that normally wouldn't happen in Ontario for example.

I consider myself a Québécois. I don't think I've ever questioned that. Because I came here when I was eight years old, I learned to speak French. I'm perfectly bilingual. My wife is French, not French Canadian, and we speak French at home. And I think that I can call myself a Québécois just like anyone who was born here.

Having been brought up in a place like Noranda, having worked in Sept-Îles and a lot of other places, remote communities especially, I'd say there is no danger to the French culture because the people speak French. There is no problem with immigrants going to English schools. Maybe enrolment drops a bit because of the decline in the birth rate, but there is no artificial swelling of the English minority with immigrants. It's in Montreal that we have the separatist problem basically, because it is here that the French feel that they are threatened. Why? Because there is a very powerful English community and the magnet is all the stronger because of the economic benefits. Therefore all the immigrants coming into the province won't go to St.-Jean, which is 35 miles from here; they won't go to Sept-Îles; they go to Montreal, and they want to speak English because they think that this is where the economic opportunity lies.

I don't think there is anything wrong with asking immigrants to speak French. I can speak confidently on that subject because I am an immigrant. The problem is that the French have to realize that they have to accept immigrants more, which they haven't been doing. Take my case. When I came to Canada, to Quebec, I was in a community where most of the people were French, and they just didn't want anything to do with us. They didn't understand us, I guess, whereas the English, they accepted us. The French kids were hostile, but for some reason — it's a mystery to me — the English kids would play with me and try to understand me. I didn't speak any English when I came here. And yet to the French kids I was a Polack. And I'm not because I'm a Yugoslav, and there's some difference. I guess it's a little better now, but 10-15 years ago anybody who spoke a Slavic language was a Polack. They didn't realize that you had all kinds of nationalities in Eastern Europe. I've never understood why it was like this — maybe it's their school. There is no emphasis on world geography and things like this. Now the French are coming to realize that if the immigrants are going to integrate into their communities, they are going to have to accept them more openly.

Since the Parti Québécois election I kind of wonder a little bit because the French-language charter seems to be saying that the only person who could be a Québécois is a native-born francophone. That disturbs me a great deal because I contributed as much as any individual can to the life here and I feel a part of it. There is something very wrong in defining a Québécois as someone who speaks French: that can lead to a sort of prejudice against anyone who doesn't — in jobs or whatever. I don't have to worry about my job but I can see for a labourer, somebody who hasn't got skills, if they don't speak French they will probably be in big trouble in this province. You may have heard that the Quebec transportation department has decided that anyone working for the road gangs has to speak French. Now that's totally and utterly ridiculous. They don't need language to work. They can understand if someone wants them to paint something. Just point and it'll be done. But the government is sticking by their guns. It leads to a lot of discrimination. It's not going to foster any understanding.

I think it was very tragic that the Liberal government completely lost contact with almost every segment of society; it lost total contact with the unions; it had even alienated business. There was just nobody who believed anything Mr. Bourassa said. On the other hand, you had the Parti Québécois, who have been yearning for this election, who were organized to the hilt, who, with a lot of collusion from the media — including the English-speaking media — managed to run a campaign that completely masked their objective of independence. I didn't really know what the choice was. And I think a lot of people didn't know what the choice was. So a lot of people voted for the Union Nationale, which was and still is an unknown—a party that had died and by some freak accident managed to come back on the political scene. Because of the Union Nationale, the Parti Québécois did so well. If it had not been there, people would have had to make a choice between the Liberals and the Parti Québécois. They would have probably eliminated the Liberals anyways, but this definitely split the federalist vote.

The referendum? I will definitely vote against it because I think that Quebec can achieve what it wants within the federal framework. I think that constitutional talks were under way but somehow there wasn't any heart in it. If they had tried harder they would have come to some agreement, with Quebec getting some cultural guarantees and maybe some additional powers. In fact, in terms of economic policy, I think that all the regions of Canada will have to have more power because our economy is so diversified that it is difficult for one government to set a national policy on anything. One policy may help one area of the country, but not another. I definitely think that something can be done there, that some sort of arrangement can be worked out.

And another thing. A sort of a gut feeling I have about Quebec is that Quebec is what makes Canada different and if Quebec were not part of Canada, well, hell, what would distinguish Canada from United States? It's French Quebec that makes Canada different from the Americans.

I don't think that the PQ can win the referendum, but if they keep dragging it on, anybody can win anything. The tragedy would be that if the PQ loses the referendum and wins the next election because that would economically destroy the province. If we had to go through another referendum the uncertainty would be ridiculous. Anything Ottawa does now, the Quebec government say is wrong and the federal government is to blame and blah-blah-blah. Then we've got all these Quebec government communication centres around the province and it's just like propaganda, what they are doing. They've got the educational TV system, and I've noticed the change in it since the PQ won. I mean so much more nationalistic. Their announcers are so much more pro-separatist. They no longer speak of Quebec as a province, it's 100 percent a country now. At least before they would say Quebec province or the province of Quebec. Now it's *pays, mon pays,* and all that. Which I guess means Quebec is a country within a country.

If the referendum does go through, I will stay for a while. And if it works out I will stay in independent Quebec. But if I found I couldn't function, if I didn't feel comfortable, if I didn't feel wanted, I would leave. It's as simple as that. But I won't try and sell my house and run away now. I think that for a lot of people it's slowly sinking in that they've got to stay and see this thing out. At the beginning people panicked and put their houses up for sale. I think now English people are starting to stay. They've convinced themselves that they are going to stay and see what's going to happen. And I think that's a good sign.

Angelo Montini
Teacher, Montreal
(F)
"I wonder if I'll be called a nigger now because of my Italian accent."

Angelo Montini has integrated into the French side of Quebec life, teaching psychology at a French CEGEP (community college), and yet he is a bitter opponent of Bill 101 and its educational provisions, which oblige immigrant children to attend French schools. There are approximately 250,000 Italians in Quebec, over 200,000 of whom live in greater Montreal. Our interview began with some difficulty in English until Mr. Montini switched to his lightly accented but effortless French.

I was surprised when I came from Italy to study at the University of Montreal because I thought I'd be attending an English university. All the papers they sent me were in English, all the documentation was in English, all the correspondence was in English. So what was I to think? I never believed Montreal was a French city. I came over by boat and then by plane from Halifax, and I went to the university the day after I arrived in Montreal. It was very strange, I walked in to register and they were speaking this strange language.

Well, needless to say, I lost a year. I started but couldn't follow the courses, so I took some courses in French literature. Now French is the only official language that I know perfectly.

Later I married a French Canadian girl, and since I had been living in Montreal for several years and I liked it, I thought it would be easier for me to adapt here than for my wife to adapt over there, so we decided to settle here. It's easier to open more doors here than in Italy. Possibly because I am a foreigner, I try a little harder. In Italy I would have been told, "You are just like me. Wait." These are some of the reasons why I am staying here in this country, but the basic reason is that I personally find it easier to adapt to Quebec than my wife would adapt to a new life in Europe. But we go back to Italy once or twice a year.

I really do like Quebec, but now, since the independence movement has got rolling, I am referred to as an immigrant. This word leaves us tainted. Are immigrants really equal? Do we have the same rights, culturally speaking? Look, I am a citizen of Canada, therefore I should be a full citizen. But sometimes I don't feel at home now. I don't think I like nationalism.

As for personal relations with the French, it used to be a lot easier previously. I have become involved in politics and the linguistic debate, seeking justice for the Italians, the right to go to English schools. But I am seen by the French people I know as someone who threatens francophones; consequently there is instant distrust. I wonder if I'll be called a nigger now because of my Italian accent.

The whole freedom-of-education problem is a matter of quality of education rather than language. If I had a guarantee that my children would become bilingual—functionally bilingual—in a French school, I would send them there. But there isn't that guarantee. The reality is that, at the present time, the only school that can make them bilingual is the English school. There, French is taught beginning in grade one on a daily basis.

We Italians are not thinking of running away from this problem. We are out to stay here and fight to keep what we need our children to have. Even if we have to pay the full shot to put them in private schools we will do it. I know many Italian parents who last year sent their children to the United States or Toronto, where it is much more expensive because you have to pay room and board. But they were willing to spend everything they had so that their children will become bilingual. We are immigrants and we know from personal experience the necessity of having two languages.

It would seem that we are in an independent Quebec already because even anglophones from Ontario are considered foreigners and have to go to a French school. But in all the other provinces, especially in Ontario, you see the opposite thing taking place. If a Frenchmen from France settles close to a French school in Ontario he will have a choice. But not here. The politicians take us immigrants for asses.

Quebec will never be unilingual, never! Even though there is a statute that says that French is the official language, we will always speak English, we will have to learn English. The francophone himself does not accept his new unilingual status. Many francophone parents want English to be taught in French schools from grade one. They want their kids to be bilingual. Look, the real economic power in North America is held by English Canadians or Americans. We live in an industrialized world, not in a world where you live only by ideas or culture. I think food and machines come before culture, and this is why I cannot conceive of us becoming unilingual in Quebec.

Marthe Beauregard
Genealogist, Montreal
(F)

"Quebec has one of the most complete birth, marriage, and death records of any country in the world and we are very proud of that."

Founded in 1943, La Société Généalogique Canadienne-Française is the oldest genealogical society in Quebec. From her Montreal home, Marthe Beauregard, who offers courses to society members in Quebec genealogy, discusses the reasons for the growing popular interest in Quebec in tracing family trees.

Our society has grown very rapidly in the last few years, and these days a lot of Québécois are interested in retracing their roots, in going back to the source. We have a lot of people coming to us saying, "This summer I am going to France. I would like to go back to the country of my ancestors. Can you help me discover who my ancestors were, where they came from?" And sometimes, you know, it is really complicated to do that. There are several ancestors, perhaps, who had the same name and you have to go back from one generation to the next, searching through marriage records to discover who the correct one is. Take the family Roi for example: there are 40 or 41 first ancestors, descendants with the name Roi. So, if someone tells me, "I am going to France to discover my first ancestor whose name was Roi," it is necessary to do a lot of work before that person leaves. If he doesn't have the proper information he won't know where to go and he will waste a lot of time.

The members of our society come from all social classes and all ages — we have people from 14 to 90 years of age, and some who have university degrees and others who scarcely know how to write their own names. We even have members from the United States, Europe, South America, Argentina. These people are all interested in identifying with something. They want to be someone. They want to know who they are. They want to know their roots.

You know, in genealogy, it is not just a matter of tracing dates; you also pick up a lot of interesting information about people's ancestors. Genealogists are also historians to a certain extent, students of common history. We deal in lawyers' records, in census records, in all sorts of documents to find what our ancestors did — how they came here; how they lived; what land they possessed; what kind of profession or craft they had; whether they got into any problems with the law while they were here. You can end up building up almost day-by-day profiles of people's ancestors and their way of life, and in the end these people that you are doing all this research on really become your friends. You know them as well as you know the characters from a novel.

My own family background? Well, on my mother's side, the family was the Guchereau-Duchesnay, one of the oldest families in Quebec — they arrived here back in 1634. My paternal ancestor was a Monsieur Faribault, who was a notary in France and who came here as secretary to Governor Duquesne in 1752. Another one of my ancestors, the Honourable Joseph Edouard Faribault, was a member of the government in the 1840s, and we mustn't forget my ancestor Guillaume Lévesque, who was one of the *patriotes* in the rebellion of 1837. I can also mention Alexandre Faribault; he founded the town of Faribault, Minnesota, 40 miles south of St. Paul. I have visited the area. The Faribaults founded several villages in Illinois and Minnesota, so really I am very proud of my ancestors.

You know, in Quebec, it is much easier to trace a person's family roots than anywhere in North America. Quebec has one of the most complete birth, marriage, and death records of any country in the world and we are very proud of that. This is due in large part to the clergy and the Catholic Church, which were assigned by the French government in the colonial days to maintain these records and this system has continued right up till the present day. They are paid for that. There are two registers of births, marriages, and deaths in Quebec: one that is made at the parish church and a master register kept at the Justice Department in Quebec City. These registers give the names of the parents, the names of the spouses, where they came from, and often their occupations, and other information can turn up as well. Anyone who wants to trace his family tree begins with one ancestor and then follows back from that person through these records, so he can trace his family tree right to its first roots in France.

Things are more difficult though for the English of Quebec and for the French Protestants living here because until very recently the names of the parents in a marriage were not mentioned in their records. So there are real problems in Quebec in tracing the family tree of Protestant people, especially before the twentieth century, when the parents' names were not entered in the marriage register. Of course there are other ways of doing this if you know other names in the family tree, but it's much less organized than simply going to the marriage records.

It's interesting that those records show very distinct periods of major immigration in Quebec. The first one started in 1634 with a group of new arrivals, who came from the area of Perche in Normandy to Quebec City. Then after that there were different waves of immigration coming into Montreal. There was one in 1653, another one in 1659, many coming from Laflèche. Some immigrants were actually French soldiers who were sent here to fight the Iroquois. The King of France made it possible for them to settle here after their enlistment period had ended, and helped them start families by sending women who were called *les filles du roi* [the daughters of the king]. This was around 1665.

After this, into the early and mid-1700s, there were no major waves of immigration, just a steady stream of immigrants — mainly people who came to join members of their families who were already here and soldiers and other settlers looking for land. During the war between France and England, many soldiers of Montcalm married here while they were defending the City of Quebec and many stayed after the Conquest. Many artisans came here as well because they were badly needed, of course. One thing that I find kind of amusing is that back in the late 1600s and early 1700s there were a lot of wigmakers in Quebec— in fact back then, wigmakers were more important than carpenters.

After the Conquest in 1759, all immigration from France stopped completely, and many Quebeckers returned to France—not so much the ordinary people but the officers in the army, the professionals, many from the higher levels of society—and they left 65,000 French-speaking *Canadiens* here completely on their own.

You should realize that from that point on, all contacts from France were completely cut off. In fact, I have seen in the attic of a very old Quebec family a dictionary that was copied by hand in small notebooks because they had absolutely no French books and this was the only way that that family could preserve the language. The dictionary was copied out by hand and then passed on to someone else, who probably did the same. People back then, you know, really struggled hard to hold onto their heritage. It wasn't until the mid-1800s that the first ship from France actually returned here to Quebec. It was called *La Capricieuse* and there was a fantastic celebration in Quebec when it arrived.

You ask me if I think the measures that are now being taken to preserve the French language are necessary. Well, my answer is definitely yes. For the last few years here we have been facing a lower birth rate because of the Pill. Also, many people in Quebec are emigrating while others are being assimilated by the English culture. It was really necessary to take these measures and I think that the government did the right thing. In all political situations, you have to go a little to the extreme in order to come back to the middle ground. If you don't go a little farther than you really intend, then you'll never achieve what you are really after, and I think this is what the government is doing now.

Look, I am going to tell you something: I don't think this problem would be facing us today if the English people had really taken note of the problem beforehand. I think they let matters deteriorate; I think they closed their eyes to the problems of the French Canadian people and tried to pretend that nothing was wrong.

Language is important but our way of thinking and our way of looking at the world—our complete cultural base—is very important and, I think, completely different from that of the English. This has to be recognized. I know people who have studied in French at university here in Montreal, and then who went on to McGill University to study in English. They did well in their studies when they were working in French—but when they tried the same thing in English, they were completely cut off. They didn't succeed because the English way of looking at the world and of viewing things academically was too different for them. You must realize that in the French culture, people are more individualistic intellectually and like to create things by themselves, on their own. Now, the English way of thinking is much more concrete and specific. Let's agree that both methods can be excellent but it's very difficult for someone who has grown up in one tradition to simply switch over to the other system. This way of thinking and our entire intellectual tradition is maintained by our writers and our culture and it is all connected to the French language, which we want to preserve.

I believe right now that we are moving in the direction of independence but how rapidly we go, I think, depends on the attitude of the rest of Canada. At the present time their reactions are totally negative —they understand so little about our problems that I think really this is helping the separatists. It is just so obvious that the English don't understand. I read English and French newspapers—I read four or five newspapers every day because I don't want to be limited to a single point of view. I read the letters to the editor in the English press, and it makes you just want to throw up your hands and forget about the whole thing because you can see in black and white that they just don't understand what we want, they don't understand where we are going, and they twist and misinterpret what is happening here.

Pierre Trudeau had a very poor idea when he wanted to impose French on the rest of Canada. In British Columbia they don't really need to speak French any more than we need to speak English in Quebec. For example, I think trying to put an English television station in the Saguenay region, where there are very few English, is just going to lead to anglicization of the population. People there feel that this is a move to impose the English culture and they resist it.

Now personally, I don't see complete separation in the future, but I think that people in English Canada have really twisted Lévesque's ideas. Lévesque is a man who really sees far into the future. I don't agree with everyone in his party, but him, I admire. I like his idea of sovereignty-association, where we will take care of the matters that concern us directly, where we are different from other people and provinces. I think that this is the real solution to our problems. Today, government in Canada is much too centralized in the hands of Ottawa. If the rest of Canada would only admit that we are different, let us control the areas of provincial concern, and together share the things that concern us all, I think that then we could have a real solution to our problems.

Fred McNeil
Chairman, Bank of Montreal, Montreal
(E)

"The one requirement for a head office is the ability to speak English."

The Royal Bank of Canada, the Bank of Montreal, Royal Trust, and many other financial institutions have one thing in common—a Montreal head office, many of them located in the city's financial centre, St. James Street. Here in this short sombre street of soot-blackened Grecian columns, armoured trucks, and purposeful pin-striped pedestrians, domestic and international commerce is discreetly conducted—usually in English. For many Québécois, St. James Street has come to symbolize the financial domination of Quebec by English interests. Fred McNeil, the chairman and chief executive officer of the Bank

of Montreal, is an approachable unilingual Saskatchewan native who joined
the bank 12 years ago. After passing by the commissionaire, armed guard,
and his secretary, I spoke with Mr. McNeil in his office suite overlooking
St. James Street.

My first reaction to the PQ victory was surprise, I think; although during
the latter phase of the election campaign it was quite evident that the PQ
were going to do better than people had thought. I listened to the head of
the Union Nationale the other day. He said the PQ wants to do next week
what should take a generation to accomplish. He pointed out that it is
only 20 years ago that the shift of emphasis on education in Quebec
occurred. Up to that time young people were expected and encouraged to
be notaries, doctors, lawyers, and only about 20 years ago they began to
go into engineering and business programs. Of course the proportion of
French-speaking people in business has gone up in the last decade. In our
own Quebec division it's gone up from 60 to 90 percent. Great progress
has been made.

Criticism has been made that the English controlled the economy of
Quebec for the last 200 years. I really don't believe that. This province
has been run, legislatively, by French Canadians since the beginning.
There's never been a majority English government here and it's
governments that create the universities The French chose not to set up
professional and business schools; it was a cultural phenomenon.

Amongst my business colleagues, either French-speaking or
English-speaking, there's a distaste for the coercive aspect of the
language bill. Many of them do not believe you can legislate culture or
legislate language. The second thing is, there's great unwillingness on the
part of all business francicize their Quebec operations.

You see, there are two distinct groups in business: the national and the
multinational. The one primarily based internally doesn't present much
of a problem. Our Quebec division operates nearly all in French. Myself?
No, I don't speak French. But the second group presents a very
significant problem for the head office of a multinational company. In our
case, 10 to 15 percent of our assets are in Quebec; the rest are in other
parts of Canada and around the world. The language of communication
in international business, and particularly international banking, is
English, so the one requirement for a head office is the ability to speak
English. There's certainly a substantial advantage if our representatives
also know the language of the country, as a matter of convenience to our
customers. Now in South America, they are bilingual in Spanish or
Portuguese. In Southeast Asia, which covers an immense variety of
languages, the language of common communication from India to Hong

Kong is English. Same thing in the Middle East — primarily English, outside Arabic.

Payment orders, which circulate world-wide, are in English, international financial conferences are in English, and so on. Now, insofar as Bill 101 inhibits our ability to attract people from our operation in other parts of Canada and overseas into coming here and having freedom of choice in education, that will be a significant handicap for running a successful head office. This is of particular concern to middle-management people in the 35-45-year-old bracket with children in secondary school.

Personally, I have no problem because my children are all grown up, and so I enjoy the bicultural atmosphere of Montreal. It is a tremendous town, a very beautiful city. And even though I don't speak French, I enjoy French culture. I like French people. They're very courteous.

But if Quebec separates, I don't know what reason the other parts of Canada would have to protect Quebec industry anymore. As you know, in Western Canada, one of the historic objections has been the high tariff on manufactured goods. If Quebec separates, someone in Calgary will say, "Why should I pay 25 percent more for textiles?" And as far as an economic union is concerned, what's the incentive if it is now a separate country? Why would the rest of Canada buy from this separate country at a premium? I also think that Quebec probably places undue emphasis on its natural resources — electric power, asbestos, and so forth. The more one travels, the more one realizes there are immense natural resources in other areas too. So the assumption that is rather common in Canada that we have immense natural resources and that the world's going to come knocking at our door, that is a profound error. This is being repudiated every day by less developed countries.

You ask if the new Bank of Montreal office tower in Toronto is a preliminary step to leaving Montreal if the referendum passes. My answer is "No." We have been decentralizing for a decade. And of course the Ontario market is by a long shot the largest in Canada, so it's natural that you put your marketing there. We've also been decentralizing our foreign operations. In the last three years we've set up regional headquarters that parallel our domestic headquarters, establishing head offices in London, New York, and Nassau. Every institution has to be concerned about a too rapid growth of its head office, but now every time we send anybody to Toronto it becomes a *cause célèbre*.

Mario Bari

Company president, Montreal

(E)

"I do believe that the referendum is going to go through, and I'll tell you why."

One of the most readily apparent changes to be brought about by Bill 101 is in public advertising. To accomplish the francization of the market place called for by the new regulations, thousands of advertising and information signs in Quebec must be changed. Certain private companies will profit directly from PQ policies, and the outdoor advertising industry is clearly one of them. Mario Bari, president of the largest sign company in Quebec, is a businessman caught between the attractive financial prospects presented by the PQ victory and his own political beliefs.

I have been with this company for 32 years and work in both languages every day. I started here in 1945 as an office boy, went through all the operations of costing, inventory, control, accounts payable, estimator, sales rep, sales manager, and today I'm president. This is the only job I ever had since graduating from high school in 1945 — St. Patrick's here in Montreal.

My company makes neon signs for the whole province of Quebec. Outside of Montreal, the signs are always French — very, very little English except in the Eastern Townships area. In Montreal, prior to 1974 and Bill 22, we made a lot of English signs for English districts, like the West End of Montreal, the Lakeshore area. When Bill 22 came into effect, the law said that signs must be French only or bilingual, so people who at one time bought only unilingual signs had to go and buy bilingual signs if they wanted English. Now this has all changed again. Bill 101 stipulates that most public signs, whether they are for one's own place of business or outdoor advertising signs, all these signs must be only in French, and company names must be French. A lot of companies are going to have to change their names, and there will be a demand to have signs changed from English or bilingual signs to French only. There will be a transition period where people will have anywhere from one year to four years to make these changes.

Of course, there'll be a few problems. Let me give you an example. Take an international chain like the Holiday Inn, which people who travel all over the world know. Let's say the motel wants to advertise its services, the good things about the establishment. Here in Quebec the signs will have to be only in French, and the tourists travelling into this province won't be able to read them. I don't think that's fair to either the Holiday Inn or the tourists, who bring us a lot of dollars. They should be able to come here and read a sign of English. We are not a separate country, we are a province and we are part of Canada. Canada says we've got two official languages; I say we should be using two official languages. With Bill 101 there is no freedom of choice; this I do not accept as a businessman.

If Quebec ever does separate, it will be very, very unfortunate for Quebec and for Canada. I think we can be a rich province, in a rich country, by being part of Canada. As much as we may want to negotiate with the other provinces for special arrrangements, special deals, I think we are going to be the losers. Sure, we've got strength, we've got resources, but we can't live only on that. We have to live on good trade with the rest of this country and with the Americans. But I do believe that the referendum is going to go through, and I'll tell you why.

There are five million French Canadian people in this province. You remove the million and a half or two million from Greater Montreal, that leaves three million in the rest of Quebec. Prior to the politicians getting hold of the language issue, for the past 10 years, there was never a language problem in Quebec. The French spoke English and some English spoke French. The fact is that the politicians made an issue of this thing; they have been preaching freedom of speech, freedom of language, freedom of our country, to all the Quebeckers of this province, and they should because it should be predominantly French. But when the referendum comes about, the three million people that I'm talking about outside of Montreal will probably say to themselves, "You know, if I don't vote separation, I'm going to lose my heritage, I'm going to lose everything, I'm going to be once again controlled by the English. I'm going to be controlled once again by the Americans. I'd better vote separation because I may lose all my rights." I think for that reason the referendum will go through.

In my work, I travel a bit in this province and I've also got a cottage 120 miles from Montreal where it's all French, and I can tell you the attitude of the people around there. They are very happy being French and figure they should only be French. "We don't need English. We're comfortable at home. Why do we need English?" So they'll vote for separation. I don't know about the public opinion polls that say 30 percent are for separation and 70 percent are against. Is that 70 percent in Montreal or are they people in the province at large? Because the smaller cities, the smaller communities, don't speak English because they don't need

English at all. They speak French. I was in Quebec City shortly after the elections, and a restaurant that I visited at one time used to have bilingual menus. Now they've changed their menus to French only because they believe that the province is French. So we were given a menu completely in French. I had no problem reading it because I do read and speak French, but there were people who could not read it.

There is so much potential here — it has been proven with Expo '67, the Olympics, the roadways, all the big industries that came into this province — but if the province becomes independent, I would say the economy will be in trouble.

What would I do personally? Look, I was born in Quebec and my roots are here and it would be very, very difficult for me to move out of this province. Sure I'm a Canadian — but I'm a Quebecker too.

Leon Teitelbaum
Clothing manufacturer, Montreal
(E)
"I'm not a betting man, but I'll bet anybody the PQ don't do better than 35 percent."

One of the most vocal groups in Quebec opposing Bill 101's provisions for francization of business is the English-speaking business community, particularly in Montreal. Leon Teitelbaum, a unilingual anglophone clothing manufacturer for the past 38 years, spoke to me in his factory-office in downtown Montreal.

I've lived in Montreal 50 years, and for the most part of my adult life I've been involved in the Jewish community, mainly in the field of education. I was president of the local Jewish private school for five years. I've been involved with the Canadian Jewish Congress for practically the last 10 years. My children have all grown up here, gone to university here. They are very much a part of the Quebec community. They actually went to the Jewish school that I headed up eventually, the Jewish People's School. In the years they went to school, French was not taught to any great extent. As a result they have come out actually speaking primarily English, with some knowledge of French.

Since about 10 years ago, when Jewish schools began getting grants from the government, the French program in the school has been intensified and the children coming out of the school have an increased knowledge of French. Since the PQ government has come into power, they have been demanding more French in order for us to qualify for the grants. We are trying to accommodate the government. We feel strongly that in order to be able to live and work in this province everyone will have to know more French than previously, but I think this should be done through incentives, not forcing it on the people that come here or live here. I think that children of English-speaking families coming into the province should be able to go to English schools, but they should have better French education programs in English schools and vice-versa. I employ 35 people in my business and about two-thirds are francophones. No, I'm not bilingual myself but over the years I've been in business, 37-38 years, I've learned words that belong to the trade and I communicate with them. We have no problems. But I can't really say that I speak French.

Do I see any possibility of discrimination in the bills the PQ has introduced? You're talking about anti-Semitism? No. I can say with good authority that there has been no trace of anti-Semitism whatsoever, but I do think that the legislation affecting business advertising is an unnecessary hardship for small business people. In other words, large corporations can always cope with anything, they have the staff, the resources, but the laws pertaining to language and francization are a hardship, a hardship on smaller companies.

If I have to change my invoices, if I have to communicate with the government in French, that creates a problem. If I get a letter in French, I have to look for someone who can translate it for me, and I just don't have the time or the people to do it. Now you multiply that many times a year, it's an unnecessary hardship and an unnecessary expense. If I have to have francophones in executive positions — well, I can only have people who are qualified. They can be Chinese, they can be Italians, they can be French. That's the only criterion I'm going to use. And if I'm forced to put a francophone in an executive position only because he's francophone and I've other people that are more qualified, then I'm out. I'm out. I just leave here. In other words, that's no way to run my business. I have to run my business as profitably as I can.

Yes, I would be prepared to leave Quebec because we do 80 percent of our business outside of the province — and that applies to most people in our industry. If you have a base of 80 percent of business outside of Quebec, you don't have to stay here because if I went to Toronto, for instance, I would always pick up the 20 percent somewhere — Toronto, Hamilton, Windsor. I speak for the majority of the people in my type of business. We are not going to be pushed around. We're going to cooperate; we think French should be the predominant language, but I don't know why it should be the official language. There should be two languages. Not those laws, not those francization laws. Not force out anybody. When a person has a plant of 100 people, which according to the government legislation has to have a francization committee that includes the workers, well, I'll buy that when the unions will take management into their deliberations.

If a guy came into my place like he did to the doughnut place and confiscated the bags that were in English — did you hear about that? It was Mr. Doughnut or something like that. He had take-out bags, thousands of them, in English only. A fellow came in, went through the back of his establishment, found the bags, backed up a garbage truck, and threw all of them out. Now if that happened to me — first of all, I don't think he could do it, he'd have to have a gun to get my things out of here — but supposing he did. Supposing he came in here with detectives, and he said, "Look, you know, we're with the government and we're taking away your letterheads and throwing them out." I'd put a lock on the door right there and then.

I think the PQ are gonna lose the referendum. By a large majority, as a matter of fact. I don't think they can get better than 30-35 percent. I'll vote, sure, I plan to work on behalf of federalism. I'm not a betting man, but I'll bet anybody the PQ don't do better than 35 percent. They will need 60 percent of the French Canadian vote to overcome the ethnic vote. They can never get 60 percent of the French Canadian votes because the people who voted PQ were 40 percent of the total votes. I say that 50 percent of those people did not vote for separatism, they voted for a change in the government. I think 50 percent of those 40 percent who voted PQ are opposed to separatism.

And I tell the people we have to pray for René Lévesque's health because if he goes, God knows who else will take over. I think he's the most rational one of the people in the government. He's been in the government before, he's more mature. He can see the pitfalls much better than these people who just came into the government. They never expected to form the government and I don't think they are quite ready.

Reverend Paul Chan
Minister, Montreal
(E)
**"Some of our people find it very
difficult to speak French fluently."**

*A native of Montreal, the Reverend Paul Chan at an early age returned to
China where he was raised and educated before settling permanently in
Montreal. He has been minister to one of Montreal's most cohesive immigrant
communities at the Chinese Presbyterian Church for the past 38 years.*

There are over 30,000 Chinese people in Montreal, but most of them are
younger people who were born here. In the early days there was an
immigration law that restricted the Chinese from bringing their family to
this country. In 1947 the government changed the immigration laws to
permit the Chinese to obtain Canadian citizenship, and after that they
were allowed to bring their families to this country. So I must say we had
no Chinese community across the land until 1950. Today we have over
30,000 Chinese in Montreal, over 4,000 Chinese families. We have
thousands of Chinese attending university in Montreal and thousands of
them attending high school here, and I must say the Chinese are doing
very well in school.

Of course the community is really changing rapidly. In the last 10–15
years we have more professional men. Laundry is in the past.
Restaurants still seem to be going very strong, because Chinese food
attracts so many people. But now we have many Chinese that go into
different businesses, different fields. I remember when I first came to
Montreal in 1940, we only had one Chinese medical doctor in Montreal
and now we have 100 medical doctors and 150 or more Chinese nurses. I
remember we didn't even have one Chinese accountant; now we have
about 20; now we have about 80 architects. So you see, the community is
changing. We have service centres now and besides what the church can
do, we have different organizations to unite the Chinese people together
so we can help each other. And at the same time we can deal with any
problems that concern the Chinese people in the province of Quebec.

I find there isn't very much discrimination against the Chinese today.
The Chinese people are well received. In fact, I get many phone calls
from different companies, different offices, wanting to employ Chinese
girls to work. So it is not too bad regarding the racial problem. But now

that we are facing a big change in the province of Quebec, this will affect the Chinese too. Many of them are from English-speaking countries like Hong Kong, Malaysia, and other East Asian countries. They find it quite difficult to learn French fluently, and some of them they worry about their futures. So some will probably move out of this province, go elsewhere to look for a job and a future.

Especially if you have a family, you know, you have to worry and plan ahead. For instance, here at the church we plan to engage a new minister to assist me and gradually I will retire. But see, here's the problem right away. If I engage a minister from Hong Kong, he speaks English but his children must go to French school. He will want them to go to English school. That gives you an idea. It's pretty hard for me to engage a man to come from Hong Kong to accept this job. A minister today must know some French too.

Mind you, I'm not worried a bit about the younger generation. I'm telling you they will learn French, English, German. No, I'm not worried about our younger generation. What I'm worried about now is the first-generation, second-generation people. They find it difficult. Now I remember even during Expo in Montreal, 1967, many millionaires from Hong Kong or East Asia passed through Montreal and discovered they must know French to establish or build up their business here. So many of them just didn't stay. Many of them went to Toronto or Vancouver or Calgary or Edmonton. Today many, many Chinese are building up big industries and businesses and buying properties, especially in Vancouver and Toronto. Some of our people plan to leave here. In fact, I tell you some of them have spent a few weeks in Toronto, Edmonton, but they find it difficult to secure jobs.

The government should realize the facts and understand the problems of an ethnic community. They should not force us to learn the language, or at least give us time to learn the language. When people come to a certain age, it is difficult to learn a new language. Also, we want to have some Chinese with money and brains come to this province and build up some industry or go into different kinds of professions. We'd like to build up a strong and bigger community ourselves, you see. But in this situation it's just very difficult for them to come here. They'd have to use three languages — French, English, and Chinese. So you can't blame them for feeling a little bit uneasy in a situation like that.

I consider myself a Canadian, you know. And naturally I love this province, I love Montreal. I have been here for so long. I like the French culture. I think the people are friendly as a whole. The Chinese get along with the French people very well, you know. In fact many of our people even marry French girls.

I have a daughter and a son and they both are working in Montreal and so of course my plan is to remain in Montreal here. But I hope this government will concentrate on building up a good government so we can live here peacefully and comfortably.

Rose Rose
Waitress, Montreal
(F)
"I can't read my sons' consciences but I'm proud of them."

October 5, 1970:	*British trade commissioner James Cross is kidnapped in Montreal by the FLQ. Demands: freeing of FLQ prisoners in Quebec jails; $500,000; mass-media publicity for FLQ manifestoes; safe passage to Cuba or Algiers.*
October 10:	*Quebec labour minister Pierre Laporte is kidnapped by a second FLQ cell.*
October 16:	*War Measures Act is invoked by Prime Minister Trudeau. Canadian civil rights are suspended; internal military alert; hundreds of suspected FLQ sympathizers are detained by police without being charged.*
October 17:	*Pierre Laporte is found murdered. The hunt for his killers and Cross kidnappers continues.*
December 3:	*Police locate James Cross and kidnappers in suburban Montreal duplex. Cross is liberated in exchange for passage to Cuba for kidnappers.*
December 27:	*Paul and Jacques Rose are arrested in hideaway 20 miles from Montreal. In a subsequent trial, Paul Rose receives one term of life imprisonment for murder and a second life term for kidnapping. Jacques Rose is sentenced to eight years' imprisonment for complicity; i.e., aiding his brother in hiding.*
	They join 12 other convicted FLQ members currently in federal penitentiaries in Quebec for crimes including murder, kidnapping, armed robbery, and bombing.

October, 1977: *Premier Lévesque makes public a letter sent to him by the Cross kidnappers living in exile in Paris, requesting a pardon and permission to return to Quebec.*

The most traumatic political experience in Canada since the execution of Louis Riel has not yet passed completely into history despite efforts in many quarters to forget the events of October to December, 1970. After making preliminary arrangements with her lawyer, I met Mrs. Rose Rose, mother of Jacques and Paul, in her small bungalow in the Montreal suburb of Longueil. A small, intense woman, Mrs. Rose is campaigning actively for the release of her sons from prison.

My son Paul is in Archambault Prison; that's a maximum-security prison 35 miles from Montreal. The living conditions are not bad. Jacques is at St.-Vincent de Paul, and conditions are not very good there. It is an old place, nearly prehistoric. It was opened in 1873, I think. I see my boys every week. Look, I have pictures of them—here.

Paul Rose at Archambault Penitentiary (left), Jacques Rose at St.-Vincent de Paul Penitentiary, Montreal.

At St.-Vincent de Paul you're allowed to visit one hour a week. They are quite restrictive all along but at Archambault it is better. The visit might last, say, three hours if there are not too many people, or even three and a half hours. The regulations just aren't the same. I don't understand it because they are both maximum-security institutions, but each jail has its specific rules—it seems to depend on the director.

Jacques was out of jail for awhile because he was acquitted three times, but then they started trying him over again, just like Morgenthaler. The same trial, the same evidence, nothing new. Finally he was sentenced to eight years for having helped his brother build a closet—that's all. And there is no parole; they aren't getting parole.

How did they feel about November 15? They were very happy because my sons want independence. Paul told me, "Mother, I am very happy because November 15 shows that Quebeckers will be proud of themselves and it shows that we will have a country of our own someday. It is an opening on the entire world, and if it is done without violence, in a democratic manner, that is very good. Afterward there won't be too many wounds to heal, so it will be possible to negotiate with the federal government without too much bitterness or hate."

Jacques felt the same way. All the political prisoners did. They were waiting for that. It was euphoria for them sitting in jail. Paul had told me previously that the Parti Québécois would win because even the Italians in Quebec who wanted to negotiate with Mr. Bourassa found it didn't work out. Mr. Bourassa first said "Yes" and then said "No." So they said he was a traitor and they voted for the Parti Québécois.

Paul's morale is excellent; the same with Jacques. They are people who have an ideal and they are all educated. Perhaps they have too much education. I can't read my sons' consciences, but I am proud of them. I am proud because they are young people with such high ideals. They were seeking better rights for Quebeckers, a better way of life, they always thought of others.

Even before 1970 Paul was a militant. We used to watch television and listen to politicians, and we might say, "So-and-so is good; he will do this; he will do that," but Paul said, "Mom, come on. You don't understand. He is no good. He is not good for anything." Paul used to explain things to us—that's when I began to think that the children know more than we do. My husband and I didn't even use our vote, we didn't bother with politics at all. But Paul had been in political science, he had been a teacher, he was aware of a lot of things and he was a militant.

No, I don't think they regret their actions in October, 1970. It was done spontaneously at that time; at least that's what I think. According to all I have been able to see and hear, it was spontaneous. The FLQ was never an organized conspiracy, no matter what the politicians say. It was made up of separate cells acting independently. Maybe one cell's actions spurred the next one on, but it was never what you could call an organization. It wasn't a planned insurrection, as the government tried to make out. The FLQ angered a lot of people afterward but it took something strong to get Quebeckers to stand up. They had been living like sheep, always following, showing no initiative in any field.

You ask if I think the death of Mr. Laporte helped the cause of independence. Probably not immediately. I don't think so because it was a shock. And when there's a death it is always hard for both sides, as much for those who do it as for those who are the victims. The boys had no interest in killing Mr. Laporte; when they kidnapped him, it was to get the political prisoners out of jail. Some of them had spent two years on death row with reprieve after reprieve — that was inhuman, it was like killing a man slowly. They had no visitors, nothing. The boys wanted those FLQ political prisoners to get better treatment because nobody was paying any attention to them. That was their aim. They had no interest in killing Mr. Laporte. None whatsoever. Possibly they threatened that to push their demands, but I think his death may have been an accident.

When we finally get to the bottom of things, I think a lot of things will come out in the open. You know, there were two autopsies done on Pierre Laporte. I went to the trial and the first autopsy report was never produced in spite of the request by Robert Lemieux, the boys' lawyer. Why did that report never come out? We don't know how he died. In my opinion Laporte's death must be an accident, but I wouldn't trust a judicial inquiry run by federal judges. We would probably end up with the same verdict.

I have never discussed Laporte's death with Paul because I have never seen him elsewhere than in jail. I have seen him only through glass, so I have never even touched Paul since he has been in Jail. And the place is bugged—in fact, it is indicated officially when you enter that the place is bugged—so I would never discuss the Laporte affair. I am not his lawyer. They admitted that they kidnapped him—Paul said so—but killing him, that was not their intention.

I think Mr. Trudeau was hypocritical the way he applied the War Measures Act. Remember, they pretended to negotiate for a week while Mr. Laporte was agonizing. It was deceitful to say, "Yes, we will help you," and then not give any help. And all the while they were preparing the War Measures Act. That's what I find hypocritical on the part of the government. At the very beginning they should have said, "No, we cannot negotiate, we cannot negotiate with terrorists," like they said at the end. Bourassa was nothing during the crisis. Trudeau was the boss in Quebec! But he's paying for those actions now.

I was jailed myself, you know. They came here to this house to get me at nine in the morning — I had driven my husband to work and was having breakfast. Police officers and army people just came in, the street was blocked off with busses. They led me out handcuffed. It was quite a show! I was incarcerated for a week and they questioned me. They didn't beat me but they did beat my daughter, who was 16, not quite 16. She was jailed too. Only the 11-year-old was not taken to jail; they left her alone in the house when they took us away. Left her all alone.

My neighbours, people at work, are very kind to me. In fact, I have held press conferences which my neighbours attended. Neighbours said that Paul and Jacques were like their own children. And I have had no problems whatsoever at work. I was well treated, but I must say that we were well known already in Longueil before October 1970. We had plenty of friends and they didn't let us down afterward.

We are preparing a petition for the boys' release, and things are going well. As for the future, when they come out, I would like to see them work like anybody else, like the man in the street. That's all.

When Jacques was first acquitted he founded a cooperative garage and that was going very well. But then they convicted him and he had to go inside. But if he should come out again, he wouldn't be dangerous. I don't see why they won't let him out. He would be far better off working in a garage. He did it for close to eight months. He could do it again.

Paul was a teacher. In his case it will take longer to get out; he received two life terms, so that is twice seven years, possibly twice ten years. The possibility of parole for him depends on whether Mr. Trudeau is still there, in my opinion. Possibly if we were to have a new government it would be easier for political prisoners. Even Clark or the NDP coming into power I think would be less harsh on the political prisoners than Trudeau is because he is prejudiced. Of course, if Quebec were to separate I think there would be no reason to leave the political prisoners in there.

Mr. Trudeau says that there are no political prisoners in Quebec or in Canada. Well, according to law there is no such thing. But there are cases where men are kept in maximum security three times longer than the others. After three years they should be allowed in medium security, just like other prisoners. What I want is the same law for all prisoners. We are not asking for anything special; we want them to be paroled when they can be paroled. Paul, well, it's seven years now and he is still in maximum security, in super maximum security. And Jacques is still in maximum security and he should have the right to medium security. So all I ask is that the political prisoners have the same conditions as other prisoners.

Yvon Deschamps
Comic, Montreal
(E)
"I guess I've thought independence is the right thing for Quebec since the late '50s."

Yvon Deschamps is by popular acclaim the funniest man in Quebec. A writer-comedian-actor who describes himself as simply a "comic," Deschamps' one-man show at Place des Arts in 1976 played for 13 consecutive weeks to some 90,000 people and was still sold out on the final performance. A bilingual performer who is still much better known in Paris than Toronto, Deschamps had to wait until the 1976-77 television season for his first invitation to appear on an English Canadian network (the CBC).

Like many comedians, he is a very serious and sensitive individual beneath the professional exterior. Deschamps, who is married to an anglophone, is one of Quebec's most politically conscious performers and does not tailor his opinions to suit any audience. When this surprisingly candid interview was recorded amid packing cases in his former Montreal home, Deschamps was in the process of moving to a new house in Westmount where, he pointed out with undisguised glee, real estate prices had recently taken a turn for the better.

I never did actually decide to become a comic. It just happened. I was an actor — I'd been a theatre actor for close to 15 years. At one point a few of us just got tired of having to act in translated French plays or American plays. In a theatre in Montreal if you play Shakespeare or, like we did, Molière or classical theatre, there would be about 25,000 to 30,000 theatregoers and they're the elite. They were the best plays and everything, but it's very hard for an average person to relate to what's going on — it has nothing to do with everyday life.

So one day in 1968 myself and a group of fellow actors decided that maybe we could write skits or revues using everyday situations. So we started doing that, and for two or three years I was always the straight man because there were already two comics. I always made jokes about the guy who had a good boss and a steady job; then one day Clémence Desrochers, who is one of our best writers, wrote a skit with that character. I felt so good in that part and was able to improvise for the first time. I was funny. So I decided to write a few things myself. And it worked. And I haven't stopped since. I think I was even more surprised than the people. Pleasantly surprised. It's the best thing that ever happened to me. For the past eight or nine years I've always played at least 250 performances a year. So whether I'm at Place des Arts or on the road, I'm on stage somewhere for at least 10 months in a row.

As a comic, I wouldn't want to perform in the Olympic Stadium. It's a little big, you know. You have to be close to the people. When we had the St.-Jean Baptiste last year and the year before, we had 300,000 people on Mount Royal in Montreal. It's very hard for a comic to talk to that many people! Charlebois, Vigneault, Leveillé, and 300,000 is a lot of people, let me tell you. We played two nights. One night in Quebec City to 150,000 people and one night in Montreal to 300,000 people.

My appearance on English television? Oh, it just happened that I knew Peter Gzowki, so when he had his try-out for the talk show, he phoned me and said it would be great if I could do one of my monologues that people could relate to. The first one I did was "Grandpa" 'cause I think that's a situation that can be lived anywhere in the world. I could do it in Chinese, I think, if I spoke Chinese, and they would relate to it. A grandpa is a grandpa....

No, there hasn't been much interchange in the arts between Quebec and the rest of Canada. For comedy it's difficult because the audience has to understand French. For singers it's a little easier. I think that Canada heard about Robert Charlebois probably a year or six months after he made his first hit here. I think it is very hard for comics to be universal. If I perform in the United States or England or anywhere, there are things I'm sure in some of my monologues that they can relate to and they can have fun hearing and everything, but never as much as a Quebecker because it will give a Quebecker flashes of his life and that won't happen to anybody else.

Yes, I like some of the comics from English Canada. But I think that people who have talent to write or perform comedy in Canada quickly go to the United States. Of course, it's very hard to say no to American money. You know, many of the American TV shows we see are often written by Canadians. Many of the U.S. TV series that often we say, "Only Americans can do a thing like this," we find out are by those guys from Toronto. When you go to the States you find that a lot of people working for television and movies are Canadians, Australians, and British as well as Americans. In fact, I even met one TV producer who was an American. Ha-ha-ha!

But it's the same thing with the singers, you know. If you make a hit and sell a million records, or you get a few hundred thousand dollars from the United States with one record, you can't wait to go there. That's why, for instance, in Toronto I don't know of any English Canadian singers like the singers we have here—Vigneault or Ginette Reno. They can play Place des Arts for a month, you know, and have 40-50,000 people. Now I don't think you could have that in Toronto even. Gordon Lightfoot plays only six or seven performances at one place. But at the same time, he'll be giving 200 shows anyway that year around the world, so maybe it comes to the same thing.

But on stage, if you're a comic like I am, it's preferable to stay in your province or country. Yes, I like performing in English but I couldn't perform on stage yet. On television it's all right. I'll do one monologue that's really a monologue. But I talk and people listen, so in English I couldn't do what I can do in French, playing with the audiences. You know, I have different types of monologues involving social problems like intolerance and violence, which are very hard on people, even if they know me. Ninety-five percent of what I do is not funny — it's everyday life. Some people love what I do, but sometimes people walk out on me. They just can't take it. So I couldn't do that in English.

Sure, there are prejudices between the English and the French in Canada. For instance, a Frenchman thinks an English person is someone who doesn't know how to cook, never eats well, thinks only of money, of power, and things like this. But since November 15 I wouldn't do anything about prejudice because it's too touchy. Instead, I'm working on things like *la fierté*, pride—how proud we are of what we are. I'll work more on that kind of thing now. I'll try to make the people laugh about their proudness, about the fact that we think that we're different and that we have something that others don't have and try to bring it down to a reasonable state of mind. I'll say we need independence but we're just people like anybody else, and we want to have fun with everybody, and we want to be part of what's going on in the world and Canada, United States, anywhere. We don't want to have a war over Quebec. And we're not different. This is the paradox about life — that every individual is different. But together we're all alike. So in my show I'll try to go ahead in time to when Quebec is independent and we can laugh at the crazy things we do now that we have control over what's going on.

Yes, I think that we do take ourselves too seriously, but at the same time, you know, it might get a lot more serious if we don't do anything now. I'm a believer in peace and tolerance and everything, but I know that if nothing is done, because of unemployment, social problems, and the rest, then it can become revolution or a civil war. Either we take up the responsibility and look at the problems and find solutions or else it will get very, very dangerous. Remember, the federal Liberals won two seats in the by-elections, which means that Quebeckers today are sure of what they want. They want an independent Quebec in a strong Canada. Ha-ha-ha!

I was happy about the November 15 election results. I'm aware like everyone else that the people here voted for a change of government more than anything else. Many didn't think about independence — they just thought the Liberals had to go. But people want independence, that's for sure. Even those who are not ready to admit they want it. I want it and we'll get it too. It's just a question of time. As long as Mr. Lévesque is there, he'll achieve it, I think, with a lot of tolerance, a lot of patience. He's a nice man. There are people in the PQ that are very extremist, to the left, but as long as Lévesque is there, everything is fine.

I guess I've thought independence is the right thing for Quebec since the late '50s. Then with the B. and B. Commission in the mid-'60s many Québécois really thought federalism was finished, only independence was left. All those millions of dollars to arrive at conclusions in their report that we had been talking about for at least 10 years before that. Like the fact that we're really disappearing, and very fast. Like the fact that French Canadians, in Canada, rate thirteenth in the average income, which is not right; in Quebec the higher income goes to an English unilingual. So what do you do? It's like the point of no return. There's only one way out and it's independence.

We thought that after the B. and B. Commission the federal government would be shocked, moved, enough to say, "We'll have bilingual areas in Canada but Quebec will become a French province, with one language and the English Quebeckers will have 10 to 15 years to switch to French. They will go to French schools, so Quebec will stay in Confederation." But they didn't take any action; they just said, "Okay, Quebec is bilingual, compared to other provinces, which will stay unilingual." So I think that the federal government lost its last chance there.

Was this good or bad? I don't know. Maybe it'll be good because this country needs a new federation and a new Constitution and maybe there's only one way to get it: fight it out. Politicians don't do anything unless they're forced to. No, I don't think the federal government's policy of bilingualism in the civil service has done anything to ensure the survival of Quebec. I don't know what good it will do for Quebec if you have 100 civil servants who speak about 100 words of French working in Moose Jaw or anywhere else. In Belgium they've been fighting, and they will fight for another 100 years, because they have two languages. I don't believe in bilingual countries. The only country that really seems to get it on is Switzerland because they have four languages — but they have four regions, and each one is unilingual. There's not one bilingual region in Switzerland. If you go to German Switzerland, if you don't speak German, you can't get a job. And if you go to French or Italian Switzerland, the same thing.

I think that if we have a special status here in Quebec, with control over immigration, language, and culture, sure it can work out. The rest of Canada has to know that if you come to Quebec, you have to speak French, you have to work in French. It would be a lot easier to get along as good neighbours rather than to stay in the same house. It's like when you have a kid, you know. He loves you but when he becomes an adult, he wants to move on — not because he doesn't like you but because he needs to live his own life. So Quebec has come to a point where the people want to live their own life, and live it in French.

Sometimes I'm frightened of what is going to happen because even if I'm optimistic in one way, I think that people are different today. They are more tolerant, they understand more, but at the same time, there are still people that are ready to take a gun and fight. So, it might be a lot harder than we think. You have to be a nationalist. You have to believe in something, but where is the line? When is it good nationalism and when does it become a fascist-type of nationalism? It's very hard to decide. Most people in Canada are not nationalistic. They don't really believe in that country called Canada, but they will become nationalistic if they think that maybe they'll lose part of that country that they didn't really care about. They haven't cared for Quebec for 100 years, but now something is going to happen, so they won't let this happen.

Also, you have to contend with the younger Canadian or Quebecker who doesn't want to hear about nationalism: "We're citizens of the world." This is dumb. You're not a citizen of the world; you live in a very specific place called Canada or Quebec, and maybe you can travel and have fun and everything, but the guy next door, like the United States, if he needs something, he'll take it if he can. So you have to protect yourself. In Quebec it's the same thing. If we don't do anything now, in 10 years it will have gone too far and we won't be able to reason with anybody and there will be a revolution.

What to me is the Québécois identity? It's inside...it's in the guts. We don't speak like anyone else in the world, not even the French. And we have a very short but very intensive history, these past 300 years. We lost the war in 1759 and this is all present to a Quebecker. It's all everyday life.

What is unique about Quebec is that it is the only place in Canada where you will find that a majority, 82 percent of the population, has the same roots, comes from the same place. In the rest of Canada, today, the WASPs don't represent 25 percent of the population. You know, even in Toronto they may be 15–20 percent of the population; the rest are new Canadians. There's nothing wrong with that, but it's a lot harder to get a consensus about something because people don't have the same roots, they don't come from the same place. They're not there for the same reason. The immigrants had a lot of problems in their own countries; that's why they left. Now they are Canadians, they have a good life, they love it, and they don't want anything to change.

It may be that people here in Quebec are a little more politically inclined than other parts of the country. If you go to Alberta, the province is so rich at the moment and everything is going so well that nobody cares about anybody else and that's normal. But problems bring people together. Take the air traffic controllers' situation. I can't see the point about safety. You know, there aren't that many crashes in France because if you're French you bring your plane down in French; if you're from another country you have to do it in English. The planes go down and they go up, and it's all right there. In Quebec, if the controllers are fluently French and the pilot is fluently French, why should they have to speak in English? To me, it's more dangerous to make two French guys communicate in English.

Yes, I think people remember the October Crisis, oh yes. I was a member of Amnesty International; now I'm part of the committee to free political prisoners in Quebec. We still have 11 of them in jail. People are still afraid of that. They're afraid of violence, and they're afraid that if they get out, the FLQ will start again.

François Schirm has been there for 14 years now; he did the Bleury firearm hold-up. He was eligible for probation at least four years ago, but they won't let him out. And Pierre-Paul Geoffrey, his sentence is 126 times life imprisonment, plus 10 years. That's quite a sentence. I think he should be in the *Guinness Book of Records*. They caught him after a bombing and they had had 126 bombings occur in the past six or seven years and he pleaded guilty to every one of them. He didn't do every one — it's impossible — but he said, "I'll have life imprisonment anyway, once or twice, why don't I have it 126 times?" And that was it. Jacques Rose, who was never convicted of the murder of Pierre Laporte, could have been out too, but he won't ask for probation. He'd rather do his sentence. He still has a year to go. And Paul Rose has life imprisonment and another 10 or 20 years, but he could go out on probation in January '78, I think.

I've talked with Jacques and Paul Rose often, but mostly I've worked a lot on François Schirm's case, trying to get him out of there. I also perform in jail regularly; not only to political prisoners but to prisoners in general, 'cause I'm against jails and I'm against the judicial system.

I think that everybody — Paul and Jacques Rose and François Schirm — are very happy about the November 15 election. Most of the guys think that what they did was something absolutely necessary at the time, but it's not anymore. Now there is another type of work to do, and that's getting the people involved in politics and doing it really democratically. Now they know that, but they know at the same time that what they did advanced things here in Quebec by at least 10 or 15 years.

I don't know about the FLQ members who are now in exile in Paris. I worked there last fall [1976] but I didn't hear about them. I think it's even worse to be in exile than to be in jail here. Exile is the worst thing. They're not part of what's going on in Quebec anymore and the worst part of it is that we forget about them. We can't even remember their names. I know all of the FLQ people in jail, but I can't remember the names of the ones that were involved with the kidnapping of Mr. Cross.

It's very bad, what happened to Mr. Laporte. It was murder in a way, but at the same time it wasn't murder, because what happened to him was an accident. I talked to every guy that was involved and it was an accident in a way. Nothing happened to Mr. Cross because he accepted the fact that he was a prisoner and they treated him very well. They got him his medicine and everything. But with Mr. Laporte, it was very different because Mr. Laporte was afraid of the government. He was to be named Minister of Justice and it didn't work out because they found out that he had a meeting or two with very important people in the Mafia. They didn't know what was going on and they still don't know. But Laporte had lost the confidence of the Cabinet and they wanted him to become a judge or anything but get out of the government. So when this thing occurred, he was afraid and a few letters he wrote prove it. He was paranoid, and he tried to escape a few times a day. So at one point they choked him. They didn't want to choke him — they just wanted to stop him from trying to escape. If he had just stayed there, the same thing would have happened that happened with Mr. Cross: he would have got out of it.

There's a funny story connected with the October Crisis. Gaston Miron, he's one of our poets and he's very funny, he's been an *indépendantiste* for 20-25 years now. He knew Pierre Elliot Trudeau very well at the University of Montreal. They were friends and in 1965 Gaston went to Paris for about a week and on the street he met Trudeau and they had lunch together. Gaston was talking about independence and the fact that we needed to be independent and things like this. And Trudeau said, "I'm against independence because if Quebec is ever independent you will lose all of your rights as an individual." So it ended like that.

Five years later, at four o'clock in the morning, in 1970, at Gaston Miron's place, there's a knock on the door. He opens it and it's the police. And he's naked and he wants to go back to his bedroom and get a robe or something, and they say, "No, sit down and shut up. You're not allowed to talk." And they start searching his place and he doesn't know what's going on. He wants to know, so he asks and the guy, the policeman, says, "You're not allowed to talk. You have lost all of your rights." It was the War Measures Act, but he didn't know. So Gaston jumps up with joy and yells, "Hurrah, we're independent!!" That really happened. Ha-ha-ha!

Don Arioli
Cartoonist, Montreal
(E)

**"So we called the film "Parlez Blanc"
because we thought it was
a nice twist..."**

*A native of Rochester, New York, Don Arioli immigrated to Canada in 1962
after leaving the U.S. Marine Corps. He joined the National Film Board as a
writer and cartoonist in 1966 and the following year his NFB film "The
House That Jack Built" was nominated for an Academy Award. He received
an Etrog at the Canadian Film Awards for writing "Hot Stuff" (1972) and
"A Propaganda Message" (1973).*

*The issue of bilingualism has apparently joined wife-beating and food
prices as a subject one just doesn't joke about, as Don Arioli explained to me in
his NFB office.*

I think that film work is probably one of the few places where you can
communicate something about the French and the English. We don't do
enough of that. I think we're kind of dragging our ass on that. Look,
Canadians have a great sense of humour. They do. I think we haven't
given it a chance. I think a lot of people who control the media are just
afraid.

Maybe I shouldn't mention any names — I don't want to blaspheme
anybody — so let's just say I was approached by a certain well-known
government ogranization that had seen some of my films, and they had
liked them because they were open, loose, and free. "A Propaganda
Message" was one of them. They said they were great films. These
people said that they had an audience in mind that they wanted to reach
— the civil servant. They wanted very much to make an animated film
that would deal with this whole language issue as it affects the civil
service, so I started to work closely with them.

I kind of liked the idea. I figured I'd take the bull by the horns, so I
said, "Let's take a character, say he's 50 years old and he's got a fairly
responsible job in the government but he just refuses to learn French. He
had a closed mind, he just doesn't want to know." So we called the film
"Parlez Blanc" because we thought it was a nice twist and because that
whole prejudice thing is in there and it's emotional. I'm sure the same guy
going as a tourist to France would do his best to speak French because
there is no threat there.

I'll tell you the whole story of my film, which never was produced. I show him being kind of rude in this office when someone walks in and says, *"Execusez, monsieur, j'ai un problème."* "Eh, eh, no capiche! Hold on there, buddy! We got a guy here, a French guy, who can deal with you! Jean Roger, Jean Roger!" He's calling Jean Roger, but Jean Roger is not there. "Those French guys are always taking their break." He keeps speaking broken English to him very loud, like most tourists do when they are in a foreign country. They don't understand, so they turn up the volume. He's stupid. Anyway the French guy gets mad and walks out of the office.

Then shortly the civil servant gets a memo from his boss, and it's in French. He's chuckling: "What's the youngster up to? I'm older than the boss. He's probably trying to impress me with his newly learned French." So he goes into the boss' office. And the memo says in French "If you can read this, don't bother to come and see me. Don't bother to ask for an explanation."

So right away he goes to the boss and says: "What is this?" and the boss says: "Ah, that's exactly the reason why I sent you the memo. We would like to send you on a one-year, all-expenses-paid French course." "Hey, hold it. I can't leave the office responsibilities. Can't teach an old dog new tricks. I don't want to . . . " whatever. All the excuses. He just doesn't want to learn French. The boss interrupts: "Look, we're a government agency. We deal with the public, the public is French and English. It's our mandate. You're not going to lose anything by it, you're going to gain." "Don't give me that, I ain't got time." "Don't worry, young Pierre So-and-so will look after your job."

So the civil servant gets really scared. "Ah, let me sleep on it, okay?" And he leaves. As he's walking by young Pierre's desk, the phone rings and Pierre answers it bilingually, "Hello, *bonjour! Comment-ça va?* How are you?" And he can see the image of his job flying out the window. All the fears, the real fears. Most prejudice is based on fear. That is simplifying it but that's what it boils down to.

Anyway, on the way home the civil servant is getting more and more angry. He stops in for a beer and he hears this group of French Canadians laughing and joking and he thinks that they are making fun of him and he insults them and runs out of the bar. By the time he gets home he is in a complete state of paranoia. There's a few other things that happen. His kid starts singing a song he learned in school, *"Frère Jacques."* He tells the kid off. His wife has just cooked a wonderful Cordon Bleu recipe and he says, "I don't want none of that. I want roast beef. Give that whatever it was that you cooked, the soufflé or something, to the dog." And the dog goes *"ouiii!"* He says, "Don't give me that *oui* shit! I want *woof-woof* from you."

Finally he goes and takes a nap on the "chaise lounge" as he calls it and as he drops off to sleep he says, "We've already done too much for them! Why should we bend over backward for the French Canadians? If they had won at the Plains of Abraham, they would have made us slaves, or they would not have been as good to us as we are to them." Then he drifts off to sleep and he dreams the ultimate reversal.

We open up his dreams on the battle. We see how the French win and the English lose. And then cut to Victoria — only it's now called Josephine, and everybody is dressed in eighteenth-century French uniforms. And they are all playing croquet on the lawn. And one of them smells something and it's an Englishman! It is the civil servant, sleeping on the bench. And they call for the *gendarmes*. The cops come with these giant French poodles and they chase him and he's running and he steps into Albérta and onwards to the pea fields of the Prairies. All of North America is French and just Quebec is English and of course all the names are changed. Ontario is Auntario. Amatoba instead of Manitoba. Saskatchewan is full of "q's." The United States is also French, and there is a sequence with French American television: they still switch to it.

Anyway, we follow him through kind of a surrealistic trip through Victoria and he's being chased all over the province because he's English and nobody can understand him. When he finally ends up in the waving pea fields of the Prairies, he gets caught up in one of these great combines and he gets sent to a pea-canning factory and he gets put into a can of peas. Cut to a restaurant in Auntario...*très élégant*. A customer has just ordered some French pea soup; he sticks his spoon in the soup and out comes our hero. Customer says, "*Garçon*, there's an *Anglais* in my soup." And then they chase him and he ends up somewhere in Toronto where the bishop is just giving his blessing in City Hall.

Toronto is very Catholic and City Hall is really a cathedral, and there's a huge Bingo game going on. In Toronto he gets involved with a small group of separatists. He gets chased out of the province and he finally ends up in Quebec, which of course is English. When he gets home his wife is having an affair with a French cook. Nobody can understand him. His kids all speak French and they don't know who he is. They chase him away. He goes back to his old job and because he can't speak the language they give him a menial task, which is cleaning the toilets.

That's where he meets the English separatist. The separatist shows him all the problems of the English minority, and they have this big uprising and he gets caught and put in prison and there is this great thing in court where everything is in French and he doesn't understand. They ask him, "Guilty or not guilty?" in French. And he says, "Huh?" So it's "Off with his head." Then we cut to the guillotine. And by this time all his appendages are speaking French except his tongue, and his tongue says, "I won't desert you, I'll speak English." He gets the chop and the next thing you see him going to paradise where St. Peter welcomes him with: "Ah, *bienvenu au paradis!*" The civil servant says, "Pardon me?" Says Peter: "*Maudit Anglais!* Go to hell!" Of course, in hell everybody speaks English. Then he wakes up: "Thank God it was all a dream."

Then there's one frame in the film where everything is beautiful and it says underneath MESSAGE. "Gee, I guess this is what they must be going through, those poor ... I'm going to learn French right away." Six months later, six *intensive* months later, he's back at his job and the same French Canadian co-worker walks in, who has since learned English. He says, "I got a problem." "*Eh, eh, en français! En français,*" our hero replies. "No please, I got a problem, I want you to help me." Anyway the French Canadian wants the Englishman to speak English, and the Englishman wants the French Canadian guy to speak French. The point I was making in the film is the English guy is still obnoxious, but now he's obnoxious in two languages!

Our government sponsor said, "We disagree with that. He's got to be — he should be — it should be a happy ending." I said, "It is a happy ending. He speaks two languages, but he's still a schmuck." I mean, just because you speak two languages doesn't mean you're going to be any better. It just means you have possibilities of a better, fuller life, more books, more movies, more people. It's obviously like a Dickens story — the guy wakes up Scrooge. The government sponsor liked it but it was too close to home, too touchy. I tried to explain that people will see it as a cartoon, so nobody is going to really object. A cartoon defuses the whole issue. Anyway, the government said no to the film.

So I thought I'd try it out here at the Board. Some of the people here really liked it and thought we should do it, but in the end I got totally destroyed. I couldn't believe it. Four out of five people hated it. They called me a racist. I walked out of the story meeting scratching my head and thinking, "Jesus, what did I do?" My reasoning now is that these guys were super liberals and they were afraid that the French Canadians were going to be insulted, but they were criticizing it for the wrong reasons. They didn't understand that it's just an attempt to satirize the language situation by exaggerating it. So the proposal is still just sitting there.

I'm from the States originally and I've been in Montreal since '66, with the National Film Board, and in Canada for the last 15 years or so. The thing that really impressed me when I first came to Canada was how self-conscious Canadians are.

It still stuns me when I think about it. I'm not particularly nationalistic, but this is a great place to live. When you're travelling in Europe, anywhere, and people ask where you are from and you say

Canada, right away they smile. If you say the States sometimes they smile, sometimes they're not sure. But you say Canada, they smile. Canada must be doing something right. It's got such a good image. Canada isn't a super power and Canadians don't have to go out and prove themselves.

Yet, when you think of it, a lot of the best comic writers and a lot of the best comic directors in the States are from Canada. It makes you wonder. Being born an American doesn't make you funnier. It's just that there are more opportunities. There's more of an outlet for that kind of humour, I guess. The only way you can develop that kind of thing is if you have two or three series going, or a couple of humour magazines or a couple of comedy shows that are current, really regular. You have to get maybe three or four of them going.

I think things like that are really happening in Toronto now with a lot of the cabaret groups. It's happening. We don't have the head start that they had in the States. And in England of course, that's where you get the ultimate laughing at oneself. I think the reason some people can laugh at themselves is that the more you've gone through as a nation, the more you've experienced, the more you see of life, the more you see humour as your own way of relating to the world. The older people get, the more experience they have, the broader their sense of humour is — the same with countries. England's experienced everything.

North America, on the other hand, has never been attacked by anybody, so we've never known what it's like to wake up tomorrow and find our city bombed or attacked. We've got this incredible feeling of security just because we're so big. The States is 10 times bigger because it's so powerful. As an American, it took me a long time—and maybe I'm never going to get rid of it — before I could understand why everybody didn't want to be an American. It took me a long time to realize that not everybody wants to go live in the States. It was so inborn and inbred in me, it took about 10 years for it to sink home and to get rid of the feelings that I had.

You know—all kidding aside, I really like Montreal. It's a great place to live. By the way, you don't want to buy a house, do you? Cheap, real cheap. A bilingual house. No, really, Montreal is a great city. We live in the garlic belt. There's every possible nationality you can think of on our street. St. Lawrence and Mount Royal — it's called the Main. It's supposed to be notorious for killings and prostitution but not where we live anyway. It's a real ethnic area, very friendly. You get to know your neighbour . . . we let each other know when the cops come, before they put the tickets on our cars. Our block is Portuguese, Greek, Chinese, French Canadian, a couple of Jewish families, one Hungarian, and a hairy Italian. That's me. It's terrific. There are a million kids. This city is a real turn-on. I read comic books, tap dance, ride my unicycle, go to small restaurants, eat garlic. It's a full life. And where else can you get six and a half rooms for 90 bucks a month?

Ron Garofalo
School principal, Montreal
(E)

"In a few years St. Rita's may not even exist."

The real impact of Bill 101 on the English school system can be clearly seen by looking at one elementary school, St. Rita's, in the north end of Montreal. Under the jurisdiction of the English Catholic system, St. Rita's has an enrolment slightly in excess of 500 students drawn mainly from immigrant families. Ronald Garofalo, principal of St. Rita's for six years, feels that the continued existence of his school is directly threatened by Bill 101.

We are very sensitive to the word "immigrant"; for example in my case, although my name is Italian-sounding, my grandfather came here in 1888, so we are no longer immigrants. Many of these children are not immigrants. They are children of Canadian citizens. If you want, call them anglophones, if not anglophones or francophones, call them allophones. But they are not immigrants — this is the word we are fighting.

There was discrimination. The Bourassa government's Bill 22 insisted that only children who had a sufficient knowledge of English could be instructed in English, and therefore they had to pass a special test from the government to prove that they had that language knowledge. If your name was Smith and your father was an Australian who was not yet a citizen and your mother was a French Canadian and you could not speak a word of English, you would not be tested — because your name was Smith. But if your name was Rossi and your parents had been living here for maybe three or four generations, you would be tested.

It just didn't work. It is impossible to test a five-year-old to discover whether he or she has sufficient knowledge of English. After proving that the tests were invalid, we went to the government and tried to put some pressure, lobbying and so on trying to get them to change this thing. The result was that during the 1976 election, the Liberal government finally allowed those who had brothers and sisters already in the English system to go to an English school.

After November 15, of course, all that changed. Bill 101 allows into the English school system only children with at least one parent educated in Quebec in an English elementary school, and this law is retroactive. But the people who were here before the law are just as Canadian as anybody else. Even an English person whose parents had sent him to a French school would not be allowed to go to an English school because he did not attend an English school. And take the case of an Italian who immigrated around the '50s. Let's say the family decided to send the oldest son to work, but his younger brothers and sisters were sent to an English school. In the future, the children of the oldest son cannot go to an English school because he did not attend school here — but the children of his brothers and sisters, who went to an English school, will be eligible to attend an English school. So you have divided families this way. It is discriminatory as well as being retroactive.

The problem is not in going to the French school but in the fact that you have no choice. If you don't meet Bill 101's criteria, you don't have all the rights that other Quebec citizens have. Parents are worried about the prospect of sending their ciildren to a French school because English as a second language is not taught until grades five and six, and not by specialists. But in an English school, French is taught as a second language as of grade one, and by specialists. Students at English schools must be able to pass French tests by the time they graduate from high school; whereas high school graduates of French schools do not have sufficient knowledge of English, so they will be unilingual.

The Italians want their children to be bilingual. They say, "You live in Quebec, so you must speak French; you live in North America, so you must speak English." It is the mobility that they want. When they left Italy they were sort of stuck, and now that they've immigrated to this new land, they want their children to have a good chance to succeed. St. Rita's is an English school, and enrolment will definitely drop in the next few years. It has already dropped somewhat because of the lower birth rate. Now add to that the children who will not be allowed to come to an English school because of Bill 101 and it will be disastrous. We feel that within three years most English schools like ours will not have sufficient pupils to remain open — they have to be at least 65 percent full to be able to continue.

In kindergarten, St. Rita's used to have about 80 children; this year we have 48. So that means next year we will have only two grade ones instead of three. And that carries through so that in three or four years the enrolment will be about half of what we have now. That means there will be no assistant principal, and it will also be hard on our teachers: those who have not completed their two years have no tenure and therefore have just been dismissed. I'm losing one this year and next year some teachers with tenure will have to take a job elsewhere in the province.

In a few years St. Rita's may not even exist. We may have to amalgamate it with a neighbouring school about five miles away—that's how schools disappear. Then children will have to be bussed to other schools, maybe as far as 10 miles away. And I think the whole thing is a shame because it is not necessary. The latest demographic surveys show that the birth rate of the French sector is not being decreased and by 1980 it will increase again. Eighty percent of the people in Quebec are French-speaking. There is no danger of their losing their French language.

I've lived here in Montreal all my life. All my relatives are here, including my parents. It's a great place to live. We're fighting, but we are not moving out. I think most French people are reasonable, you know. This elite that is now in power is certainly not a reflection of what the French population is like. They're very warm people. I'm certainly not ready to move out of here, even if Quebec votes in favour of independence. But I think that the referendum will be defeated; the people will vote "No." What? You haven't heard of St. Rita before? Who is she? Well, she's the patron saint of impossible causes.

Kevin Lane
Teacher, Montreal
(E)

"I voted PQ because I think the French are not aggressive enough."

Only a few Canadian schools offer a second-language immersion program starting in grade one. And even fewer schools make immersion programs available starting in later grades. The Regina Caeli English language elementary school on Montreal's West Island is one such school. For grade-six students who are voluntarily enrolled in this program, the entire school day is conducted in French. Teacher Kevin Lane is pleased with the results, but concerned at the anti-French climate he encounters on Montreal's West Island.

I've been teaching with the school commission for nine years, and I've been in the French immersion program four years. It's my second year in this particular school. I spoke French as a child and I reinforced it by going to school. I got my degree in French at St. Francis College in Brooklyn. My mother's side is French; my father was Irish. Both my parents were born in the States, and there wasn't much of a French atmosphere in New Jersey, where I was. I've been in Canada about 14 years and I consider myself a Québécois. To me, this is my home, this is my country. When I go back to visit my family, my sisters and brothers, in the States, I don't feel as at home there as I do here. I love it here. I love Montreal.

I thought the election of the PQ was fantastic! Of course I couldn't stand the other government. I thought they were very corrupt, hypocritical liars. I thought they were in power much too long. They had lost contact with the people. And most people have a lot more confidence in this particular government. I voted PQ because I think that the French are not aggressive enough. I think I have an objective point of view, coming from elsewhere. I think the French should be much more forceful for their own rights. And I find that they have been very fair to the English population of this province — the English have been privileged, far more than any group anywhere that I can think of. Many of them seem to have a colonial type attitude, but this is changing very rapidly now. When I first came here and tried to talk to English-speaking people in French, they didn't like that at all. But now, now they seem to want to practice their French.

It's a fact that English have dominated in the business world and financial matters, while the French always took a back seat, but now they're coming forward to take their place. I hope things go along in a tranquil manner. I'm opposed to violence of any kind. Can't see any point in that.

I'd like to see the French situation very strong and secure in Canada and if Quebec has to be as a separate country for that to happen, well, that's all right too. I'm a Canadian but I'm a Quebecker first. So if they separate, that doesn't change anything as far as I'm concerned. I have no reason to go anyplace else in Canada. In fact, I would probably prefer to go back to New Jersey rather than go to Ontario or anyplace else.

I have never felt rejected here in Quebec. I'm not a French Canadian but I have always been well treated. I've always enjoyed my French friends. I don't like arguing with people. I don't like arguing religion. I don't like arguing politics and I very seldom express my views because I don't like to lose friends over it. But I think I have lost some English-speaking friends who think I'm too French. Sometimes you end up getting dragged into conversations where your opinion comes out and I found that some of the English-speaking people have been totally obnoxious and said the most terrible things against the French — extremely hateful.

I have found this more on the part of English-speaking people than the French-speaking people. They are very prejudiced against the French; they don't want to see French people getting ahead or getting equality or anything. For example, I have a friend who's been a very good friend for 10 years. He's born in Quebec — the Gaspé in fact — but he's extremely hateful against the French. Whenever anything about the French comes up in a conversation he says a rhyme of curses. To me it is totally irrational. I just laugh him off, I don't take him seriously, but still it's a reflection of a deep-rooted sense of superiority. I've never had any kind of incident like that among my French friends. I'm not saying it doesn't exist among French people, but I've never had an incident of that nature.

You know, the French culture is always on the defensive. It's a totally abnormal situation here. When immigrants come into a country and assimilate into the minority group, which is very extremely powerful as far as cultural, business, and economic pressure is concerned, that's an abnormal situation. If you go to any country to live, Denmark, for instance, Danish is the language of the country, so you learn Danish. You can learn English or any other language also, but Danish is the language of the country. Well, 80 percent of the population is French in this province and it's a real putdown when immigrants come in and many of them are not interested in the French culture. They are more interested in assimilating into the English community.

Most of the children in the French immersion program at my school come from English-speaking families. They've been introduced to the French sounds, to some French vocabulary, because they've had French throughout their schooling, a half-hour or 45 minutes a day. But our program is tremendous because it puts them right into the atmosphere and they use French in everything. They see it as a practical thing of life, as a means of expression, and they are very successful. They enjoy. They may be apprehensive at the beginning and have a hard time understanding, but at the end of two months they've relaxed and begun to function in French.

I had one particular student who was extremely negative at the beginning. He thought he was being forced into the class and he was doing very poorly. He refused to speak French or try at the beginning, and I even suggested to his parents that he be put into an English class.

But since Christmas he's just opened completely, he speaks French very well now. And this is common. You see kids opening up. From reports we have had, these students become even more keen as far as their listening skills are concerned, and they do just as well, if not better, in their tests as other kids who do not go into the immersion program.

I think that everybody in Canada should speak French and English, and I hope that as many people as possible will have the opportunity to learn both languages. But you have to have bilingual schools; you have to step up the program. You cannot expect children to come out of a school bilingual if only one subject is taught in the second language.

Claire Vines

Single parent, Montreal

(E)

"I don't know what my daughter is going to face in the year 2000."

While most of the pressure for access to the English school system in Quebec originates in the anglophone and immigrant communities, there are also demands for admission from the French population. This is particularly evident in Montreal, where the economic and social advantages of bilingualism are most obvious. Claire Vines, a young French Canadian single parent, lives in the predominantly French suburb of LaSalle. In lightly accented English, she explained her attempts to enrol her daughter in the French immersion program of the local English language elementary school.

I am a French Canadian. I was born in Montreal and raised in Montreal. I went to a French school, Mary Queen of Hearts. I have four brothers who don't speak very good English and a sister who is bilingual like me. I married an English guy, so I ended up being bilingual and sort of knowing a little bit of both sides of the question.

You know, I think in English, I dream in English. . . oh yes, it's true, I think more in English now than in French. But if I am with French people, then my mind will still switch to French. Which language is more difficult? Well, a lot of my friends are bilingual and if you learn French when you are young it is not hard. It is only for adults that it gets harder because French grammar is difficult. A friend of mine is a secretary and perfectly bilingual — she has beautiful French and beautiful English — but she doesn't know French grammar, so she cannot take dictation. That is the part that is hard in the French language. In the English language the grammar is easy, but English pronunciation doesn't really make sense to a French person sometimes. For instance the "o-u-g-h" in "thought" and "through" are impossible to figure out, so you just have to know it by heart. And a French person can never be sure of Tuesday and Thursday, which is which.

I have a four-year-old daughter. I don't know what my daughter is going to face in the year 2000. I want her to learn both languages, to know English grammar and French grammar.

I'd be happy to send her to French schools if they had a very good French program *and* a very good English program. But even the French in our French system is second-rate! But in the French immersion program at the English school, the French is very well taught. It is well pronounced, very slow, and it is beautiful to hear. That is the way French should be. Listen to the kids around here that only go to French school and their French is not as nice as the French that English kids speak. It puts the French kids to shame!

I learned English by talking and working with English people and by reading a lot of English books, not in school. I am very proud of the fact that I am bilingual, but I could not write a book in English because I do not have the grammar—even though I can read easily enough. I want my daughter to have more than I have. I want her to be able to go around the world if she wants to, in both languages. But I don't know if I can get her into the English school system. An English person can send his kids to French schools, no problem—but a French person cannot send his kids to English schools. In order to do so, at least one parent had to attend an English elementary school. I didn't but my former husband went to grade seven in English. At that time seventh grade was considered the last year of elementary school. Now, of course, it's first year high school. So I'm still waiting for a ruling on this. That is the problem I am facing now.

Personally, I didn't think the French language was going down the drain. But if it is, it's because the French cannot speak proper French, not because they have been influenced by the English. And I don't think bilingualism is a threat to the French. Of course, French Canadians want the right to speak French and not *have* to speak English in order to get certain jobs. If English people can get jobs without being bilingual, we should have the same privilege. If the PQ could negotiate those rights, everyone in Quebec would have the same opportunities.

Oh yes, I plan on voting in the referendum. A lot of people I talk to say, "Well, separation will never happen," but if people are too easy-going, the referendum *may* go through — just like the election. People said, "The PQ will never come in," and then they did come in — very, very strongly. A lot of people misjudged the ability of the PQ.

If the referendum does go through, I'll probably move out of the province, but not without giving it a fight. I am proud of being French. French people here in Quebec identify with the country, the place we live. I find most English people identify with Britain or America but not with Canada; they don't have a sense of belonging to this country. Maybe that's one good thing the PQ is doing: making them realize that they do not belong in England or in the States but here in Canada. Whether you are in the Northwest Territories or in British Columbia, you are part of this country. If Quebec separates ... I don't know ... even the word *Canadien* is originally French, don't forget. We were here before the English — about 200 years before. So we have a sense of belonging that I find most Englishmen, at least here in Quebec, don't have. So maybe the election of the PQ isn't a bad thing. It may make English Quebeckers realize that they love Quebec and want to stay in Quebec. A lot of English persons are starting to say, "I was born here, and I love it tremendously and I am going to stay. I am going to fight for my rights." Maybe 15 years ago they would have never felt that way.

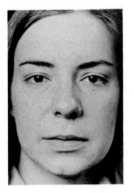

Anne Webb
University student, Montreal
(F)

"At the dinner table in our family there are two languages going all the time."

Anne Webb, a third-year University of Ottawa student, lives in a family situation that is very Canadian.

I live in the Côte des Neiges area of Montreal and until going to the

University of Ottawa two years ago, I didn't speak a single word of English. In fact, I never wanted to speak a single word of English in Montreal, but I think that was a mental block on my part — it really didn't have very much to do with politics. It was a family thing. I refused to speak English mainly because of some problems with my stepfather, who speaks only English. He doesn't speak a word of French and this has resulted in some little conflicts in our household.

It is very difficult because the English mentality is completely different from the French mentality. My stepfather has his language and his way of looking at the world and I have my life and my mentality, so when we talk there are often problems in understanding what the other person is saying. My stepfather tried three years ago to learn some French and began speaking French a little bit at the house, but then the elections of November 1976 came around and the PQ won and that was it as far as he was concerned. He stopped speaking French entirely.

My mother has talked to him only in French for the last four years and now he speaks only English, but they still understand each other. I don't know how they do it but they do! At the dinner table in our family there are two languages going all the time. It's really kind of funny because Mom will say something and my stepfather doesn't completely understand it — in fact, he will often understand something completely different and be shocked by what he thinks my mother has said. Just the fact of trying to understand the conversation keeps them at the table for a couple of hours!

There are two televisions in the house. No problem there. But I think the funniest problem of communication in our household is still to see my mother saying white and him understanding black. It's really funny to see them trying to untangle it all, but sooner or later they manage it. In a way maybe our family situation is a mirror of the Canadian-Quebec situation.

It wasn't until I went to the University of Ottawa, which is supposedly bilingual, that I began to learn English but I didn't pick it up in my courses. I prefer to speak English with the average people. My landlady in Ottawa is English and I talk a lot with her. That really helped remove this mental block against English that I picked up in my family — otherwise I don't think I would have ever gotten over that. You know it's funny but I have the feeling at the University of Ottawa that there are no English students there. I know they're there — they are almost 40 percent of the student body — but I feel they don't exist; you have little communication with them from one day to the other. My social life revolves completely around the French circle. All my courses are in French. The English are the minority at the university and I just don't see them.

You can live in French in Ottawa. I don't have any problems and I've lived in that city for three academic years, but I would like to have more contact with the English community, to improve my English because it really isn't that great. If I don't want to use it, that's my problem, but if I have it for the purposes of working or travelling, it could be fairly useful. I think it's important to have two languages. Now, if I was really pushed by the university to learn a second language, by taking more courses, I would do it, but that's not the case.

Look at the schools. I think it is completely normal, more than normal, that immigrants who come here should be directed to the French school system. We're French in Quebec, aren't we, and basically I agree with it. As far as English Canadians moving into Quebec are concerned, I say, "Okay, let them send their kids to English schools but only if they have a good program of French as a second language. Then their children would come out of that system knowing their French and their English." I also think it should be reciprocal: the French schools should have a good program of English as a second language too. I remember very well the sister who taught us English for the first year at school in Montreal. She wasn't even able to get us through the final exam because she didn't know enough English herself. She didn't speak a single word of English even though she was teaching it to us. It was completely ridiculous!

I am not a specialist in politics but I have my personal opinions and personally I am for independence. Why? First of all, for cultural reasons. I think we have a beautiful culture here that has been developed over many, many years, and if independence can help reinforce that culture, and show that Quebeckers are more than water boys, then so much the better. Economically, I think that Quebec is going to have problems with independence though. The English industrialists and owners may dismantle their factories and take them elsewhere. The owners know that you can always find labour anywhere in the world, so leaving Quebec doesn't pose great problems.

What I would really like to see would be independence with economic association, just like the PQ are proposing. I don't want to see strong barriers set up between Quebec and the rest of Canada. If there was a frontier set up right away between Quebec and Ontario, I would really feel as if I was living in a bit of a prison with a political regime which was stifling me. If we had independence with economic association, there would be a mutual dependence between Quebec and Canada, so it would be important that we be represented in the Canadian Parliament.

Most of my friends and the people I know at home in Montreal and at university in Ottawa, I think, are undecided about independence. They are saying to themselves, "Am I for independence or am I against independence? What would be the advantages and disadvantages?" I think we are waiting to see how the PQ proves itself in the months ahead. If the first question on the referendum is, "Do you give the government of Quebec a mandate to negotiate independence for you?" then they will get my vote. I am in agreement that the government should at least have the possibility of negotiating these things with Ottawa. But if the referendum simply says, "Are you for or against independence for Quebec?" that is another matter. There is a difference between giving a politician permission to negotiate and giving complete support for outright independence.

Robert Beaudoin
University student, Montreal
(E)

"I suppose you could say that what has happened to me is what Mr. Lévesque and his government are trying to prevent."

Robert Beaudoin, a McGill University arts student, is an assimilated French Canadian—or more precisely, someone from a French Canadian background who left his French heritage behind at a very early age. Like French-speaking Robert Blackburn, whom I interviewed in Quebec City, his surname is one of the few remnants of a now irrelevant family past, a misleading flag signalling the wrong nationality.

The reason I went to an English school was that my parents preferred it that way. They thought that I would pick up French along the way. I didn't. All my life I associated with English students, English friends, so I just never learned the French language.

My father is a French Canadian from Montreal, and of course my name is French Canadian, but my mother is British, and I was brought up by her most of my life, so the French didn't rub off. My upbringing has been an English one and my values are basically English values.

As a person who likes Montreal and likes Quebec as a province, I feel that not knowing French hurts my cause in whatever field I'm going into.

It would be very difficult for me to learn French now, so I've resigned myself to the fact of not being bilingual.

Of course, the drift right now is toward bilingualism, and the people who are not bilingual, unless very rich, will suffer, so I feel that the time is ripe for me to leave the province. I think in the very near future, unless something amazing happens, politically or personally, I will leave, perhaps to the United States. I'm interested in television and Montreal is not the mecca of television in Canada. Toronto is. And Toronto is English-speaking, so if I want to stay in Canada, I could go there. But I believe there is more opportunity in the U.S. in my field, and in other fields as well.

I know a lot of people didn't like Bourassa but I did. I think he took bad advice from his people in a lot of things. I also think he did positive things for Quebec. For instance, he and Mr. Goldbloom helped iron out a lot of the Olympic problems. The reason he was defeated was that there was so much corruption within the party. Naturally, I wasn't satisfied with the corruption but I did like the man. I just had a gut feeling about him. I don't care what anybody says about him. He may have seemed cold and aloof to people but a lot of politicians do. People are going to be forgiving him in two years, as they are going to forgive Nixon in two years for what he has done. The whole process is pretty silly, but that's politics. . . .

What do I think of Lévesque? Well, as a former Liberal — which I always like to bring up — he seems to be a relatively moderate politician. He has certain goals, he seems to be a man of integrity, which of course everyone likes in a politician. I would say I trust the man, again as a gut feeling. But the people he has surrounded himself with, that's what worries me. I don't trust the people in the Parti Québécois. I don't like what they are doing in terms of creating a French elite. And if that happens, there is no question that separation is possible. In fact, it would be inevitable. If there is a French elite, I couldn't see why they would want to be involved in a unified Canada. It would be ridiculous.

Yes, I suppose you could say that what has happened to me is what Mr. Lévesque and his government are trying to prevent. They're concerned with cultural assimilation, and they are trying to make sure that the sovereignty of Quebec is a reality rather than just a talked-about dream. Culturally, economically, politically, and socially, they are trying to move in that direction. Now if I was a French Québécois, I would probably support the Parti Québécois. I'd probably be a zealous supporter. But I'm not. I don't like what they are doing and I'm not supporting them. I voted Liberal in the last election, and I'll vote Liberal in the next election, if I'm here. I don't think I'd feel any regret in leaving Canada though. After all, we are brought up with U.S. television, we are brought up with American foods and American values. I guess I even feel slightly American! And I don't think if I went to the U.S. there would be a substantial change. Oh there might be some differences that I would not like, but I think overall I could adapt quite easily.

Hélène Gratton
University student, Montreal
(F)
"I feel more Québécois than Canadian."

A young education student at the University of Montreal, Hélène Gratton is a commited separatist. Her experience of an awakening Québécois nationalism that developed after her first trip to English Canada is one that was recounted by many young PQ supporters. In the same sense that young Canadians often return from summer trips to Europe with a clearer sense of the national identity and distinctness from the United States, many young Québécois seem to find English Canada a catalyst for their own nascent nationalism. Student exchange programs may lead to greater understanding, but not always the type Ottawa wishes to promote.

I came from Outremont, which is a privileged area of Montreal. It is quiet, there's a lot of green space, and I was brought up in private schools, which I didn't always agree with in principle, but my parents sent me anyway. They really believed that it was important that I receive a good education, and I am now 20 years old and a Bachelor of Arts student in education at the University of Montreal specializing in learning difficulties, because for me education is a very fundamental thing. I'm very attached to the city of Montreal and to the province, which I consider more like a country, because I feel more Québécois than Canadian.

My parents are perfectly bilingual. I can make myself understood rather well in English, even though my pronunciation is bad and I may sound like a Spanish cow, but that's really just a detail. I think there is a great advantage in having more than one language and I've even studied

Spanish and German, but I've remained extremely attached to my first language, which is French. I'm really glad that finally we have a worthwhile government as far as this question of language is concerned. It's about time. We were in danger of losing the French language sooner or later.

I don't have any animosity at all against the English. That isn't the problem. I've visited Canada and I've met many Canadians. In fact, I've gone all the way to the most westerly point of the country, Long Beach, British Columbia. I miss not having visited the Maritimes though. I found the country very beautiful, but for me it was like going to the United States. I have visited the Eastern seaboard, around Maine. I mean there is a very real difference between language and common culture. For me it was like visiting a foreign country. Of course, language is a big factor here. I'd say if there really is a difference between English Canada and the U.S.A., it may be that the Americans seem prouder than other peoples. American nationalism is very strong and to be an American is really a big thing. I felt that much more than when I was in English Canada.

I don't remember feeling aware of being Québécois when I was very young. I think it began when I was a teen-ager, going out on my own, taking an interest in what was going on. When I went out West, at the age of 14, I realized I didn't feel truly Canadian. I wouldn't say then that I really felt Québécois, but I certainly felt a difference. I began to think about my roots and at the age of 17 or 18, I realized I belonged to a specific culture that was different from that of the English. The difference was in the way I was raised, the language that I speak, the people I spent my time with. I went on other trips with the English. My parents were really stuck on the idea, so they sent me to English summer camps and any other place where English was spoken. And every time I'd end up with French people who had been sent there for the same reason. It wasn't that I didn't like the English, but our interests were different and I just got along much better with the French kids.

Our daily life is made up of all sorts of minor things — food, slang expressions, personal tastes. Our roots as a people are also important, especially when you become aware of what's gone on before. And maybe we are a little more combative. We take pride in our identity and in fighting for something better. In the last few years we have really started to come into our own in this respect. It began with a political awakening that found expression in the arts, in the songs, the cinema, in all the mass media.

For me the PQ victory was absolutely incredible because I had worked very hard that day in the polling booth for the party, and obviously everyone working in the campaign wanted us to win. I really didn't believe such a thing could happen. I really didn't believe it was possible. And then I turned on the television and the PQ was ahead! I jumped up and down. It was really exciting ... almost euphoric because we hadn't anticipated it.

The PQ wants to create a unilingual state because that's the language of the majority. When immigrants arrive in France I'm sure they learn French; when people immigrate to Spain, they learn Spanish. I think the Charter of the French Language is justified to correct a situation that had become distorted. In Montreal you couldn't work if you didn't speak English. It is a little disgusting when you think that 80 percent of the people of the province are francophones and we were protecting their English language.

Of course I recognize there is a definite advantage in having more than one language, especially these days, and above all English is very useful and important with the United States and Canada close at hand. We can keep English as a second language, but we mustn't forget that this is going to be a French country.

Alain Gaudreault

Graduate student, Montreal

(F)

"I have the impression that the Parti Québécois doesn't want independence, contrary to what might be thought generally."

Twenty-two-year-old Alain Gaudreault is a graduate student planning a career in the media. His reason for voting PQ is the most common one cited by the many Péquistes in this book: intense dissatisfaction with the Liberal government of Robert Bourassa. Gaudreault discusses a question frequently being asked today: "Is the Parti Québécois really in favour of complete independence?"

I once spent nearly a month on a trip in English Canada. You have to recognize the very real differences between the French and English in this country. I can't write English but I can speak it fairly easily. I am short of vocabulary, but I can still get along. I found the English Canadians are more pragmatic than we are. They plan a lot. They have a concrete sort of mind. French Canadians have more of an abstract mind. If you look at folklore in Quebec and compare it to the folklore of other cultures in other parts of Canada, you see that they refer to more abstract things than the legends of English Canadians do. I think this is part of our search for identity.

We have been stuck for 200 years not knowing our real identity. We lived, at the same time, under a francophone regime and under an anglophone regime. We had Confederation with anglophones without ever knowing where we stood as Quebeckers. We don't know who we are. And we have been using the French language to find out who we are. But the language is not really what represents Quebec the most. Let's not make an error about this. Language is something that is being used to create a kind of identity.

I voted for the Parti Québécois because I no longer wanted the Liberals. I knew some things that were taking place within that government—all the conflicts of interest, for instance, and people being given honorary appointments because they were friends of the party, or they were close to the party, or had a lot of money to give to the party. A lot of things like that took place within the Bourassa government. So it was important to get the Liberals out.

I was astonished at the PQ victory because, just like everybody else, I did not expect such strong results. Some said that the Parti Québécois was not going to come into power. Others said it would have a minority government through a very small margin. Very few expected such a resounding victory.

Mr. Lévesque deserves to be where he is at the present time. He has worked enormously; he is hard-headed; he is extremely calm, collected. He thinks on a very long-term basis. He is not impulsive and he doesn't exploit his image like Mr. Trudeau does. Mr. Trudeau uses his image to justify his government's policy. He doesn't mind exploiting some aspect of his private life or his personal image to obtain something. Mr. Lévesque won't do that.

Now, on the subject of independence, let me tell you something. I have the impression that the Parti Québécois doesn't want independence, contrary to what might be thought generally. Over a few years I think that the Parti Québécois will try to get the people to understand that Quebec cannot operate within Canada without being a separate country in the sense of specific programs. They are trying to see what agreements we can come to with the federal government — and when it works they will say so. I believe that at the next election they will tell the people,

"Look, the essence of what we wanted to do we have done — without resorting to independence. We don't need it and we won't do it. All we need is a particular status."

They can't say that openly now because it would be in contradiction of what they campaigned for. Of course, we first have to see how this particular status would work out. At the present time I have the impression that it would work all right, but things will depend largely upon the next couple of elections. What will happen at the federal level we don't know. If Mr. Trudeau, for instance, loses the leadership of Canada and is replaced by Mr. Clark, I think it could change a lot of things at the level of federal-provincial relations.

What I would really like to see is a Quebec that would be managing its own resources, its own capital. If we must have bullshit, I would rather have it made locally than imported from elsewhere.

Stors McCall
Philosophy professor, Montreal

(E)

"What worries me now is not so much the PQ, but that all my fellow Quebec anglophones will pack up and leave or will gradually drift away like a cake crumbling over the edges of a plate."

English-language McGill University has grown from its beginning in 1829 to today's institution boasting 14 faculties and 15,062 full-time students. Future enrolments at McGill, particularly in faculties like Education, are bound to suffer directly from Bill 101's restrictions on Quebec's English school system. McGill philosophy professor Stors McCall personally faces two problems created by the election of the Parti Québécois: (1) the spectre of faculty cutbacks necessitated by falling student numbers and (2) a continuing exodus on the part of Montreal's English population.

Our children are going to an English school that has a French immersion program. All their studies are in French, but they speak English with their friends, walking to and from school and at recess. It's an ideal combination: there are no social difficulties of any kind, but at the same time their studies are in French. It's a compromise, quite a good compromise, because they do learn French quite well but at the same time they're not taken out of their milieu. Most of the kids are fluently bilingual by the end of grade six. Mine are in grades one, three, and four now.

Most children from English homes are able to adapt beautifully to the French immersion, but a few have trouble and it's not clear exactly why they do. But for any child who has a problem with immersion, the option of returning to the English-language program is always available.

I hope my children will be totally bilingual and able to live and work here, just like any other children, so I'm personally committed to the future of Quebec, but I don't want to live in a unilingual French community. I want to keep the genuinely bicultural, multilingual aspect of Montreal. That's the environment that suits me best. I like the cosmopolitan kind of society that Montreal traditionally has the reputation of being and I want to preserve that very special character of Montreal. So I personally was surprised and a little alarmed on November 15.

What worries me now is not so much the PQ, but that all my fellow Quebec anglophones will pack up and leave or will gradually drift away like a cake crumbling over the edges of a plate and in a few years' time we'll only have a token representation of anglophones in the province. This is a bad dream. Only in the worst possible scenario would this come to pass, but that is nonetheless a fear that all of us have, I think.

So it's not so much a fear of the Parti Québécois as a fear as to how our fellow citizens are going to react to the Parti Québécois. You see lots of *For Sale* signs in my neighbourhood now. Maybe they're just trying to sell their houses because they are afraid that they will lose their investment and they plan to move into an apartment. You know, one doesn't question all one's neighbours to find out exactly what their motivation for this is, but I think a lot of them feel they just can't take the hassle. The way they put it is: "Why the hell should we bother ourselves with all the effort that it's going to take, filling out forms in French, making sure that our company promotes enough francophones, being sure we communicate with all the right people in the right language?"

But a lot of people also leave perhaps because they've come from a European country and experienced this kind of state control, currency control, and things like that, and they want to take their money out while they can. You know, we don't think bank accounts could be frozen here but they didn't think it could happen in Hungary or Poland or Czechoslovakia. Some people have been burned once, and they're not going to be burned again. And I guess you can sympathize with these people. I don't have any of those feelings myself, but I have to respect the way they look at the problem.

I have a great faith in Quebec. I intend to stay and if necessary I can give my lectures in French. They won't be as good as they would be if I gave them in English, but I could certainly work them up and certainly lecture in logic, which is my subject. But there are certain realities that must be faced. I'm afraid that the pool of potential students on which McGill draws may be reduced radically and if so the university will have very hard times ahead, and so will Concordia and Bishop's—they are the two other anglophones universities in the province. I suppose McGill could stagger along somehow or other, drawing on more francophone students and on students from other parts of Canada and the United States. McGill has always traditionally had a large percentage of students from outside the province. But it wouldn't be the same.

Another thing—because I've moved around so much I'm not yet tenured at McGill. If enrolment does drop seriously, that could mean a reduction of maybe 30 percent of the teaching faculty — and of course then the question would be: Who goes; who is going to stay? That kind of pressure on a teaching faculty can be very agonizing. It can arouse all sorts of internal antagonisms and difficulties with a university. I belong to the McGill Association of University Teachers. We don't have a faculty syndicate, or union, here but our faculty association is working on this problem, trying to outline, if possible, some rational and sane guidelines as to how you would effect a reduction in staff if you had to.

Anyway, I think that the voters of Quebec will reject the idea of independence or separatism, or whatever you want to call it, when it comes up in this referendum. My own scenario for the future is that the Parti Québécois knows this is going to happen. Their ostensible aim is separation but their real aim is to make Quebec as French as Ontario is English and there are many things they can do short of separation to achieve this.

There is a school of thought in other parts of Canada that says something like the following: "We can preserve Confederation, Canada can be saved, if we allow the Parti Québécois and the nationalists in Quebec to achieve their legitimate aspirations short of separation. Let's give them a free hand to make Quebec as French as possible; but still remain within Confederation. We can loosen up the constitutional structure of the country in such ways to allow them to do this."

Now this is fine, Canada is saved—*but* the people who lose out in this process are the anglophones of Quebec. Canada is preserved, but at the expense of Quebec, and particularly Montreal, losing its multicultural, bicultural ethnic aspect. So I think that we can say that there are two kinds of separation. There is legal separation, which the people wish to avoid at all cost, and then there's also de-facto separation, whereby Canada can be preserved by having a totally separate French Quebec and a totally English rest of Canada. I don't regard that as a solution to Canada's problem. I think this is really giving up on Canada as we traditionally know and love it.

Daniel Latouche
Political scientist, Montreal
(E)
"The PQ will win the referendum."

Daniel Latouche is one of those "experts" that the electronic media like—well informed, able to speak understandable French or English without academic obscurantism, and possessing a gift for the memorable phrase. A McGill University political scientist specializing in public opinion survey research and French Canadian studies, he was guest commentator on that most memorable night in Canadian television history — November 15, 1976. Since he has designed and carried out numerous public opinion surveys, his comments on the forthcoming referendum deserve careful attention. Professor Latouche is not only an experienced pollster but a PQ supporter.

I remember the night of the November election very well because it got a bit confused. I was invited by CBC TV as a commentator to discuss the election night for the English network. But when I got to the Montreal studios of CBC I realized right away that there are actually three separate CBCs, each corresponding to three countries. There was the French network with its massive organization, dozens of people, carrying the thing live for the Quebec population and also for the French networks across Canada. Then there was CBC English Quebec, also carrying the thing live, but with more limited coverage and a smaller staff. And in a small studio in the back was my spot — with a team of CBC people from Toronto covering the election in a two-hour special for the rest of Canada. The week before, they might have been covering the elections in Prince Edward Island, but this week was the Quebec elections. The other commentators were Eric Kierans, former minister of the Liberal government, Premier Hatfield of New Brunswick, Professor Dale Thompson from McGill, and Maurice Pinard, a McGill sociologist who was important because of his very pro-federalist public position. I was the token *séparatiste*.

So the show started. At first it was simply a few jokes and then a result came in. The first result was Liberal leading in five and PQ leading in three. And suddenly, 10 minutes later, there was a PQ leading in 15; then the PQ leading in 40, and then everybody was a bit nervous. And the interesting thing is that of all these professionals covering the thing, no one really knew what was happening—but in the next studios, the French CBC and the English Quebec CBC, people knew very well what was happening. On the faces of all the technicians from Radio-Canada smiles started to appear suddenly. There were about 200 or 300 teletypes manned by two students each, and these students were starting to cheer, but the professional journalists from Toronto didn't know what was happening yet.

I got more and more excited as the evening went on, and I was less and less of an objective political scientist. The only problem was that I was with at least seven guys all around me who obviously felt they were losing. Richard Hatfield was sort of slowly falling apart in front of the camera. Thompson was gloomy; Pinard couldn't believe what was happening. His surveys had been predicting for the last six or seven years a 7 or 8 percent separatist vote in Quebec.

I'm a product of the Quiet Revolution. I'm the first generation of Quebec students who went to study abroad. We espoused all the causes of the world, the blacks, the anti-Vietnam war, everything, but we often lost on these causes. Of course you also came out for Quebec independence too, although you'd studied in English, but on this issue you're finally winning! My God! It was a real ordinary day-to-day electoral victory that happened dozens and dozens of times in the world — but this time it was happening to your team. It was Charlie Brown winning and Lucy shutting up for a change! So you can imagine how excited we were. Nobody could believe it, and the roof of the CBC just exploded when it was announced that Gérard Godin had defeated Premier Bourassa in his riding. I mean, people were shouting! It was funny because on the French network you could hear the shouting and the anchorman was trying to keep his professional cool. I got so excited after a point that I shouted "Hooray!" and spilled my glass of water over the poor anchorman. I was a catastrophe in terms of cool presentation of the facts to an English Canadian audience, but I was too excited to keep my cool.

There's debate within the university community as to whether or not the PQ is a broadly based political party. Well, it is. It's a mass party. Some people argue that those who are young, urban, well educated, are the backbone of the PQ. But the 1973 election clearly showed that the PQ succeeded best in the poorer areas of Montreal.

It's a massive vote spread all across the board. Of course it's stronger among men and stronger among urban people, and it's stronger among French people obviously. But it's not confined to one region, one group of people. Secondly, it's a vote that is not a one-shot thing—that is to say, if you vote for the PQ, you vote again for the PQ. Thirdly, it's an ideological vote—that is to say, maybe it is true that if you vote for the PQ you're not separatist. There is also a debate as to whether or not these people are separatist or not separatist. And of course people in Ottawa like to believe it's a protest vote. This time the PQ succeeded both in attracting the separatist vote and the real protest vote.

My surveys have indicated that, once you vote for the PQ, you tend to line up your ideology with the ideology of the PQ. For example, you're very unsatisfied with Liberal government, so you say, "Okay, I'll try the other guy." So you vote for the PQ and what do you do afterward? If you're satisfied with the way they're running the government, you will tend to adjust your own views and say, "Well, maybe the independence thing is not that bad after all." And so you become a separatist even though at first you didn't vote for the PQ for separatist reasons.

It's like if you go to a used-car lot and you want to buy a car. You don't really trust the salesman but you know it's a good deal, so you buy the car. The car is perfect and two years later the same guy comes to see you and offers you a radio. You tend to say, "Well, he was honest with the car, so I just might buy the radio," although the radio hasn't got anything to do with the used-car lot. It's the simple PQ strategy. It certainly hopes to be able to sell independence to an audience which is already available to be sold something. It is a pure question of marketing.

French Canadian nationalism isn't a new phenomenon, but the election of the PQ is a turning point, the first turning point since 1837. In a way it's a repetition of the 1837 armed rebellion, which at the time was as ambiguous as the PQ victory. The 1837-38 rebellion was a complex matter because it was also the rebellion of Upper Canada and not a purely French thing.

The only thing that was not complex about 1837 is that it failed, miserably. Quebec nationalism, which had been simmering since the Conquest in 1759, was cut off in 1837. And you know what happens when a movement, a rebellion fails: people fall back into a survival ideology. From 1837 to 1970 nationalism in Quebec really became an ideology of survival; a way of preserving the culture. By 1960 and the change to Lesage liberalism, Quebec had become urban and industrial. It did not happen in 1960 — it was simply recognized then. The protest movement picked up again with negotiations with Ottawa, just like back in 1835, when Papineau was negotiating with the British Crown. Then in the late '60s there was a transformation of a protest movement into a political party, the Parti Québécois, a few defeats, and finally the 1976 victory.

In a way the November election was really the Declaration of Independence. It's saying to English Canada, "Okay, we are going to do whatever we want to do, when we want to do it. We've waited 100 years so you shut up and wait and we'll send a telegram saying okay we want to negotiate, we want to separate, we want to do this or to do that." This is why Quebeckers since November are really enjoying this time. Now it is no longer just a survival situation.

Now if Lévesque loses the referendum, I can already see the headlines in the *Globe* or the Winnipeg *Free Press*: "Quebec Problem Solved." Well, it's not going to be like that! Lévesque has already stated that if he loses, he won't quit. He'll have an election afterward and two things can happen at the election: he can either win or he can lose. If he wins, we're back in the ballgame. It's the Joey Smallwood scenario, with a second referendum. And if he loses, I suppose the Liberals are back in power. And if the Liberals are back in power in Quebec in four years, English Canada is going to wake up to an incredible shock when they realize that the Liberals will also want a new Constitution right now, in one month or two months. I've always said there's very good chance that the Quebec Liberals will declare Quebec independence and not the PQ. So if the PQ loses the referendum, it changes very little. I think the movement has started now in the mind of young Quebeckers. They are no longer *séparatistes*; they're already *indépendantistes*. That means you live in a separate, independent country. For them the question is solved once and for all. At the first congress after their electoral victory, the PQ didn't discuss the referendum. They discussed abortion, foreign investment, all sorts of things relating to social democracy, but not independence.

What is the best way out of the situation? I think that Canadians and Quebeckers are probably the best-equipped people in the world in terms of their traditions to get themselves out of this impasse. It's very simple. I think that everybody should look very carefully at how Canada was created. Go back to the Charlottetown Conference in 1865, when the Maritime colonies called a meeting for Maritime union between Prince Edward Island, Nova Scotia, and New Brunswick and just out of politeness, invited Canadian delegates to attend. The Canadian delegates saw their chance and they came with a plan to convince the Maritime people: "Forget about this Maritime union, let's talk about a bigger union." They simply turned around the agenda of the conference.

If you look at it on paper, they came up with the most Wizard of Oz type of country. The new country has no jurisdiction at all over its foreign affairs or its military affairs. If you put up the BNA to a panel of constitutional experts, they would say that this is not a country. What I'm driving at is that the PQ suggestion of sovereignty-association is far less impossible and ridiculous to achieve than Confederation was in 1867. In 1867 John A. MacDonald and a few others had a lot of political imagination. There are dozens and dozens of solutions available to us, and we have an unbelievable history in Canada for figuring out things like that. Not with people like Pierre Elliot Trudeau in power though.

I favour political independence, re-creating some kind of arrangement with the rest of Canada. But this implies recognition of two equal sides. There will have to be an entity known as English Canada, nine provinces, 24 districts, whatever, and they will have to come together with one voice or many voices in the same delegation. What I'm saying is that at one point there will have to be a meeting between Quebec and English Canada.

Quebec could eventually be a new country in the form of, say, the Ukraine, within a new Canadian Community. Everyone knows that the Ukraine is in the United Nations, but everyone knows that it was to give the U.S.S.R. another vote. So we could get two countries in the United Nations and this would be a great benefit to both Canada and Quebec because we would have two votes. Canada would become known as the Canadian Community, with provision for a joint delegation.

Another constitutional alternative is to follow the Common Market setup, where there is a rotating presidency or chairmanship shared by equals. There is no reason why we couldn't adopt a similar system. Every six months or every year or whatever, Lévesque and Trudeau would alternate in the presidency. There are dozens of possibilities open to us, but we can't just try to negotiate the areas of conflict, like communications or immigration policy, one by one.

I don't think that English Canada has accepted the registered letter that November 15 is. I don't think that English Canada is willing to sit down and negotiate one to one the future of this country. And I think the entire problem rests there. For some crazy reason, Quebeckers are not really taken seriously. Maybe if 24 hours after the election, Lévesque had declared Quebec independent, they would have taken us seriously.

There's also the question of dignity for the Quebeckers. For 300 years the Quebeckers have never had their own country and the opportunity to make their own mistakes, do their own thing. It's a question of national maturity.

Why are men like Trudeau, Pelletier, Marchand, Wagner, Caouette, federalist? That's a good question. I don't think they are all federalist for the same reason. I think, for example, some of them are federalist for exactly the same reasons that some people have joined the PQ: because they wanted a political career and the opportunity was there. Then they rationalize their actions afterward. Secondly, some really think that the future of the francophones in North America is with Canada, not with Quebec. All these people that you've mentioned define themselves as French Canadian. They still have not made the jump from 1837 to 1960: they still think that Canada could belong to the French and so on and so forth. They live in a dream, Ottawa being a dream capital of a dream country. You just have to walk around Montreal to see how far from reality Pierre Trudeau is. He's completely cut off from Montreal and the Quebec reality.

You think I'm dismissing these men as just careerists? Okay, I'm saying that, for some of them, it was an element. When Pierre Trudeau, Gérard Pelletier, Jean Marchand made the decision that they wanted to get involved in politics, the field was full in Quebec. The only place they could go was Ottawa and if they'd really wanted to stand up for their ideas, they would have joined the NDP. Trudeau *was* a member of the NDP! No, they wanted power because it's with power that things get done.

It's time for Canadians to face a few very hard facts about themselves, and Quebeckers have started that process. If English Canadians are not ready to face up to that challenge, that's their problem. Independence is a process, and for me that process started on November 15. I can see very well that Mr. Trudeau's game is to press for that referendum, because he doesn't want to negotiate. He's the only one who's got something to lose. He had nine days to save Canada, between the election and the naming of the new Cabinet. One letter would have solved it all. If Pierre Elliot Trudeau had sent a letter to the nine premiers of English Canada calling them to form a joint delegation to negotiate with Quebec in those crucial nine days, we would be at a completely different point now.

And people think that the PQ might lose the referendum? Do you really think that a party which has been able in its first six months in power to assemble $1.3 million, 80,000 subscribers, 146,000 card-carrying members, do you think that a party like that can lose? My God! I mean the PQ will win the referendum. They know that they will win the referendum. They're already thinking what kind of victory they want. Do they want a 70 percent massive victory, but on a very ambiguous referendum text, or do they prefer a smaller victory and a more specific text? This is what they are discussing in Quebec City. They're not discussing, "Are we going to win or lose the referendum?" In their minds, it's done. And they're in power, don't forget that. These people are in the business of winning. They're not in the business of moral victories. They've had a taste of power and they like it.

Laurier Lapierre
Writer, broadcaster, historian, Montreal
(E)

"It is a very traumatic thought that in
two years from now I may no longer
be a Canadian."

The best-known French Canadian outside Quebec during the mid-'60s as co-host of CBC television's This Hour Has Seven Days, Laurier Lapierre is an historian at McGill University and an active contributor in both languages to this country's media. Working in the world of words, ideas, and popular communication, Lapierre has proven himself professionally effective and personally comfortable in both languages and cultures over the past dozen years.

Like everybody else, I was quite surprised that the PQ had won and that Bourassa had been defeated so badly. That was my first reaction, and after that I think I felt a sense of relief that we were rid of that government and that finally the matter might be settled, once and for all, so that we would stop talking about it.

Somebody asked me yesterday, "Are you a federalist?" I said, "No, I don't go to bed as a federalist every night, you know. I am a Canadian. This is my country." That's all. It is a very traumatic thought that in two years from now I may no longer be a Canadian. That's what I am, that's what my fathers have been since 1634, and I'm not prepared to give it up.

I haven't voted federally since October, 1970, so I did not vote in the election of '72 nor the election of '74. In October '70 I said, "Fuck your systems. If that's what democracy means — that people are going to be arrested in the middle of the night — then I'm going to behave as if I was living in a dictatorship. If all human rights and civil liberties are suspended because some idiot wants to liberate me by killing people or some other idiot wants to protect me from these idiots by putting me in jail, well, I don't have any choice in this goddamn system. And I want no part of it." So it was my way of saying screw off and I didn't vote.

But I'm not an *indépendantiste*. Why not? Well, because I'm a Canadian. My roots are firmly implanted in Canada. I'm a citizen of this country. I'm not a Québécois, I've never been. I don't know what that is — nobody else knows what that is either. They are talking about French Canadians, they are talking about the Canadian culture, which expresses itself in different languages. There are differences, but they are more of style, I suspect. That's essentially what they are talking about. It's important for them to have the word "Québécois." Recently I was in Quebec City talking to civil servants and I asked them what is it to be a Québécois? What does it mean? None of them could answer. And there were 25 of them in the room.

A French Canadian really belongs to a group of people who have been here permanently since roughly the middle of the seventeenth century and who have opened up this continent to their brand of civilization. A generation after they had been here, they had an empire that stretched from the Gulf of St. Lawrence to the foot of the Rockies and from Hudson Bay down to the Gulf of St. Lawrence to the foot of the Rockies and from Hudson Bay down to the Gulf of Mexico, and which was all fed and regulated from Montreal and Quebec City. And these people eventually transformed themselves from Frenchmen into Canadians, or *Canadiens*, and after a while they had to learn to share their continent and they became more and more shrunk, both psychologically and territorially, into the province of Quebec. That accounts for their schizophrenia and also for their limitation of vision.

From time to time in history the word "insular" has been used to describe the Quebec outlook. But it has been used more by English-speaking Canadians to explain their insularism, their incapacity to deal with it, than it has been with the French Canadians. French Canadians have never been that sort of people; they were certainly not in the years of New France. They may have come in the nineteenth century to accentuate the land and the agriculture and limited their vision to a hundred acres of land. But basically there will always remain, I think, this tremendous vision of openness and of space which makes us very bad Frenchmen, I suspect, because the European French have a tendency to contain. French Canadians have a tendency to think they are American. There's no doubt about that. We're profoundly American.

Almost 60 percent of the programming on Montreal's Channel 10 is translated programs. Pick up *La Presse* and look at the movies . . . 95 percent are translated from the United States. Ed Sullivan used to be a national celebrity as important as Madame Julien must be today. I think there is basically an American culture that expresses itself in the French language. I suspect that people will tell you that there is a Quebec sound just like there is the Atlanta sound and a New York sound. But look at the values that are current today. At one point or another this is essentially what one must ask oneself when one talks about culture: What is the content? What are the values of the culture? I do not see that the values are vastly different between Madame Laframboise who lives in the East End of Montreal and Mrs. Yablonski who lives in the Bronx. And I do not think that the language, even if she is quite unilingual, has in any sense isolated Madame Laframboise. So when people talk about Quebec being insular and all that, it is a lot of nonsense. Just pick up a box of Corn Flakes, pick up any consumer product. You know they have all been manufactured, or thought of, or developed in the United States of America and sent up here. And this has been so since time immemorial, so I cannot see where the differences of mentality are, really.

I cannot see that the French Canadians are less materialistic than the Americans. Are the French Canadians less attached to the great American dream of having two cars in every single garage than the Americans in the Bronx? I suspect not. I see no difference whatsoever between Outremont and Westmount. I see truly no difference between the suburbs of the French Canadians and the suburbs of the *Anglais* in the West End. None whatsoever! In St.-Bruno they are running out of water because they put too much water in their swimming pools, and that ain't the English. There is a swimming pool in every yard.

French Canadians are Normans. They are stubborn mules and Normans don't share. They appropriate what they think is theirs and if they can't get away with it legally they take what is somebody else's. I cannot see that the French Canadians are more cooperative than the English. The cooperative movement may have had some development in Quebec, but its real life is really lived in Western Canada more than it is here. The advances that have been done in the cooperative movement as a social force have come from Antigonish, from Nova Scotia. The Caisses Populaires Desjardins is a massive bank which is as impersonal and as intractable and as bureaucratic and as interested in building mausoleums as the others. Look at the Desjardins Complex in Montreal. The cooperative movement is, after all, a capitalist venture. And to try to transform it into an instrument of socialism or even social democracy is overdoing it a bit! The people in the cooperative movement have bought shares from which they want a return, and this is why the cooperative television station in Hull failed so miserably: because there were no profits to be distributed.

The French Canadians and the people who call themselves Québécois have this kind of innate feeling that they are a people set apart for reasons that are at times a mystery. But they are a people with a kind of distinct will and capacity to live the way they want to live, and they have done so for 300 years and they want to do so for quite a number of years yet. What has happened to French Canadian nationalism is that it's like patriotism, it is the refuge of scoundrels. And the scoundrels have been largely the elite and the professional class, the clergy, lawyers, and notaries, the politicians who lived off this, and now the new elite, the new professional class who lives off it too — the technocrats. Nationalism becomes always an *instrument de classe*, an instrument of class, of class warfare.

I think Quebec nationalists are those who can live off the state, people I describe as parasites. Politicians, first of all, people who are involved in public service; people who are involved in the parapublic sector of schools, hospitals; technocrats who are largely unilingual and who cannot find their way in a multicultural pluralist world and society; writers, authors, for whom the emotion and sentiment are more important than the reality in which they live; people who can live quite well sealed hermetically from the rest of mankind. No doubt three-quarters of the members of the PQ will send their children to English schools eventually because if everybody else is to be unilingual, surely not they! It is very important that they should not be, because there must be a class distinction between those who vote and those who are governed. And that has always been the will of the French Canadian elite: to put itself between the rulers and those who are ruled, and to explain the former to the latter and the latter to the former. And to carry messages back and forth. French Canadian politicians have been by and large messenger boys. There is no difference today. The PQ would be the messenger boys for the kind of society that they want and the kind of American capital they need to expand.

You ask is the PQ a party of serious political reform. I don't think that there is a shred of evidence to suggest that. Not a shred! In fact, there is considerable evidence to suggest otherwise. As soon as the PQ was founded and began to talk seriously that they might take power, they began to fall over each other knocking on the door of Mr. Rockefeller in New York. And we were led to believe that Mr. Rockefeller was a better capitalist than other capitalists because he spoke French — as if that mattered very much. If I tend to be rather harsh on them, it's because I think that the Parti Québécois lies more than the other political parties we have. All politicians lie. I think that's an axiom.

I know that many people who voted for Lévesque say they voted for him because he seems like an honest man. Yes, he seems so. No doubt he *is* an honest man, and an open man, but that would not prevent him from being quite ruthless and manipulative, should it suit him. No one exercises power for public service. You exercise power for the pleasure of it. Because you happen to like power and because you can utilize power for whatever purposes you prefer. And some purposes are very, very noble, I have no doubt. I'm not saying everybody else is better than we are; I'm not saying that at all. I think everybody else is also as bad as we are.

And I do not see any difference between Mr. Lévesque and Mr. Trudeau. None. None. They are highly practical men, pragmatic people. They are both brilliant. Exceptionally brilliant. They are imense manipulators of public opinion. And they have concepts of societies which are about the same, you know. I think it is only an accident that has made Trudeau a federalist and Lévesque an *indépendantiste* — a sovereignist, to be fair to him, because he is not an *indépendantiste*. Because in the final analysis what Lévesque is talking about when he talks about association is federalism. He is talking about federalism and he thinks that, after he has fragmented English-speaking Canada, he is going to have an association with Ontario, an association with the West, an association with the Maritimes. But he's got another thought coming. And he ought to be intelligent enough to sense that. Really.

What I'm trying to suggest is that the idea of independence, the idea of sovereignty, is built upon the accentuation of the most retrograde feelings and sentiments, which always tend to be nationalistic, and which are hopelessly outdated in this last quarter of the twentieth century. I'm overwhelmed by the very fact that in 1977 one should be using words like "independence" and "sovereignty." They are meaningless words! They are meaningless words for the United States of America, they are meaningless words for Russia, and they are meaningless words for any other society. What Lévesque is really talking about is provincial autonomy: there are powers that are exclusive and therefore the prerogative of the provinces, and the provinces in the administration of these powers are sovereign.

We are a small, insignificant people. We really cannot affect the course of mankind one way or another, and we cannot really determine empires anymore or anything like that. We don't even own 85 percent of our own province! Our natural resources don't belong to us. Our manufacturing doesn't belong to us. Our commerce escapes us.

Eighty-five percent of the people of Quebec work in French 100 percent of the time. The Gendron Commission demonstrated that beyond the shadow of a doubt. And of the other 15 percent that is left, the vast majority work most of the time in French; there's only a very small minority who works purely in English, and they do so in areas like international finance or international firms that count. Therefore it is a false problem. We're told that the French language is menaced. By what?

As for the immigrant children in the English school system, that is a political power. Essentially, the government is saying that the population is not growing fast enough and that we will become a minority. What they want is the *politique de natalité*, to encourage the birth rate. But since encouraging the birth rate is not politically possible, well then, you have got to assimilate the Italians and of course you are all right doing that because everybody else in the world has done that.

I see absolutely nothing whatsoever about immigrants that has threatened the French Canadian culture. Montreal in 1840 was an

English-speaking city. We used to alternate mayors between French and English, which we don't do anymore. Are we so weak that one million English-speaking Quebeckers will threaten five million francophones? What is the rate of immigration into Quebec on a year or two-year basis— 40–50,000 at the most? We're going to be threatened by that? What is all this nonsense?

I think that racism and insularism are being encouraged today; I think that the Parti Québécois has made up its mind that it can stand half a million to a million people leaving Quebec. They will manage it, too, if they keep stressing that size matters. They want a smaller country rather than a big one. And they don't want any immigrants until such time as they have been able to establish French as a fundamental language of work. Realizing all of their linguistic objectives should take them at least four or five years, so I think that over the next four or five years they have accepted the fact that over a million people are going to leave. And this is why they want to control immigration too. They know perfectly well that nobody from France is going to immigrate here and nobody from Brussels is going to do so either—nobody from the French-speaking Western European world is. Why should they? Come here and babble in French in the wilderness? Their trains run faster than ours! Their standard of living is as high as ours! They have jobs! Now why would they want to come here? They have all the television stations through satellites. They would not come here to better themselves—if they want to do that they go to the United States of America. That's where the manifest destiny is—the dream, the hope—not here.

I claim to be a man who's quite open and therefore I have no difficulty outside Quebec whatsoever. I think it is people of very little imagination and vision who are screwed up by travelling to English-speaking Canada. I don't expect problems and therefore I am not bothered by things. I don't expect in Vancouver that somebody is going to babble to me in French. I don't expect that. And therefore I am not upset if they don't, although now I find that with the bilingualization of the federal service it is quite conceivable that I might eventually, if I lived there, have services in the French language. But I don't think that I want that at all. I don't want two melting pots in this country. I mean, one is bad enough. Two must be worse. Three must be awful! The essential reality of this country is its diversity, its amazing geographical diversity, its amazing cultural diversity—that's what life and the world are all about. You're not going to make Englishmen out of Chinamen! People are people.

I have said Canada is of the heart. That's what the whole country is about. It's a sentiment, it's a feeling. I know there is a lot of disappointment and bitterness and anger across Quebec about what has been done historically, what could be done now and should be done in the future. But in the final analysis, you put all those together and what are you left with? Just look around you. It is something very beautiful. Very beautiful... Something which makes you soar, which makes it possible for you to believe that on a plot of land that stretches from the Atlantic to the Pacific people can find in their hearts and in their souls and in their heads a kind of a capacity to create equality. That is what life is all about. To create equality. Not equality of opportunity, but equality. So microcosmically a crisis of mankind is being played out here. How can I, and the people to whom I belong, possibly partake, truly and completely? And not only me, but the Maritimes and other people. I think it can be done. It can be done if we stop being a nation of bitchers. We are the greatest bitchers on earth. But it can be done if the will can be rekindled by the reality that this is a good country, one that serves everybody equally and one that recognizes that the rights of a minority are guaranteed.

I'm very cynical. And skeptical. But I'm not pessimistic at all. No. Look, this country has never been tested, nor have the people been tested. There are people dying in Lebanon for what they believe, there are people dying in Israel, there are people dying in Northern Ireland, in Uganda, in Chad. The test of my national belonging is the test of my living with other men in a society that is mine. But it takes a ludicrous form in Vancouver, where with 15 potential TV channels people want another American one instead of a French one. Is that the test of sane men? Is it a valuable human objective that you should build in Montreal a tower that is bigger than the CN Tower? Are these human values? You see what I am talking about? Are we really going to transform Chinatown here into a French town? Do the people of Lac St.-Jean and the Crees and these people have no longer any claim to their territory, no longer any claim to their language? Is it right for me to assimilate the Italians and despoil them of their roots and of their continuing life? In the name of what justice do I do that?

Churchill used to say there was a kind of collective wisdom in people and that is why you have the old adage, you can fool the people some of the time, et cetera. These are words of wisdom. There is a fundamental wisdom in people and sooner or later it is going to come pass. But I'm too old now to care.

Jacques Godbout
Writer, film director Montreal
(E)
"We don't want to be loved and we don't want to be a pain in your neck."

From the arrival of the Jesuits in New France in 1634, the Catholic Church has played a more important role in the history and political development of Quebec than has been the case in any other part of North America. Until 1964, for example, when the Liberal government first established a Department of Education in Quebec, schooling was almost totally controlled by the province's Church. One of Quebec's best-known novelists and a prominent film-maker, Jacques Godbout has been a long-standing critic of Quebec's Catholic Church, as he explains from his National Film Board office in Montreal. Two of his most popular novels, Hail Galarneau! *and* Knife on the Table, *are now available in English translation.*

I was born in 1933, in a Catholic, French Canadian family of the petite bourgeoisie. I was happy enough to study in what was called a "classical college," Jean de Brébeuf in Montreal. There I met most of the people who were involved later on in politics because a classical college was very specialized in dealing with the sons of the rich. But then, living with those kids, I discovered that the only richness that I had was language and that I could overpower them with language, but not with my father's chauffeurs. My father had no chauffeurs as they had.

After discovering the power of the word, I slowly but surely became a writer, publishing poems and writing for radio to start with, and then writing novels and so on. Then I got a job at the National Film Board of Canada, first as a translator, then as a film writer and director. It's been a hell of a lot of fun.

In 1959 when Maurice Duplessis died and the province opened itself up, we had a small literary magazine called *Liberté*. I started fighting for lay schools, nondenominational schools. I wanted to get the clergy out of the goddamn province and that was a hell of a fight for five or six years. I started fighting the Jesuits, who had been my teachers in college. In 1906 France passed a law saying that from then on the schools would be non-Catholic, so the priests and the brothers and the sisters, who were controlling education in France, had to leave he country. Between 1910 and 1920 these goddamn Catholic teachers came here by the thousands. They infested the province! They decided that we would be the Catholic

France. From here they would send missionaries throughout the world to save everyone who was bing lost without them. And they said to be poor was a great thing, because in heaven we would be rich. The goddamn Church prepared cheap labour, which the English astutely and intelligently used! Sure, I have it against the Church. I am told once in a while that it's too bad, I should forget it, it's all past. All past my ass! It's *not* in the past. We're still living with it. And not only that: there are some priests in the PQ. There is some Catholic thinking in the PQ that could bring us back.

That was the beginning of *la révolution tranquille,* but I was still fighting Jean Lesage, who had said, for instance, to writers, "There will be a Department of Education in Quebec over my dead body." Of course, a year later, a *ministère de l'education* had to be created because we had not stopped asking for it. Our elder brothers then were Pierre Elliot Trudeau, Gérard Pelletier, Jean Marchand, and the lot of them were still Catholics and are still Catholics. We usually met once a week or once a month at book launchings. We had discussions about the future of Quebec and we used to put them on because they were still churchgoers. They didn't like that and so finally they got so damn mad about it that they all decided to go to Ottawa, in order to go to church and not be bothered—which probably is 50 percent of the reason why Trudeau, Pelletier, Marchand, and so on went to Ottawa: to recreate a sort of apostolic way of seeing the country because they were losing the unanimity elsewhere which they call "Canadian Unity" today.

They were also involved in *Cité-Libre,* which was a liberal Christian ideological magazine fighting Duplessis at that time. Most of the jobs they did was impressive and interesting, but it was still within the limits. They wanted to liberate Quebec from its medieval outlook but still keep it inside a Roman Catholic organization. They assumed when they went to Ottawa that they had to save us from our sins. We were becoming slowly autonomous or *indépendantiste,* so they wanted to save us. In my generation anyway, not many of us followed them. I was never impressed. I'm still not impressed.

I think Trudeau's vision of federalism is stupid, and the best proof is that since 1951 or '52, when the first issue of *Cité-Libre* was published, Trudeau has not changed an iota in his way of thinking. Now I believe that a man who from 1952 to 1977 does not change a single comma about his way of thinking about a society does not think. That's why I tell you it is sort of a Catholic approach in the sense that there is a dogma, and that dogma is the way Trudeau interprets Confederation. I think we have been very, very lucky in Quebec and Canada that this stupidity has not yet brought us to civil disturbances of a serious kind. I think his stupidity in 1970 was very clear, now that we know what the real FLQ was, compared to what he thought it was—which is the best proof that he doesn't know a damn thing about what is happening in Quebec anymore.

And I think his way of provoking the Parti Québecois pushes us near to a civil war—not between English Canada and French Canada but between French Canadians. This is not impossible because Trudeau is a man who likes to dominate. He acts in Parliament the way he acts at home. His need for dominance is the same. His need to be right all the time is the same. He's a mule. Proof of that is that there are no more French Canadians around him. What of his ex-friends, from Pierre Juneau to Gérard Pelletier to Jean Marchand? They all had to leave him because they are no more even on speaking terms. He's a solitary, stubborn, conceited, political Casanova.

French Canadians are probably the most British people in the world. There are a few things that the British have given French Canadians, and one of them is the notion of fair play. I agree with you, that's not a bad thing...far from it. The French Canadian is not treacherous in any way, and his approach toward independence, toward autonomy, toward sovereignty has been a fair-play game. So it was sort of a shock, the way that Ottawa and our Catholic friend, Mr. Trudeau, reacted, sending us troops from Rome. But the October Crisis helped the cause of sovereignty a lot.

You have in Quebec two main lines of thought. One is a nationalist one, and the party in power always has to be nationalist because we consider ourselves a nation and whether you find it true or false is completely academic, because we think this is a nation. So if you want to be in power, you have to play the nationalist string, and you also have to play the liberal string in the sense of progress. French Canadians want to go forward, but not necessarily rapidly. It is a peasant culture, so when the Liberals, under Bourassa, stopped being nationalist and just kept on being progressive, they were replaced by a progressive nationalist group, which is the Parti Québécois, and you will not replace the Parti Québécois unless you find a group that represents better ways to be more progressive.

I have known Robert Bourassa since the age of six or seven. I went through school with him, and I've kept on knowing him. I also have known Réné Lévesque for a long time. Bourassa's Liberal Party was composed of a hell of a lot of morons—some good fellows but a majority of morons. And it was subjected to blackmail on the part of the federal government. Trudeau and the federal Liberals just toyed with Bourassa. One time Trudeau even came to Quebec to meet with the premier and then he called him: "*Ti-Pit*," "the hot-dog eater." That was not accepted by anyone, it was too much.

Quebec needs some form of sovereignty and only the PQ can provide us with that. We cannot live without an association, but already Quebec is more separate from Canada than Canada is from the United States, as far as culture and economy are concerned. So let's not fool ourselves. We want the possibility of being ourselves in North America, which means that we want to control immigration. It's incredible that up to now we have been submitted to the immigration laws of an English majority, which has managed to get and keep in Quebec a certain percentage of English-speaking people in order that the balance would not be upset. Now when someone says Quebec should be as French as Ontario is English, that's normal. In Switzerland, where there is a confederation, when you go from one canton to another, you have to change languages. There are no French schools for German people in the German canton. We are subjected to a lot of bullshit. There are a lot of areas where sovereignty can be given to Quebec or taken by Quebec. It will not take anything away from the English Canadians. We're all in favour of a Confederation, not a federation. Even René Levesque and Claude Morin and Pierre Bourgault and Jacques-Yvan Morin are federalist. When they talk about *une souveraineté-association* it's a federal approach. There is not just one way of being a federalist, although right now, it seems that only Trudeau's way of being federalist is called federalism. That's quite funny!

What do I think of the argument that Quebec is American? Laurier Lapierre said that? Well, if he thinks Quebec has become as Americanized as English-speaking Canada, he is right and at the same time he's full of shit. The technology available to us is of course American technology, but that is also true in Europe. Except for the skidoo in Quebec and probably the cuckoo clock in Switzerland and a certain number of other folklore objects, the technology is mainly American. But as far as the way of using that technology is concerned, that's another matter altogether. You know, the same car put into the hands of an Italian doesn't make the same noise and doesn't go around the street the same way it does when it is put into the hands of a fellow called Smith in Ottawa, where you can even jaywalk without being in danger. Culture is the way you use that technology. So when Laurier says that we have the same material things as the Americans, of course we do. But I think that he is wrong when he says that we have the same values. This is too simple. Even the Americans don't have one set of values. There's a west coast and there's an east coast and there's a hell of a lot of small countries in the United States, so let's stop talking about the Americans as a vast entity which is submerging us.

Look, we know basically who we are in Quebec. The language permits us to recognize ourselves, and don't forget we are five million grouped more or less around the St. Lawrence, so if one wants to meet his parents, he can do it in a day or two. Most Quebeckers are related in one way or another, you know. After all, Quebec started from 10,000 families. There's always an uncle somewhere. When you sleep with a woman you are not sure if you are sleeping with your cousin!

I suppose that the black in the United States who was kicked around for years had a better notion of what blackness was than the white people who were kicking him. Being kicked in the ass and being told to "speak white" and being turned down for a job because you don't speak English and feeling ill at ease in many circumstances, you tend to say, "Christ, who am I?" So a minority describes itself much better than a majority. Look at the Jewish communities around the world. Look at any minority.

Ireland is the comparison that should be made with Quebec, much more than with any other country. In Ireland, the Irish are not separated by a language but by two ways of being Christian. Here we are separated by two ways of being Christian plus a language. If Protestants and Catholics cannot live together in Ireland, how the hell do you expect us to live together here? Like Ireland, we may be going toward a situation where our political leaders, our spokesmen, might tend to overstate a number of things and get us into trouble. I think Trudeau is the worst in this respect. He's the worst prime minister we could have. Political careers can be built on or against nationalism.

We French Canadians tend to be more aware of the dangers of uniformity in the way of thinking than the English. We tend to be more critical about whatever comes from the American money-making cultural side. Language helps us. We see the American message coming, while the kids in English Canada tend to take it as it comes. One thing that made me sad personally was to discover that English Canadians prefer American television. They don't even look at their own television. That makes me sad because I have the impression that Canadian kids are becoming Americans whether they like it or not.

But there are similarities between English Canadians and ourselves. We're not a violent people, I don't think the English Canadians— whether Irish, Scottish, or whatever origin you want—are violent. When I meet English Canadians in London or in Addis-Ababa, or in Paris, we find a lot of things in common. We even find a lot of things we hate together! And that's okay. When we come back here I suppose we should go live in our own way. We don't want to be loved and we don't want to be a pain in your neck. I couldn't care less what happens in Toronto and the fellow in Toronto shouldn't care what happens in Montreal. We should just live and let live. Except that there's always a politician in Ottawa who thinks he should control what happens in Toronto, in Vancouver, in Montreal—trying to make sure that we have the same great Canadian attitudes in Toronto, Vancouver, and Montreal. Who cares, for Chrissake? The fellows in Vancouver are living so far away from us that they should live the way they want to live. And that's all we want, too, you know.

André Fleury
Film producer, Montreal
(E)
"Lévesque was a very professional journalist."

Any visitor who stays in Quebec longer than several weeks will discover a society on surprisingly intimate terms with itself. Nor do Québécois transfer into and out of their province like other Canadians. A shared, almost family, identity and personal contact are present in Quebec to an extent that English Canada will never experience.

In view of this, perhaps it should not be surprising that I was continually meeting people who personally knew René Lévesque, whether in Montreal, the Gaspé, or Rouyn. It suddenly became possible to learn more about his background, temperament, and personality than what is being presented in the media. André Fleury, the owner of film production and sound-recording studios, is one of those people personally associated with René Lévesque.

My company doesn't dub any feature films. We mainly dub television series, documentaries, shorts. I would say this year we are going to dub about the equivalent of about 300 hours of series and films, most of them are television series for the French networks. What programs? Oh, Mary Tyler Moore, Hawaii Five-O, Cannon, Medical Center, Que Sera Sera, The Odd Couple, a few National Geographic specials, and we will be doing about 100 made-for-TV movies. Most of them are American shows, but we have dubbed a substantial number of films, feature films and shorts, from the East European countries like Poland, Czechoslovakia, Rumania, into French and English. Now this year we are dubbing a Czech film called *Tanto* for CBC French television.

We use international French, not Joual. Most of the contracts are written with American distributors and in the contracts there is always a clause that French has to be dubbed without any accent — they call it international French. At the beginning the French people kept telling us they did not understand it, but of course, I don't believe that. A few years ago we had a TV series to dub, and to make sure that the dubbing produced here could be used in France, I imported the writer and the main actors from France. And the French television people said they had accents and they told us the script was too Québécois to be used in France when it was their own! Well, I don't think that there is ground for that because, you know, French is French, even if you might have some accents. I mean, because you have an accent doesn't mean you speak bad French. And you go to France, people in the south have a different accent than the people in the north. The same goes for United States — you have the Western accent, the Eastern accent, Southern accent, but they all speak English. So the same goes here. In Canada it's the same, we have different accents — Cockney, Scottish, British, American.

Here in Quebec we don't make it a point to talk Joual. The French-speaking culture we want to keep is certainly not based on Joual. We talk proper French and, at times, with less accent than the Parisians themselves. We in Quebec are trying to sell our films and TV programs on the international market, but it is hard. We are coming out soon with a film based on the legends of old Quebec. We had Félix Leclerc present those legends in French and Vincent Price do it in English. With this film, we think we might open a fair market. And in the U.S. television market we have had good response for a series of animation specials of Quebec origin which are of international quality. So in certain fields we might attract an international market. Then there are other films, like *Lies My Father Told Me*, which had a fair success in the U.S. and it was a typically Montreal situation. So I think in time we will get to this market.

No, we have no success at all in France, but the problem there is that the French people consider Quebec a colony; they think we are Guadeloupe. And they think that we see Paris as the metropole. This will have to change, and we are taking steps now. I'm going soon to France with the Quebec government to meet the French minister of cinema to get access to their market in the same way they have access to ours. They come here and dump a lot of French films and there is a good amount of money going from Quebec to France — but there is no reverse traffic. We want to discuss this problem because we are not their colony; we have our own economy and we want to have a share of their market.

You have to realize that in Quebec we have developed our own French-speaking television production much further and much bigger than Canadian production on the whole, and we are much less numerous.

We are smaller than the rest of Canada, but still we have no problem in meeting the Canadian content quotas. Long before the CRTC rulings on music we had our own composers, our own songs, our own music, our own poets, our own writers. There is no problem for any Quebec television station or radio station to meet these standards. We surpass them! We just don't like the same kind of programs, and this is why it is so hard for English Canadians to interest French Canadians in their series and their programs and vice-versa. We just don't enjoy the same thing. Listen to the music in English Canada. It's more Western American in flavour than Canadian. It is composed by Canadians but it is American music made in Canada.

I think it is time that we put our foot down and say that this is a French province. Let's face it, what attracts the Americans and other tourists here is the French flavour, and we would be stupid to ignore this. It is an asset for us. It is part of the Canadian community as a whole and I don't see why we should compromise on this. We have a very strong culture here, much stronger than the rest of Canadian culture, and we want to keep it. And I am all for it on all grounds.

But I don't think people in Quebec are quite ready for separation. You know, the day after the election, people expected to become independent, rich, better off, and all that; but obviously it is not like that. We are worse off than we were before, economically. We have more unemployment, more economic problems, and we have international market problems. So I don't think that people will buy the idea. What can be done to reverse that? Well, that's Lévesque's problem now. But in two or three years, who knows? We might be so much worse off that people might be inclined to say "Yes" to separation.

I know René Lévesque personally because I used to work with him when I was working at CBC. I was part of the crew that worked with him on *Point de Mire* — Target Point in English. That was a public affairs show, and we travelled around the world making documentaries and covering news. We went to France, to Italy, England, Cuba, Mexico.

I feel that I got to know the man from behind the scenes. Lévesque was a very professional journalist. He was always concerned with impartiality. He wanted to cover all aspects of a question. Before he would make an editorial statement, he would make sure he got information from all sources. He was a great popularizer. He could take any international situation, very complex, and he could simplify it and make it understood by the ordinary people. And he was straight, a very straight journalist and a very hard worker. Oh yes, he wouldn't stop, he wouldn't count the time, and he was a very hard worker.

He was also very organized. When we used to work together he would give us the schedule for the next day, or the next week, and then he would go his way digging out information. I remember in January of 1960 we went to Cuba for the celebration of the first anniversary of the revolution. We couldn't get interviews with Castro at that time because, you know, it was still very unsettled. There were armed people everywhere, and millions of people walking. We had to travel by jeep and it was a two-day ride. That was very, very hard coverage.

After working with him, I'd say Lévesque is an honest man, a straight fellow. I like him. I kind of trust him. The whole idea of separatism is not my belief, but this man is a good man so, my first reaction on November 15 was to wait and see. Couldn't be worse than what we had before.

André Major
Writer, Radio-Canada producer, Montreal
(F)

"As long as there is no cultural security for Quebeckers, I shall be an *indépendantiste*."

André Major is a well-known Quebec writer and Radio-Canada radio arts producer who published his first book of poetry at the age of 19. In the early '60s he worked with the publishing house of Parti Pris, then spent two years in France, wrote for Le Devoir, *and joined the CBC French network in 1973. His novel* The Scarecrows of St.-Emmanuel *has recently been published in English. Mr. Major received the Governor-General's 1976 fiction award for his novel* Les Rescapés. *We spoke in his office 20 floors above Dorchester Boulevard in the CBC's impressive Montreal headquarters.*

I was born in Montreal, very close to CBC here, near the Jacques Cartier Bridge. My mother is of Scottish origin—she was a Sharp, like the former Minister of External Affairs, Mitchell Sharp. There is no relationship, I think, between the two by the way. We spoke French at home because my mother had become francophone. I had a rather privileged education in one sense—my father was a teacher of chemistry and mathematics in the Catholic School Board. I didn't finish my Bachelor of Arts Degree. At 14 or 15 years, I wanted to become a writer.

Around the age of 18, I left college and followed courses in journalism and philosophy and I finally wound up becoming a journalist and I started to publish in the year 1961 when I was 19.

Yes, it was a little early, perhaps a little bit too early, but I published poems anyway. I was one of the founders of the publishing house Parti Pris — I was there one year. I finally left Parti Pris because I was not a Marxist. I was an *indépendantiste* but never a Marxist as far as doctrine was concerned. Marxism seemed to me a philosophy which was somewhat outmoded. My comrades at Parti Pris were hard-line Marxists and wanted revolution against the family. But I always had a very good relationship with mine. My father encouraged me to write even when it was difficult. And when I left college he told me he would support me until the day I could support myself. So I got along just fine with my dad.

My mother had a definite Protestant side to her which was very rigid, very puritan, and I had a great deal of conflict with her. She wanted a secure profession for me — insurance agent or notary.

As I said, I am an *indépendantiste*, I am for making Quebec French as quickly as possible, but in temperament I am nevertheless far more Anglo-Saxon than Latin. In literature what interests me is not French writers. I don't like people who talk a great deal and who do nothing. I am far more pragmatic than most French Canadians that I know. I don't feel at ease with people who are theoreticians, even in literature. I like Scandinavian literature a great deal; I like the Russians — Nordic literature, if you will. Also among my favourites are Swift and Robert Louis Stevenson. I read *Treasure Island* two or three times a year and am now producing a radio program on *Treasure Island*. But as long as there is no cultural security for Quebeckers, I shall be an *indépendantiste*. The day we have that cultural assurance and security, then independence will no longer be of interest to me. You see, I write in French, but from 1960-65, I must say frankly that I was wondering if in 10 years I would be read. It's rather horrible to have that spectre before you. That is one more reason for becoming an *indépendantiste*.

I studied for a year in a cosmopolitan area of Montreal, in a Jewish quarter on Pine Avenue and Parc. It was unbelievable because I had always lived in a French Canadian milieu and to be transported into quarter where only English was spoken, with signs only in English, completely disoriented me. Here I was in the heart of Montreal and the Prime Minister of Quebec couldn't have spoken French with the merchants there. These were my merchants! That was a shock. A feeling of inferiority develops when you find out you *have* to learn English in order to be of value. That played a large role in my political development.

Then of course there were other things. For example, bilingualism from A to Zed I find an aberration. I can understand very well how

English Canadians in Vancouver would resist becoming French-speaking: it has no meaning for them, no practical meaning. For reasons of pure principle you cannot decide to establish bilingualism. True bilingualism must be a necessity of life; it cannot be just a theoretical or political decision. I have the impression that federalism has become a question of principle. You want to keep Canada as it is — not to disturb anything—and in the final analysis, there will be 10 percent of us left who will still speak French. There is a whole political attitude which seems to be false here. I am not a separatist in the sense that I want to cut all my ties; I think you have to be intelligent in your nationalism. But in the cultural field you can't negotiate—there has to be full cultural autonomy, which means education and immigration. If you don't control immigration, in my opinion, there is no use bothering with communication.

Now here in the CBC building what we have really is two separate networks — French and English. Change the CBC? No, I don't think that's necessary. In my daily experience as a producer we in French radio do our work without any problems at all and the English Canadians go about their work. I am happy, I do what I want, and I do my work without any problem.

A much better example of bias than Radio-Canada is CFCF Radio in Montreal, the English station that led the campaign against Bill 22. A very violent campaign, a campaign where there was no objectivity. There were 46 hours of propaganda against Bill 22, and the listening public were asked to send in money for the campaign. The station asked people to come and speak against the Bill but when people who were for it phoned, they hung up on them. There was no objectivity at all. It was simply a political campaign, and the CRTC publically censured them. But the operating permit of CFCF was renewed. In none of my programs have I ever used the air time like that. You just don't do that.

At Radio-Canada I have rarely seen cases where information was distorted or abused. They are accusing the CBC of manipulating information, of not being objective, but this is just a case of reading meanings into smiles or gestures. Inquiries will just find that men are men. In our November 1976 election coverage I didn't hear any commentator or any journalist announce that he was an *indépendantiste*.

I'm involved in arts programming. Of course there is no outright promotion of the Canadian reality. On the cultural plane if it happens, it happens accidentally. I produce a literary and information program called Book Club — that's rather amusing, eh? We use an English name for the show, because there isn't a direct equivalent for Book Club in French! Anyway, we regularly review books from English Canada that are available in translation here in Quebec. Recently we've reviewed new works by Robertson Davies and Margaret Atwood; we just take it for granted that they are part of our cultural world.

Now, as far as public affairs on radio is concerned, as soon as something happens in Newfoundland or Vancouver, we know about it. They cannot attack Radio-Canada on this plane because it is really a Canadian network. For example, I listen to a program which is called *Le Présent National* in the evening when I drive home. It's on from five-thirty until six o'clock and covers what's happening everywhere in Canada, so we are pretty well informed. The politicians interpret our CBC mandate to mean publicity for federalism, but good journalists have to report what is happening honestly—and that doesn't mean being a PR man.

I think that Quebec is divided in two. You really have to admit that Trudeau and his crowd are reacting against what they see as the conservative nationalism that has often been ours in the past. Duplessis in particular and people like him fought against any nationalism which resembled socialism or social democracy. These people don't understand. They have an attitude which, in my opinion, a great many French Canadian federalists have: a very strong inferiority complex. They see equality with others in being a Canadian, and to be a Quebecker is to be a rural guy, a farmer. In this way of thinking, Quebec cannot have its own destiny, cannot have its own reality. This is really despising yourself, in my opinion. It is the attitude of the colonized. The only way to escape from the minority inferiority complex is to espouse values of a stronger people or a people who appear to have more important values. For these people, nationalism is reactionary and so they latch onto federalism.

The Trudeau government is far from being a very progressive government. It is a government which calls itself liberal but which in fact is very conservative. Actually, Canadian nationalism is a very conservative nationalism and is in no position to accuse Quebec nationalism of being conservative and reactionary.

What I hope for very deeply is that the referendum will give the government a very specific mandate to negotiate with Ottawa to find a very practical solution, so that after 20 years we can deal with other things and not just spend all our lives speaking about this particular problem.

But it would surprise me a great deal if Trudeau ever negotiated a new agreement between Quebec and Canada—if that happened I would change my mind about Trudeau. What he wants is to have his own way. He wants the change to come from Ottawa. He cannot admit in his own egotism, as a politician, that the change might come from Quebec, that it might come from us, because he has given himself a mission to save

Canada; it has become a sort of obsession. He does not want to negotiate that idea. Trudeau doesn't know whether there will ever be a new Confederation but he wants to be the father of it if it does come about.

Guy Rondeau
Canadian Press bureau chief, Montreal
(E and F)

"We would have real problems convincing any reporter to accept a post in Toronto or Vancouver."

The largest news agency in Canada is the Canadian Press, which collects and distributes news to virtually all the major mass media outlets in the country. A nonprofit cooperative owned by the country's newspapers, CP is divided into separate French and English divisions, supervised by Montreal Bureal Chief Guy Rondeau. Among other questions, Mr. Rondeau discussed the inadequate coverage of Canadian affairs offered the Quebec public by Presse Canadien.

My father was from a family of farmers, from near Montreal. He was not very long on the farm; he went to Quebec City very young. He became a travelling salesman, working for an outfit that sells foods. Our family was just a middle-class family; we lived in the upper town in Quebec City. Our ancestors came from Brittany in France. Both sides.

I think I'm a true Quebecker. I was born in Quebec City in 1924 and I have always lived in Quebec province, except when I was in Ottawa for three years. I've always been in journalism. I began my career in radio in Quebec City and then went with Canadian Press for almost all my career except for brief periods with *Le Soleil* and the Quebec government.

To be a Quebecker is to be part of a really distinct part of this country, to experience a dynamic, living culture. But there should be no frontier —you can live here as a Quebecker but still be open to the other provinces. When I was working in Ottawa, the feeling among the Ottawa reporters was: "There's no Quebec problem." Quebec was a part of Canada. Part of a melting pot, as a matter of fact. I don't think they caught the difference. It was a matter of ignorance and nothing else.

Personally I have always had good relations with English people, but I have to say that they didn't understand Quebec.

Before 1950, CP had only English reporters in Quebec City. French reporters had to translate all the news that came in over the wire into French. Finally, in 1950, news service in French was established. CP's translation service is in Montreal. We have around 10 people doing the translation of CP English copy that we get from across Canada. Reuter's has an international service in French which we use here in Montreal. We have seven reporters in Quebec City, three in Ottawa, and two in Montreal. There's also a French correspondent in Paris. And that's it.

We have a problem at CP sometimes when we want to transfer a French reporter to Ottawa. The problem is to find someone who is willing to live in an English milieu. Maybe it is a kind of fear. I don't understand that kind of fear, but it is part of the reporter's mentality, part of his background, probably. We have to offer a better deal financially, in order to get someone to leave Quebec. We would have real problems convincing any reporters to accept a post in Toronto or Vancouver — even for a year or two. They simply prefer to remain here in Quebec.

If the papers were ready to pay for it, CP would have French reporters everywhere in Canada. CP is the property of the papers. If the French papers here in Quebec were seriously interested in getting somebody outside the province, probably they would be ready to pay, but my feeling is that they are not very interested. It's too bad. If you take a look at the French papers, you don't see many stories outside Quebec. Even on the international scene, they are not very interested. I think the papers are trying to survive and they are becoming more and more regionally conscientious. In Quebec you've got a lot of small papers. I have to agree with you that the French newspaper publishers are neglecting their responsibility to cover the rest of Canada. I'm not saying that they are *not* covering Canada, but it is not very satisfactory. However, they seem pleased with the way it is done right now.

And of course there is the other question of biased news coverage. I think we have to be careful when the politicians make charges that the media — Radio-Canada in particular — are biased in their news coverage because personally I'm not always confident of the intentions of those politicians. But maybe there is something true behind the charges. Of course we have to recognize that the media in the Quebec province are sympathetic toward the PQ government and the separation of Quebec. I don't want to hint that all newspapermen are biased. I would say instead that there is some kind of a sympathy toward the Parti Québécois. They are just reflecting the desire of the population. Look, every French Canadian, every real French Canadian, is a *séparatiste* at heart. It does not mean that he wants to separate exactly, but he would like to be recognized just a bit more. As I told you earlier, to be Québécois is to be identified with a culture, to want to live that culture, so maybe the reporters, the newspapermen, are reflecting that feeling of the French Canadian.

How did I vote November 15? PQ, that's how. Yes, I will explain why. Like many other Quebeckers, I wanted to get rid of that Bourassa government. That's the first reason I voted PQ. Also, I voted PQ because they had the best candidate in my constituency and he was elected. I've watched Lévesque working through the years and I'm confident that those guys are going to give Quebec good government. As far as independence is concerned, I didn't vote for the PQ for that reason. I'm not sure that independence will be a good bet for Quebec. Nobody has convinced me yet that it will be the right way for Quebec to go. I think that we should get a new federalism. Quebec is now in such a position that we can negotiate with Ottawa and get maybe more autonomy on more fronts, more freedom. I think that in the end we aren't going to go all the way to independence — I mean complete separation. Of course, even Lévesque wants association with the rest of Canada.

No, I don't know Lévesque personally. I covered him, of course, as a reporter. I find him a very honest man, as a matter of fact. What struck me is that he always uses the same language, whether he is speaking to Quebeckers or he is speaking outside Quebec. And I think that is why he is really respected in Quebec, and also outside Quebec. He's not afraid of going outside Quebec to explain his views and that's very good. But if Lévesque disappeared tomorrow, I don't know what would happen, because he's a kind of catalyst inside the party, relating the left and the right of his party. The man is a moderate.

Michel Roi
Publisher, Le Devoir, *Montreal*
(F and E)

"Is it too little, too late, as Mr. Lévesque says?"

Le Devoir *is the leading federalist voice in the Quebec media as well as being highly respected for in-depth news analysis, arts coverage, and its editorial page. Yet as anyone can see for himself by reading the newspaper for a week, its coverage of Canadian politics outside Quebec and Ottawa is superficial, haphazard, and usually second-hand. This inadequate Canadian news coverage is the rule in the French language press in Quebec. Before discussing these matters,* Le Devoir's *publisher, Michel Roi, reminisced about his childhood in a Quebec military family.*

My name is an easy one in Canada because it's Roy in English or Roi in French. If I'm in Toronto, it's easier to say Roy.

My family is Québécois. My grandfather was a merchant in Lévis, near Quebec. My father was a colonel in the Canadian army during the First World War and also for part of the Second World War. So being in the armed forces, he was in Ottawa where I was born. And he worked in the Governor-General's house as aide-de-camp for a few years.

My family moved to Montreal in the '30s and I was raised there. My father being a military man, I was raised in an atmosphere that was not exactly the same that all the Quebeckers had during the war. I mean my father was in favour of conscription and Quebec participation in the Second World War, and so as a kid I was a witness to all these political fights we had in Quebec about conscription. In those years, 1939, '40, '41, '42, it was a very divisive issue.

I was only 10 when the war started and 15 when it ended, and my main regret was that I was too young to go to Europe and fight myself, so it gives you an idea of the climate in which I was raised.

My father was anti-nationalist and he was angry with those who opposed conscription. As a kid I was not able to understand clearly the reasons why these people opposed the war. Only many years after, by reading and personal contact, did I begin to understand what really happened. I realize now that the Quebec people didn't feel that they were part of that war. To them, it was an imperialist war, a war in which Canada had to fight because of England. But I think a few years later Quebeckers understood that it was not only a war for England; it was a war involving all the countries in Europe, involving a certain idea of life, society, and civilization.

I think they also had the feeling of being strangers among English-speaking soldiers of their own country, of not being recognized as French-speaking Canadians. This is an old problem and I know this was a fact because my father told me about that. I remember him telling me stories about Quebec military men arguing with their majors and colonels in order to be recognized as French-speaking soldiers of Canada. They wanted to use their own language and be understood by their officers in French. At the end of the war some regiments, the Chaudière, the Royal Twenty-Second Regiment, finally got the French language recognized, but it took a few years. It certainly was not easy at the beginning.

I was educated at St.-Jean de Brébeuf, the college where Mr. Trudeau, Mr. Bourassa, and all those people studied. The professors and the Jesuits themselves were pretty nationalistic then. They saw Quebec as being in kind of a state of siege; the Jesuits pushed the idea that Quebec could not go very far if the French language was not recognized in this country as equal to the English. But the French language was still associated with *emploi subalterne*, with bad jobs and poverty. It was very difficult to escape the impression that you could not go very far in life without English.

This is very important to understand. So many of the young people of my generation had the impression that, in order to succeed in life, you would have to forget about your main language, French, and try to work in English, and succeed in English. That was the success language.

English was taught at Brébeuf, but not very well. This is an old problem we have had in Quebec for a long time. The only way to learn English, I feel, is to live with English people for a few months, a few years, at camps for instance. This is where I picked up whatever English I have today—by spending the summer with English kids in the Laurentians. Middle-class kids would go to camps in summer to learn English. Even today my kids are at school in Montreal, and in order to get fluent in English, I send them to an English summer camp. In fact, I'd like my daughter to go to Scotland for a year or so. That's the best way unless, unless our *ministère de l'éducation* in Quebec can think of a better way to teach English to Quebec boys and girls.

One thing I find interesting in terms of different English-French perceptions is the Olympics. There was a great deal of controversy and criticism over Mayor Drapeau's Olympic schemes and the money spent on it. The line that our paper adopted was that the spending for the Olympics was much too high and that other priorities were much more important than this one. But today the Quebec people are very proud of the results because the stadium is there and it's a fine place, a huge place. Of course we now have to pay for it and as Montrealers we're paying extra taxes. For instance, my rent went up last year by 15 percent; this year it was 20 percent and it'll go up and up again next year. The landlord can justify these increases because of all the extra taxes he's paying to reduce the Olympic deficit. The Quebec province is also paying part of the deficit. It was imperial, it was very beautiful, but it was costly.

The thing is, Mr. Drapeau is so convincing, as you know, that people bought his idea and even today, I think, they would re-elect him. Well, I'm half-joking but when he's at a public gathering with Mr. Trudeau, I think the applause is much greater for Mr. Drapeau than for Mr. Trudeau. He's a very popular man with the crowds here.

You think some of these different ways of perceiving public events are influenced by different standards of news coverage? You may be right. I'll admit that Quebec's press coverage of the rest of Canada is inadequate. I am astonished that a large paper like *La Presse* doesn't have a correspondent in Toronto, another in Winnipeg, a third one in Vancouver, and probably one more in Moncton or Halifax. *Le Devoir* has no full-time reporters, but we do send people at times across the country. For instance, we had a reporter covering the Ontario election and sending stories every day on it. We are not doing as much as we should, but our resources are limited. We could not dream of having people all over the country. Here at *Le Devoir* we interviewed all the provincial premiers when they came to Montreal. Whenever one of them makes an important statement on any issue relating to Canada, we make a point of printing it in *Le Devoir*. We translate it. This is how we're doing our share.

What we need is good stringers all over the place to cover this country, and this is one of our objectives. I must say, though, that we are receiving Canadian Press, which of course sends stories from all the provinces on a daily basis. But all journalists know this is not enough to really cover the country. But the second aspect of this question, to be very frank with you, is that the Québécois are not overwhelmingly interested in news from the other parts of the country. They want to read anything relating to Quebec, to national unity, but they don't pay much attention to provincial stories that have no direct bearing on their own lives.

We just cannot go on in Canada like we have been. Even people who oppose separation, who I think are the majority in this province, are in favour of some changes in the Constitution in order to have more autonomy in Quebec. It is not very precise yet in which fields, but at least in the cultural field. This is one of the main tasks. I've been listening these last months to programs, open lines, coming from Toronto or Winnipeg or Vancouver, and one thing that strikes me is that people are honestly trying to find new solutions, new arrangements. Is it too little, too late, as Mr. Lévesque would say? I really can't answer that because the younger generation is almost entirely in favour of separation and so many of them are living as if Quebec was already independent. It's not easy to go against that trend, which is very deep and strong.

If Quebec does become an independent state, I suppose I'd stay here. I like to travel, I like Ottawa and Toronto, but my real home is here, in Montreal.

Gilles Marcotte
Writer, professor, Montreal
(F)
**"Canada is one of the freest countries
in the world."**

*Quebec's intellectual community, while often pro-independence, contains
many federalists, including University of Montreal professor of French
literature, Gilles Marcotte. One of Quebec's most prominent literary critics, he
is also a former associate and personal admirer of René Lévesque, while
remaining a committed federalist for various cultural, political, and historical
reasons.*

I arrived at Radio-Canada in the late '50s and I worked for two years in
television with Mr. René Lévesque. I was a producer of a daily interview
program called *Carrefour*. Lévesque was very good, undoubtedly the best
interviewer they ever had at Radio-Canada in Public Affairs. He was
extremely conscientious—prepared intensively for his interviews, and in
fact I heard him chide his staff occasionally when they weren't properly
prepared. He was an absolutely top-rate radio and TV man and it was a
pleasure to work with him. René didn't leave his interviewees in peace
until he got what he was after. He worked very fast and occasionally even
I produced programs where I did not know or just barely knew the
content! He just forgot to tell me about it. No, he was responsible for the
programs. I played a small role there.

In my view, television has played an enormous role in our cultural life,
and I think a lot of things have taken place in Quebec that were
influenced by television. Radio-Canada first had a strong influence
during the Duplessis government. It was the voice of opposition,
together with *Le Devoir*, and personally I was at *Le Devoir* at that time.
Another example of TV's influence is in the matter of language. When
television arrived we had a lot of public participation shows, much more
than in English Canada, and CEGEP students were beginning to be
invited to programs. At the beginning, the language standard was fairly
bad, because people weren't used to expressing themselves in such
circumstances, but in a few years we saw enormous progress—very
striking. So, there is a connection between the influence of television and
the extreme importance gained in communication in Quebec in all areas.

Most of my friends are separatists—writers and so on. I am not a
separatist because I think every time that nationalism appeared in our

history, it played a dirty trick on us. Nationalism has always been an alibi for us: whenever we had real problems, instead of dealing with them, we said, "We can't solve them—they're caused by others."

My position is similar to that of Claude Ryan of the *Le Devoir*—that there are obvious problems and Quebec must be more French than it is now, but I am somewhat scared of the mandatory measures in Bill 101. I don't agree that the French language in Quebec is losing any ground. I think it is quite the opposite; in fact, my personal experience shows that the French language has never been in such a good shape in Quebec as at the present time. I am willing to make a very long speech about this! English Canadians in Quebec in the past 10 years have made a very considerable effort to learn French.

I spend most of my life in French; I very seldom speak English, but I do read in English quite often. I have just read Robertson Davies' trilogy, for instance. I enjoy the poetry of Margaret Atwood—I don't like her novels but her poetry says a lot to me. I read *Maclean's* Magazine, and sometimes I read *Saturday Night*, though a lot less because it is very Torontonian. I often watch English programs on television. I make a space for English in my life and I think that if I didn't I would not be a very good Quebecker because being a Quebecker is also living closely with the anglophone world. What really strikes me is that Lévesque himself is much more bilingual than I am. He speaks English a lot better than I do and he has a wide experience of the English world, which is extremely important for him and makes him a Québécois.

A Québécois is not a Frenchman and it's not just the physical experience of the North American setting that does it. It is also having lived in Canada with Englishmen and English institutions. Not much importance is given to that but I find it extremely important. A Quebecker who goes to France and has to come into contact with a political or police or judicial structure there soon realizes that he was formed and molded by English institutions in Canada and he has assimilated these institutions perfectly.

People now are setting their minds on constitutional changes, which are completely beside the point. Marshall McLuhan has said, "Quebec is already separated," which does not mean that McLuhan is a Quebec separatist, but that he made the distinction between software and hardware—between culture and structures. We already have a different culture, but does that mean the software, or cultural separation, must be followed by changes in hardware, or political structures? I don't believe so.

Politics to me should create structures, spaces to live in, but it is absolutely essential that politics not try to provide everything for man. That's one of the major ideas of Pierre Trudeau and I think it is very important. It is essential that politics not try to solve all problems of collective life.

The present-day world is becoming a world of minorities. Ten years ago we thought we were going to see a great world unity in which cultural differences would disappear. Well, we have realized that quite the opposite is happening now: even in France, which is the country of unity, you have the Bretons who are agitating; you have the Corsicans; you have people in the south; you have Basques. The claims of cultural regionalism are stronger now than they have ever been! Now to create politically and economically independent countries in these different regions would be chaos.

I think that the Canadian problem is not the Canadian problem — it is the world problem. It should be possible to have large units based on economic necessity and at the same time have very strong cultural units at the regional level.

Frankly, I don't know exactly what Lévesque wants. It is fairly ambiguous at present. Sometimes he speaks as though it's not complete sovereignty he is after, but other times he makes declarations indicating that, yes, he is seeking full sovereignty after all. I think he will have difficulty getting out of that because his party is seeking full sovereignty. This whole idea of sovereignty-association is still quite confused. Sovereignty for me would imply, for instance, counting the rolling stock of the Canadian National Railway and keeping part for Quebec and giving the rest to Canada and that I don't accept. You know, the things Lévesque proposes — the things that the PQ party wants at least at the cultural level — can be accomplished without changing a single thing in the Constitution!

Being a Quebecker, it is obvious that my emotional attachment is first and foremost in Quebec. That having been said, I also think that the structure of Canada is the best for me as a Quebecker. Canada is a country that I respect, a country that preserves things which are very dear to me. Canada is one of the freest countries in the world. It is a country where you can live a fairly human life. I think we tend to forget that.

Mike Gonzales

Self-made man, Montreal

(E)

"If people shit on the English long enough, you are going to have the same type of FLQ thing in reverse."

The stereotyped English Quebecker often presented in nationalist rhetoric in Quebec is as far away in style and substance from Mike Gonzales as René Lévesque is from Leonard Jones. Of course in English Montreal it is still possible to find real-life versions of Mr. Lévesque's "Westmount Rhodesians," but in anglophone quarters of the city, such as Pointe St.-Charles or Verdun, the typical English Canadian is working class or often unemployed. Mike Gonzales is third-generation Irish on the maternal side, and has lived his 40-odd years first in Griffintown and now in Pointe St.-Charles. A self-made man, having risen from runner for a bookie to founder and director of a nonprofit community employment agency, Mike Gonzales is very much a product of English Montreal.

Most of the people who settled in Griffintown came over during the potato famine and they were sheltered in sheds along Victoria Bridge, along Victoria Pier, as it was called. And most of them ended up working on Victoria Bridge or for the CNR, which was also down in this community. Back in the '60s Griffintown was rezoned—people out, warehouses and parking lots in. I moved over here to the Pointe, which is sort of next door. But Christ, Griffintown was where English Montreal started! Sometimes I come back just to drive around the old neighbourhood. You look around at this place that was a part of you and you want to cry. Your home, everything, gone. And what for? Warehouses, vacant lots, small businesses—it shouldn't have been allowed, but there it is.

It was a very Irish community at one time. St. Anne's Church was built right after St. Patrick's Cathedral and it was the main parish for the poorer Irish immigrants who came to Montreal. Eventually the ones who "made it," they moved out; they went to Pointe-Claire, Montreal West—the better neighbourhoods. The ones that didn't make it, well, they stayed down here.

What do I think of the rich English Montrealer stereotype? Well, that's horseshit. As far as this area is concerned, most of the people I know are definitely not rich and any of them that have businesses probably work in the business themselves and maybe have a brother or two. There are very few people I know in this area who have a lot of money. Even today very few lawyers or doctors come from here. Most of my friends do labour type of work. There are a few who are in offices, but most would be checkers down at the harbour maybe or working in the elevators. A few would be taxi drivers—not too many people rush to be a taxi driver; it is not a good-paying job. I worked as an inventory control clerk for seven or eight years, then I just sort of bummed around for maybe four or five years. I did nothing. I took odd jobs, helper to a bookie, things like this. Horse racing I like, so I became a runner for this bookie named Porky, collecting bets, phoning them in, and paying off the winners.

Oh Christ, when the bookies were around here it was a good area we had, and you couldn't get a better person than Porky for a bookie. He bailed more people out. With nothing to eat at home, they would come running down and the wife would come and grab hold of Porky and he'd hand her a fiver or something. Very seldom did he ever get paid back, but that's the type of person he was. At one time he was wide open—when the city was open, he was open. He was doing very good. Maybe $5,000 bet a night, that sort of thing. This would be around 1960, before Drapeau got elected. Drapeau's great accomplishment was to close all the bookies. The police just started raiding them.

Everybody has got the idea that a bookie is a big businessman. If he does $5,000 worth of action a night, they think that that's $5,000 he puts in his pocket, but you know, out of that $5,000 he may lose money, or he may at the end of the night wind up making $102. They work on a very small percentage. It is 10 cents on a dollar—you know, if you are betting on a hockey game and you bet $110—like two people, one betting on one team and one on the other—well, the bookie makes $10.

Porky had a list of who he owed money to. I also carried a few dollars and we'd know between us who to pay off. But those days are gone. You'd never get a person like him anymore. There is no compassion today like he had. Eventually Porky went broke and today he stays at home 'cause he's nearly blind.

When Porky went out of business I was left just standing on the corner. I guess maybe I was down. A lot of people get down on themselves when they're broke and go into a sort of depression. I guess I was like that. I went for a job but I only had seventh grade. A lot of people were on welfare, so I decided that I should have something in my pocket. I was reaching an age when I couldn't get a job—coming close to 40—so I went to the Welfare Department and they told me I should be working and they gave me a list of private employment agencies to go and see. And I went to work a day for these agencies and they paid me I think it was a buck thirty. Then I found out they were charging about $3 an hour, and I was sort of pissed off about that. I was doing the work and they were making more than I was!

So I joined citizen's groups and one of the things I advocated was that we get some sort of employment program going because unemployment at that time was really high. In 1970 a lot of people in this area were on welfare and you know we are getting back into that same situation today.

Anyway, I knew most of the people and certainly knew the ones who didn't want to work and a lot of them that did want to work. So I got together with a friend of mine and we came up with the concept of The Fair Share Temporary Employment Agency. The difference would be that the actual monies that we collected, less what we had to give the government, would go to the worker. For the first four years we went with the aid of the federal government and now they have cut all funding, but we're still trying to get by.

What do I think of the election of the PQ? Well, I think it was a mistake. I voted Liberal. I think a lot of people were up tight. They weren't satisfied with the proposed language bill that the Liberal government were trying to put through, so I think a lot of people in anger voted against the Liberal government. A lot of people said, "Look, Bourassa is an ass . . . can Lévesque be worse?"

Another thing. The Liberal government was sort of a, you know, sort of a high-class government — never reached the people at all. Bourassa might have been a sincere person, but he never reached the people. I listened to him and I really couldn't get on the same wave length, whereas if you listen to Lévesque with your eyes closed you might believe what he is saying. But I think a lot of people are opening their eyes now. They make excuses for Lévesque. He is the moderate and you know many extreme left wingers — or nationalists or whatever you want to call them — are trying to push and he is sort of balancing things off. He wants to separate but he would like to separate just by saying to Ottawa, "That's it; we are finished, you. Give us some sort of a document saying Quebec is independent."

Now that's not going to happen. People are going to fight. You are going to see a lot of confrontation over the next couple of years. A lot of the English are going to move out, but some are going to stay and say, "Who are you? You're not going to push me around because I have been here a long, long time and you know I deserve as much of this province as you do. We didn't lose the war, you did."

I consider myself a Canadian. Québécois, that's just a word they invented. I don't think we're ever going to separate, but I think things may get much more bitter over the years. I don't think that you can just come along and tell me to leave the province. And if you want me to leave, I think you are going to have to compensate me. I think the federal government has a lot of responsibility in this. There is boatload after boatload of immigrants coming into this country and yet the poor English Canadian in Quebec is being treated like a piece of shit and he doesn't deserve that. Not by the Quebec government and not by the Canadian government. I am a little pissed off at this stage. The federal government again—if we go back—are at fault for not helping us English Montrealers learn French. Because at one time they gave grants and had training courses for immigrants to learn French, but they wouldn't allow English people from Quebec to take those same courses.

Now, as far as the federal government is concerned, I would like to see more programs dedicated to providing employment. I would like to see them maybe not lean so much toward business but lean toward people. I have to say that the federal government is the real culprit. And they are trying to create an issue—language-wise—to cover up high unemployment and various things that they are doing. You know that really should be looked at because this Trudeau government hasn't been a strong government at all. If there was no national unity debate Trudeau would have his arse burning right now with people asking, "How come unemployment is so high? Why are taxes to high? Why is the civil service so big?" You go down to Ottawa, all you see is people bumping into each other and more and more ministries trying to create a bigger bureaucracy. And why were civil servants given the right to strike? Christ, I have never heard of postmen owning taverns before. But two of them here, you know, got together and bought a tavern. Well, that's great, you know. But in the meantime are they going to take the time off from work to serve beer or are they going to deliver the mail? That's what we'd like to know. If they can afford to buy a tavern, why are they postmen? There are a lot of people who can use those jobs.

Bill 101? Personally, I don't like Laurin—I think he's a puke, if you understand what I mean. He doesn't like the English, let's face it. He would like to see the English disappear from the whole continent, if it was up to him. He just is not very bright. He just doesn't realize that he is surrounded by 250 million English-speaking people, and someday if they do separate and they cross the border, a lot of people who have moved out of Quebec or have been pushed out of Quebec are going to remember and they are going to make it tough for French Canadians in other parts of the country. This is one thing that a lot of people don't realize. As far as I am concerned, no way should we have any change as far as the rights of English-speaking people.

I was born here, my friends are here, my enemies are here. It is something I have built up over 43 years, and if I went somewhere else I would have to start all over and I don't think that is what I want. I am not in any big rush to let Camille Laurin push me out of the country.

What people don't realize is that for every crazy Frenchman there is a crazy Englishman. If people shit on the English long enough, you are going to have the same type of FLQ thing in reverse. Bombs went off in Westmount a few years ago. Maybe in five years, bombs will go off somewhere else. And they may not like it.

Rudy Loeser
Advertising executive, Montreal
(E)

"Hell! What this country needs is a corridor between Quebec and New Brunswick."

Federalists in Quebec are discussing a wide range of options designed to meet the challenge of independence. However, federalist Rudy Loeser is pursuing a different course of action. Proceeding from the assumption that Quebec will in fact become politically independent, Mr. Loeser is planning the further partition of Quebec to allow English-speaking areas to remain part of Canada.

I'm an immigrant. I left a European country which has in its history a great deal of suppression, and came to Canada at the age of 21 with probably a naïve belief in the fact that democracy is shining example of a society. Perhaps it is naïve but the fact is that I can't stand any undemocratic use of a democratic power.

I escaped East Germany in 1951, before the Berlin Wall was built, but of course the border had been established — wires and so forth . . . How did I manage to escape? I made my way through the underground system into West Berlin and was flown out in an American aircraft from Tempelhof to Hamburg.

I left East Germany for the same reason a lot of French Canadians are leaving Quebec now. Don't forget I was a very young man at the time. I had lived the first 15 years of my life under the Hitler regime and the next five years under Communist regime. I went to school, of course, and I was fed a certain ideology and all of a sudden, because the war is over and the Russians are here, we are being fed a totally new ideology and told this is the right ideology. Well, any thinking person at that stage said, "Just a minute, I have to make my own judgements here somewhere; I have to sort this thing out." In no way, shape, or form could I buy this Communist propaganda they were giving.

I speak several languages, but French is not one of them at this moment. When I first came to Quebec, four years ago, I enrolled in an immersion course and according to my teacher, did quite well. But then Bill 22 came out and I just had a sort of red-neck reaction to that and said, "To hell with you; nobody is going to force me."

My first reaction to the PQ election? I said, "Hell! What this country needs is a corridor between Ontario and New Brunswick." Maybe about 10 miles wide. It was only later on that the idea crystallized of going farther. I prepared a brief called "The Province of an Eleventh Community of Canada," and then I got in touch with Dr. Shaw, Member of the Legislature here for Pte.-Claire, and we had a founding meeting. And so the Preparatory Committee for an Eleventh Province was founded. And we spent the next two months holding sessions, attracting more people, and finalizing the shape of what we thought should be the eleventh province.

We are dealing essentially with a government that I personally doubt is a government of good will. I firmly believe that they will further their aim to separate Quebec and they will use any legislative tactic available. Whether such legislation deals with economics or welfare or what have you, it is all feeding into the final goal: separation from Canada. To me this is a highly dangerous thing for Canada as well as for Quebec, and I don't think it can be allowed to happen.

If Quebec votes in favour of separation, we would create an eleventh province and we would demand first of all the return of our language rights for both French and English. Freedom of choice is what we want. Not necessarily bilingualism because we don't force anyone to speak another language, but freedom of choice. Let the French speaker speak French, unilingually if he will. And the English speaker speak English, unilingually if that is his choice. This is to be done in a definite geographic zone that is to be established. I would say it should start in West Quebec, run past Hull, include Hull, the Ottawa River Valley, come in the Laurentian Auto route, include a good chunk of Montreal, then proceed up the river to include the Eastern Townships. And of course you have the business community of Montreal, which has said time and again that English is a necessary tool of communication in business. And the same situation exists south of the river. Many areas are predominantly English-speaking or English is spoken a lot even though they are predominatly French-speaking. And a lot of French Canadians, of course, adhere to the principle of bilingualism.

The PQ don't like this idea one bit. Lévesque has stated that the borders of Quebec were established over 100 years ago and cannot be changed. But Mr. Trudeau made a speech in Verdun a few months ago in which he pointed out the basic fault in Mr. Lévesque's logic; he said that if Mr. Lévesque thinks that Canada is divisible, then Quebec is divisible. That is what Mr. Trudeau said, and we believe him! In case of separation, I think we would absolutely have no hesitation about taking our documentation to Ottawa, to the government, and saying we wish to be protected. Our rights and our citizenship must be protected. And we are talking about two and a half million people here.

At this moment Quebec is not a separate political entity. If it were, it could do as it wished. But at the moment it is still a part of Canada. Now then I submit that it is highly immoral to force anyone coming here from another country or another province to send their children to a French school. What the government is really saying is this: "We can't save our culture ourselves, we must now have the Italians, the Yugoslavs, the Poles, and whoever else coming in save our culture." But if you look at the graphs of growth of the French-speaking population in this province over the last 100 years, you cannot by any stretch of the imagination think that the language or the culture is in any great danger. There is just no way! I'm sure that in past years injustices have been perpetrated on the French Canadians. But when you talk about a French Canadian woman going into Ogilvy's department store and being served in English, I don't really call that an injustice. I call it stupidity on the part of the merchant. Right? And that is being rectified.

But it is stupidity to begin with. If I want to do business, I should endeavour to speak the language of my customers. And if five million of them happen to be French Canadian, I should damn well speak French. And if I don't, well, then in the spirit of free enterprise, it is up to some enterprising French Canadian to open his own department store in French and get all the business. Isn't that the easiest way? Historically it would have been possible, don't you think? If business had been taught in French Canadian schools, I think we would have a very healthy business climate in French today. If it didn't work out that way you cannot just say, "Let's blame the English for that." They simply happened to have a different educational system, so they developed the banks, the stores.

This situation reminds me very much of pre-war Germany, to tell you the truth. Very much so because the type of legislation that was brought out then, in 1935, 1936, shortly after democratically elected government came to power, was very much the same way because it was based on restriction. It was based on intimidation of a different minority. Let's go back to the basic thing. If I happen to establish a business because of my enterprise or initiative, nobody should be able to come along and say from now on 80 percent of your executive echelon has to be French. That is just not done. It is my goddamn company!

I think, incidentally, that economic association is a most immoral use of the concept for propagating your aims, furthering your aims. It is being stated by a lot of people both outside and inside the province that we don't want any economic association. I think we must get this most important message across to the French Canadian who listens to Lévesque and says, "Well, yes, maybe we can have our cake and eat it too." Separation with economic association is like your wife leaving you and still wanting alimony. If this damn referendum goes through, I think there will be a considerable number of people in business who will say, "Well, I will not have anything to do with Quebec at all." Even if it means some sacrifice.

I have a friend and client who is in the real estate business. He was into real estate developments in the Laurentians and for the time being he has made a switch to Florida. And he was greatly astonished to find that most of the people who are buying his condominium units there are French Canadians. They say, "Look, we got the message, we're taking our goods, getting out—and these are business people. It's not just because they like the sunshine. Oh no. For myself, if Quebec separated and the Eleventh Province didn't become a reality, I would leave immediately for Toronto or Vancouver.

I think René Lévesque is a dreamer. I think he is being badly used by some people in his party who are shrewder than he is, who are deeper than he is, and possibly vicious in their approach to Canadian politics. Lévesque is an honest man, I believe, but fairly superficial in terms of philosophy. And I don't think Mr. Lévesque is in control of things any more. Mr. Laurin I wouldn't trust as far as I could throw a piano; I don't think I would trust Mr. Charron very far or Mr. Morin very far.

As for Mr. Trudeau, I think I have to subscribe, like the rest of the people in Canada, to the belief that Mr. Trudeau is going to pull the chestnuts out of the fire for Canada. He's the only choice we have. Mr. Clark just won't make it because I think he is trying to waffle. He has not made any commitments to any firm policy. He doesn't emerge as a leader at all.

If you believe in something, you have to work for it. I'm working on this committee to set up a zone of choice because I know nobody else is going to do it for us. Those of us in this group—and there are quite a few involved—we believe that what we are doing is the only answer at the moment to the threat of separatism and the unity of Canada. And rather than paying lip service, we decided to be very concrete about it, and to work as hard as we possibly can.

Pauline Julien
Singer, Montreal
(F)

"If the referendum doesn't go through, what are we supposed to do, die with a smile on our lips?"

The past 15 years have seen the emergence of an extremely popular and nationalistic group of chansonniers, or popular singers, in Quebec. Félix Leclerc, Gilles Vigneault, Robert Charlebois, and Pauline Julien speak directly to the young Québécois and have become the engine of the cultural revolution in Quebec. Like the other chansonniers, Pauline Julien has achieved wide popularity in Quebec without the initial benediction of U.S. approval that English Canadian performers are often forced to seek by a culturally colonized public at home.

I was in Europe on November 15, on a tour in Paris. Like most Quebeckers, in my deepest heart I had a great deal of hope, but I didn't want — well, after having seen a failure in previous elections, I did not want to start hoping again. I would rather say, "Okay, fine, there will be some progress from the point of view of the number of voters, but certainly we won't win. But if we really win I would be very happy."

The first time that I was phoned from Quebec I asked, "Are you sure? Don't call me again until you're certain." We knew that it would come one day, but it was a surprise because everyone was convinced that we would gain a great deal but not necessarily win. But we did! But we are very realistic and this victory is just one step. There is a great deal to be done; it will mean long and hard work.

I did not become an *indépendantiste* until 1962-63 because I came from a small town where one is very, very passive. I had lived in Europe for six years [from 1952 to 1959], cut off from the reality of Quebec. When I did come back in 1959-60 I noted a great deal of change in Montreal. A great many things were going on and it was then [1961, '62, '63] that the idea of an autonomous independent country really took hold. We were not Canadian like the others, so we called ourselves French Canadians. Still, this wasn't a satisfactory way of seeing ourselves. Several years later we understood that Quebec could be independent, could be autonomous, could be self-sufficient. At that point we thought of ourselves as Québécois—that is to say, we were no longer Canadians, no longer French Canadians, we were Quebeckers, Quebeckers living in a country which must and should and does call itself Quebec.

These last 15 years have been a renaissance, or a revolution, a period of extraordinary ferment for Quebeckers. Popular music has been quite an important factor in the development of a national consciousness in Quebec. No more important than the other arts, but music can be very quickly spread in little time. Of course, it is less durable than film and a book; it will die out more quickly—but it is on the street corners more quickly too.

Many of the leading performers in Quebec are *indépendantistes* because they are able to express themselves and because anyone who is not blind, deaf, and dumb can see the urgency of the situation. Expressing oneself doesn't mean just talking about little birds or making love on the beach in the sun. You speak about how you feel, about what is happening around you. If you feel colonized or you don't feel at home in your home, you say, "We don't feel free." If you feel abused, you say it. That's how singers are. I think that an artist is never behind the times. I think that by his very nature he is rather like a poet—a little bit ahead of his time. He sees what is: he tries to anticipate and also express his own desires. Perhaps most of the time what he feels is what everyone else feels, but he has the opportunity of voicing it.

After the October Crisis in 1970 we became more convinced than ever that the only way to feel at home was to be autonomous and be independent. We found that the so-called "fair play" of our comrades— anglo Canadians and particularly Trudeau and his government— disappears automatically when the least thing happens that endangers it. Remember that one man's fears sent an army that raided 1,500 people and detained 450 people. They put six million people in a state of fear— basic fear. I was imprisoned for eight days. There was no reason, without charge. It's revolting but that's the way it was. It's not just my case which is revolting: it's everything that happened.

Prime Minister Bourassa was Trudeau's little dog. They wanted to exterminate anything that could be called protest in Quebec, which was really just the desire to express oneself and the will to change something. They wanted to scare people, and it worked for a month or two, but after that people woke up and said, "They want to crush us." I don't believe that it affected us for very long.

Trudeau is an intelligent and cultivated man, but I think he has a strong appetite for power and I think that he panics in the face of Quebeckers who want autonomy. He loses his head completely. I tell you that you just don't send in the army like he did. He is not capable of considering Quebeckers as human beings to whom one can talk. But a change has to come about. And if there is a change to be made, it will be through discussion — it will not be imposed. Oh yes, Mr. Trudeau *is* a Quebecker, but there are other Quebeckers throughout the country, the colonized country. There has always been a percentage of people who have sold their souls to power to gain privileges.

Mr. Lévesque, I think, is a great man; persevering, honest, and very much a politician. That is to say, close to the people. He might perhaps be too cautious if anything, but I don't believe that's important because the party is there, and as the party is formed of a great many people, the party is the voice of the people. I think that the party is going to try and help him to go in the direction that the people want. The last PQ election proved that.

We said that the election was one step. The next step, you will understand, is necessarily autonomy, autonomy with socialism. It is autonomy, and working toward constant progress to improve the standard of living of Quebeckers, which is generally pretty low. Unemployment is terrible and it's not the PQ's fault. When they took over, unemployment was already there. Women's rights, equal wages, day-care centres — that's the social side. Very, very important.

I know there is a great deal of money in the federal government which doesn't come back to us. We don't control all the social programs that are already in operation. I believe that all this money could be recovered for us and transferred to build Quebec. Maybe we could do these things if we had a sovereignty-association, but only in the way that we want it, designed not in the way the others want it — just a few crumbs from the cake.

If the referendum doesn't go through, what are we supposed to do, die with a smile on our lips? No — if it doesn't work this time, it will work the next time. If we haven't succeeded in liberating our country, we know that our children will do so.

I am realistic. It is going to be difficult. You won't make it easy for us, and that's normal. This is an inevitable struggle, but we are confident because independence is our right.

Chapter 2

Eastern Townships

I*t is easy and perhaps natural for the non-Québécois to generalize about Quebec and see the place as a sort of enlarged village with a uniform history, culture, and political outlook. But this cartoon of a complex and constantly changing society is, of course, grossly inaccurate and inhibits real understanding between Quebec and the rest of the country. Perhaps the best way for the outsider to fill in his sketchy Quebec picture with real detail and humanity is to just travel and meet the people. Since Quebec is Canada's largest province (1,540,680 square kilometers) this will take some time, but it will be an experience never regretted.*

The short journey south from Montreal to the Eastern Townships is a trip back in time to an area that was once more English than French, with place names proudly lifted from the map and history of England: Windsor, Stanhope, Ascot Corner, Cookshire, Stoke, Stratford, Stornoway, and Disraeli. Towns like Stanstead, with its 100-year-old wood frame houses and expansive lawns and shade trees, could have been unrooted intact from rural Nova Scotia or Ontario—except for the Quebec flag flying over the Palais de Justice and the French names over the storefronts and service stations. These are friendly, inquisitive towns where the newcomer is noticed on the streets, where young girls cycling and old folks front-porch-rocking give out fine open smiles that make you want to pass through slowly.

The first settlers were New England Loyalists who arrived here in 1784 after the American War of Independence and were followed by veterans of the War of 1812 who were granted land in recognition of service in the British Army. At the same time, French Canadian settlers had begun to claim portions

of the rich agricultural land in the northern section of the Townships, and by Confederation there was a substantial French-speaking population. Through natural increase, the French became the majority over the decades, and towns like Drummondville, named after Canadian Governor-General Lord Drummond, saw their English character virtually disappear.

Drummondville (population 29,286; 97 percent French) is the first city I visited in the Eastern Townships after a fast one-hour drive from Montreal on one of Quebec's superb autoroutes. Drummondville can be a very misleading city to the first-time visitor: its clean streets, pleasant parks, and well-kept houses and lawns give no hint of the 20 percent unemployment rate, high incidence of divorce, and union militancy. A clearer, more representative picture of Drummondville begins to emerge in the local bars, factories, and households where I met people directly affected by Drummondville's economic problems.

Every community in the Eastern Townships does not suffer from a severe unemployment problem. A short drive southeast from Drummondville leads to the bluntly named town of Asbestos, where a highly paid work force enjoys job security and winter vacations in Florida, thanks to the world's largest open-pit asbestos mine. The name of this town became a household word in 1949 during the bitter and now-famous asbestos strike that is still well remembered by many workers.

Since there seems to be a lively interest in borders these days, after visiting the regional capital of Sherbrooke, I drove south to the border we share with the Americans. Here on the Quebec-Vermont border I explored two communities that exhibit in microcosm some of Quebec's severest linguistic tensions: Stanstead (population 2,700) and Rock Island (population 1,200). These towns, almost equally composed of French- and English-speaking residents, also had a very interesting involvement during World War II with the anti-conscription Bloc Populaire movement, as described in the words of the only anonymous interviewee in this book.

On November 15, the voters in the Eastern Townships sent 10 PQ, seven Union Nationale, three Liberal, and one independent deputy to the National Assembly.

Mrs. Marjorie McWilliam
Widow, Drummondville
(E)

"I don't know how to say it exactly, but we have noticed that the English population has decreased in the last three years."

The English of Quebec are too often presented by their political critics and sections of the media as self-interested latecomers to Quebec who have exploited the French economically and culturally. Mrs. McWilliam is an English-speaking Québécois who can trace her roots in Drummondville back to the War of 1812.

My great-grandfather on my father's side came from Scotland, from Sutherland. His name was George Sutherland. His tombstone is in the cemetery over there, St. George's cemetery.

He was with the foot soldiers in the War of 1812 and after the war he settled here in Drummondville. His regiment was disbanded here and a great many of the soldiers were given grants of land by the Crown. And of course some families still have them; some of them have come down, but there's not very many English left.

The Sutherland farm was built in 1837. Well, really, it had been built earlier, about 1815, but it was finished and enlarged in 1837, something like that. George Sutherland passed the farm on to his son—my grandfather—Donald Sutherland. He had five children, I think. My father was the second son. My father was Donald Sutherland and he had a brother, George, who went down to the New England States and went into the ministry. And there were three sisters; they were scattered through Massachusetts and Vermont.

Yes, the farm was handed down to my father and I was born there on the 27th of August, 1902. I had an older sister. We were seven children, but one little brother died. That's a large family. My father passed away in 1927; my brother Douglas was there and he was married and he lived on the farm until, say 1944, something like that. Then the place was sold. The house is still there—the main house—but the barn and the outer buildings have all been taken down. It's changed a great deal. The trees have all been cut down, there were a great many maples and butternut trees, and elms around the house, but the trees have all been cut down.

When I was growing up, my father did what you would call clean dirt farming. He had hay for the animals, and he planted grain also, and there was a mill up around near Richmond, a place called Dennison's mill, and in the fall the wheat was taken there and ground into flour. He had milk cows, usually about 12. It wasn't a very big farm, you see. He had work horses, and everything was manual labour. There was a cheese factory not very far from where we were, where you sold milk. But don't forget that that was back in the early 1900s. Farming was very diverse and hard — usually you had hay fields and you cut the hay in the summer to feed the animals in the winter.

In those days there was a fair number of French people in Drummondville. There were more French than there were English, I think. Couldn't tell what the proportion was then. I know we were the only English family for over six miles from Drummondville.

Oh yes, my father was perfectly bilingual, my mother even more so because she had been to the convent. She was a good, very good scholar. My father's education had been in English. He went to Bishop's for three years. I am bilingual, but my French is only passable. I can't read or write French. There was an English school. When I went with my brothers and sisters, there was just one teacher, a one-room school. It wasn't high school. We went up to possibly grade 10. Finally the new high school was built, in the '30s, I would say.

I went to school in Montreal for a while — I stayed with my aunt and uncle. But as for going shopping, as we did a few years later, you know, you never even thought about going to Montreal then. It was just too far; it took four hours by train, and there were no cars until 1915. I can remember the first car in Drummondville. Somebody who owned a shoestore bought one, and it was a Ford. It certainly created quite a stir around here, and it made a lot of noise too. The roads were not very good; especially in the spring they were terrible. There was about six inches of mud.

I was married in '28, to Derrick McWilliam, who was a Marconi engineer, a wireless engineer really. Now I'm not very sure about these dates, but it was approximately 1923 when the wireless station came and we lived there, about two miles out of Drummondville. My husband was in charge there for about 30 years. I remember there were two guards on duty all the time in the war.

I worked very hard, cooking, bringing up two children, doing housework. My husband's work was very exacting really. You know, the station never closed down — they couldn't — and that's why he lived so close to his work. He had radios all over the place and whenever he heard a strange noise or strange sound he dashed over.

Oh yes, there have been a lot of changes in Drummondville over the years. It's fantastic, really and truly. I well remember the war in 1914. I remember it being quite difficult to get news, but the weekly newspaper came on Wednesday and of course somebody would go to town and hear a little more. But as for daily news, well, you only got a weekly paper and that was it.

When the Celanese plant came into Drummondville in early 1929 — I'm not sure about the date — it brought quite a lot of people, a lot of people from England. I don't know how to say it exactly, but we have noticed that the English population has decreased in the last three years. I think a lot of them have moved away and Celanese is not employing as many, and quite a few English people left last summer because there was a strike here at Celanese. I'm very much afraid there will be even fewer English people coming to Quebec now — after the PQ election.

It's sad, very sad, you know. We struggle very hard here to keep our old St. George's going, the church, but it is getting to be a problem because there are so few English now. The land for our church came from Heriot, Frederick George Heriot, in 1815. He was the founder of Drummondville. He gave the land for the English church and also for a Catholic church. St. George's Church is the Anglican church; St. Frederick's is the Catholic.

General Heriot is buried in our Anglican church. Did you notice the little iron railing in the corner as you come in? That's where his tomb is. Some of the schools around this area asked if they could bring the children to see the church last summer, and this man who sort of looked after it, he was telling us afterward that many of the small children asked if General Heriot was in that tomb, that odd-shaped thing in the corner.

My roots here are deep and being a Québécois means a great deal to me. It means everything in a way. I feel very badly about the situation as it is because you couldn't have kinder neighbours anywhere. Even just around here. Certainly, when we were growing up, I remember if anybody was ill . . . there was an elderly neighbour. She was a midwife, a nurse, and as Mother said, she'd rather have her than any doctor. It was six miles to go to town to get the doctor if there was an accident. If anything happened, you went to the neighbours, the neighbours came to you. And we were the only English family within six miles, so it is a strange situation now. I don't understand it at all.

Gérald and
Joanne Coderre
Unemployed, Drummondville
(F)

**"When you're in the U.S.A. you speak
with your hands."**

Gérald and Joanne Coderre, a young couple in their mid-20s, are unilingual. Like most Quebeckers, they are very aware of the inconveniences and limitations faced by any unilingual francophone who decides to venture outside the province. Without exception, all Québécois in this book, bilingual or not, support the idea of personal bilingualism. While the anglophone may also support bilingualism in the interests of national unity or cultural enrichment, the francophone generally offers more pragmatic reasons, like the ones below.

Gérald: At first I had no particular goal in life, but when I was 15 or 16, in grade 10, then I started thinking about getting a job. I was the eldest in the family and we had a large family — nine children — so my father needed money. I thought I should help him, so I left school and found a job in the textile industry. That was seven years ago, and I've worked since then. I dyed materials, like your shirt, for Consolidated Textiles; then last month things slowed down and I found myself out of my job.

Now I am waiting. I am looking. It sort of shakes you up after seven years because in Drummondville salaries are not high and everybody is looking for better wages, and you have to start out at the bottom of the ladder every time you change jobs.

Joanne: I went to school in Drummondville up to grade nine and I quit. I went to work — that was five years ago — and when I left I was getting the minimum wage and I had been working for five years, so they don't pay very much. There were no increases at all. I worked in a place where we made nylon stockings. Then they decided to cut back; now it is only men working there, so we lost our jobs and I've been on unemployment since then. I'm looking for another job, if I can find one, but there are not that many available. It is difficult when there is not much money coming in. Many couples have to work nowadays to make ends meet. If they don't work they have to tighten their belts.

Gérald: I was working nights for five years and Joanne worked days. I'd come in in the morning at seven and she had already left—she started at seven A.M. I would go to bed, of course. She finished at three, so I'd get up when she came home. Either she was ready to prepare supper or damn near it at four o'clock. On shift work people lead two different lives—one lives at night and the other one lives in the daytime.

Joanne: When I went to bed, he left. I would go to bed about 10 o'clock. But it is a way of life and you get used to that. When he starts working again, it will be more difficult because now I am used to having him with me all the time. But when he starts working it will be nights again possibly, because when you start out in any industry, you have to start on the night shift.

Gérald: We don't have any children. We have been married for three years now and if I had a more stable job, more regular — you know — I wouldn't mind, but it is not stable enough in Drummondville, especially in the textile district. We would like to have children. It would be nice to have a child, but I guess we'll just have to wait.

Joanne: Our families live around here and we would miss them if we left. It's hard to just pack up and leave. In a new place you don't know anyone. Here in Drummondville people talk to each other. I like it that way. Gérald might find a job in Montreal but I don't want to live there. I don't know, you walk on the street and you can get robbed. I would rather not go. I don't think he would like to go either. At night especially — at eight or nine at night — it is getting dark and on those small streets thefts and all kinds of things happen. In Montreal, you never know . . .

Gérald: That's right. Montreal is more wide open. Here you have a different mentality.

The last provincial election? I voted PQ . . .

Joanne: Oh really? You didn't tell me. I voted Créditiste like my father.

Gérald: Well, I knew the PQ had a chance of coming in and I thought they'd provide more work and help young people mainly because of that pension thing at age 60 and lots of things that they haven't done yet. If people had their pension at 60, younger ones who come out of school or university now and can't find a job because work is scarce would be able to get work. But I am not in favour of independence.

Joanne: Me neither. We don't have enough economic development in Quebec to be independent from the rest of Canada. There is not enough — we have to export and import from other countries. Quebec by itself would be a very difficult spot economically.

Gérald: I say that the language policy is good, though. It is really normal that immigrants should learn French because in Quebec the language is French. But for industry and business, English is a good second language. So you need both. When I went to school, we didn't have any English till grade eight.

Joanne: The same with me, so we don't speak much English — very little. So we can't really travel very much outside Quebec. We have been to the United States—to Atlantic City and Old Orchard Beach—but it is very hard to get by. People just don't understand us.

Gérald: When you're in the U.S.A. you speak with your hands. We know a few words of English here and there, but we don't know how to place those words in a sentence or make a full sentence in English. We have to get along with a few words, so we make gestures. But you know what the advertisements say: "Visit Quebec first"! It used to be that Quebec was only bush and nothing else, but now there are parks, there are a lot of tourist attractions, in each city there is something to see. In Quebec City there is Parliament, the Plains of Abraham . . . Maybe we'll take our next vacation here.

Joanne: I have an uncle who lives in Ontario and he speaks both languages. When he comes over here he speaks French, but over there he speaks only English because his wife speaks only English. I also have an uncle in California and an aunt who is bilingual, but she hasn't come here for a long time. She can't speak French very well now. We don't have any English friends here in Drummondville.

Gérald: The English live mainly in their own area, they stay together. They are maybe 4 or 5 percent of the population, at the most.

As Québécois, we have our own language, but looking ahead, I would certainly like our children to be bilingual because when they go into English areas they could get along better than we do. But will they have the chance to learn it now?

Yves Garièpy
Union leader, Drummondville
(F)

" . . . what really counts is helping the workers in Quebec —that's what counts."

The politics of Drummondville is the politics of competing foreign textile and clothing imports, tariffs, quotas, and economic protection—all federal responsibilities. A national tariff policy that favours the manufacturing industries of Ontario has produced the same anti-federal feelings here that have been present in the West for decades. Partly as a protest against what is seen as federal inaction on import protection, Drummondville voted PQ on November 15, 1976.

Yves Garièpy, the 25-year-old president of the 1,100-member textile workers union, is pleased with the PQ victory, and equally proud of Drummondville's support of his union's recent seven-month strike for higher wages. Mr. Garièpy and his union see that strike as a community effort against the company, the federal government that created the hated Anti-Inflation Board, and the national import policy.

My father and his father were honest hard-working Quebeckers. Dad was a bricklayer who built a lot of houses for a lot of people but never had a house of his own. That's the story of a lot of people around here who have to work, and work hard to earn their living. Soon after starting to work in the textile industry I became interested in the guys I was working with who were stuck in the system the same way I was, so I became active in the union, and last year I was elected president of our local of 1,100 members. My age? Twenty-five. This word "president" is just a title—what really counts is helping the workers in Quebec—that's what counts. The title doesn't mean anything.

Do you know, I'm not even sure who owns the Celanese Company! I think it's American, but I don't know for sure. One thing I am sure of, though, is that Drummondville people really help each other out. During our last strike last year there were collections throughout the city. Things went well; people were helping each other out. Those are Quebeckers for you—people who help each other. You will find that especially in smaller cities. Now in larger cities such as Montreal for instance—Montreal I know a little—people don't speak to each other much. Everybody stays in his own corner. But in Drummondville everyone pitched in during the strike to support the workers.

The owner of a theatre company opened the doors free to Celanese workers one day a week and said, "Come on in; you need recreation too." There were merchants who gave away their merchandise—clothing, shoes—some gave every week. In the public market they were giving away meat. That strike cost the Confederation of National Trade Unions $1,600,000.

In Drummondville now there is lots of unemployment—22 percent unemployment. The textile industry here has been hurt because of foreign imports. It's caused a major problem. Salaries are at the minimum salary level, so you have some people who would rather go on unemployment.

There have been statistics prepared saying that a man with two children and a wife — a four-person family — should have about $150 per week to make ends meet. Well, we don't have that much here. So what happens is that workers who can't make ends meet have to borrow. They still can't make ends meet and now they have debts. What does that produce? Strikes for more money, that's what.

We want the federal government to limit imports of textile products, even if that might hurt the Westerners who export their wheat. We think that the Quebec government should have the right to control not only its immigration but also its imports. Of course, Quebeckers, like everyone else, will walk into a store and buy what's cheaper. So a $5-shirt imported from another country will sell better than a $10- or $15-shirt made in Canada. Our textile industry can't compete with those prices, so companies close their doors and that creates unemployment.

I hope that the election means that an awakening has taken place among the people of Quebec. Now is the time to wake up! Not only should the party do something to protect the industries in Quebec; it should also help us become respected in our language, although that's not a major issue here because the percentage of francophones in Drummondville must be about 98 percent. The survival of French here is not going to be a problem. The PQ in Drummondville won all the seats probably because of the dissatisfaction with the government at the time.

What does being a Quebecker mean to me? Lots of things! To be a Quebecker for me is to talk in French. To be a Quebecker means having economic problems, being held down by the finance companies, by American industries, by multinational companies. To be a Quebecker means to be short of money, to be short of capital to build up our own industries. To be a Quebecker means to want cooperatives, to want Caisses Populaires. It also means the will to work, not to sit down and watch the others work. That is what it means to be a Quebecker.

No, I don't speak English, but it is not a lack of good will. There are lots of people in Quebec who speak English because they had the chance to get an education. I didn't. I guess a lot of people would like to be bilingual, but it is costly; it takes time.

But language has created a barrier between the two people. How often do you hear it said by anglophones, "Look at the pea soups"? Or the Frenchman will say, "Look at the square heads!" That shouldn't be. I am not a racist but if I come into another province, why should I have to speak English? This is an officially bilingual country but the fact has not been accepted by anglophones. I as a Quebecker am convinced that, without a policy of unilingualism in Quebec, we will be assimilated. It's that simple, and that's why I'm for Bill 101.

As for the future, I am 25 years old and I have a lot of confidence in the

Lord. He is the one who placed me here in these circumstances and I am waiting for the future and will see what happens. I came to build and not to tear down.

Roger St. Pierre
Cinema owner, Drummondville
(F)

"We are Canadians too and we are not ready to separate."

Quebec today is officially unilingual, and a large majority of the francophones in this book, including, Mr. St. Pierre, support the PQ government's French-first policies. However, as the following interview shows, it is misleading and incorrect to conclude that this pro-French sentiment means a rejection of the English language by Quebeckers.

The vast majority of the young people are Péquistes. I think they were politicized in the schools to start with because teachers are for the most part Péquistes. So I would imagine that it is easy for them to be able to interest young people in the PQ — not directly, but indirectly. You can always get a message across without people really knowing it. And that's how it happens. Look at René Lévesque. He wanted to lower the voting age to 16. So if the voting age had been lowered to 16 — and it had been a time to vote for separation of Quebec — I think that he would have gotten it because the 16-to-30-year-olds would be almost the majority of the voters.

I was never a PQ, although I had some sympathy for the Péquistes because in the province of Quebec you can't deceive yourself. Even in the time of other governments — Liberal or Union Nationale — things weren't going all that well. Here in Drummondville our PQ candidate was elected. And he's a charming person in his late 20s, rather conscientious, and he does good work. I have nothing to say against him, and I think that people from Drummondville are pretty well satisfied for the time being with our provincial member of the National Assembly.

The PQ, of course, is a new party and there are a lot of competent people in it. You have to admit that. Very competent.

The social policies of the PQ are okay, but independence—that's the only thing I don't like. I claim that a country with a population of seven million isn't feasible. I don't think it can compete with the other provinces or with the United States. There is one thing that I find not quite fair and that is the Quebec minimum wage: it's $3.15 an hour. That is the highest minimum wage in the world. With the girl working at the candy bar to sell chips and soft drinks for 25 cents apiece at $3.15 an hour, there is no way that I can make any money. I am not talking about large business, of course; it's small ones that cannot pay salaries of $3.25 and $3.50 an hour.

So what happens? I will have to change my system in the snack bar. I shall have to put in automatic machines so that all the clients will serve themselves—which means that two weekend employees are going to be out of work. Here in Drummondville $3 for a movie is a real luxury for many people. Even if you earn a $150 a week, insurance, heating, taxes, everything costs a lot; so if you calculate two people coming to the cinema, that's $6 for the tickets. With the restaurant and the baby sitters, an evening out can cost $12.

You know, before having the theatre here, I worked at Canadian Celanese for 17 years and I went through a strike in 1960. We were out on strike for two months and when we started back to work I left Canadian Celanese to take over the cinema. So when the Canadian Celanese workers went on strike again I knew what it was like. Life isn't easy on $25 or $30 a week when you have three, four, or five children. So during the last strike I opened the cinema up free one day a week to the workers. I thought that it was a good idea for people to have some leisure once a week. It was not very much, but while they were looking at a film for two or three hours at least they were not thinking of their problems. It pleased them; it pleased me. Every Thursday evening people came with their wives and I charged them nothing as long as the strike lasted.

Today we hear a lot from the government about Quebec being officially unilingual. I have two daughters—Kathleen, who is 17, and Gislène, who is 12. They speak only French. They don't really realize yet how important it is to be able to speak English, but one day they will discover when they go outside the province of Quebec, if they can't speak English, they won't go too far.

This is the unfortunate thing about the PQ. I don't think that people can be unilingual in the province of Quebec. If people decide to become unilingual, then they are going to have to stay put right here. If you want to travel the least bit, whether it be on vacation or anything else, if you don't speak English, then you can go nowhere. No more complicated than that—you can go nowhere. You can't get any information. You can't communicate.

I am very proud to be a Quebecker—just as any American is proud to be American or an anglo-Canadian is proud to be a Canadian. But on the other hand, I am not the type who is closed in on the province of Quebec. I am happy to stay here, but I say that we cannot live all by ourselves in isolation. We can't be separated from the others and say, "Well, we are going to get along alone."

Certainly there should be changes in Confederation. We have to start by looking over the Constitution and making changes on it. They have been talking about that for a long time. Mr. Trudeau wanted to have a meeting with the provinces to discuss it. In the province of Quebec it is understood that we would like to control our own language. French should be the working language, the language that everybody speaks. I have always said that if I go into Ontario I won't ask people to speak French. People will talk English, of course, and it is up to me then to learn to speak English—but when people from the West, from Ontario or the United States, come into Quebec, I would think that it would be very normal, if they want to stay in the province and work in the province, that they have to learn French. I agree with that. What about the managers of the Bank of Montreal, or the Royal Bank, who work in Montreal, in English? They don't even *read* French. These people have been living in Montreal, which is a French Canadian city, for 25 or 30 years and cannot read or speak French! I fail to understand it.

I know a whole host of French people who went to work in the United States and to Ontario and elsewhere and at the end of a year, when they came home, they were speaking English. It is just a question of will. Any person who has lived in Quebec for 25 or 30 years and still does not talk French just didn't want to learn it. That's clear. I worked at Canadian Celanese 15 years ago and there were some people in management who had been there for 25 or 30 years who didn't know any French—and Drummondville was 98 percent French Canadian.

As far as I'm concerned, immigrants to Quebec—except English Canadians—should go to French schools. The Italians, Germans, and all those, I agree with the Parti Québécois that these people should go to a French school because they don't speak English any more than French. But if English Canadians want to move to Quebec they should be able to educate their kids in their own mother tongue.

No, I don't believe that independence would be a solution to Drummondville's economic problems. On the contrary, I think it would make things worse. This is a personal opinion, of course, but as I see it for the next three or four or five years industrialists will not be ready to come to Quebec. They are going to wait and see what is going to happen first.

The same goes for English Canadian or American investors. It would be very bad for the economy of the entire country, but we are Canadians too, and we are not ready to separate.

Gaudiose Leclerc
Mine worker, Asbestos
(F)

"We picked up "Death to the cows!"
from Trudeau and it became
a sort of slogan."

Asbestos, Quebec, is a living monument to man as mole. Twenty-four hours a day the huge trucks enter and leave the enormous open pit. The 1949 Asbestos Strike united for the first time labour, the clergy, and intellectuals against big business and government in the form of the U.S.-owned Canadian Johns-Manville Corporation and the Union Nationale government of Premier Maurice Duplessis. After five months of bitter, often violent confrontation many of the union's demands were finally met. One of the many outsiders walking the picket line in support of the workers was the young Pierre Elliot Trudeau, who stood shoulder to shoulder with men like Gaudiose Leclerc.

I have worked in the mines for the past 30 years, and I remember the 1949 strike very well because I went through it. I was about 22 at the time.

The first reason for the strike was to improve working conditions. We used to work eight hours a day, six days a week—48 hours a week. Salaries weren't very high. We got $1, maybe $1.10 an hour, I think. Everything was done by hand, there was a great deal of dust in the air. Asbestos dust in the lungs is dangerous; that was one of the reasons why the union was asking for improvements.

The strike started on February 13, 1949. We were visited often by Mr. Trudeau, Gérard Pelletier, Michel Chartrand, and Jean Marchand— these were the leaders of the strike in 1949. They used to have meetings with the workers and make speeches to us. They told us to hold on, and that we had to beat the provincial government of the day, which was the

Union Nationale. They helped us to politicize the strike a great deal. At the time Maurice Duplessis was premier of the province of Quebec, and probably in the upper echelons among the trade union leaders they wanted to get rid of that government, which was anti-union. I think that Maurice Duplessis himself took sides with the company but his minister of labour was sympathetic to the workers. After the strike we learned that the labour minister was really at odds with Duplessis.

You know, as workers we used to have meetings, and we would discuss things pretty openly with the leaders both during and after the meetings. We workers especially liked Jean Marchand; he was the union organizer and a brilliant speaker—we had confidence in him. Personally, I think that Trudeau was a socialist at the time. He was certainly avant-garde and you really have to admit it, he was for the labourer, the working class. He believed that Duplessis was the real problem and I think it's true that the premier was anti-union. One thing I can remember to this day about Trudeau—he had just arrived from France and he brought back an expression: *mort aux vaches*. In France the strikers always yelled to the policemen, *"Mort aux vaches!"* "Death to the cows!" We picked up "Death to the cows!" from Trudeau and it became a sort of slogan. During the strike, whenever we met provincial officers we used to say "Mort aux vaches!"

But the Pierre Trudeau I met in 1949 is a different man than the one you see today. His ideas have changed. Maybe he was a socialist back then but today? Oh yes, there is a difference. He is no longer the same man. He said things to workers during the La Palme strike in Montreal that he never would have said at Asbestos. Remember? He said, *"Mange la merde."* Still, Trudeau will be recognized in history for having given a place in government to French Canadians, which they didn't have before. Before Mr. Trudeau came into politics as leader of the party and leader of the government, government departments rarely had French Canadians in high positions—it was people from the West or people from Ontario. But since Mr. Trudeau has been there, we must be honest and say that a great many French Canadians have had economic portfolios. Trudeau, Pelletier, and Marchand really believe that French Canadians must have their place in Confederation.

I voted Conservative in the last federal election although I voted PQ provincially. I don't strongly believe in the Conservative Party but it was a response to Trudeau's arrogance. Mr. Trudeau is convinced that Quebec is 100 percent federalist and Liberal. Well, it isn't.

We need more of a balance from Quebec federally. When Mr. Clark was elected leader of the party, he impressed me. His acceptance speech made me think that he was a young man who had scope. But I've been a little disappointed since then—he's not the leader that I expected. Mr.

Trudeau—whether you are for or against him—is frank, whereas Mr. Clark skates quite a lot. He is not definite enough. He should say if he is for or against things, the way Diefenbaker did. You have to admit he was one Prime Minister who always stuck by his ideas. He always said, "One Canada." People in Quebec knew what to expect—we knew that he was against separatism, that there was no way to reach any agreement with him on that. We knew what kind of a man he was. But I don't think he understood Quebec. Among the Conservatives the one who best understood Quebec was Mr. Stanfield—he is the man who could have really communicated with us French Canadians. I got this impression from his speeches and the way French Canadian M.P.s spoke about him, but we'll never know what might have happened because he never got to power.

As for René Lévesque, I think he has the potential to become the greatest French Canadian ever. We will know better in a few years what he was able to accomplish on our behalf. Lévesque is committed to real economic reform. Now, I personally am against complete independence for Quebec but I am ready to see negotiations with the rest of the country toward a new economic union. I think we need more control over the Quebec economy, but let me say this doesn't mean nationalizing the asbestos industry here. I think that would be an extreme step.

What we want is to see the asbestos companies do more of their processing and manufacturing here in Quebec, but wages are generally good today and working conditions have improved tremendously over the years. The basic wage here is around $250 a week and more with overtime, and at the workers' credit union we have about $15 million in assets. A lot of our guys take Florida vacations in the winter. We don't need any nationalization program here.

Jim Bullock
Factory worker, Rock Island
(E)

**"I'd drive myself insane if I took a
pessimistic view of it."**

Rock Island and Stanstead are two small adjoining communities 133 km.

southeast of Montreal on the Vermont border. The international border runs through the middle of Rock Island—in fact, right through the operahouse and library built in 1902. With a population divided between French and English, people here are as highly politicized on the language issue as they are in Montreal and other communities with substantial English and French populations.

Jim Bullock in one important respect is the exception in the Eastern Townships—a unilingual anglophone, he has chosen to send his children to a French school.

The cutting-tool plant I work in here is kind of unique. The building sits on both sides of the river, so you can walk from Canada to the U.S. without leaving the plant. Who owns it? The Americans. Anyways, like I was saying, you can walk across the river inside the building and go from Canada to the U.S. but you shouldn't leave the building. Once you leave the building, by law, you're supposed to report in at the customs—you know, give 'em your answers as to where you're going, how long you're going to be there, and what you're going to do.

Some of the Canadian workers work on the U.S. side in the U.S. division of the company, but they have to obtain a work visa to work over there. Now, if I was going across, just to visit somebody in the plant and come back without doing any work, there's no problem. But to go across and work I have to obtain a work visa.

The town itself is divided the same way. Some of these older houses were built before they found out that the border was actually running through them. I suppose they didn't bother to move the building because of the expense and that's how it come to be. But nowadays you cannot build a building straddling the border.

There's a big house on the corner that's in that situation. Half of the residence is in Canada and half in the state of Vermont. The border runs right through the middle of the house. Now, if the owner buys furniture for the American side of the house, he has to buy it in the States and maintain it in the States side of the house. If he buys furniture or appliances for the Canadian side, he has to buy them in Canada. This way, he doesn't get any problems with crossing merchandise from one side to the other border, and therefore his customs duties are nullified. But he has to pay property tax on both sides.

My own family? The Bullocks were from England originally, but I think they came into this area as United Empire Loyalists. They settled mainly west of the lake here, and, oh the story goes, my great-great-grandfather in the wintertime decided to move into this immediate area, on the west side of the lake, and he came across the ice in winter by double team and sled. He hauled all their belongings over the ice one night, you see, and he came to a place near one island and the team stopped dead in their tracks. Wouldn't budge. It was after dark then, and he had to get off with a lantern and see what was holding him up. Well, it was actually open water in front of them. So he had to turn around and go around the island, which detained him for another mile or so, but they went around the island and eventually landed on this side of the mainland and then set up housekeeping.

I consider myself a Québécois. Yes, I do, in the sense that we live in Quebec. I've lived my entire life here in this area in Quebec. I'm only 33 years old, but my point of view is that I am a Québécois and I'll remain that till such time that I'm either dead or forced out of here. Which I doubt we'll ever see. Not in this area.

But to be honest, my reaction on the night of the PQ election was panic. Since then, though, I've thought it through and I thought to myself that René Lévesque is a damn smart man; he's one smart man. I didn't vote for him but I've got to hand it to him—he's damn smart. Now if he can just hold his head tight to his shoulders, sort of not become beheaded, as we say, and he can hold his followers down . . . He was smart enough to get that many votes, so I think he's smart enough to hold the lid on things here until things cool off. Now that's my opinion.

I speak some French. My wife is French Canadian. I have one daughter in school. My oldest daughter is seven years old; she's in her second year. We're sending her to a French school here in Rock Island. Since the children are all brought up Catholic and I do want to give them a good chance, whether we live in Quebec or not, they should have two languages. Therefore they're learning their French. Although the children are perfectly bilingual, they'll get their schooling in French, as far as I can manage it.

I think there are a great many, especially of the younger generation, here, with children just pre-school age and beginning school that are thinking along the same lines. I have many friends my own age that are starting to send their children to French school. The Protestant schools today are not run as the Protestants schools were when I was in school. When I was going to school we had the leather strap and the hardwood ruler and you can laugh if you want to but, by God, it worked! It worked. Now today if Johnny wants to get up and run around, Johnny's just left on his own—he can get up and run around. In grade two, three, four, five, up to seven, pre-high school, this does not work. Even in high school it does not work.

Elementary or high school, I loathe the permissive system that the English schools have now. This is one reason why I've sent my children to the French school, which, to this day—and I hope it continues—is maintaining the hardwood-ruler ethics in school. The second reason is the second language. I do wish 'em to have their second language and the easiest way to accomplish that is to educate them in French.

French is the second language here in Quebec for us English-speaking people. Now it's the official language, but this does not mean that you're going to lose your English entirely. As I see it, they can always attend either a high school or a finishing school or a university or college after their high school is done. Of course, if Quebec became a separate country, I don't know . . . I hate to think of it.

Right now, I'm thinking personally that it'll never go through, and even a few of the French Canadians that I've talked with are hoping that as well. Mind you, in some of the French schools the kids have it preached into them—propaganda—that separation is the only way to go, separation. I know that for a fact. I know one fellow that's in a university, and it's preached to him at the university level. Now I won't say all the professors do it, but some of them do it. But if it goes independent, I don't know what I would do. My decision then would be based on how much pressure they would apply to me personally.

Right now the English and the French people here get along just fine. Oh, you may find one or two in this whole area here who would be willing to give problems to some chap just because he's English, but I think it's a very minor sort of thing. Now, further north, toward Quebec City, where it gets more intense, you're going to find it a little bit different, but in this area we have no problem whatsoever. At least, myself personally. Now we have, mind you, a few bad eggs on both sides of the fence here. It's not just a question of one side. But I'd drive myself insane if I took the pessimistic view of it. Right at this present time I'm remaining optimistic, but I hate to think what would happen supposing the referendum did go through.

Anonymous Interview
Rock Island
(F)

**"Now I'd rather remain anonymous
because I'm afraid of getting into the
same sort of mess all over again."**

If you're interested in politics here, I'll tell you what happened to me
during the war. It's not a pleasant story but maybe it's worth telling. My
wife and I lived here in a beautiful apartment—right in the centre of
town—that cost $12 a month. I had a good little home-delivery business
going. I wasn't interested in working for the customs or at the plant—I
was content right where I was. Okay?

Then in 1943 in the middle of the war we had a federal by-election in
the riding here because the member, Mr. Davidson, had died.
Conscription was the big issue then. I entered the campaign, made
speeches, and worked as an organizer for the Bloc Populaire Canadien.
We were against conscription and against the war for Quebeckers. We
didn't want to feed the sharks in the mid-Atlantic. As far as we were
concerned, the war didn't concern us at all—to be dominated by
England or Germany was all the same to us, and Stanstead County was
completely against Canada taking part in foreign wars, no matter who
was involved. Our candidate was Mr. Armand Choquette, a very
well-known farmer, and we worked quietly but hard for him. We had
meetings everywhere—in people's kitchens, in some of the churches; we
went from door to door just talking to people, making sure they knew
what was going on. Then voting day rolled around.

I was working as a scrutineer for the Bloc Populaire and one thing I had
to do was keep tabs on the voting list. It was a long one, and I noticed
there were some names added by hand, including a Liberal senator in
Ottawa, who is dead now, and his son and servants. When he came to
vote I asked him to swear that he had been living in the riding for at least a
year. He hadn't. He refused to do it—said he had already been sworn in
by the King of England and he didn't have to do it again. Well, as it
turned out we won the election with our candidate Choquette, and he got
a majority of 1,700 votes, as I remember. The Bloc Populaire victory was
quite a surprise to a lot of people here, I can tell you! It's funny looking
back—if Lévesque's referendum on independence had been held back
then, why, it would have passed here with no trouble at all.

Then, the very next day after the vote, I received a registered letter
from Ottawa telling me to report to St.-Jacques Street in Montreal to take

the medical for entry into the army. So I went there, passed the physical, the heart check-up, all of it until the final test where they discovered I had flat feet. It's something I've had since birth. Anyway, it means I was turned down by the army. So I returned here. And what do you think happens next? A lot of the customers on my route—maybe 80 percent— were English, and the next morning after I get back from Montreal, I hear: "No delivery today. Don't bother coming back. We don't like your politics." et cetera, et cetera.

I was forced to give up my delivery business, sell it for the value of the truck. A used truck at that. I couldn't find work here. I moved to Montreal—a city I don't like—and took a job on the railway with Canadian Pacific. Fifteen years I stayed with them, until the diesels came in and we were laid off for good. Then I returned here and went into a small business. But remember why I lost my livelihood in the first place —over politics! The English in this part of the province, even today, when it comes to questions of language rights they always gang up against us. An experience like I went through marks a man for life; you can understand that, can't you? I was forced to leave my home—and I was content here—to live 15 years in a city I hated, almost like an expatriate. Now I'd rather remain anonymous because I'm afraid of getting into the same sort of mess all over again. Do you blame me?

Today, Trudeau isn't much better than Mackenzie King, if you ask me, with his current talk of putting Quebec "in its place." Quebec should have a special place in Confederation—we must regain our legitimate rights on land, on the sea, and in the air. If Ottawa doesn't want to give us—I should say return to us—what is rightfully ours, then we will have to think about other ways of getting our rights. The Englishman has the right to love England and his Queen, but I am a French Canadian and I also want the right to my own unique country— with the rest of Canada or without it, if it has to be that way. A lot of changes are needed in this country. A lot. And no matter what happens in the years ahead of us, I know that Lévesque, Parizeau and the rest of the PQ team are 100 percent for Quebec . . . 100 percent!

Don Prangley

Customs officer, Stanstead

(E)

"We have more right to the Eastern Townships than the French do."

This interview is the result of an illegal border crossing. The Canadian-U.S. border at Rock Island is not just the undefended border; it is also the unobtrusive border. I didn't realize I had entered the U.S.A. until the first American flag appeared, and after I turned the camper around, it wasn't clear that I was back in Canada until a siren was sounded by Canada Customs officer Don Prangley at the border post I had inadvertently passed. After asking some questions of his own, Mr. Prangley a life-long resident of the Eastern Townships, agreed to this interview.

I lived here all my life, which amounts to 50 years. Prangley is an English name. If you hit any Prangley, you know we're relatives, we're that scarce. My parents came from England and I sometimes consider myself English. I shouldn't but I can't help it. My wife is the librarian in the only international library and operahouse, I believe, in the world. The border goes almost down the middle. The audience in the operahouse is in the States and the stage is in Canada. During World War II, Ottawa and Washington both agreed that they'd pretend that the damn place didn't exist because the question of amusement tax came up: who was going to get the amusement tax when the performance was Canada and the money was collected in the States? They couldn't decide who got it, so they pretended to forget about it.

To enter either the library or operahouse, one has to come in through the United States. The reading room is half in Canada, but the stockroom, where all the books are, is all in Canada. So an American person who wants to borrow the book has to come to Canada, and a Canadian wishing to use the library has to enter by the States. No one has to report though. It'd be too hard to control. So the Canadian and the American Customs and Immigration pretty well ignore it.

I sat in on a unique hearing last summer. Three Canadians, who had been apprehended by the Americans on drug charges, were brought here from Minneapolis to be testified against by a Canadian, who was being held in Kingston Penitentiary. I happened to be the only person around who was empowered to swear in the Canadian witness. He sat on the

Canadian side of the operahouse, literally within four feet of the three accused, who would have dearly loved to have seen him dead—which was very obvious by the looks on their faces. And they had an American sheriff, the state police, three lawyers, a district attorney, and assistant district attorney, who were all flown out. How they discovered this place, I don't know, but it was the only way they could get a deposition from the Canadian to take to the U.S. to use in their case.

There is a lot of contact back and forth here between us and the Americans. We have the Border Curling Club with membership from both countries. And we've got the only international Masonic Lodge. This year we celebrate our 175th anniversary here as Masons. We have French Americans who speak damn little French, English Canadians who speak very little French, and a great many French who are fluently bilingual. They've intermarried with each other and families have split up. Some have moved to the States and pretty well lost French, but they still come up and visit relatives whose language is French.

The French here have brought a damn lot of their troubles on themselves. When I was a kid here, I think the highest any French kid could go in school was about grade six. They weren't encouraged to go any further, you know. A lot of them weren't even encouraged to go beyond grade four.

Our school system is still mixed up. You have, naturally, your French Catholic system and we have our own Protestant public system. The nearest Protestant high school is 32 miles away. My daughter is bussed there but I don't like the idea. We also have Stanstead College, which is a private English boy's school. Down in Newport, Vermont, there's a convent that caters to American Roman Catholics, and also their Protestant system. So closely knit is the border that a fair number of Canadians send their children to school in Vermont rather than bus them the 32 miles to attend a Canadian school.

The balance between the number of French and English in this community is just about 50-50. If anything, French might have a slight edge. In the main, they stay pretty well amongst themselves and we stay amongst ourselves. I'm supposed to be bilingual for the sake of my job, but I'm not. I don't think a person is bilingual unless he can think in both languages, and the number of people around here who can do that can probably be counted on one hand, and as far as I know they're all French. They're all fairly well educated too, brought up more or less in an English milieu.

I was quite surprised when the PQ got in and I suppose I felt disappointment and probably anger. I was as glad as anyone to see Bourassa and that damn bunch kicked out. But I really believe that Lévesque and his lieutenants are going to destroy this province in four years. They're well on their way already. They don't realize what the hell they're doing to themselves. They're cutting their own throats and don't realize it, with their policy of revenge and not worrying about the cost. Camille Laurin said that he was prepared to sacrifice the jobs of 23,000 French Canadians in order to attain this language goal. My biggest reaction to all this is that the PQ is destroying what could have been one of the nicest provinces in the country to live in. But as so often happens, if you are out for revenge, you're filled with hate, you're blinded. You know the old saying: "He whom the gods wish to destroy they first make mad." I think they, the French people, were driven mad by their own politicians.

The Church has to take a great share of the blame for it, and this is not supposition on my part because I grew up with a lot of French kids here and they told me that the Church had preached the song of hate about the English. They are beginning to show sparks of intelligence now. I think the initial objective was to stamp out the English language and if they could drive all the English out of the province, all the better. They never stopped to consider that, if the English left—this may sound conceited— they're going to lose a hell of lot of technical know-all, intelligence, cash, connections. If they want to get ahead they'd better learn English—and there's a lot of French that realize that. Unfortunately, the politician doesn't.

Young people aren't worried, but the older ones are. The younger ones are taking the attitude of "What the hell, I'll get out and I'll go to the States." They are mobile. For instance, I said goodbye to a young French Canadian yesterday. Fluently bilingual, it's true, but he said, "The hell with this place, I'm going to Alberta where it's a little more settled, a little calmer." And you can't blame him. Things are not exactly good here.

For one thing, property values are definitely dropping. My own property, which at one time I could have gotten three times or more what I paid for it, I think since November, 1976, the value has dropped right back to what I paid for it. And people who are putting their houses for sale just aren't getting any nibbles at all. There's a house across the street here for sale that's worth about $50,000. I don't think you can build it for that today. As far as I know, he's only had one nibble at that. There's an even bigger house, and a better house, very similar to my own, much better condition and much newer—my house was built in 1846, but this other one was built, I guess, at the turn of the century—and if you could put it on wheels plus the lot and take to Toronto, you could sell it for $100,000 easily. They're asking $39,000 and they're not getting any takers at all. And that's a lot 100 feet wide and 200 feet deep, a two-story house with a two-car garage, probably 10–12 rooms in it, extremely well built, right next to a school.

The best solution to the problem in Quebec would be if someone, either in the federal Liberal Party of the federal Conservative Party, had the guts to stand up and say that this is going to remain one country. If provinces want a little more autonomy, fine; but decentralizing can be carried too far. It could destroy the country just as quickly as outright separation. I think we've got to have a strong central government—that's one area where I agree with Trudeau. A country this vast has got to have a central control.

I don't know what I'd do if the referendum vote was in favour of separation. I'll cross that bridge when I come to it. But I'm strongly in favour of taking the south shore of the St. Lawrence, or at least the Eastern Townships downstream of New Brunswick, and telling the Péquistes that no matter how that referendum goes, that area is going to stay as a bond between the East and the West. If we did that, I'm sure that it would make the Péquistes back off some and also reassure the English to a great extent.

But this policy of sitting back and waiting—well, hell, you're not old enough to remember 1937 or '38—I was just a kid myself—but I still remember the talk then: "Well, let's wait and see what Hitler does next; let's wait; let's wait." And what happened then? That can happen all over again. You can't wait! I damn well consider myself a Québécois too! I've as much right to be here as anyone. We settled this area—we opened it up, if you want to know. We have more right to the Eastern Townships than the French do. This was predominantly English until the turn of the century. So I'm just as much a Quebecker as any of the French Canadians.

What keeps me here? First and foremost, love of the countryside. In spite of anything that someone from B.C. or Alberta might say, I think this is the prettiest part of North America right here—the Eastern Townships, the southern part of the Eastern Townships. To me the West Coast is nothing but snow-capped mountains and trees and nothing else. Nowhere else can you get the vistas you have here. I can go to the widow's lookout on the top of my old house and I see at least three lakes, probably four. I can see what we call mountains—the Westerner would say they're just hills—but to us they're mountains. I can see open fields. I can see the United States and I can see Canada. I have snow in winter, hot summers. You name it, we've got it—there's just no other place in North America like the Eastern Townships.

Henri Doyon
Retired, Stanstead
(F)

**"Let me tell you how I became a
Péquiste after retiring."**

*Henri Doyon, the proud descendant of a 325-year-old French Canadian
family, was a federalist until his mid-60s. His retirement in 1969 coincided
with the passage of Canada's Official Languages Act, and he felt that people
outside Quebec would be more receptive to the French language. In this flush
of optimism he set out on a cross-country tour by car with his wife.*

My ancestors came from France to Canada around 1652 or 1653. There
were three brothers who came here. One was a farmer, the second a
merchant in Quebec City, and the third was a soldier. I have always been
interested in history, so I commissioned a study of my family tree back to
the twelfth generation. Some branches moved up the Chaudière River,
others went to Île d'Orléans, some went up to Lévis, and still later others
came to the Eastern Townships here. Some were craftsmen,
blacksmiths, carpenters, sailors, and many—right down to my father—
were farmers.

In the spring of 1920 my father decided to sell his farm in this area and
emigrate to the United States because economic conditions were better
there and he had a large family—10 children. So he immigrated to
Vermont, just a few miles away. He had a big farm and all the family
worked there. The economic situation in Quebec wasn't good. As for me,
I got married in the United States to a Canadian girl and I stayed there on
a farm that I worked with my brother until the 1930s. It was a big farm,
about 300 acres. We had livestock and a lumber business on the side,
supplying telephone poles.

During the depression I returned to Canada when it became
impossible to live in the United States. Things weren't that much better
here, but they were still better in Canada, so we moved back here to
Stanstead. The depression caught up with us a little later, about two
years in fact. We had only one son when we moved here in 1930, but after
that we had more children for a total of four boys and a girl.

A lot of French Canadians went to the United States but now a lot seem
to be coming back. Today the economic situation in the United States

isn't all that good and, in Canada, social programs are much better, especially hospital insurance. You don't have to pay for the doctor here but, of course, in the United States you do. And the French who have stayed in the U.S., I've found have just been absorbed into the American melting pot. I have three sisters in Hartford, Connecticut. And now just a quarter of the family can even speak French. Of course, to please me the grandchildren try to speak it but they don't speak French very well. American French—it is really neither French nor English.

I am very proud to be a Québécois, you know. To me that means living here and surviving. We have lived, we have evolved. We are nearly five million people and we are conscious of ourselves as a people. Of course there is a lot left to accomplish. We want to preserve our Quebec identity. And we have had our political differences with the English, even quite recently. During the last war the French were against conscription in this part of Quebec. People didn't want to go and get themselves killed in an English affair. Why should they? In this area we even elected a candidate for the Bloc Populaire which was the group opposing conscription. I worked for the candidate and it was very interesting. Just a quiet word-of-mouth campaign with no public advertising, no posters — just word of mouth. And then, on election day, we won! Some people were very surprised, let me tell you, but the movement didn't last long at all after the war. It was just a flame, a passing thing.

Oh, I was very happy with the PQ victory. But, you know, after the election here, some people withdrew their savings and transferred them across the line to American banks. Now that's pretty ridiculous, isn't it? Of course I voted PQ. Let me tell you how I became a Péquiste after retiring.

Back in 1969, like most Canadians, I thought that eventually we would become a united country and there would be harmony from one coast to the other. The Royal Commission on Bilingualism and Biculturalism had submitted its report and the Official Languages Act had been passed and I personally was full of optimism for Canada—I was a committed federalist.

I wanted to make a trip West with my wife after retiring, and we set out by car to drive all the way to Victoria, B.C. We wanted to meet a lot of people and we did—from Ontario, to Manitoba, to Saskatchewan, to Alberta, and finally British Columbia. But after this trip I was obliged to completely change my attitude toward Canada. Bilingualism and biculturalism just didn't work. The moment we left Quebec I realized that nobody spoke French.

I speak English better than some people around here, but I discovered on that trip that in Ontario, Manitoba, Saskatchewan, Alberta, and British Columbia, if you want to speak French, people actually get angry at you. Really quickly! In Calgary I went to get gasoline at a garage—by this time I was speaking English to people from the start—well, the guy there saw that I had a Quebec licence plate. He says, "How come there is no language barrier between us?" I said, "Well, if I was like you, there would be." Just like that. I said it just like that. I learned that the people out there don't really want to hear the French language spoken. When they hear it, they get angry. That trip showed me that. Pierre Trudeau will never persuade me that bilingualism is going to work.

Look, I was a Canadian and a believer in federalism until I retired and took that trip out West. I am 73 years old now and I think the only solution for us is independence, with an economic association along the lines of the European Common Market. Now, it is not going to happen all of a sudden. But at least for my grandchildren, I want to see a Quebec that's master of its own destiny. Master in its own house. Not dictated to by Ottawa or Ontario. As things stand now, to be accepted by the rest of this country, we have to think like the others. We have to speak English. We have to go along with the other provinces. Well, that's just impossible. They can't make us do that. They can't impose what they think on five million people.

We are in a good position here in Quebec, between Ontario and the Maritimes. We have got a lot of mines and natural resources. We have our own hydro-electric power. We have everything we need here. And yet the English want us to be assimilated, to be absorbed into the melting pot, like in the United States. In the U.S., a Russian or a German is 100 percent American. But we don't want that here. That's the difference. If the English think they are going to assimilate us, well, they've got their work cut out for them.

Another recent example for me was the air traffic controllers' situation in Quebec. Now, in Europe, many languages are used in aviation. English is the international language and in addition, the home language of each country is used. But, in Quebec, the air traffic controllers and the pilots can't use our French language. Why can't they? Why?

Someday I am going to write my autobiography. I have only got as far as the title so far. Do you want to hear it? "A Loyalist Until the Eleventh Hour." That trip out West was the twelfth hour.

Brian Blain
Musician, Waterloo
(E)

"A lot of English people in the entertainment field voted for the PQ."

The PQ does not rely entirely upon French Quebeckers for its support. A small minority of anglophones have also voted PQ for various reasons. In Brian Blain's case the PQ vote was not so much a party vote as a vote for an alternative approach to politics. A 30-year-old singer and guitarist who performs primarily in English for mixed, often predominantly French audiences, he provides some first-hand insights into the possibilities and limitations confronting an artist working in a language that is largely foreign to his audience.

I was born here in Sherbrooke and I lived here until 1967 and then spent eight years in Ontario. For the last two years I've been back here. I went to a private French elementary school. We spoke English mostly in the household but, because my mother was French and my father English, I guess they decided to split it up and have me get an elementary education in French and a secondary and university education in English. So I went to this French elementary school and made a switch at grade seven or eight into an English Catholic boy's school run by the fathers. Mass every morning, eight o'clock. A different kind of regimentation than I had in the one-room school. After high school I went to Bishop's University in Lennoxville, but didn't make it really — dropped out after a year. And after doing various jobs I took up playing full time for a living. I play with a group — no heavy electric stuff; more lyrical.

My music is very English-oriented: not just the lyrics but the concepts don't fit in with the kind of music that's happening in French Quebec. Blues has seemed to work very well here; even traditional blues goes very, very well. There's a connection between French Quebec and the Cajun French in Louisiana. A very definite style in music in Louisiana that the French Cajun people are into. It's very blues-oriented, and there's been a sort of influx of that lately in the French Quebec music scene. But it's very difficult for an English song writer to get his feelings across to a French audience.

One thing that does seem to go over fine in English in Quebec is if you can play the top forty type songs. In fact, if you can play them just like the records, then you can sing in English and they'll love it. There's no problem there at all if it's something they hear on the radio. French radio stations, especially the FM stations, play English records. But you've got to keep the music very beat-oriented or just concentrate on the instrumental part of it, because the lyrics are not going to get through, even if you do like Bruce Cockburn and print translations of the lyrics on the back of your albums. It still doesn't get across on stage.

Maybe the time will come when French musicians will be as well known in English Canada as English Canadian musicians are in Quebec. There's a lot of first-rate singers and groups here and there's a certain momentum building now. It will be interesting to see how far it goes but I don't know, there's a real basic block. Language is a very important thing, you know and if you don't understand the words, there's a good percentage of what's happening that you're missing.

I voted for the PQ. No, I wasn't relating it to independence a whole lot then; it was just a reaction against the government that we'd been having. A lot of English people in the entertainment field voted for the PQ. I guess I was making a kind of statement for individualism. I am opposed to nationalism, any kind of nationalism. I guess probably the out-front reason for that is that my generation hasn't gone overseas and fought in the war or anything like that. Most of the people in the PQ government are individualistic people.

I shouldn't use that word "individualist" so freely, but I can't think of another label to use. My vote was for René Lévesque the individual, and a lot of others that had come out of a different background. Most of the PQ were just people who had made it to the top of their respective professions using their heads. They all seemed like people that had their heads screwed on right, you know? I got the feeling some of the PQ members are real freshmen — you know, brand new to politics.

But when it comes to the question of independence, I don't know. I wonder if it could come to the point where I would vote "Yes" to separation in a referendum? I can't say right now that I would absolutely *not* vote against it. It will depend on the arguments that are presented. I've travelled all across Canada and there's a real bond of affection, you know? Jees, I don't know...

On the other hand, there's a certain adventure to being part of a new country. I'm sure a lot of the black African states are very exciting. This is something that hasn't happened in North America since I guess the United States did it. But I'm not too politically oriented and I wonder if I would really take part. I can remember when I was 16 or 17, hanging out with a kind of beatnik crowd here in Sherbrooke, listening to John Coltrane records in a basement with sunglasses... and no lights either! I also remember going to a little café in Montreal and hearing guys plotting to put a bomb on the hull of some British vessel that was in port—real heavy separatist kind of people. I was always very careful to speak French in those kinds of situations.

I have a slight English accent now but then I didn't. I'm sure I'll get rid of it though. I'm really concentrating on it. I talk French more often now than I talk English. But the word "Québécois" doesn't seem to lift my heart or anything like that. To me, it's more a label geographically.

It seems like it's been some kind of class struggle going on. The French Quebeckers felt that they were oppressed by people that spoke English. Now they're finding out that they're being oppressed by people that are bilingual because you have to be bilingual to really steal from the French. When I was in high school there was street fights. It was French against English—the English guys going to beat up a Frenchie and the French getting even. There was always that division. Wow! But that finished about the time I got out of high school. As soon as the balance got more in favour of the French, I guess, the English decided to cool it. But I always picture the English as being the aggressors.

Marcel Bureau

Director-General,
St.-Jean Baptiste Society, Sherbrooke
(F)

"You never know your wife until you have gone to bed with her. well, that's true in politics too."

In the English Canadian imagination, perhaps no other voluntary organization in Quebec is more closely associated with the nationalist movement than the St.-Jean Baptiste Society. For many the very name, which is never printed in translation by the English-language press, carries an almost sinister connotation, encouraged no doubt by the wide press coverage accorded the annual June 24 celebrations, which have occasionally turned violent. However, as Marcel Bureau explains, this conception of the St. John the Baptist Society is inaccurate and ignores the ideological split within the organization that developed in the late 1960s. (See also the interview with Bruno Roy of La Société Nationale des Québécois on page 184.)

In 1908 the Cardinal of Quebec City asked His Holiness Pope Paul X to name St.-Jean Baptiste as the patron saint of French Canadians wherever they are in the world—not only in Quebec but French Canadians all over. The Pope granted this favour. The St.-Jean Baptiste Society had been founded previously, but since then we have been organizing celebrations on St.-Jean Baptiste Day, June 24. It is something that we are proud of! We organize great celebrations and we want people to participate as much as possible. This year the PQ government decreed St.-Jean Baptiste day the National Day of Quebec, but we still feel it is the day of French Canadians everywhere. We won't argue over terms but I think the same people are trying to remove the religious nature of June 24, which I really deplore.

The St.-Jean Baptiste Societies have always worked for the advancement of French Canadians. Some years ago—maybe 15 years ago—we began being infiltrated by political groups, the RIN (Rassemblement pour l'Indépendance Nationale) and all kinds of movements which gave birth to the Parti Québécois about 10 years ago. Many of our societies were taken over by these groups, but the Sherbrooke Society never accepted that situation. We don't belong to any political group, however good it may be. We want to represent all French Canadian people, no matter what their political beliefs are.

Now personally, I am a federalist and proud of it. My ancestors came from France in the 1600s. I am a Sherbrookecois, a Quebecker, and a Canadian. I am also an American since I live in North America, if you want to start putting adjectives to it. I am also very happy for the Parti Québécois. They wanted to be in power and they are. You know the saying, "You never know your wife until you have gone to bed with her." Well, that's true in politics too. Here Mr. Lévesque has been knocking on our doors for a long time saying that he could solve all our ills. Now he is in Quebec City; we will see what he can do. I am very happy that he is there. People will finally know what it is like to have that government. If they give us the good government they promised, so much the better. But people did not vote for independence. I don't believe that more than 30 percent of the population are in favour of separation.

It should not be forgotten that the Parti Québécois is there to serve the interests of the province, not just its own party members. There are some very nationalist, even racist, people in the PQ, but I think a sort of equilibrium will be reached.

Chapter 3

Quebec City
-Trois Rivières

It was late June when I drove from the Eastern Townships north to Trois-Rivières, (population 52,500; 96 percent French). Midway between Montreal and Quebec City, Trois-Rivières is Canada's second oldest city but one that too few tourists visit. Some of North America's most illustrious explorers came from here: brave, restless men like Radisson, des Groseillers, and La Vérendrye, men who explored and gave names to a continent and called Trois-Rivières home.

Today, the visitor is first apt to notice the sweet sulphurous smell of twentieth-century success — the pulp and paper industry. The senses tell you that this indeed is the world's largest pulp- and paper-producing centre. One-third of the area's work force is employed in this industry and many of them helped elect a PQ member in what had until 1976 been a non-PQ city. This blue-collar centre, where well-paid shift workers picnic beside their expensive cars along sandy beaches, was selected for this book since it reflects the recent shift of a sizeable portion of Quebec's working class to the Parti Québécois.

One hundred and thirty-three km.east is the city that gave its name first to a colony, then a province, and soon — some hope — to a country. Quebec City, founded by Champlain in 1608, is the site of the continent's first college (1635) and seminary (1663), and takes its name from the Indian word Kebec, meaning "where the waters narrow."

To walk the narrow streets of Quebec is to lose the feeling of rootlessness common to many North American cities. Here at last is a place with a past that can be seen in its architecture, heard in its music, sampled in its cuisine, and *enjoyed with its people, direct descendants of North America's first settlers. If Samuel Johnson could say of the infinitely varied but often grey and reserved English capital, "When a man is tired of London he is tired of life," then it should be said of Quebec's capital: "When a man is tired of Quebec he is tired of people." Despite repeated annual onslaughts of tourists, residents of the capital remain open and friendly, exhibiting none of the mercenary surliness of their distant Parisian cousins. Quebeckers have somehow learned to open their hearts without selling their souls, which is a beautiful thing in any language. However, the fact that these people are genuinely friendly to visitors should not lead anyone to conclude that this is federalist territory. On November 15 the PQ swept five of Quebec City's six seats.*

The drive 33 km. northwest of Quebec City took me from New France to Old Ireland. Being of recent Irish descent, and therefore one who appreciates good conversation and refreshment, I set out in search of the descendants of St. Patrick in the New World. It wasn't necessary to look far. The small community of Shannon was settled by Irish immigrants forced from their homes by the potato famine of the 1840s, and their descendants still farm the land here. After leaving Shannon I drove 33 km. south of Quebec City. Outward appearances change very little but with the short journey I was back in several of the oldest-settled parishes of Quebec, dating from the mid- to late 1600s.

Alphonse Piché
Poet, Trois-Rivières
(F)

"I feel that everyone is a poet."

The works of the poet living in a modest trailer in Trois-Rivières are included in anthologies published in the United States, England, Australia, the Soviet Union, and Japan. In 1976 recognition came from his own country when he was awarded the Governor-General's prize for his collection, Poèmes *(1946-1968). At 60 years of age, Alphonse Piché fills his days with poetry, church singing, sailing on the St. Lawrence, and conversations over brandy with his visitors.*

L'infini de la neige ô pays éternel
De l'infini des champs à l'infini du ciel
Tu élargis mon âme au creux de son mystère
Et fais battre mon sang au rythme de la terre.

From "La neige," Alphonse Piché, 1977

My maternal grandmother came from Ireland. My paternal grandfather was a sort of industrialist, a nomad type, who built sawmills and construction companies around the province. He even went as far as Gaspé, which at that time was something. He moved from city to city 12 times. At that time he used to say to Granny, "Sell everything, we're leaving. We're going to start a lumber company in Matapédia." And they would sell everything including the silverware. On top of that, he had 17 children. They were extraordinary men and women in those days! When he died, Grandfather left over a million dollars. Then his boys, who had been brought up in the style of princes, squandered all that. But that's all right.

I was born in Chicoutimi in 1917, but the following year we moved here to Trois-Rivières. Trois-Rivières is the hub of the province. We are next to the St. Lawrence. I love the water. It is my life, my passion. Water and women. I've always had boats. My last boat was a 40-foot, two-masted schooner from Lunenberg, Nova Scotia. A real Bluenose. I recently sold it and bought a smaller 20-foot aluminum motor-sailor.

Trois-Rivières is a sort of small village with a village spirit. In the past there was very sharp differences separating the classes. There was the upper class, or class of property, the bourgeoisie, and the workers. As far as I can remember, at the beginning we called our boss the "Bourgeois." We would say, "The Bourgeois is coming," "The Bourgeois is here." That's what we called him. This social-class difference is still quite marked even though poverty has practically been eliminated. The poor labouring class that I spoke about in my ballads has practically disappeared and the artists and writers of this region have helped bring the social classes together.

Things today are not as they were in the '30s. I remember helping my father when he was director of social services in those days. The lawyers and notaries, whom one called the shamed poor, came to get their welfare assistance by the back door because they did not want to show up in the regular line-up of poor people. It was I who handed it to them. That was a frightful period.

Today you can see the improvement just by looking at the neighbourhoods in Trois-Rivières. It is one of the most spread-out towns in Canada, about 20 miles long. The residential areas in this town today have houses worth between $30,000 and $50,000 and they are owned by working people, my friend. We have a lot of workers at Wabasso cotton, and the three pulp and paper companies—all English money, by the way. No French capital.

We French are not the sort of people who will start up a business or invest our savings in factories. If we make a little money we put that in the Caisses Populaires. We are economical. Why? Because we have been uprooted so much. We've eaten a lot of shit. This is the big difference between us and the English. The *Anglais* is an entrepreneur. He will risk his capital and savings in factories, business, and the stock market. That isn't our mentality.

But we are enterprising in terms of adventure. When the first French came here and got to know the Indian women, they took off into the forest with them and didn't return, because these were real women. It was very sad for their wives who lost them. That was the way it was for our guys like La Vérendrye, Pierre Radisson, D'Iberville. These guys were giants, incredible adventurers, to leave by canoe and reach the Rockies and descend to the Mississippi. *C'est formidable!* We were the original owners of the land here in Quebec. That's understood. We succeeded in not being assimilated by the English—not because we detested the English, but we were a more agrarian people. We lived in the country, and though we went to town from time to time, we kept our language and our customs.

Then when the villages began to grow into towns the Québécois migrated to them because this isn't really an agricultural province. It is more suited to mining. They began to leave the countryside for the cities and factories, they didn't become anglicized, but began to speak a bastardized form of the language which became Joual. That's Quebec. But all the same we remained attached to our land because basically we are Latins and French. We want to keep what we have.

In the cultural domain, the Latins have a lot of imagination, sentiment, and passion. That's what makes us creative and the type to have a certain passion and a certain *je ne sais pas quoi*. We are lovers of women, lovers of beautiful things, of flowers. The English would make large parks with beautiful flowers. That is not the French way. We stop by one flower, maybe a daisy, and admire it as you would a woman. And all of that develops the imagination. And after all creation is just a question of imagination.

As a poet, I feel something of what everyone feels, and have the possibility of translating, transcribing, and expressing this. I feel that everyone is a poet. Everyone has some poetry inside them because without that we would not live. We would be like machines. It is surely because of this personal poetry that we can live and survive. And people read and understand my poetry because of this basic poetry that everyone has inside themselves.

Now, people seem to be looking for happiness through material possessions. The material things of life are necessary but boring. Consider the person who gets a lavish house, modern furniture, a chalet, two cars, a boat, and a summer cottage. He won't be any happier. The poor guy has to earn all that by the sweat of his brow. He must direct all his energy to earning the money that he needs to cover his expenses. It's a sort of indentured labour. The more that he possesses, the more he is possessed by it and the more he wants to possess.

French Canadians haven't been badly used by the English. They have been exploited by their own bourgeoisie. In other words, the professional class — the lawyers, the doctors, the notaries, and the priests — has lived the good life, always at the expense of the working class. The employers took trips, bought houses, and lived in luxury and style. That always made me sick! My father had a good business, but he remained human. Everything he did was for his children.

As a Québécois, I found the November 15 election necessary. We had come to the point where it was absolutely necessary that we establish our rights to Quebec and that we demonstrate our resolve to live in French here. I should say not in French, but in Québécois, because I don't have any great attachment to France. Most French Canadians don't care about France. France abandoned us here. If they are interested now, it is because of the mines and natural resources, because apart from that they wouldn't be interested.

I very much doubt that things are going to go any further. I don't think we are going to break up Canada. At the present time we are passing legislation, here in Quebec, that will really make us master of our own house. Immigration is still left to be settled and certain details like that. I'm not talking about money — it is ridiculous and secondary. But with control over immigration, a full system of education without federal interference, and taxing powers to a certain point we would need little else. That would be a sort of federation instead of Confederation.

Lawrence Turcotte

*Factory worker and part-time
garage attendant, Trois-Rivières*

(E)

**"I wouldn't change places with
anywhere else in the world."**

*Lawrence Turcotte is a federalist who was surprised at the PQ victory and
unable to comprehend his son's election decision.*

I work in the wire company—I'm what you call a wireman. We make
articles for paper mills all over Canada and even in Europe; we sell wire
too. I also work in the garage as a little sideline. It's a towing operation.
When I'm finished at the plant, I come here to work some nights.
Sometimes the weekend, like today, I help out. It gives me a little bit of
spending money. You notice the sign? It says 25 HOURS A DAY, and that
means we work a lot. Instead of going 24 hours a day, we're going 25
hours.

My father's French, my mother's English; she's from New Brunswick.
They decided that I go to English school, so I went in St. Patrick's
School. And the French, well, I learned it with the kids here.

Oh, I've travelled a little. I've been down New Brunswick, I've been in
Ontario too. Well, that's about it, New Brunswick and Ontario. But I
love it here. It's just like a family here. I wouldn't change places with
anywhere else in the world. But one thing I'd like to do is go for one week
in Las Vegas. Spend a little bit of the money I'm earning here. But I love
it here; everybody knows each other. There's about 70,000 people here,
but everybody's together, I guess.

Yes, I was surprised at the November election. I knew they'd get a lot
of deputies in there, but not that much. The Parti Québécois, I don't
really hate them. I'm glad they're there. It's going to show the others, like
the Liberals, the Union Nationale, and Progressive Conservatives. You
know it's about time we have a change because to me it is just to scare
them off. Well, they are trying to do their best. But I don't think it will
last. To me they won't come right back in for another term.

Here, they went for the PQ. I don't understand that. They've always
been Liberal here, strong. But during the last election it was 1,500 more
votes than any other for the PQ. I was surprised! And this time nobody
was talking about the election, nobody was saying anything. We used to

have Liberals, Union Nationale, bugging each other and all that, but not Québécois. This time even my son voted for Québécois. Well, I respect his vote. But if I would have known that, I would have told him a couple of things. So he never told me he was going to vote Québécois. He told me the night the election started. He was very happy about that. Not me though.

Personally, I vote for the man, but I've always been a Liberal. My father used to be Liberal. Come the next election, I'm probably going to vote Liberal. They have good men in the Liberal Party. The Parti Québécois, they came in not because of the candidates — it was just the name Parti Québécois. People trying to say, you know, "We're Québécois."

Independence? It'll never come in. It'll never come in. It it comes in, boy, I'm moving to Ontario! No, even my son's not for separation, he's not for a separate Quebec, not right now. A lot of people at work I know now they voted for Parti Québécois, but they're not for a separate Quebec either. They want Parti Québécois to scare the government, to say, "Well, it's about time somebody took notice of us."

Sure, I'm Québécois — but I'll say I'm a Canadian too. Can I ask you a question? Are you Ontarian or are you a Canadian? That's it — we're Canadians. But some people here are saying that they're just Québécois. Why, I don't know. Just because they live in Quebec? I know guys at the shop they're Québécois, but they're for staying in Canada. What are you gonna say? I'm a Quebec Canadian?

Quebec's in Canada, so let's stay together. Why separate like that? I don't know what we'll gain. To me we'll gain nothing. Oh, they say, "We give money to the federal." They think we're giving money to the federal and getting nothing coming back. To me it's not like that. We're getting money back. We're giving and they're giving.

If they want to speak French, okay, I'll go for that, I'm French myself. I speak English and I went to an English school. But my name is Turcotte; I'm French, you know. But I'm not for saying, "No more English." If people want to speak French, speak French; if people want to speak English, speak English. Sometimes I will talk with my son and we'll be speaking English in front of somebody else and they will say, "Hey, we're in Quebec. Speak French." And I'll tell them, "Well, I speak French. But let me speak English if I want." They're not going to tell me which language I can speak. This is a free country here. Let me speak the language I want. Maybe that gets them mad. Too bad.

One day I went to a restaurant with my wife and we heard Italians and Greeks speak. I couldn't understand them. They were laughing, but I know they weren't laughing at me. They were telling a couple of jokes. I just wanted to know what they were talking about. What's the joke? I'd like to be in on the joke too. Why just keep the fun just for them, you know? Maybe that's the way the Frenchman who doesn't understand English thinks too. "Hey, I want to know what they're saying." We're very snoopy. We snoop in everything. Nice town, but, "What's going on across the street there? Hey, who's the guy with the girl there? Must be a new girlfriend." We're snoopy.

I don't hate Lévesque. I hate what he wants to do, separating Quebec from Canada. As a man, what he has to say, he says. I like that. What I have to say, I say too. Lévesque's a good man. There's only one thing that I'm against and I'll always be against it. He wants to separate Quebec. I know he won't realize it though. When I'm 72 I'll be against it. I think we'll have over 90 percent going to the vote.

What'll come out of it? I think about 35 percent will vote for it and 65 percent will vote against it. And that will be the end of it. Unless Lévesque wants to have another vote, and if he does that, then the people are going to say, "Hey wait a minute! You asked for an election and you said after the election you would hold a referendum. The people put you there, and you got your referendum. It didn't pass. Now forget it."

Marcel Pilotte

Factory worker, St.-Louis de France

(F)

"In 1949 in Newfoundland they had two referendums before they joined Confederation, so why can't we have more than one to leave it?"

It is important to recognize that the decision to become a separatist taken by many of those in this book was exactly that—a conscious decision. No one here "inherited" his separatist philosophy from the family, which is not surprising in view of the relatively tender age of the independence movement in Quebec. Personal experience often becomes the bedrock of later political belief and action, as Marcel Pilotte, a committed separatist, demonstrates. Both Mr. Pilotte and Fernand Gauthier who follows live in the suburbs of Trois-Rivières and work in the city.

What led me to become an independent? Well, back in the 1950s — '50 –'52 — I was working for a company in the Abitibi area and there was a group who decided to take a weekend trip into Timmins in Ontario. We went into a hotel and of course were speaking French. And a couple of hours later — I don't remember exactly — I went to the washroom and while I was there I was accosted by a big guy, an anglophone, and he said to me, "Here we speak English. I see that you were speaking French, but you won't be in a little while." And then luckily one of my friends came into the washroom and the other guy left. One of our guys was a boxer but we didn't want to start any fights.

Anyway, that's when I discovered that in Canada, outside of Quebec, the official language is English. Others were saying that Canada is bilingual, but only in the province of Quebec are people bilingual. In the other provinces signs are in English, but the minute you come into Quebec, you'll see two languages. And English is always on the top. If people speak English, then we speak English to them, but for the Quebecker who speaks French, he can't get along in other provinces. No, I'm not perfectly bilingual but I know a little English.

Anyway, several years later, I went around the Maritime provinces. Moncton was a little bit bilingual because part of it is francophone, but particularly on Prince Edward Island I didn't hear French spoken at all. I visited the building, you know, where Confederation began in Canada. It's true that you could press a button and get a French commentary on tape but the guides didn't understand us at all. There was an information centre there and when I spoke in French there the women and a man even said in English, "We don't speak French."

Then I went to Stanhope Beach campground on Prince Edward Island. That's a federal campground but they told us our campsite numbers in English only. So of course a French Canadian who doesn't know figures in English won't know where to camp for the night. We spent five days there and even then on the boat when we crossed over to get back to New Brunswick — it is supposed to be a federal boat — not a word of French. The same thing in Cape Breton. So I got fed up with Canada.

Personally, I was glad to see the PQ Party form the government. In 1949, in Newfoundland, they had two referendums before they joined Confederation, so why can't we have more than one to leave it? I am very proud of the PQ because since the party has been the government, things are happening in Canada like never before. Before that the Union Nationale or the Liberals went to Ottawa and said, "Well, things in Quebec are going well." Of course they weren't. But the PQ tell it like it is, they're not shy! Quebec is a province that isn't like the others. I was listening to TV not too long ago. An anglophone from Toronto said, "I like it when I go to Quebec because it is a province unlike the others, you don't have the same culture." And he was speaking French.

My own personal idea is that Quebec is a country because of its unique culture. Quebec can become an independent country with association with the other provinces of Canada — it seems to me that it would be a very natural thing. They are not going to put up any barriers like they do in the U.S.S.R. I claim that you shouldn't be afraid of anything because the Parti Québécois wants to do everything democratically. There's no question of hypocrisy and so far I think we have acted very well.

I want to see a francophone country here for my children. It's a beautiful dream. The future will tell of course. Time will tell. But I'm very optimistic. I believe in it!

Fernard Gauthier
Paper mill worker, Cap-de-la-Madeleine
(F)

"If the rest of French Canada outside Quebec had been treated as well as we've treated the English, there would be no separation today."

One of the most forceful and committed indépendantistes in this book, Fernard Gauthier is a door-to-door campaigner for the PQ. While the Bourassa Liberals were largely dependent upon corporate, large private donations and paid workers in the November 15 election campaign, the PQ relied on small individual contributions and volunteer workers like Mr. Gauthier.

I work at the Consolidated Bathurst paper mill as a heavy-equipment operator. The manager, of course, is anglophone, but the labour force are French Canadians. There are people who are partially bilingual in management at the present time. In the department I work in, a great many of the documents were in English, but now it's becoming more and more French because of the legislation that was passed. I am in favour of that 100 percent.

I am a confirmed *indépendantiste* because I figure that we are sufficiently adult to be able to govern ourselves without being controlled by the federal government in all sorts of ways. I read a great deal and what leads me to independence is all the injustices, the frustrations, we suffer from the federal government. Take, for instance, the air traffic controllers in Quebec—they don't even have the right to speak their own language. In all other countries controllers can speak their own language; why then in Quebec should we not speak our own language, which is French? They said that it wasn't safe, that it was a safety factor, but really this is just hiding the truth. The truth is that if they accept French, it will mean more work for French Canadians than anglophones. We want justice and the means to get it is to stop federal government domination. Understand? That's what is needed. So, we have to separate.

Separation is not a question of putting up fences around Quebec. We will continue dealing as equals because, at the present time, Ontario sells about 40 percent of its production to us and we are interested in keeping that. We can sell to them; they can sell to us. And, in the rest of Canada, it is the same. But with the present system of government, everything favours the rest of Canada, to our detriment.

When anglophones come here, we try to be nice to them and kind to them, to be polite. But if you go into Ontario and you don't speak English, too bad. They don't try to be helpful there. At the present time the English here have more rights in Quebec than the French have rights in the other provinces. Here they have schools. In the other provinces a great many don't have schools, and from what I have read, up until just a few years ago, the French had to pay double taxation if they wanted separate schools, which wasn't the case in Quebec for the anglophones. But the English here had privileges that we didn't have elsewhere as a matter of fact. If the rest of French Canada outside Quebec had been treated as well as we've treated the English, there would be no separation today.

We figure that the PQ victory of November 15 was the first step, but there are still many more steps to be taken before the final victory; we must convince people that this is the solution required to manage our own affairs. And we will start in the schools. Now Quebec students will learn more about their own history and economic exploitation than ever before. The classrooms will help open the eyes of the young in Quebec, and the independence struggle will forge ahead much more quickly because of it. Oh yes.

Propaganda says that headquarters of the companies are moving, but they only have three or four employees and they are not listed even in the telephone directory. I figure that before the referendum they are going to try to demoralize people—they want to start a reign of terror. Personally, I could lose my job for political reasons because now they are talking about closing down the Cap-de-la-Madeleine plant, which belongs to Consolidated Bathurst and is managed by English imperialists. It is an entire establishment of anglophones who manage it. Of course, they are not going to lose anything because production at this plant would be spread to the other plants, but it will have impact because people will say, "Look, the PQ is in power and look at the plants that are leaving now." This is all planned in advance; we expected this. But we are going to fight just the same. Perhaps in a few years the standard of living will not be as high as it is at the present time, but we fought and we are going to continue to fight and this isn't going to stop us and it isn't going to make us change our minds.

It would be rather difficult to tell you why francophones like Trudeau, Marchand, Caouette, are federalists, but in my opinion, they are well served by federalism, so they accept it. It is more or less a personal advantage for them because they are part of the federal government. They are people who live a little bit like the English people. Their people are no longer the French Canadians. But I could turn the question around and ask you: Why is René Lévesque in favour of separation? And Jacques Parizeau, who is an economist, an influential economist, who could get a position anywhere? What about Madame Payette, who used to be on the CBC and had a salary of maybe $50,000 or $60,000 a year and now has less, of course, as a Minister? Their aim is for us to become a country.

As a politician, I think that Trudeau is just about the best skater that ever has existed. Once in a while he says to Quebec, "Well, we will give you what you need, so you won't be a separatist," and then he will turn around and say to English Canada: "Nothing is to be given to Quebec." Frankly, I don't like the way he talks. He sure can skate around the issue. On the other hand, Mr. Lévesque, I think he takes a stand and he sticks to it, like for example, when he left the Liberal Party. He said to Jean Lesage, "If you don't want this idea of sovereignty-association to be discussed, I am going to withdraw from the party." A lot of people have said that Lévesque was chased out of the Liberal Party, but he wasn't. He withdrew.

I started waking up, when I was 15, when Louis St.-Laurent was Prime Minister. Even back then, a French state in America was a dream, an illusion. But I swore that it would not be an illusion and that's why I am working. It is not a dream, it is realistic and ever since I was young, I have been in favour of this. I don't worry about the financial aspects. I have been working for three election campaigns for the PQ now and it is all volunteer work. My day is completely theirs because I am convinced that this is the most honest government we have ever had—and I shall support them for as long as they are honest and do honest work.

I even took time off from my job to help the party. To show you just how convinced some people are, when Operation Finance took place in March, after our election victory, they collected $1,300,000, donated by ordinary people, not companies. No company has a right to subscribe. And individuals can't give more than $250. Now there is money from the grass roots! I went around door to door and explained the point of view of financing the PQ and renewing memberships and after renewing the membership, I asked them if they wanted to give money to finance the Parti Québécois. Even if the party is in power at the present time, it still needs money to continue its operations and to make it work. There was no problem collecting money from people. No problem. Some people gave me up to $24—you know, $2 per month, or $10, $15—it varied. Others gave a little bit less because they earned less, but to show you just how convinced they are, they gave something.

We have had enough! We don't need any more Quebeckers on their bellies in front of the federal government. A lot of people in the Liberal Party here are down on all fours before the federal government; they don't care about the people. Please understand that this is not a question of saying, "We don't like the English Canadian people." You are English, Rick, and you are just as sympathetic to me as any French Canadian. You speak with me in French, and I'm really glad to see that. And believe me, I don't have the same positive feelings for some privileged French Canadians who are working against us. No, this isn't a simple anti-English matter at all. It's just that in so many ways— economically, politically—we've had enough.

Yolande Bernier
Artist, Quebec City
(F)
"I am not a Canadian..."

As a young street artist in Quebec City, Yolande Bernier sees the face of English Canada every summer. Of necessity, she has acquired some English to deal with the unilingual tourists, but insisted on being interviewed in French.

And like many of the Quebec nationalists who appear in these pages, she first of all wanted to know if this book was being supported or subsidized by the federal government or the Canada Council. When satisfied that it was not, she agreed to be interviewed.

I was born on the island of Orléans and live here in Quebec. I sell my paintings here on Rue du Trésor. Oh yes, we are the treasures.

I studied oil painting but water colours I learned myself, by trial and error. That' how you learn the best, as a matter of fact. And that's how I started painting. It was something I liked to do in my spare time. What painters do I like? Two Quebec artists are special to me—Jean-Paul Lemieux and the primitive painter, Arthur Villeneuve from Chicoutimi.

In Rue du Trésor we have a special place where we leave our paintings, so we go and get them in the morning—if it is cloudy we put plastic on them. We talk a bit, have a coffee, wake up a little bit, and then we start talking with people. Mornings go by pretty fast because we get here about 10 or 10:30, and by the time of course you have got the stall all set up it is 11:30 or 12. So we go for lunch to a small restaurant, where it is not too costly and the food is very good. After lunch the day's work really begins. You are selling, you are there until 10 at night, often longer. When it rains, of course, it is very difficult, particularly when you have water colours. Everything can be destroyed in two minutes' time. You can lose $200 in a couple of seconds if there happens to be a quick rainfall, a cloudburst, unless everything is covered over with plastic. Sometimes it goes right underneath the plastic, as a matter of fact. You know, with the wind the paintings fly off in every direction, and at the same time you are trying to sell, it is very difficult. What is difficult, too, is to have to talk with everyone because I do serious things and they have to be explained.

It's pleasant here because everyone working on the street likes what he is doing and of course we are mostly young people, with our own individual characteristics and personality. We are all about the same age —from 20 to 30. Our customers? We meet a great many from Canada and from the United States—New Jersey, New York, Massachusetts. They like this or that according to their own personalities. But tourists from outside Quebec like the Chateau Frontenac, for instance. People like to have a souvenir of a place they visit. Quebeckers like my work because I do have water colours of Quebec homes and houses. Sometimes they even buy a series. But you have to tolerate all kinds of remarks from people who don't understand what you are doing. They all think that they are experts!

I would say about 5 percent of the tourists speak some French, maybe it's only 3 percent. I only see a few. I am talking about the Canadians, of course. Three percent is not very much in a country that is supposed to be bilingual. The only ones who speak it a little bit are the public servants. Maybe people are afraid to try to speak French, but it's not by being bashful that you are going to learn. You have to try. You are going to make mistakes. In Germany I try to speak a little German even if I make mistakes. It will make them laugh but it will please them and I will learn. They will correct me. You can't be shy about it. But judging from the Canadian tourists I meet every day, Canada is not a bilingual country. That really makes me laugh!

If people ask me what I am, I will say Québécois. That is what we call ourselves. If you say, French Canadian, no. "Quebeckers," you really shouldn't say either. You should say Québécois.

We have wanted more autonomy for 300 years. We have always been under the English or under the French regime or under the clergy. We are always under something. Why then would we not try by ourselves? With the PQ party they said it was going to be disastrous, it was going to be a catastrophe, it was going to be like Biafra. But I was pleased to see that we have taken — we have made one step. We have been afraid and a closed society for too long. Oh yes, I know that when there is a referendum — when they say do you want to become independent — the answer is going to be "Yes" because we have made a step forward by putting the Péquisites into power. This was really very important for us. Now we are beginning to be less afraid. People are beginning to get around to accepting that idea. There are positive energies and I know the answer is going to be "Yes." It is impossible to be educated to any degree and be opposed to the Parti Québécois.

I am not politically minded, I know nothing about politics, but I know I am not a Canadian because we don't speak the same language, we don't have the same culture, the same religion. We have our own films, our own writers, we are far less conservative. We are not as cold precisely because we have Latin blood in our veins. No, I am not a Canadian. I am international or I am a Quebecker. There are so many beautiful countries in this world. In Europe I say I am a Quebecker; we are very well liked there, particularly in France. They are very sympathetic to us, very sympathetic to our cause. They say, "Oh, the beautiful little Quebec women!" It is not just because of that, of course, but the French just adore coming here, because Quebec City resembles France and Europe. They can't get over how free we are here. In the countries I have seen I think the freest country in the world is Quebec.

Robert Blackburn
Buggy driver, Quebec City
(E)

**"I may have an English name but I'm
as French as anyone in Quebec City."**

*Robert Blackburn is a bilingual francophone. The assimilated Frenchman in
Quebec is quite rightly the focus of much attention and political debate, but the
fact that English Quebeckers can also be assimilated into the French
community is sometimes overlooked. From his vantage point as a calèche or
buggy driver, Robert Blackburn offers some insightful observations on that
common Quebec City species—the North American tourist.*

I was born about two miles away from here, in a suburb called Ste.-Foy.
My parents are French Canadians from Malebay—we call it La Malbaie.
They came here around, I don't know, they were about 25–28 years old.
My father learned English because he worked for an American company
then; but it's now a Canadian division. My mother is still very French
Canadian, she hardly speaks any English. My father has a quite large
vocabulary with a very beautiful accent. It's quite amazing to hear him
talk. If I speak English, it's just because I practiced on the buggies. I may
have an English name but I'm as French as anyone in Quebec City.

My ancestors? They came somewhere around the year 1790, a few
years after Wolfe. They were two lieutenants in the British army, the two
Blackburn brothers, and I would be the seventh generation. These two
original Blackburns both married French girls and over the years the
families just became more and more French and less English. My
grandfather was totally French Canadian — I remember him and he
couldn't speak a word of English. We are all totally French Canadians.
My kid brother's nine years old and sister 12 years old. She doesn't speak
a word of English. What she speaks, she learned in school, but she can't
make any sentences or, you know, understand everything that is said on
TV.

But there are still a lot of people here in Quebec that don't speak any
French at all. I know a guy who works on a buggy, the most amazing and
powerful guy that I've seen. Big heart, much guts, you know, and believe
me, he never learned French and he's lived here in Quebec City all his
life. His mother, his friends were probably all English so he didn't really
need to learn any French.

On the buggies the French Canadians, they call me Irish. But I have to tell them that I am French Canadian because I speak French and only French at home. I never speak English at home but on the buggies, that's all I speak. Yeah, I like the work. I like to work outside in the summer, and I like to talk with people, that's for sure. I've been working on the buggies for six years—since I was 18—and as I got experience I got better rigs and better horses. You work with two horses all the time; you switch every day. They have names just like you and I. I work with Bill and *La Puce*, the flea in English. Quite an amazing horse—huge, large.

I worked with *La Puce* for the past three summers, nobody has touched that horse because it's my boss's favourite horse. No kidding, if I don't work the horse doesn't come out. It's like that. The boss has had it for the past six summers, so it was eight years old when he got it; it was very young and very healthy. It's still very good but naturally slowing down a little.

Now Bill, the other horse, has very long legs, a fast walk, and is not nervous at all, which makes it beautiful for the buggies, because you do have crazy horses that might worry you or give you a lot of fun. They need to be quite calm, quite calm, with a good heart for all these crazy hills, and they need good legs to stand up to the hard pavement. A horse that never limps is a beautiful horse because they do get to limp. There's cracks in the streets and the horses step on them.

In winter the old drivers bring out the buggies — not more than six a day. Most of us younger ones are back at school, so we don't drive at all then. Some guys come out for the Easter holidays, but the busiest time would be July, August, naturally.

Yes, I go to university. A welcome change after working 15 hours a day in the heat and the traffic! I'll be back next year—it's a good summer job. You know, we have four or five girls driving buggies right now. Yeah, but that job is very hard for a couple of them. You need to be strong to hold those buggies on the hills sometimes, and you have to be able to handle horses in any situation.

And I guess you have to like people on this job — we get all kinds! I especially like people from Montreal. Americans are pleasant too. People from California are extremely educated, I notice, and they have a little more money, so it means they either work a little harder or the average pay is a little higher. Their minds are a little more open. They'll never tell you they got nicer buildings or the nicest places. Like people from Ne York will tell you that very often. They will tell you that with a 32-story building, they'll put cars in that. Everybody knows they have 110 stories, but who cares? We don't need that up here. We've got something different and very pleasant.

The people from France are extremely annoying and unpleasant. They boss you around and tell you where to go; you can't go where you want to go. They talk about what they have at home. If there is somebody that comes from France, you notice it right away because they speak very loudly, so then the buggy drivers go away. We don't wanta take them. Most of us, we'd rather die than take people from France.

We can't generalize about the people from Ontario; they are very, very special. If they come from Toronto, they're even more special. How? They won't pay a cent more than the going rate and they make sure they get the most out of it. They'll say, "You will tell us everything your little memory knows about this city." How would you like that?

People from other provinces are very pleasant. British Columbians are very, very good tourists, I would say. They come from far and they've seen a lot — they're not just passing, you know. People from Manitoba, they don't travel too much. They don't come up here. I don't know where they go. Alberta, they're a little richer right now. They tip more, that's for sure. Alberta, you get a dollar or two. When you get a dollar from an Ontario person you're really surprised. People from the East don't travel that much... once in a while, someone from Newfoundland or New Brunswick. And when they come from New Brunswick we always have a good time with them. They speak Acadian, so they're very pleasant, very funny; we just laugh a lot, you know. That's a laughy tour. But when we get the huge Italian people there, they just laugh all the time.

You get people who are too big; you get some, they can't even go in between the two seats. You have to push them like you do with a bag of oats! You just push and everybody laughs and she laughs and these people, they're big people, they laugh all the time. So you just push and they squeeze in. Your springs go down and you hear your buggy cracking, *craaack-craaack*, and every hole you take you just hope nothing breaks because one fat lady or a man is heavier than four people of average size. I mean four people if they weigh 150 pounds, they balance the rig better. But one "fatty" can nearly tip you over. No, I've never seen a buggy tip over — you'd have to go really fast to have that happen.

I don't like to go too fast anyway. I do a "social" tour — that's what I call it. We talk about everything — the snow, religion, history, politics. Especially now, politics, but I don't get involved personally in that subject too much with the customers! The landmarks I like to point out are the Armoury, the Parliament, the walls of the Citadelle. I think Quebec, this area, is beautiful.

Roger Demers
Pilot, Quebec City
(F)

"Why are you English always 25 years behind us?"

The immediate political issue most frequently mentioned by the Québécois I met is the use of French in aviation. Several people went so far as to say this one issue made the difference between a close race on November 15 and the strong PQ victory, and after extensive travel in Quebec I tend to agree.

In June, 1976, just five months before the Quebec election, Canada's airline pilots began an 11-day walkout to protest the proposed extension of French in the cockpits and control towers of Quebec. The use of French in Quebec aviation is restricted to visual flights, which in practice usually means private aircraft. For commercial instrument flying, including all Air Canada's operations, English is the sole language of aviation in Quebec and elsewhere in Canada. Unilingual Quebeckers, or those who insist on working in their first language, are therefore ineligible for most jobs as commercial pilots or air traffic controllers. The English-dominated Canadian Air Traffic Controllers Association and the Canadian Airline Pilots Association both favour maintenance of this system, which is under review by the federal Department of Transport, the final authority in the matter.

Unable to form a separate union, French-speaking pilots and controllers have joined together in an organization called L'Association des Gens de l'Air (the Guys of the Air). One of their most active members has been pilot Roger Demers, whom I met in his Quebec City office.

My family has been here more than 300 years. My father took part in the third-century celebrations of Quebec City in 1908. At that time they published a fairly impressive book on the celebrations themselves and on most of the older families of Quebec City and they traced our ancestors back to 1648. They came from Dieppe in Normandy, which I visited, incidentally, early in June when I went to France. I went to the Air Show at the Le Bourget via London and Paris, and I spent a weekend going to Dieppe to visit the beach where the landing took place. I visited the Canadian Cemetery and the municipal archives to look up the origins of my family. I also learned that it was from Dieppe that three nuns set out in 1646 to found the first hospital in Quebec City.

Anyway, I'm the first pilot in the family. I learned to fly during the Second World War. In fact I joined up at 17 and I had to wait until I was

18 to be sworn into the RCAF. I was part of the Atlantic command, stationed at Halifax. At that age I became acquainted with other parts of Canada and I also learned English, of course, which I did not know at all when I started out. I guess that's obvious from my French accent. I feel more comfortable now speaking to you in French than I would be in English.

After the war there was no civil aviation to speak of and Air Canada had just begun. Of all the pilots from the wartime perhaps one out of 100 could find an opening somewhere. They were a dime a dozen! So I went into electronics and worked in that field four years before becoming a pilot in 1950. I haven't stopped flying since then. Now I work for the Quebec government. They have a small fleet of planes — just last week I took Mr. Lévesque from Montreal to Quebec City, in fact. Of course all my spare time is spent working for L'Association des Gens de l'Air. We speak for the French-speaking pilots and controllers in Quebec but we're not a union recognized by the Labour Relations Board.

The only thing you hear about in the media is safety in the air, and it's all very confusing. But you don't hear about politics and job security, which are very important here as well. The political overtones should be obvious. As far as job security goes, some controllers are afraid of a fully bilingual system because they might not fit in. But if it's introduced properly, this needn't be a problem. Still, all you hear about is safety — so you want to look at safety? Okay.

In the early '50s when the Ministry of Transport got organized and began increasing technical facilities at airports by putting up air traffic control towers and control zones, they did it only in English. When they first started to build new control towers, it would have been easy to start the right way in both languages immediately. If they had done that, the problem would not have exploded in our faces today, but they didn't do it. And the great injustice of the whole thing of this is that French-speaking pilots who use these airports and who are supposed to be Canadians, full-fledged Canadians, first-class citizens like everybody else, they have been pushed aside and no longer have the right to use many airports with control towers because they can't speak English. This happened sort of gradually. Every time an airport was equipped for tower-to-pilot communication, the private pilot was pushed back to smaller visual-flight airports if he couldn't speak English. This happened at Baie-Comeau, Bagotville, and many other locations.

I recall the case of a francophone pilot coming back from a trip to Mexico in his small plane. He was on his way to Bagotville, across the Laurentian Park between Quebec and Bagotville, and here he ran into a bit of difficulty because of weather. He was going around in circles in a valley with a heavy cloud cover and couldn't find his way out. It was a very serious situation but he was able to communicate with the Bagotville base. Of course he was under such great stress that he was using French, but luckily at the military base in Bagotville there were pople who spoke French and so they sent a helicopter out to him with a French crew and they guided him out in French. Due to the fact they could communicate in the pilot's native tongue, he was able to get down safely.

Safety is based on two things. It is based first on understanding between the control tower and the pilot in the airplane and secondly on the adherence to air regulations by the pilots. That's where safety resides. If you have a large number of francophones in the Quebec air space who don't understand English — as many private pilots don't — safety is threatened if the tower doesn't speak to them in their own language. Think of the controller as a bilingual telephone operator: you radio in French or English and get service back in your mother tongue. This is what we have been fighting for — and this is how it's done all over the world.

Now there are 60 aviation schools in Quebec and you just can't force all those people who are learning to be pilots to learn a second language. This sort of injustice can no longer be tolerated. Either we are first-class citizens or we are not. It's very straightforward.

I have heard people saying that the PQ victory may possibly have hinged on this dispute — that it made a difference of 5 or 10 percent in the vote. I agree with that because the issue of language made it possible for a large segment of the Quebec population to become aware of this problem. The spectacle of federal French-speaking civil servants in Quebec and French-speaking clients in Quebec airspace having to speak English, not able to use their own language, is odious.

And another thing, even today at the federal level — in Transport Canada — even now, there is still an obvious attempt to deal with this matter as a purely technical matter. But is not a technical matter! It is a political question. You can't get out of that. It is a matter of justice. It seems that Parliament cannot get its messages through to the public service. There is constant blockage, obstruction, delay, unjustified delay that takes place in all kinds of decisions. Public servants must understand that you can't treat one-third of the population of Canada as second-class citizens. You cannot keep them outside such a major industry as aviation and tell them, "You are not welcome in this industry; you have to learn a second language to be able to work in your own country." We are talking about the right to work and the right to use our mother tongue in our work, at home.

I recall as a young lad when I went to primary school, our teachers made us sing "O Canada" and even then we were campaigning for our own national anthem and that's 40 years ago. We were campaigning for a

Canadian flag and for a national anthem back then! Why are you English always 25 years behind us? Nowadays, all of a sudden, you are discovering Canadian nationalism. Now people in English Canada are saying, "Let's sing 'O Canada' instead of 'God Save the Queen.'" Well, we have been doing that for decades. But for English Canada, the light just came on! But in the meantime a lot has happened and French Canadians had become somewhat discouraged. It is a case of too little too late.

Jacques Guay
Professor, Quebec City
(F)

"In grade four I cried when I learned that we had been beaten on the Plains of Abraham."

The Parti Québécois has succeeded in attracting the active support of Quebec's intellectual community on a scale reminiscent of the Democratic government of John F. Kennedy in the early 1960s. To fit the image of academic respectability that the PQ has acquired, even the previously rumpled Mr. Lévesque now wears well-cut suits, ushering in the new substance with the new style. While still a left-wing critic of the Parti Québécois, Jacques Guay, Laval journalism professor, is clearly pleased with their November 15 victory and, like many of his university counterparts, optimistic about Quebec's future.

My ancestors arrived in Quebec around 1640-1650. On my father's side, the Guays established themselves about 20 miles east of Quebec City on the south shore of the St. Lawrence. My maternal ancestors were Nadeaus who established themselves on the island of Orléans around 1660. Back then the king of France sent ships with young ladies because they had to populate the colony — they were called *les filles du roi* — and my roots go back to that period.

I was born in 1937, in Montreal, and I lived there until I was 24. The northern part of Montreal on St.-Hubert—north of Metropolitan Boulevard—where I lived was almost rural at that time. We used to go down to the centre of town perhaps once or twice a year—we'd go to see Santa Claus at Eaton's and we'd to to the St.-Jean Baptiste Day Parade on St.-Joseph Boulevard, but that was about all. My childhood memories of Montreal in the late '40s are of a much more anglophone city than today. I can remember that at Eaton's and in the large department stores there was almost no French spoken.

I also remember the blackouts in Montreal during the war when we had air raid exercises, and I was aware of the conscription crisis. We talked about it a lot at home and I heard about all the forced marriages at the beginning of conscription—one way of avoiding the war was if you were married. There were hundreds of marriages in 1944 to avoid being conscripted. Our neighbourhood was very French. I remember that one of or neighbours left and sold his home to an anglophone, and people didn't like that at all. The poor man who moved in came from either New Zealand or Australia because I remember there was a boomerang in his parlour. Anyway, he made special efforts to become integrated. He had the first power mower in the neighbourhood and he used to lend it to everyone. Yes, he did everything to try and integrate, and he almost succeeded. But then he moved on or I should say up to the town of Mount Royal.

It's really strange now to go back to my old neighbourhood. It has become almost totally anglophone. The Italians who moved in after 1950 sent their children to English schools, so today you hear Italian and English spoken there, and practically no French. The phenomenon of Italians going to English schools is a postwar phenomenon. Before the war, when I was growing up, the Italians living there used to become francophones.

Here's something rather interesting that people forget. When I was growing up we called those who spoke French simply *Canadiens*. That term didn't refer to those who lived in Ontario or the Western provinces: they were the English. The expression *"Canadien"* was like in the song *"un Canadien errant"* — it was a French Canadian, a Québécois if you will. That's the same origin as in the Montreal Canadiens hockey team. Today of course we're all Québécois.

I have always had that feeling of being *Canadien* and I must admit that in grade four I cried when I learned that we had been beaten on the Plains of Abraham. I thought that we had nothing to do with the English. I thought that they lived elsewhere. When I listened as a child to the king of England speaking on radio, I thought we heard him because there was no king in France and we were being given the king of England as a substitute. I hadn't made a political connection at all. I remember going to Ottawa when I was quite young. I really felt that it was a trip abroad. I knew that it was not home.

Throughout my childhood the English were just people who didn't want to speak to us in our tongue and who forced us to speak another language if we wanted to buy something. My mother almost started a riot one time at the beginning of the war because she was being spoken to in English at Eaton's by the son of a British family who had been sent here to avoid the war. My mother got mad and said, "Our sons are going to fight in England for a cause which isn't our own and you haven't even got the guts to fight. You come and take refuge here." Just then a student came along and said, "You are right! It is disgusting!" Finally it took the police to restore order. But these were the feelings that existed in Quebec.

Politically, I woke up at university. Around 1957 I worked actively at the University of Montreal in the Social Democrat Party — it was the Quebec counterpart of the old CCF party—because, as you can imagine, Cooperative Commonwealth Federation had no meaning whatsoever in French! So we had formed the Social Democrat Party. I worked actively in the Socialist youth with a young fellow called Robert Burns, who is now the PQ House leader.

In the final analysis we weren't nationalistic—we just hated Duplessis' guts. But slowly I discovered that the only way for us to keep our identity was to go for social reform in Quebec, not from another country or from Ottawa. I did not go through flag-waving or through the St.-Jean Baptiste Society. I just thought that it was the only avenue for our collective good. I never could believe that we could improve our lot by going hand in hand with the government of Canada for the good reason that French Canadians would always be second-class citizens in Canada, like the blacks in the United States and somewhat like the Algerians were before independence. It is a question of decolonization of a territory which is our own.

You see our colonial position even in the FLQ situation today. The Cross group is still in exile, the Laporte group is still in prison here, and other remnants of the FLQ before that are still in prison. Let's face it, they are political prisoners and have always been. If a fellow had done his time for a common law crime he would be freed by now. But not the FLQ. I think that one day or another the government will have to deal with the cases of these individuals — not counting the fact that first of all we don't really know what went on with Cross and Laporte. We do know one thing and that is that Laporte died. That is all we know. We don't even know how he died. There are too many doubts that still survive with regard to that murder. We are not even sure that the Rose brothers were the ones behind it. It is all very unclear. I think an enquiry should be started.

And look at the press coverage of Quebec politics today in the English press. It's unbelievable! When I see *Maclean's* Magazine pushing stories about the Christ agony of the Quebec anglophones and the tearful children, it is obvious to me that *Maclean's* are doing precisely what *Time* Magazine did with Vietnam or *Paris Match* with Algeria. This is colonial journalism.

But all that doesn't change the fact that the people here have great confidence in the Lévesque government and if things continue the way they're going, in two or three years, Canada as we know it will no longer exist. We won't be living in the same Quebec or the same Canada.

Eddie Conway
Carpenter, Shannon
(E)
"We're an island of Irish surrounded by French."

If a self-contained French community can exist in western Newfoundland (the Port au Port Peninsula), it is somehow appropriate that an Irish enclave should exist in Quebec. In Shannon the people speak with a remarkably authentic Irish accent after some 150 years of settlement, cut off from outside influences by the French surrounding them. Eddie Conway is a former carpenter and the mayor of Shannon, whose ancestors have been in the Shannon area since the 1820s. He has never visited Ireland but he has a much stronger Irish accent than my father, who emigrated from county Dublin at the age of 21.

Yes, I was born here in Shannon. In fact, my grandfather was born in this area. My people originally came from Ireland, from Kilkenny and Wexford. This area was settled by veterans from the War of 1812, and they had to go overseas to be at Waterloo, so they were veterans from Waterloo too. On my mother's side, they were Murphys and my great-great-grandfather fought with Nelson at Trafalgar. He got a pension of 10 pounds a year. He was quite a well-off man! Then her people in Ireland, most of them took part in that uprising in 1798; that would be 22 years or so before they left Ireland.

I've never been to Ireland but I intend to go. I imagine I could find the old farm the way my father described it, and the way his grandfather described it. I think I could find the exact location, you know. I've been told I have an Irish accent. Everybody here would have that accent. Yes, if you could spend a few days here, I could show you some people with a *real* Irish accent. I had a fellow from Ireland here a while ago and he said, "If I had a tape recorder and taped that fellow's voice and took it to Ireland, they'd tell me exactly where his ancestors came from, the exact district." Here it's as if we're on an island, you know. We're an island of Irish surrounded by French. We have some social contacts but not very much really. Not that much.

We have a St. Patrick's Day show here every year. It starts traditionally with the children. Like all Irish concerts there is supposed to be a play, so they have a short play. We have traditional Irish dancing too. In fact, we have a fellow from Ireland here who teaches Irish dancing. There is a fiddler, an accordion, and maybe a flute. And we mustn't forget the licenced bar!

Shannon is a close community. If you enjoy what the people enjoy, you just fit in, like a hand in a glove. But if you wanted topless dancing or something like that—not that they wouldn't enjoy that too! I mean that's not exactly what we're sponsoring here. Some people say we're not too sociable with outsiders, but others would say the opposite. I guess it depends on what sorts of social activities you like.

I was born and raised in Quebec and I love this place, but I have to admit they're more efficient in Ontario. Oh sure, they're so efficient there it'd make you sick! I was visiting a friend of mine at his cottage in Ontario awhile back on the day he was expecting the hydro to put in some power lines. He said he'd called them a few days ago and they promised to be there on this particular day. I thought to myself, "Oh yes, I've heard that one before." Well, sure enough around 11 in the morning they arrive, put in the lines, and leave. Now he thought this was quite normal, but I was thunderstruck. Thunderstruck! Yes, you have to admit they're more efficient in Ontario.

It's strange, but I have a lot of sentimental attachment to Ireland. But I like the land in Canada, especially the woods. The Irish are good woodsmen, you know, second-generation Irishmen are fine woodsmen of this country. I built conventional houses, you know, for a few years but I just sort of lost interest in it. But I sort of got interested in log house construction; it's more of a challenge to you. I've been very fortunate all my life from that point of view; I found work in the woods, then got interested in log construction.

I've been mayor of Shannon for 14 years, you know. I had two hitches — one six-year hitch and another eight years. No, I don't think I'll run again. I hope I'll have sense not to. It's time-consuming, you know, and then there's better-educated young fellows that sure would do a better job than me, if they want to put the time in it. It's like anything else, if you put a lot of time at it, and you do your homework, you do a reasonably good job.

I think what's happening with Quebec politics now is absolutely ridiculous. The French say they have been exploited, but all poor working people are exploited, not necessarily French Canadian. The Cockney in London was exploited, and so was the Irish Canadian and the Scotch Canadian, if you were a poor working man. We were exploited maybe as much as the Negro or the peon in Mexico. And the French Canadian, he was exploited if he was a poor workman, the same as the rest of us. No more. No less. Certainly my people never exploited the French. When we came here first, we paid rent to a French landlord. If we hired a lawyer we had a French lawyer. If we voted, we voted for a French member of Parliament all our lives — my grandfather and my father before me. So how did we exploit anybody? Half my life I worked on construction for a French foreman. Sometimes I worked on the river drive for a French foreman. Well, if the French Canadian was exploited, so was I. That's the way I feel about it. If they're afraid of losing their language, they're justified in trying to preserve it, but not at somebody else's expense. A language or a culture that can't stand on its own feet, I think, it should be let die.

At the hearing on Bill 101 there was a brief that came from working people from the Eastern Townships and they said that we never exploited the French. Camille Laurin said to them, he said, "You're guilty by association. You have to suffer because you belong to the anglophone community." That's a ridiculous theory. That's the kind of thing I'm afraid of. It scares you. A very small percentage, maybe 10 percent of the population here, are real militant Péquistes and they make a little trouble for us in the Council, but they're so weak. Actually, they have so little to complain about. In the election two years ago a French Canadian ran against me; he got 30-odd votes and I got 400. No, I couldn't say I'm bilingual, but I know some French. I have no problem discussing construction, but when it comes to talking politics or religion, I'm lost. The people I learned my French from spoke Joual. At that time we didn't know that we were talking Joual, but we were and today it's not acceptable.

You know, construction is no place to learn French because carpenters don't talk very much. You can't saw and hammer and talk. If you're a painter or a plasterer or bricklayer you might be able to do that. I don't think they're justified in accusing us of not being able to speak good French. We're lucky we talk English, you know! There was little formal education when I was young and we worked long days.

The government at the present, they're socialist but they're like National Socialist, and that's not very encouraging either, you know. I've no objections to socialism if they move slowly, but when you have National Socialism, that's what they had in Germany. We're a long way from that yet, but still it's disturbing.

As long as Quebec remains in Canada I have no fears. You know, the English language is not going to disappear in North America, that's for sure. Of course, we're pretty smug about that; its 200 million English-speaking people and five million French-speaking, so, from that point of view, I know we can be pretty smug, but never mind. If Quebec should break away from Canada, I can't see staying here. But I'd stay until they actually break away. If I can make any contribution to Canadian unity, I want to do it here. But unfortunately there's a few families that are moving. They have their future and they have their children to think of. Last Saturday night we had a party for a young fellow who works for IBM and has decided to move to Calgary. It's a pity but he asked for a transfer.

My family has been here 157 years, so I consider myself a Quebecker. Absolutely, I feel at home here. I've travelled across Canada, I've been in every province and territory in Canada with exception of Newfoundland, and I feel most at home in Quebec. When I hear the French language I feel at home even though I'm not really bilingual. I've made a couple of trips out West and when I came back and I was crossing the Laporte Bridge, I knew I was getting home. I would find it hard to move, but move I would before I would become a second-class citizen.

Jean-Guy Carrier
Writer, St.-Raphaël
(E)

"A large element in the French-English thing is the question of respect."

Jean-Guy Carrier is a former journalist (Canadian Press News Agency, CTV) and press secretary to NDP Leaders David Lewis and Ed Broadbent. Carrier's concern with family roots in Quebec is evident in his two novels, My Father's House *and* Family, *which are set in his native village of St.-Camille. Carrier has returned to the Quebec of his youth and now lives in an old farmhouse in St.-Raphaël, 33 km. southeast of Quebec City.*

I was conceived in Quebec, born in Ontario, and raised in Quebec and Ontario, so I think in that rather confused way I am Canadian—because we are all sort of jumbled. And what I am or try to be right now is a writer. On the side I am sort of a pig farmer and maple-sugar harvester, restaurateur, and whatever else will support me. In fact, I am just a jack-of-all-trades because writing doesn't support you, after all. It is a nice pastime but it doesn't make you a living very much—in this country.

I have very deep roots here. My family on both sides first came here in 1647; they have always been in this country, and they were all farmers as far back as one can see. That is some nine generations. What happened, of course, is that the original homesteads kept being subdivided as more and more sons came of age, and naturally the people wanted to be near the St. Lawrence because, especially in the early time, it was a safe place to be. But also the better lands were there. So they just kept moving south to find new land.

My grandfather was somewhat of a local politician, old style. They used to demolish bridges so they could get them rebuilt by the winning candidate. There is an actual story about this bridge, which was linked to a very remote community, across a small river. The bridge was an old wooden structure but it was sort of the main access to this village, and it very conveniently burned down prior to an election. Of course people couldn't go across with their horses; they had to walk across and go to the next village. So there was a great uproar about getting a new bridge, and of course what happened is that the Union Nationale candidate was quite conveniently able to say, "Well, if you elect us, if you vote for our candidate in this country, of course we will build you a new bridge. Otherwise, good luck!" And they voted for him and they got the new bridge. But it was made of steel and concrete! This didn't make my grandfather very happy because how could you burn down a steel and concrete bridge? Anyhow, there were elections to be fought in the future. I guess he had to find some new tactics!

This is old rural Quebec and even here the Church is really on the decline, and I think that is tremendous. When I think of the old control the Church had, I am overwhelmed that it has gone. It went all the way from politically influencing people to making people cower for generations. Just think—sometimes the *curés* used to get up in the pulpit and castigate women about not having a child. They might have had 12 already, but they hadn't had one in three years so they weren't doing their duty. Just think of what that did to people's minds when they took that kind of thing seriously! I think it is almost heaven-sent that the *curés* no longer have any power.

The villages around here are all about 300–320 years old. So that goes back to the beginning of the colony. In that sense, it is the heartland of the province. These places were settled earlier than Montreal or anyplace like that. This is really where it began. I came back here very simply because it is home for me. My family is quite large and I have a very strong sense of family and I like very much being in the bosom of that family. I have lived in most parts of the country. In the Arctic. In Manitoba. Ontario. But there is no place like Quebec for a francophone. There is no place where you can feel half as at home as in this place.

My father's family is a good illustration of what happened to people through the depression and into the '40s. I think he went up to grade five or four or something—that was normal; he was from a very isolated village in Quebec. He went to work in the woods when he was about 12 years old. Obviously there wasn't much of a future working for $1.50 a day, so when these people heard that there were jobs available in steel mills in Ontario or work in the States, it was only natural that, being young people, they picked up and left. There was a great migration about that time. Dad went to Welland, Ontario, to the steel mills. Today, there are something like 2,000 French Canadian families in Welland, all from these little villages here. And they always come back every summer, but they are all from around here. Because of my family's financial situation, I was raised by my grandparents until the age of eight and then sent to my parents in Ontario, where I was thrown into an English school system. I didn't speak a word of English then—it was a great deal of fun. I remember trying to ask to go to the bathroom and the teacher not understanding and feeling somewhat frustrated raising my hand a lot and so forth. I think I made a mess.

My parents have been away now for something like, oh, 25 or 30 years, but they have come back every summer, almost like a pilgrimage. Among those who left there was sort of a feeling that the people who stayed behind were not terribly ambitious—were somewhat even probably a little stupid for not realizing that there were better things elsewhere. And the self-respect of the people who had stayed behind of course was affected by this: "Maybe we are a little doltish. Why are we staying here?"

Well, the November 15 election was really a shock to my relatives in other provinces because this was supposed to be this quiet place, where the people were supposed to be very unambitious, and now suddenly everyone here is very involved politically, and all of a sudden they don't have any interest in how much the Ontario steel mills are paying. So now it is the people from outside who are asking the questions and the local people who are sort of smiling knowingly. For once they are experiencing the sense, the feeling: "Maybe we weren't so dumb for having stayed. Maybe these people who are Ontarians, who have chosen assimilation, weren't so smart for having left. Maybe we had a rough haul of it but perhaps in the long run it was best that we stayed." So there is a real pride about their having hung on.

I would like my children to be Quebeckers—Québécois rather than franco-Ontarians or franco-Manitobans or whatever because there they will always be a majority. It is only here that they will be masters of their own fate. I want them to speak English and all the rest of that, but I think that in terms of belonging, in terms of having roots, which is terribly important to me—you know, my family has been here so long—I want them to have a sense of the importance of that.

A large element in the French-English thing is the question of respect. In this area, there isn't much consciousness about not being respected, you know. There isn't much of a feeling that the people out there don't like us. People here respect the English and they imagine that the same thing applies vice-versa. What shocks them and where this thing called respect comes into play is when they find they may be less than respected by some other parts of the country.

The air traffic controllers' strike was a great example. This really upset people here who are farmers, factory workers, and so forth. My relatives have never taken a plane in their lives, much less been to an airport, but they were upset. They really had a feeling of being sort of struck at. My first reaction was pure outrage, of course. I could then sort of rationalize it somewhat and think about it, but finally even my last reaction was outrage. It was someone from outside telling people in Quebec how or when they could use their own language. We all understood that this was not a very good thing the people were trying to do to them.

I think cultures are always competitive. There can be a lot of sort of well-wishing and so forth, but at the heart of it, cultures are essentially competitive. A good example of this is the tough time Ontario has given its French minority in the area of educational rights. The fact that at one point I was able to go to a French school in Ontario was purely because my parents, who were both working-class people—my mother works in a textile mill, my father drives a truck—were willing to pay for it. They were not making very much money but the province wouldn't support the school. I have seen assimilation of many people that I know in Ontario and a lot of friends I went to school with. My cousins and a lot of people in my family now speak barely any French and their children surely will not speak any at all. They were given no help at school.

I don't want to kick anybody who is trying to maintain their French language and culture in Ontario or Manitoba, but as far as I can see from here, I really think by now that it is a hopeless thing. I think that they can probably hold on for maybe another generation, but I really think that the young people are just not there to pick it up.

My answer to the independence question has got to be very conditional. I think that is kind of the answer that most people would give you right now in Quebec. I think that it is a good thing that it is finally opening up and being discussed sincerely by all sorts of people, at all sorts of levels. Speaking personally, the way the power is shared right now between the provinces, I think it is not advantageous to either the Western provinces, the Maritimes, or Quebec. I really think that the system has not been working well for 100 years. It was sort of hacked out by various politicians 100 years ago and has been very difficult to define since then. I think somehow we were conned into thinking that if everybody learned French the country would be okay, but it doesn't matter to Quebeckers really. It would be nice if everybody learned French, but it wouldn't affect what is happening with Quebec that much. And that is something people should understand outside. They can do whatever they want, turn somersaults, learn French or whatever, and finally what is being worked out in Quebec is almost like a family situation that is being worked out within the family. And there is very little that people on the outside can do to influence it positively. But they can do a lot to influence it negatively. Like the air traffic controllers thing again. Every negative comment sort of rings like thunder; every positive comment goes over everybody's head. Do you understand?

Or take the Canada Day celebrations on Parliament Hill. It wasn't even faintly ridiculous, you know; it was sort of irrelevant—in this part of the woods anyway. We had a very nice quiet St.-Jean Baptiste Day. We got together in my house, my family and I; there were 27 of us and we had a great time. It wasn't any sort of great nationalist outpouring; we just had a big meal and then we danced some square dances and had a great time until about three o'clock in the morning. No one was making raging speeches about Quebec, independence, or anything else. I just wish that the July 1 celebrations could have been in the same spirit, without the political element that was injected into it. That made it unhealthy and so people just ignored it. There are not really a lot of screaming nationalists in Quebec, you know—not as many as the press outside of the province would make you think. People are leery about running up flags and embarrassed by that kind of gushiness. But you have got to understand that there is a very basic strong sense of belonging, which is a different thing from running up a flag and getting salutes and so forth.

How do I feel about the future? Well, I am in a peculiar position. I can look at both sides, which isn't an enviable position at all because although it may enable me to understand a little more about both sides, it also saddens me to see the growing differences—because I do think the differences are growing and the splits are widening. It is very difficult to be optimistic. I hope something will happen that will bring us sort of all together, but I can't say I am optimistic. I think that the only thing I can see is tolerance, mutual tolerance and respect. It will require that English Canada not feel that it is being rejected if Quebec wants a little more autonomy. Quebec should be allowed more control over its own destiny. That requires redefining the association between us in some basic ways. If the rest of Canada isn't going to do that, I don't see any hope.

You know, Ukrainians out West, English people in Ontario, Scots people in the Maritimes—all have an attachment to "the old country." They always have some other *place*. That doesn't exist in Quebec. France isn't "the old country"—it is nothing. Only a few intellectuals who have gone over to France and who have been dependent upon its production intellectually feel anything substantial for France. For Quebeckers, the only *place* is this place here.

Historically, it is understandable why this is so. The bulk of Quebec was cut off from France for 200 years. What I am trying to say really is that the experience of Quebeckers in Quebec is very similar to the experience of the Americans. They were cut off from Europe and determinedly sank roots in this continent. So the literary tradition which attracted me, which meant something to me, was the English-American tradition, and it seemed only natural to start writing in that tradition, in English. I feel it was a good choice because I hope that what I am writing will perhaps make people from outside the province understand Quebec a little better. Culturally I know where I am, absolutely. Intellectually, I am sort of straddling two worlds and hoping that what I can do is convey the one world to the other.

I am now writing a quartet of books—a sort of series of books which are all one story following Quebec's evolution from about '39 to the present. I have finished three of the books now and I am about to start the fourth. In any case, I think after my next book I will have shot my bolt as far as writing in English is concerned. What I probably will do is start writing solely in French after that.

Father Antonio Arsenault
Priest, St.-Séverin
(F)

"I have lived my priesthood during the greatest period in the history of the Church in North America."

To visit the parish of St.-Séverin 50 km. south of Quebec City is to return to a time and place largely untouched by Quebec's Quiet Revolution. Take away the paved roads, automobiles, and power lines and you are in a nineteenth-century rural parish sustained by an agricultural economy and a strong Church. Father Arsenault, the energetic and forceful curé of St.-Séverin who still wears the traditional soutane and three-cornered hat, was working in his garden behind the rectory on the sunny July afternoon when we met.

My ancestors came from Acadia. They were deported in 1755 and the waves and the winds brought them to Louisiana. A beautiful area but they had no relatives and friends there, and you know that Acadians like to stick together—families, friends, all together. So my ancestors were among those who decided to walk to Quebec. It was just a small pilgrimage of 2,000 miles—you know, through the bush in 1756-57. It took exactly three summers and two winters. There were 1,430 of them and only 750 reached Quebec. The others died from hunger, cold, and sickness along the way. My Acadian ancestors settled about 20 miles from Lévis, and the proof is if you go there today, instead of hearing of the 1st Concession or the 2nd Concession, they still say the 1st Acadia, 2nd Acadia, 3rd Acadia, and so on. When they had cleared a concession, it was known as such and such an Acadian concession.

I became a priest in 1928. Which means that in 1978, if I live that long, I will have been 50 years as a priest. I'm 74 years old and I have lived my priesthood during the greatest period in the history of the Church in North America. I say that because, first of all, we had a classical course at college — the humanities, Greek, and Latin. It wasn't dismantled like it is today. And, second, with the sacred music that was inaugurated by Pope Pius X, we had a half-century of beauty, grandeur, harmony, and concerts in our churches.

One of the two greatest causes of the confusion and disarrangement today is that in the space of one generation, 35 years, we have gone from a population 80 percent rural to 78 percent urban. This is very bad because the greatest mistress of civilization is nature, Mother Nature. And you know as well as I do that there is not much of nature in the city. You also know that what supports and feeds the nation is not the city; it is the land, the rural areas.

The other cause of our problems is the Ministry of Education. I can never forgive them for replacing 3,500 small schools with the large regional polyvalents and CEGEPS [Quebec's regional high schools and community colleges]. There has been a deterioration because the more the teachers are paid, the less devotion they have to their duty. We should praise to high heaven the old teachers who used to replace the mothers of all the children they had in their classes. They didn't have the qualifications and the diplomas of today's teachers, that's true, but they did give an education, a family education and a religious education. Whereas the CEGEP and the polyvalent school today destroys the family spirit and doesn't teach the faith. It's not much more than a Protestant organization in a public school.

Another problem is our small families today. I told my parishioners recently that in Japan, which is about one-third the size of the province of Quebec, there are 90 million people, while here there are only six million of us. We have 9 percent unemployed and in Japan there are none. The poverty of Canada and the province of Quebec is simply because we do not have enough population, and there are a great many parishes of 600 or 700 who don't have a resident priest. This is a great pity.

We have 84 families in this parish and thank God the majority of the parishioners of St.-Séverin are staunch Catholics, just like I was at their age. Three weeks ago on Sunday, June 26, 1977, we celebrated the 100th anniversary. Our honour and our life, our very soul, is the faith and the language.

There might be some good in the PQ victory. The people said to themselves, "We have absolutely nothing to lose. We may as well have a change." We shall see. Mr. René Lévesque is a man who has a great deal of willpower. I wouldn't say that he is stubborn, but he is tenacious. And he has surrounded himself with an executive which is also tenacious. But nobody can convince me that the province of Quebec will succeed in obtaining independence and living with it. Of course, it can vote for it, like the African countries have done. But as soon as independence was voted on there was civil war. That's what I am afraid of here.

Roland Mercier

Farmer, musician, La Durantaye

(F)

"All the young people get on the floor and dance when we play the old-time music!"

In hundreds of towns and villages across Quebec there are local fiddlers or accordion players, each of whom has a smaller following but one that is every bit as enthusiastic as that enjoyed by the well-known chansonniers. In the small farming village of La Durantaye, the local favourite is Roland Mercier. A soft-spoken, hospitable man, Mr. Mercier has noticed among young people a marked upsurge in the popularity of Quebec's traditional music.

I bought this farm from my father about 30–35 years ago. That house out at the back, that was my grandfather's house. It's about 200 years old. It has always been inhabited by the Merciers.

I built this house two years back when we were thinking of selling the farm, but then I decided not to sell for the time being. I don't have a son to take over, you see, but it always hurts to sell. This is good farmland, among the very best on the lower St. Lawrence. I have always had dairy cattle, so I grew hay and oats, nothing else. Yeah, well, we do have a small garden—but it's just for the family.

Life has been good here. I learned music when I was young. We were a large family—14 children—and we all used to play, all members of the family. My father played fiddle and accordion. I used to play the fiddle with him. Here, listen to this piece ... [Music.] That was called "*La Ronde Marier.*" It's not a new piece; it goes way back. I played in bands— I used to have a lot of fun when I played for socials; it's a good way to pass the time. Thirty years ago there was no television, so we had to make our own fun, our own entertainment. And you know, this kind of music has become very popular again. It's Canadian music, as we call it. Square dancing.

It's so popular that if I had the time I would be out two or three evenings a week to play, but in view of my age — and I have children — I am doing a little bit less of that now, but I am often asked out. All the young people get on the floor and dance when we play the old-time music. They really dance! I really like to see that. It's the young people today who really want to hear the traditional square dances along with the modern ones. My kind of traditional Québécois music sort of went out of style back in the '60s but nowadays it's really popular again. It's good-time music and it's our own music, maybe that's why. Yes, I think people here are more interested in the music and the culture of Quebec now than they were awhile back.

Since the November 15 election there is a lot of discussion; people talk about it. When we meet it is always what is talked about. And we listen to the news more and more. We always want to see what is going to take place. It will be necessary for us to vote in the referendum. People will have to express their opinion, but people are not all that much for independence; I don't think so. They were for Mr. Lévesque, of course. They elected him with a good majority, but if the referendum was held tomorrow, in my opinion, I don't think it would pass. He won't have a majority in the referendum — I'm quite sure of that. I speak with a lot of people and I don't think that they would be in favour of independence because, well, they are afraid.

What are they afraid of? Mmmm, I really don't know . . . maybe that the situation might get worse. Take me; I am not asking to be better off, I am doing fine as it is. So if things change, will I be better off? If I am not to be better, I will likely be worse. They say that with independence we would have more freedom than we have now. But would we? I don't think so. We are free now. We do what we want; we say what we want. We have to work, of course, but I like to work. And things are doing well. I don't have any complaints about Ottawa or Mr. Trudeau. I have nothing against him at all.

I don't know what will happen to Quebec but I want to keep the farm here for a few years, as long as I am capable. If we should come on hard times, we will always have the farm to live on, grow food on.

At the end of the day when you have done a good day's work, you feel satisfied. Doing nothing, I wouldn't live. I would rather be dead! Sure, I like to take a day off here and there. A day or two per month, I'd say. And more in the wintertime, when things are quieter. Then I play my violin . . . would you like to hear another tune . . . ?

Chapter **4**

Lower St. Lawrence and the Gaspé

A s the St. Lawrence River lowlands outside Quebec City were settled by habitants in the late 1600s, New France's expanding population began to move steadily eastward. I followed the path of settlement past Rivière-du-Loup and Rimouski into the Gaspé Peninsula. The scenery in the Gaspé is spectacular; the road follows forests and upland pastures, bordering steep cliffs that drop to rough Atlantic beaches below. It was midway around the peninsula on the shores of Gaspé bay that the explorer from St.-Malo, Jacques Cartier, planted a 30-foot cross in 1534, claiming this land for France. The cruel expulsion of the Acadians in 1755 led to further settlement, as did the U.S. War of Independence, which drove a contingent of United Empire Loyalists here in 1783.

While the Gaspé Peninsula is one of the most beautiful areas of Quebec, it is definitely the poorest. Isolated and dependent upon fishing, tourism, and limited agricultural and mineral resources, the region suffers from unemployment that can climb to about 50 percent in some communities. There is little future here for the young, who are obliged to move west to Quebec City and Montreal in search of work.

Particularly along the southern coast where Loyalist settlements like New Carlisle, New Richmond, and Douglastown are found, I was reminded of the Eastern Townships as I began to uncover political reactions from English-speaking Gaspésians that reflected the siege mentality that has taken hold in many sectors of Quebec's anglophone population since November 15. The French-speaking population of the Gaspé has grown steadily in this century to its present level of 85 percent. As Quebec's most isolated

English-speaking minority, many anglo-Gaspésians feel threatened and still somewhat bewildered by the PQ victory, which includes three of the five seats on the peninsula. The politics of the Gaspé today for many is the politics of poverty and for some, the politics of cultural isolation.

As in the Maritimes, one of the main exports of the Gaspé is brains—the late Senator Gratton O'Leary came from these parts, as do René Lévesque and Quebec Liberal leader Gérard D. Lévesque. One of the earliest places on my itinerary was René Lévesque's birthplace of New Carlisle. Lévesque's shadow still hovers—some would say looms—over this town. The people are reluctant to spend their time with visiting writers and reporters, but patience and persistent investigation eventually produced results.

Raymond D'Auteuil
Cable TV operator, Rimouski
(F)

"Part of our TV equipment is still hidden but I'm convinced the RCMP know where it is."

Mr. D'Auteuil is caught in the middle of a major federal-provincial jurisdictional dispute over the right to regulate and licence cable television. With the advent of telegraphy in the late 1800s, the federal government assumed control over communications under the section of the B.N.A. Act that grants federal jurisdiction in matters relating to inter-provincial transportation and radio. Since conventional television systems obviously cross provincial boundaries, they have been considered a federal prerogative. Cable television systems are limited to a more restricted area; however, on this basis, the province of Quebec, with the unofficial support of several other provinces with similar interests in the cable field, is challenging this federal control in the supreme court of Canada—and in the living rooms of Rimouski.

I work with a cable TV company, which at the present time is in litigation between the federal and provincial governments. We operate with a permit from the province of Quebec only. It seems that we are trying to sit in two chairs at the same time. Now that's not an easy thing to do, believe me! If there's a choice, we'd prefer to use the provincial chair.

The provincial government's philosophy about cable TV is that cable distribution, being in a very limited zone, should be governed by the provincial government, not by Ottawa. The province does not deny that the federal government has jurisdiction with regard to microwave and interprovincial communication; but in our particular case we are not using the airwaves, so it should come under provincial jurisdiction, just the way the provinces also have jurisdiction over telephone companies.

Our troubles here began when the CRTC gave a permit to a rival company to give cable coverage to the Rimouski area. Without getting bogged down in all the details, let me explain that the CRTC didn't hear our application, but the provincial communications authority did. In the end they decided to split up the territory the CRTC had granted solely to the other company, and give us the Rimouski region to serve with cable. Quebec also required that we start work immediately, which we did without a permit from the CRTC. Our competitors fought us in the courts but we went full steam ahead and finally the federal Ministry of Transport, along with some help from the RCMP, impounded our transmitting and receiving equipment, sealed it, and denied us access to it. So at nighttime we just set up new lines and installed some hidden equipment and began sending our programs anyway!

Part of our TV equipment is still hidden. I'm convinced the RCMP know where it is, but they have lost so much face they have stopped the seizures: after they had seized one antenna, another one took over!

This is a question of principle, not money. Of course, we did lose money from the seizure of the antennae but we didn't have to pay out any legal fees—we have been helped by Quebec City there. We are defending Quebec's rights. Cable must come under provincial jurisdiction. We went to a Superior Court and won, but we lost in the Appeal Court. Now we have gone to the Supreme Court of Canada to get a final decision on whether cable is to be under provincial or federal jurisdiction and also whether the act governing communications in Quebec is constitutional or not. [In December, 1977, the Supreme Court of Canada ruled against Mr. D'Auteuil, finding that licensing of cable TV is a federal responsibility.]

We've had excellent support from other cable distributors in Quebec. They all have a provincial permit as well as a federal permit. They sent us equipment, lent us all sorts of things, and said, "Don't say that we lent it to you. Don't talk about it because we have to deal with both Ottawa and Quebec." Other provinces, like Ontario, Alberta, Manitoba, British Columbia have supported Quebec. They have the same opinion as Quebec on the cable issue.

I am pleased with the election of last November because it clarified matters. Now, hopefully, Canada will come to understand Quebec better. We have had a bad press in English Canada. People in Ontario just don't know us and as for the people in the western provinces, what have they heard about Quebec? Nothing but scandal. The good things that Quebeckers have done, people are not made aware of. Things like Hydro Quebec, for instance. It is one of the best government hydro companies and what do people in Ontario know about it? What do people in the West know? All they know is that it was administered by French Canadians.

But anything bad that we have done—the stupid expenses for the Olympic Games and so on—they know about. The media see to that! So maybe if we were in their position we wouldn't be tempted to sympathize too much with Quebec either. But now Quebec is saying, "Look, fellows, you have laughed at us long enough. Now you are going to have to sit down and talk with us or else we are leaving." Maybe this will clarify some fundamental issues. And don't forget, there is a democratic process involved here.

You know it was because of the Second World War that the federal government was able to take over so many powers. It was supposed to remit them to the provinces after the war but of course never did. I think it will come. If the federal government does decentralize and give powers to the provinces, and stops spending on its own, perhaps we can work out a settlement of our differences.

But we can't have a completely bilingual country. It is absolutely impossible. You can't dream in Technicolor and you can't expect to have a bilingual government. You can't ask a fellow from Vancouver, who has a great many contacts with the Americans but who never or rarely has any with Quebec, to learn French. On the other hand, if in British Columbia there is a rather important French community and they want to have French schools so that their children can be educated in French, let them have that—just as we let the anglophones' children receive an English education. Fair's fair. But any lasting solution must not be imposed or dictated by Ottawa—that's impossible.

Gilles Roy
Social welfare worker, Rimouski
(F)

**"I married a few months after leaving
the priesthood."**

*Although precise figures are difficult to give, an important phenomenon of the
'60s and early '70s in Quebec has been the decline in the power of the Catholic
Church, reflected partly in the number of priests who have left the priesthood.
Many, like Gilles Roy, have become involved in education or social welfare
work. Mr. Roy is employed by the government of Quebec as a community
organizer.*

My first memories go back to the depression, which marked my family
very deeply. I can recall that my father at that time lost what little he
owned and we found ourselves literally on the street. Completely
impoverished. The only ray of sunshine was the coming at
Christmastime of a cousin who had a grocery in Rivière du Loup. He
came in a sleigh carrying a stock of groceries—enough food to last us the
winter. That was our social welfare. It was given with a good heart, but it
was no less humiliating to feel that we were completely dependent on
somebody else's charity.

My father was a ditch-digger; he had no education whatever. He could
barely sign his name and I can recall very well two winters when he
simply worked to earn the wood with which we used to heat the house.
That didn't put much on the table.

I turned out to be a fairly talented youth, and in those days there was
always a number of benefactors who watched out for the more intelligent
children. I had some benefactors who permitted me to start my classical
education in 1942, here in Rimouski at the seminary, when I was 12 years
old. We were all very impressed by our parish priests. Priests had an
impressive social status, like doctors and lawyers, and they played an
important role in the community, helping out everyone. They lived in
very close contact with the population. We had an old parish priest who
originated the first Adult Education Course given in the province of
Quebec, and my father attended that course. He learned how to read and
write. No, I will never throw stones at the priests, saying that they kept
the population in slavery, because I knew some and I have been marked
very deeply by them. They were extremely close to the poor people and

they gave themselves body and soul to try and get people out of their misery and ignorance.

After my classical course I did four years of theology at the Rimouski Seminary—it was traditional theology—and I was ordained in 1954. I taught first, but over the years I began to question celibacy in the priesthood and finally I concluded there is no theological justification for absolute celibacy. I also disagree with the Church on questions of birth control and female priests. So I finally left the priesthood in 1972, although I am still very close to my faith.

I was married a few months after leaving the priesthood. Unfortunately we don't have any children. We lost one during pregnancy but we would like to have one now. We are thinking of adopting a four-year-old girl—I don't know whether it will work out but I hope so. And we still hope to have some of our own.

The Church is having some difficulty in finding the role it is going to play in modern society—I think it has a social and human role to play in a society that is so technical, technocratic, logical, and everything else that we always have a risk of losing the human dimension, the true values. But as long as the Church believes that only men can be enlightened by the Holy Spirit, it will be inhuman. And its attitude toward birth control belongs to the past. The Church only has one chance, in my view, and that is to open itself onto the world of today and to renew its outward appearance, even though actually there are reactionary currents within it. But I think we will always have that.

Fortunately, the concept of personal conscience has been developed, and we are aware that basically each of us must rely on his own conscience, enlightening it as much as possible. I feel a deep social commitment—deep, because I believe that Christian values are not to be found only within the Church; they are to be lived in life as a whole, around concrete problems of humans and the basic problems of modern-day society. And in my social commitment, my Christian values are being passed on and those values are not opposed to those of other ideologies. I work with the least favoured people in this area—which is itself one of the most underdeveloped areas of Canada. Unemployment is high, and that may be one reason why the PQ won six out of eight seats in this riding.

How do I feel about the PQ? I am very happy with them so far. I've seen a lot of changes in my life and the life of Quebec recently, and it's not been for the worse, I can tell you. I am not sure that Quebeckers as a whole are sufficiently mature to become masters in their own house yet, but I don't think we will ever see a wall of China around Quebec, which is what Trudeau keeps telling the people. Mr. Trudeau constantly disgusts me and his ministers do too. When I got married it did not mean that I forgot about my parents, but it meant that I was master in my own house, and that I was in a good position to deal with my former family and neighbours. Independence does not imply that we cut off all links, that there will be no agreements and contracts with our neighbours. We cannot live without our neighbours any more than they can live without us, whatever they may think. I see a new state, a decentralized state. Then among equals we can have our own nationality, our own base to operate from. For years in Quebec we've believed that only the Americans or the anglophone element could manage the development of the economy and run the show. Well, that way of thinking is finished now.

Bruno Roy

Director-General, Société Nationale
des Québécois, Rimouski

(F)

"As long as a dog remains tied — even
if you change the length of the rope —
it is still not free."

La Société Nationale des Québécois, the radical nationalist offshoot of the St.-Jean Baptiste Society, has 46,000 numbers in its Rimouski area branch. English Canada's favourite stereotype of the Quebec nationalist is still the PQ voter who belongs to the St.-Jean Baptiste Society. However, a comparison of Bruno Roy's views with those of Marcel Bureau of the St.-Jean Baptiste Society in Sherbrooke (page 139) should help correct this outdated image.

I am the seventh son in a row in a family of eight sons and four daughters. My father was a farmer and always gave us an example of social commitment. I saw him work very hard to promote the cooperative movement in Quebec and the Caisses Populaires. It is obvious that he passed on his commitment because I discovered when I was about 20 years old that I also was attracted to social causes. And slowly I became committed in political matters. After graduating from the University of Sherbrooke, I taught school for a while and slowly I acquired a feeling of Quebec nationalism.

Why did I become an *indépendantiste?* I think that, like a vast majority of Quebeckers, I had in myself this germ of liberation, of independence. There was no one event that brought this on, it was more like a sequence of events. For me, it started when Daniel Johnson became the premier of the province of Quebec. A new hope was born in Quebec after the Liberal government under Mr. Lesage, which in its first few months had given the greatest promises and finally at the end, became questionable and was in fact questioned. The Johnson government helped open our eyes in Quebec, but after his death we had a difficult period with Premier Bertrand, who didn't continue what Johnson had started. At the same time the Parti Québécois was beginning to be heard of and was already offering a new challenge. I think another thing on the road to independence for me was this Quebecker, Pierre Elliot Trudeau, who was the Prime Minister but who did not at all meet the expectations of Quebeckers. There were several independence-minded groups like the RIN [Rassemblement pour l'Indépendance Nationale], but the PQ was the one that brought us all together in the end, and I've backed them ever since.

In many parts of Quebec, like here, the St.-Jean Baptiste Society has evolved into La Société Nationale des Québécois and there is really no difference between the two groups. Okay, I spoke with the Director of the Associate St.-Jean Baptiste in Sherbrooke too and he is not in favour of independence. True enough. But that's one exception.

This group in Sherbrooke is a federalist group and the option that they have taken is to remain federalists and to promote Canadian unity to a certain extent. It is a society that we consider a dissident society—but in Sherbrooke we've also got a SNQ, so there are opposing groups there.

The first objective of the Société Nationale is to help the people of Quebec. We help organize the national celebrations; we have contests to promote the quality of the French language; we even have a funeral cooperative here. And we do a lot of publicity work on issues like the air traffic controllers. We have 46,000 members in this region who pay $6 a year each and this is what we operate on. We have the largest number of members in Quebec and the second-largest budget after Montreal.

There are a lot of things about Canada that bother me. I have the unfortunate feeling that we are paying a lot of good Canadian money for things that for all practical purposes are only folklore, like the monarchy for example. What can the monarchy bring us? What is a crown to me? What symbolism does it have? None whatsoever! All I know is that somewhere there is a queen, but I cannot recognize her as my queen. A symbol is valid as long as it represents me. I cannot recognize myself as a British subject or a subject of the queen. What has that to do with me? Absolutely nothing. For the English, for Londoners, I am prepared to believe it means something. But for me the monarchy means nothing.

As for Trudeau, it is only since November 15 that Mr. Trudeau is finding the solutions to all our problems—problems that supposedly he's been solving since 1968. We've seen nothing in the way of concrete results from him though.

And John Diefenbaker, now there is a bull-headed Tory. Irrepressible and amusing in debate, but he is a man who is just too hardheaded. His ideas are far too fixed. But he is nevertheless a great man. For a man in his 80s you have to admit he is very sharp indeed, but these days the only thing he seems to be happy with is himself!

Do I think we will win the referendum? You bet I do! The movement cannot be stopped. The people have been held on a leash too long. As long as a dog remains tied—even if you change the length of the rope—it is still not free. And now Trudeau has been trying to get people to believe that Quebec will be liberated in a blood bath. He repeats the slogan "Independence Now" with disdain, and tries to say that Quebec intends to cut itself off from the wealth of New Brunswick, Nova Scotia, or Ontario. Well, that is just not true. We are not such maniacs to believe we can live by ourselves. Only Prime Minister Trudeau is saying that. Not us. He says, "Be careful in Quebec . . . the PQ want to set up barriers." Not true.

People like us will make independence happen. I don't have the impression that the Church will determine anything. Members of the Church—priests, religious people—will become committed, but the Church as an institution I think will take a position only afterward. Unfortunately, we are used to that.

I am sure the Prime Minister has bad dreams at night, I am sure that he doesn't sleep well. But he has no choice in what he does. Trudeau, Chrétien, Jeanne Sauvé, all of them, are completely submerged by the anglophones. But it doesn't matter. The important thing is that independence will take place. To me, what counts is that the Quebec people are now able to recognize their strengths and express them. Look, Norway and Sweden, with populations smaller than Quebec's and with less wealth in the way of forests and hydro power, have succeeded as nations. There has been no bloodshed. There was no hanging. There was no civil war. The citizens of Quebec don't want to live like princes. They want to live in freedom.

Guy Gagnon
Fisherman, Matane
(F)

"The St. Lawrence may be threatened here, but not the French language."

Many Quebeckers with good jobs and steady incomes—particularly working-class individuals less concerned with English cultural domination than their middle-class counterparts—have few immediate reasons to opt for radical change. Guy Gagnon, a married man in his late 30s with one son, is in such a position. He spent the first 14 years of his working life in paper mills in Trois-Rivières and Rivière du Loup. In 1968 he invested his savings in a shrimp trawler and has never regretted the decision. One can only speculate as to whether Guy Gagnon's political views today would be different if he had remained in the paper mill at Trois-Rivières.

My boat is the *Joel Josette* — it's my fourth — a 60-foot, wooden-hulled dragger with Caterpillar diesel engine. She's got radar, sonar, radio telephone, and a CB radio. I work with a two-man crew and we go out for from four to seven days at a time, and leave a day for unloading. My day at the dock is Thursday. We fish eight months a years, from the beginning of April to the end of November, and in the winter we go on unemployment and sometimes take courses on fishing equipment. It's not a bad life. Crew members can earn from $15,000 to $20,000 a year and the boat owner anywhere from $20,000 to $40,000, which is not bad at all. The main problem we have now is that our boats are getting old; they really need to be replaced. Last fall one of the older boats went to the bottom, luckily with no loss of life. But over-all in the shrimp fishery we can't really complain.

No, I didn't vote PQ in the November election. I nearly did but in the end I voted for the Union Nationale, Mr. Rodrique Biron. It seems that I owed something to them. I find it sad to see that party disappear. I wanted to encourage them to get back on their feet and provide some competition for the other parties.

I'm not for independence, but still I'm glad that Quebec has been putting the squeeze on the federal government, the Liberal Party, and the English. I get along in English and my wife is bilingual, but when the English bitch because they see French words on a box of Corn Flakes, then it's time to put them in their place.

Trudeau came here for St.-Jean Baptiste Day this year. Now that man impresses me. But the real problems to us are economic; I think we have the worst area in Canada, economically. Us and Newfoundland. And I don't think René Lévesque can help us much—he has too many other problems. I think the Gaspé will always be slightly behind the rest of Canada because there is not much here in the way of raw materials. A bit of wood and of course fishing.

But as a fisherman I have the impression that soon we will be fishing in a garbage can. The great St. Lawrence is becoming a huge garbage can, slowly but surely. Sometimes we lift our nets to find a barrel of oil or tar there. We have to throw the entire contents in the water because the fish stink. We find logs, bits of cable—everybody is using the St. Lawrence as a dump. Possibly too much money has been spent on the Olympics to do anything about it. They say there is more awareness in the past two or three years regarding pollution. Everybody has been made aware, fine, but the second step should be taken now: prevention.

The St. Lawrence may be threatened here, but not the French language. Most people can't speak English here, so I don't think the French language is in any real danger.

Bona Marin
Iron monger, Cap-Chat
(F)

**"Pierre Elliot Trudeau . . . is playing a
game I don't understand."**

Cap-Chat is a picturesque fishing and lumbering village on the north shore of the Gaspé where unemployment hovers in the 50 percent range. Bona Marin, as a self-employed craftsman fashioning fireplace utensils and decorative iron work, is economically independent and able to provide for his wife and young child, but still very much aware of the severe economic problems faced by many Gaspésians. His views on foreign ownership reflect a common feeling in Quebec that since the federal government has presided over the foreign takeover of the Canadian and Quebec economies, the only hope left for repatriation of Quebec's economy is an indépendantiste government.

I am a confirmed separatist. I voted PQ so that the PQ can try to negotiate what should be settled before separation takes place. But if they don't succeed in negotiating a settlement, then separation anyway. We have nothing to lose. We can't lose anything because we don't have anything. What can we lose?

The first thing to push me toward the PQ was the language issue. When I was applying for a company job a few years back, I was advised to indicate on the sheet that I spoke English. It helped. Now that is going a bit far. That is the first reason I voted PQ. The second reason is economic. If we don't take charge of our economic life now, tomorrow will be too late. In fact, it might be too late already.

All the mining, all forestry, aluminum—that all belongs to foreign interests, American, English, German, Japanese. It all belongs to everyone except to us. When we were younger and went to school we were told, "You live in a rich country." Sure, it's a wealthy country but we are a bunch of poor people living in a wealthy country. Profits don't go to us.

It won't be difficult for Lévesque to do better than Bourassa. That wouldn't be hard at all. In fact, that shouldn't be his goal. He must have more than that in mind. With 75 percent unemployment in this area, Lévesque has got to take a few risks to get things moving. Now, since the election, even Ottawa is trying slightly to do something. But only since November 15, 1976. They are scared; they don't know what's going on. They are trying to put a bit of money in here—LIP projects, and that sort of thing—but up until now the federal government hasn't done very much for Quebec.

Look, to be a Gaspésian means to be poor, to be a Québécois means to be less poor, but not necessarily rich or well off. That's all it means. I remember way back in my schooldays, someone told me a joke but I didn't take it like a joke. He said, "In Quebec you're born to have a small loaf of bread and you'll stay that way. But in Ontario if you can have the whole bakery, take it!"

I think the people of this province have been asleep, politically asleep. There are a lot of people who still don't understand what's going on now. Take the FLQ situation as an example. I say that we don't know everything that took place in 1970 with the Laporte affair. Obviously they committed an act which is reprehensible. A kidnapping is a kidnapping. Social justice doesn't develop from something like that. But I think the FLQ people in exile should all be brought back to Quebec and those here should possibly have their sentences shortened. Several should have been liberated already. Their sentences were too harsh.

Pierre Elliot Trudeau has been hiding his origins. He is playing a game I don't understand. He seems to be always attacking Quebec. Sending the army into Quebec during the October Crisis, that sort of thing that you don't take lightly. Or take the Robin Hood Flour Mills strike recently. When you are in a free country and you see workers who have been trying to negotiate a contract for eight or 10 months being shot and the federal government doesn't send a conciliator, then you just start asking questions about freedom. That whole thing was absolutely awful. Trudeau or his minister should have reacted sooner. A 10-month strike is too long, especially when you see that Robin Hood is American-owned.

What do I think of the Conservative Party? It represents the English Establishment! I don't think that Quebec will ever put Clark into power — I'd be very surprised if they did. No matter what Trudeau might do, Clark will never be elected by the province of Quebec. He represents far too much what Quebeckers have in mind as the English Establishment and Ontario. And he doesn't have enough French Canadians in his party. That is a second error. I will be very surprised if he gets anywhere.

I think that it is quite possible that there will be negotiation between Quebec and the provinces, but not between Quebec and the federal government. There has been a major agreement between Quebec and Newfoundland regarding all the electrical power in Labrador, so that proves that it is already possible. And if it is possible on economic matters, it will be possible for linguistic matters.

I think the federal government has not shown enough of an open mind to understand what is going on here, even though there are a lot of French Canadians at the top in the federal government. We are not asking for the moon. The people we elected on November 15 understand us, and they are there to ask for something much more within reach.

Carmen Blondeau
Housewife, Gaspé
(F)

**"What we have here in Gaspé today is
the two solitudes."**

The gulf between French and English speakers is very democratic — it cuts through large cities, small towns, and rural areas alike. The unilingual tribal members can be found standing in awkward silence in high-rise elevators or passing each other unacknowledged on small-town sidewalks—neighbours but forever strangers. The small, pleasant tourist town of Gaspé has its gulf too, as Carmen Blondeau, in her mid-20s, explained.

In the Gaspé there is a sort of truce between the two ethnic groups, but it is a definite separation. Personally, I've never had any close English friends. Until maybe 40 or 50 years ago the Gaspé was run by the English —money, businesses, the large houses, all belonged to the English. Then there was a reversal—the francophones became the majority. What we have there in Gaspé today is the two solitudes—in peace with each other but very much apart, even at church. There is a good proportion of Catholic anglophones of Irish descent here. On Sunday there is a Mass for the English at 9:30 and then two other Masses are for the francophones. The same priest says both Masses. The one we have now is less bilingual than the previous one, but I assume that he is sufficiently bilingual to provide service to the anglophones. Anyway, I don't attend Mass that often.

Even the bars here are segregated. There is one English bastion in particular. The other places are fairly mixed, but mainly French. Except for the Canadian Legion, of course; that's really an English club. You have to swear allegiance to the Queen to get in and all that, so there are precious few francophones—some but not many. I don't know if they would go as far as singing "God Save the Queen" though! The anglophones here have all their own radio and TV from Moncton, New Brunswick. I couldn't tell you how they view Quebec. I don't know what they think. I know that they're not separatists, that's for sure—but aside from that . . .

I really don't think the English have understood us. They haven't even tried. They have had a majority mentality, and the minority was poor, with no economic power. We stayed quiet, we provided cheap labour for the economy, we didn't bother anyone. But they did not respect us.

Where I personally felt this lack of respect for francophones was on a trip we made last week to New Brunswick. We have relations there and we go every year. My mother's family is still in New Brunswick, around Bathurst. But here's just a very small example of what I mean. I went up to buy chocolate eclairs—you know what those are? So I said, in French, *"Deux éclairs au chocolat."* The saleslady pretended to not understand. So I pointed and she said, "Oh chocolate éclairs!" Now don't tell me that she could not understand *éclairs au chocolat*! Service in stores and businesses is spontaneously English. They wait until the francophone speaks English because they know very well that francophones in New

Brunswick—at least in the north of the province—do speak English. So they wait until the francophone yields.

Now I think that francophones outside Quebec are waking up, even though the New Brunswick francophones are anti-Quebec and always have been. A Quebecker is not liked in New Brunswick, oddly enough. I have seen that a lot in my own family. My father is a Quebecker and my mother is from New Brunswick and there is a sort of . . . I don't know if it is jealousy . . . I really don't know. The Acadian seems jealous of the Quebecker, and possibly feels inferior with regard to his language because the Quebecker speaks better French than he does. The Acadian accent is very different; they use a lot more anglicisms. One thing I find maddening: they will use English terms before using the French terms. Like in mechanics, they will say "fender," or "windshield" instead of using the French word. Now I think that any language owes it to itself to be as pure as possible—not only French in Quebec but any language anywhere.

I don't speak English perfectly but I do consider myself bilingual. I learned English outside the classroom. School was no use whatever to me because the teachers we had could not even speak English! I never had English taught by an anglophone. There was one in primary school who bragged that he had learned English on Corn Flakes boxes, and believe me it showed. I wouldn't have bragged about that!

I should explain that while I am a Péquiste, my mind is not set yet with regard to the independence option. I have been voting for PQ since I was 18, but I still doubt that the PQ government, which is young, can really govern an independent country. This government does not have enough experience to do something like that and this is why I still hesitate with regard to independence. I still have a certain solidarity with Canada—I'd rather be Canadian than American, and I wouldn't like to see the Maritimes annexed by the United States. That could happen if separation took place. Ideally, I would like Quebec to stay in Canada—that would be my first choice—but with Quebec, its mentality, its culture, respected in every way. I think it is really a matter of respect.

Two years ago I was working at Canada Manpower and I met an English-speaking student and we spoke a lot about politics because he was studying political science. For the first time in my life I became aware that an *Anglais* could have respect and love for Quebec. He said he would feel cheated—I think that is the word he used, cheated—if Quebec were to separate. A real Québécois! In Ottawa his room in the university had a large flag of Quebec and in discussions with his classmates he often took the side of the French-speaking Quebeckers. That was a position I have never encountered—an English Quebecker who understood the position of francophones and who told me, "I love

Quebec too. I wouldn't want to have to go and live elsewhere." I was astonished. I have always seen them as able to leave for Ontario tomorrow and be very glad to go. I never thought an anglophone would want to stay here. That really did surprise me.

George Ascah
Nonagenarian, Gaspé
(E)

"My great-great-grandfather, Richard Ascah, fought with General Wolfe on the Plains of Abraham."

For sheer historical continuity personified, George Ascah belongs in this book. His straightforward account of the Battle of the Plains of Abraham was not learned from the books that all Canadians read in school. Mr. Ascah's descriptions come from that more intimate and very special classroom: his own family.

You know, it's true what they say: "Once a man, twice a child." You change when you get older. I notice it.

Yes, I'm 94. The secret? No secret; I've worked hard all my life. When I was young I used to take a little whiskey but no more. As for beer, I don't know the taste of it. And no soft drinks.

My great-great-grandfather, Richard Ascah, fought with General Wolfe on the Plains of Abraham. He was born March 1, 1724, and he was married at St. Paul's Church in Halifax, which is still standing. He came from England via Virginia and took his military training at Halifax. When Wolfe came out in 1758 he picked up his soldiers in Halifax, including my Richard, and he wintered in Gaspé Bay near here. General Wolfe spent most of his winter in a log hut on Peninsula Point. In 1759 he was joined by more ships from overseas and then he set sail for Quebec. Richard Ascah sailed with him as an officer and his wife went along as a nurse.

Wolfe anchored above Quebec City and one night in September he slipped down to Quebec and started landing his soldiers. General

Montcalm had his guards on and they said in French, "Who goes there?" And some of Wolfe's men answered in French, then they overpowered the guards and when daylight broke, General Wolfe had his men all lined up. He told them to put a double charge in their muskets and not to fire until he gave the orders. And the French started marching down, firing. At last Wolfe said, "Fire!" They mowed down so many soldiers that the rest turned and ran. Wolfe and Montcalm were both wounded and died. Richard Ascah wasn't injured.

Not long after the battle Richard and his wife had their first child in Quebec City, a daughter they named Hannah. She later married a man by the name of Abraham Coffin who came up from Kentucky, probably a United Empire Loyalist. Now the first son of Richard Ascah, who would be my great-grandfather, was also named Richard. Born in 1774. This Richard, the second, in 1811 married Sarah Thompson and bought this land we're on today. They have five children, including my grandfather George. He was born on June 3 in 1817. I remember him well. My grandfather inherited part of the original farm and then bought some more land to add onto it. He got married in 1846 and they had my father in 1853. I was born here on the twelfth day of June, 1883.

Roots? Roots? Yes, you could say I've got roots in Quebec.

Georgette Bujold
Housewife, New Carlisle
(F)
"I remember René as a little boy."

A widow with 13 children, Georgette Bujold lives in René Lévesque's childhood house in New Carlisle.

My husband bought this house from Mrs. Dominique Lévesque, the mother of René Lévesque, after the death of her husband 37 years ago. Mr. Lévesque died of kidney disease right here in the upstairs bedroom. He was a lawyer — very well known and liked by both the French and the English here. I used to meet him in church and so on. I knew him quite well. He was not very tall, and balding — a lot like René nowadays. He was a bit more stocky than René, and very distinguished looking. He treated French and English equally in his office.

Mrs. Lévesque was a slight person, a pretty woman and very likable. People here liked her. Mr. and Mrs. Lévesque moved to New Carlisle from Rivière du Loup.

I remember René as a little boy—he's younger than me. I'm 64; he's 56. He was a very intelligent, very active child. He read everything he could get his hands on, and he was a bit of a fighter too. That was René. He liked to argue with the English, and Mrs. Lévesque quite likely encouraged that. Maybe René disliked the English to some extent because they were more favoured than we were as French Canadians. Of course, René's father was a professional man and they lived very well, but it was obvious that the francophones in New Carlisle did not have the same standard of living as the English here. I don't know for sure but possibly René learned to dislike this. He left here fairly young to go to the seminary to study. After his father died, Mrs. Lévesque moved to Quebec City, where René was studying. That's when we bought the house.

Yes, I was happy that the PQ won. A change was needed. You see, we French Canadians were always considered as secondary people. Now we are on the map; we are respected. Since the election, newspaper reporters, the CBC, Radio-Canada, and literally hundreds of tourists have come here. Sometimes as many as 10 or 12 people a day visit the house, nice people. Some of the photographers even pay me to take pictures. And I've given interviews to some journalists. A lot of them promised me a copy of the magazine or article but I have never received anything. That's not very nice, it it? Maybe you'll send me a copy of your book, though.

People ask me what I think about separation. Personally, separating from Canada would hurt me. What I'd like to see is a stable government, a French government, but with the English being respected also. I think bilingualism is a good thing—if you speak English and French, you are rich. You can go anywhere in the world.

But no, I don't want to see independence, not at my age. When the hockey season starts on TV and I hear "O Canada"—well, that's the best part of it!

Henri and Jean-Paul Bujold

Unemployed, New Carlisle

(F)

"René Lévesque hasn't provided me with a job."

For Henri and Jean-Paul Bujold, in their early 20s and eager to work, employment has usually meant federally funded make-work projects or the armed services. As unemployed but functionally bilingual Gaspésians, most of the alternatives open to them seem to exist in English Canada. With obvious bitterness they compare their hopes of job creation brought on by the election of the PQ against the reality of moving to Alberta and British Columbia to find work. At the time of this interview, Henri and Jean-Paul were living with their mother in Lévesque's boyhood house.

Henri: At first I sought employment locally, within the region and New Carlisle itself—I couldn't find anything with the Manpower Centre. I looked in the Ottawa region and again there was no job available. The only job I had for the past two years was winter works and the LIP project of the federal government. They paid about $125 a week. Then in the summer, like a lot of people in the Gaspé area, it is unemployment insurance, except for fishermen. They work in the summer and go on unemployment insurance in the winter.

Now, I'm through here. I am going to Calgary. A lot of people from the region are in Toronto, Moncton, Montreal. Most of the young people go outside for work. In Calgary there is stable employment—something with a future—so I will be able to build a decent life, not remain on unemployment insurance as long as I live. There is no future in the Gaspé area; there is no industry and the kind of job I can get is for the government. It is not pleasant to leave your home but you have to; there is no choice. Here, there is nothing.

Jean-Paul: I left school in 1973 to join the navy. I was stationed in Esquimalt, B.C., on the destroyer *Terra Nova*. I left the navy after my term was up and I came back here to New Carlisle and then I applied at the CEGEP at Gaspé where I did a year there in human sciences and history. Then, to get work, I went north, around the Lac St.-Jean area. I worked for a while at a sawmill. It paid about $150 a week, but the cost of living is high—it's twice as expensive as here, and it is already expensive here. So I eventually quit and came back down here and was on unemployment until November, 1976. Then the Manpower Centre offered me a course in Rimouski as a machine-room assistant. They told us some nice stories: "If you take this course we'll find you a job." Well, I am still here and I still don't have a job. I have the diploma and everything else, but I am on unemployment insurance. All that happened was I got an extension on my unemployment because of the course.

Now I am waiting to re-enter the armed forces—again the navy—the same trade, fire controlman. I'd really like to find a job here but I can't. I applied here at the Ministry of Fisheries; they were looking for a man with experience in boats and all that, and I had had a course in boat machinery in the navy. But they found that I didn't have enough experience so...

Henri: I voted for the Parti Québécois but not for separation. I voted for a change of government because with all the scandals there had been I thought Bourassa was rather corrupt. So I voted for a change of government, but I am rather disappointed. I thought that the PQ would have dealt with the important matters—urgent matters—rather than trying to know whether they would speak English or French. I speak both and have no difficulty with English or French people, but when I have a job then I will be able to worry about whether we speak English or French. The language is of no importance if you are out of work.

Jean-Paul: Well, I voted Liberal because we had a good member here. The PQ doesn't have my confidence. They have good men but I don't agree with their ideology. They want to separate Quebec from Canada. I don't agree with that. First of all, I am a Canadian; secondly, I am a French Canadian. In fact, I would say I am a Gaspésian first and a Canadian second because the region is very important. Mr. Lévesque is a native of the Gaspé area and there are many people who place their faith in him because they knew him when he was younger. We didn't know him but our parents did and so did a lot of people here. They hold that René Lévesque will do a lot for the Gaspé peninsula. But I say, okay, he started the whole thing but he doesn't give the orders, it is the men behind him—they push him. He is just a figurehead, just like the Pope. He has no power.

Henri: The corruption in the Liberal government was obvious; it has been proven. There was the meat scandal; they were all involved in that, so I voted for a better government in the sense that they would be honest. Before November 15, René Lévesque had solutions to all the problems, but on the 16th he must have forgotten them because we've seen no solutions. Unemployment is still as bad as it was. Grants have been cut. There was supposed to be less income tax; now we have a 10 percent tax on children's clothing. Everything is like that. The tax on meals in the restaurants has gone up. He seems to be doing the opposite of what he said he would do and he is still arguing about the language. They are wasting time.

You know, proportionately more francophones are unemployed here than anglos. We'd like to know why! Of course here in New Carlisle the mayor is English, most of the councillors are English. When a project starts up, the same people get the work. I won't name anyone, but I know because I worked here for four months on a LIP project, and it is always the same people. There is a small clique—a little Mafia—it is the same gang who controls everything. You go and ask anyone in New Carlisle. In the LIP project there were 17 employees—14 English and three French—and the francophones are forced to speak English. The boss was English and being French we had to take orders from others, including employees who were hired after us. We had to do what they told us in English. Otherwise, no go!

Jean-Paul: You're going to get us in trouble around here, talking like that.

Henri: No trouble for me. I'm going to be in Calgary when this book comes out!

Jean-Paul: If we hadn't spoken English we wouldn't have had even the small jobs that we had; but if I am going to speak English anyhow, I would rather go to another province where everything is in English, and always work in English. When I was in the navy everything was in English, all the orders. When you spoke with another guy it was in English because francophones aboard ship weren't that numerous. I guess I am more used to working in English than in French.

Henri: There is one thing about the PQ: they haven't done anything wrong because they haven't done anything, period. But if they continue this way, they will sink themselves. There are a lot of people who voted PQ who are disappointed.

Now, if I find a good job in Calgary I'll stay. But it is always more beautiful where you were born—whether that's Westmount or New Carlisle. We were born in this house and it is a good house. We were born here and we've lived here all our lives. Sure, people come and visit here mainly to see René Lévesque's house and all that. But for us it is not René Lévesque's house; it is the house of Mrs. Wilfred Bujold. Look, it doesn't give me a job that René Lévesque was born here, so there is no advantage in that. Some people criticize us for being on unemployment, but what else can we do? A lot of people have advised me to go outside Quebec to find a job—so okay, that is what we are doing.

Jean-Paul: This *was* the house of René Lévesque, but now he lives in Quebec City and he can stay there. It is all very nice for tourists and reporters and writers like you to come and see us and René Lévesque's house, but René Lévesque hasn't provided me with a job. If René Lévesque creates employment in the Gaspé peninsula, then maybe we'll consider it an advantage that he was born around here; but otherwise he is in Quebec City and seems to be concerned mainly with Quebec City.

Paul Dallain
Postmaster, New Carlisle
(E)
"The school René and I went to here had one room at first; then later they added a second."

The calmest person I met in New Carlisle was postmaster Paul Dallain. Perfectly bilingual and with a secure job, Mr. Dallain is happily immune from the chronic employment worries of many Gaspésians, and is able to understand and appreciate both cultures in that special way reserved for the fluently bilingual. And to the extent that the child is father to the man, Mr. Dallain is also in a position to know more of René Lévesque than the public image reveals.

My father came here direct from Jersey to work at the age of 14 and later on he married my mother, who was a local girl. You see that view out there over the water? That's why I'm postmaster of New Carlisle and not Postmaster General in Ottawa. In those days there were fewer French families in New Carlisle. We spoke mostly English at home, but spoke French to my grandmother. And because we were Roman Catholics it was only normal that we went to the French school.

In those days, back in the '30s, there were Catholic and Protestant elementary schools here, but no Catholic high school. If you were Catholic and wanted your children to have high school, you either sent them to the large Protestant school, which the Church was strongly against, or you paid to send them off to a private Catholic school. We only had seven years of schooling in our system, and our parents just took it for granted they needed permission to send their children to another high school. Most of them didn't want to hassle with the Church, so if the Church didn't give permission to go, you sort of took it for granted you couldn't go. That's the way things were, you see.

But around 1938-39 things started to loosen up a bit, and there were a few French children who continued their education at the Protestant high school in New Carlisle, and there was a hell of a hassle with the bishop. It was the same hassle you get with marriages between the religions. We had a seventh grade here in New Carlisle, and after that if you wanted to continue your education you had to leave home. These were depression years and most people couldn't afford to. We were a family of seven and I was a twin. So my father sent my brother and me to Quebec after grade seven. That was difficult enough for him. He couldn't really afford that. It would have been so much easier had we gone to the high school and got our high school education, which was a lot better than the three-year commercial course I got in Quebec anyway.

When I went off to Quebec, René Lévesque, who was a classmate of mine, went off to Gaspé School, which was a classical college. The school René and I went to here had one room at first; then later they added a second. We were always in the same class right through. There were grades one to three in one classroom and four to seven in the other. This was for both French- and English-speaking Catholic boys and girls. If you were English-speaking at home you took your subjects in English; if you were French-speaking you took your subjects in French. The one teacher did both languages. For instance, doing your Canadian history, when she asked a question, she would speak to you in English, then go on to someone in French. And in the mornings we all took a dictation in French, whether we were English- or French-speaking. Then in the afternoon we took a dictation in English. Consequently we all became bilingual. We had some good teachers. They had to be pretty good to put up with us because there were times — with that many in the class, two languages and four grades — when the teachers had a hard time of it.

There weren't that many people, as far as I know, who were that close to René. But we would go to his birthday party or to his New Year's party. The Lévesques were the only ones I knew of who celebrated New Year's instead of Christmas. In those days a few French-speaking Canadians still had their gifts on New Year's Day instead of Christmas, but in New Carlisle the Lévesques were the only ones.

René spoke French and English, like we all did. He certainly wasn't known as a hard worker at school. He didn't have to. He had a good memory. It didn't bother him whether he brought his books home or not. We'd find his books under the snow at the rink in the wintertime! We'd shovel the rink in the morning on the way to school and find his books. We had hockey here in those days, but I didn't play on any team and I don't recall that he played. But my cousins had an ice rink and we would stop there and play a game with or without skates, and René would be with the rest of us.

On the coast here we take our politics seriously enough. I'm not too pleased at all with the direction things are taking, but I believe some good will come of it though. When you have troubles I believe it's because something somewhere is not right. We often hear the comment: "I don't see what the trouble is. Everything was always fine around here." You know? Well, if everything was always fine, how come we've got all these troubles?

Most people tend to not make too great an effort to understand other people, and most people don't try that much to be tolerant. In a small community no one can afford to make bad friends, but lots of people do. Personally, I can get along in English or French, so I don't have some of the problems that certain people have. And I realize that it's bloody hard to learn a second language. Take Stanfield. It was very difficult for him, it was a hell of a time in life for him to have to learn a second language. But most people are not that willing or anxious to become bilingual.

Russell Smith
Retired railwayman, New Carlisle
(E)
**"Wolfe was a leader and he came in
and he cleaned her up!"**

In obtaining interviews for this book, I spoke with hundreds of people in addition to those who appear in these pages. More than three-quarters of those I met were francophone. Nowhere at any time did I encounter, from any of them, the type of sentiment that follows. No one who knows Quebec at all would suggest that Russell Smith's views are typical of English Quebec, but it is important to recognize that this type of thinking still exists in this country.

I remember when I was a young fellow going downtown, I would meet about three French people on the street and they were servant girls for people like the sheriff of the town, the doctor, a well-to-do farmer. And that was the only three people that I knew at that time who were French. I have lived here all my life, but today I go downtown and I don't know half the people. The percentage of French has increased and the English have got to leave because they can't get work, but the French, there is all kinds of work for them, and I don't know why. That's the way it has been going for a good few years. Our Regional School Board down here is supposed to be Protestant — a *Protestant* school board — but there's half French in there. They are taking over, that's all. They are really taking over.

But they don't win all the time. I remember back in 1970 my wife said to me one day, she said, "Did you notice anything coming through town?" I said, "Now what is there in New Carlisle to notice?" I figured I knew everything that was there. She said, "The bank — the sign on the bank has changed." I said, "What do you mean?" She said, "Well, there was French on one side and English on the other, but now it is down and there is French on both sides." "Well," I said, "that's nice."

So I went down the next day and sure enough. So I asked a few people that I know had money in the bank and had been dealing there all their life what they thought of it and what they were going to do about it. "Well, what can we do?" they said. "Oh," I said, "you don't want to do anything? Well, I will have to try and do something."

So I came home and I wrote a letter to the head office in Montreal and I explained the situation and told them if that's the way they wanted to run the Bank of Nova Scotia in New Carlisle, I would take a petition out and ask that all the money belonging to the English in there would be put in the French bank. And the next day the man who received the letter phoned direct to the Bank of Nova Scotia and had the manager pick a man off the street or wherever and get that sign down. And a couple of days after, it was followed by a nice letter thanking me for the information. Ha-ha-ha!

How do I feel about the PQ victory? Well, I think it was handed to them, right in their hand, because the Liberal government was such a disgrace. They didn't know what they were doing. They were spending money right and left, and people was fed up with it, and in order to get clear of them they put the PQ in, which was a mistake. Half of them is sorry now. They are starting to wake up.

I hear the government won't let the English children go to English schools now. But if you notice, the big shots are sending their children to schools where they can speak English. But the ordinary fellow, he keeps his child home and the French is just put to him, that's all. He will have to remain for the rest of his life in Quebec. He can't go to another province because he can't speak English. But maybe by then the Prime Minister will have that changed because he is doing very hard work to get French throughout Canada. They are going to start the language program in the schools, where it should have started in the first place. That other language policy of his was the biggest waste of the taxpayer's money that was ever made law! That was a disgrace.

I have no use for the PQ. They don't know what they are talking about because as a province Quebec could never survive alone; they couldn't. No way could they. Ahhh, they can't even give a bit of work on the roads; where are they going to get the money for all that stuff?

Oh sure, I knew René Lévesque when he was growing up here. Yeah, he was radical even then. They had to tie him to a tree in his back yard because he used to throw rocks at people—English people, I guess. Yeah, he was a real bad boy. I didn't chum around with him—you know, have anything to do with him—but I know a lot of boys who did.

What do I think of Mr. Trudeau? Well, he's a hard man to understand. He says one thing one time, and turns right around and says differently another time. I remember two years ago Trudeau saying, "Separatism is finished in Quebec." Now they're in power. So he can't be very smart. Or maybe he is smart. I think he is 100 percent for separatism, and this is just his cute way of putting everything together. He is a very cute politician. And in my own heart I think that he is glad Quebec is going the way it is. That's what I think. Sure. He and Lévesque at one time was terrible good friends, terrible good friends, and they're probably still good friends, but he doesn't want the people to know that. He is just playing smart.

I think he would like to see French all through Canada, the same as in Quebec. The government in Ottawa should be stopping things like that. It's really gone too far. Pearson is the man that I blame for the whole issue, the whole issue. Quebec wanted this and Quebec wanted that . . . if there was a Frenchman in Quebec with a bad cold, he would run and wipe his nose, give him this, give him that, and give him the other thing. It started from that and once they get something—it's the same as the man stealing: if he steals a little thing it will lead to a big thing after a while if he doesn't get caught. That is the same way it happened in Quebec—started with little things, then got bigger and bigger. Now they want to separate!

I'll say, though, that the government's action in October, 1970, was all right. They had to stop the FLQ. They would have blown the whole place up, so the army had to be called in to stop them. And those guys in jail, they should stay there until their term has expired. That's the matter with our law today, they're too lenient. The law protects the fellow that commits a crime and the victim, they don't think anything of him.

The PQ would release those FLQ guys if they could. The PQ are all a bunch of radicals, and I would say that Lévesque is not the worst. It is the ones that are pushing him and if they keep on pushing him, and if he keeps on smoking, he is going to go off his rocker. He can't stand the pressure. It is real bad, real bad. We need a leader to clean Quebec up, eh? The same as back in Wolfe's time. Wolfe was a leader and he came in and he cleaned her up! So this has got to be cleaned up again and all the people now, all they want is a leader and I am sure they would follow that leader. I would follow too.

One mistake the English people of Quebec are making is picking up and moving out. They are just giving the PQ what they want. Why don't they just stay here, eh? No, no, *we're* not leaving—we are established here and here we are going to stay. But the more that leave, the better Quebec's chances are for separation.

And people outside Quebec, they don't care what happens here. Well, maybe some really care but some, like I say, don't care now—but will probably feel sorry for that in days to come. Hah! Maybe it'll be too late then. Because I'll tell you something else. I think this situation has gone that far now that it can only be settled by violence now. I truly believe that. It can't be settled no other way because the more they want and the more they get, the more they want in Quebec. Yes, I would say that it will be settled by the sound of marching feet—on the pavements of Montreal and Quebec. If they keep on the way they are going, that will come. It's not the little places like New Carlisle that are pushing things—the French people and the English people always got along the very best here.

No, it's the big places, eh? They figure that the English have got all the good jobs and the high-paying jobs. Well, somebody had to run business! If a French family had three children, two girls and a boy, the girls were made nuns and the boy probably a priest. So that wasn't business. And they can't run a business much anyway. They haven't got the brains for that. During the war they didn't want to go to war. Everybody put a dress on to be a priest. Now they are fighting with Canada, their country! If it wasn't for the English they wouldn't have a country. De Gaulle, at the time of the war, ran to England three or four times to see if he could hide. And how long did it take the Germans to march through France?

De Gaulle shouldn't have been allowed to leave Montreal. If that had happened in the States, he'd have never left there. They would have killed that right there. The big frog face. He shouldn't have been allowed to leave Montreal, coming in and meddling with another country. Should have carried him off, put him in the St. Lawrence with a big brick around his neck.

Alain and Félicienne Thibault

Alain—unemployed,
Félicienne—artisan, New Carlisle

(F)

"The English in the Gaspé are very aggressive because they are scared."

The bases of racial prejudice, intolerance, and suspicion can often be traced to that socially destructive combination: fear and ignorance. The Thibaults have experienced prejudice at the community and individual levels, as have many of the French Quebeckers in this book; but they have gone beyond their initial hurt and anger to attempt to understand reasons for this anti-French prejudice. Following this conversation I joined the Thibaults and their three-year-old daughter for lunch before leaving New Carlisle.

Alain: Independence will certainly come. It may take a while but it will come. We have been in Confederation for 110 years—it never worked, and it is not going to work now. There are always the arguments between French Canadians and English, or Quebeckers and English Canadians. Just listen to the news: they're always drawing swords. I find the English TV service anti-French. It tends to build a sort of barrier between Quebec and the anglophones. I don't say that it is always lies, but fairly often things are exaggerated. On Canada AM, in the morning, seldom a day goes by when there is not something about Quebec, and they like to give you the impression that Quebec is always arguing with the rest of English Canada. Now I don't have anything against the rest of Canada but what I want is to have equal rights. Equal rights means, for instance, the same possibility of economic advancement as the English. I want to work, you know. I'm a teacher by training.

Yes, I do think Quebec will be independent. It's irreversible! If we have to live within Confederation longer, we will do so, but personally I wouldn't like it. The English in the Gaspé have never wanted to integrate with the French. If they had integrated, they would be bilingual today, but they didn't make the effort to learn our language. This still happens in New Carlisle, where anglophones still refuse to learn French. I will go even further: the English School Board here is fiercely anti-French. I know—I worked for them for three years. The anglophones here are an isolated small minority that refuses to integrate. They are Loyalists— you mustn't forget that—and Loyalists who never learned to live with the rest of the world. In New Brunswick they even have Loyalist Day celebrations every July! I make an effort to communicate with them, but they don't make any effort to communicate with me. I speak some English; I get along. But I have seldom been able to speak French with an anglophone. You're the exception, my friend. I have always had to speak English.

My brother's boss—he's American—is very proud to say "*bon jour*," "*merci beaucoup*," "*je parle français*" —but that's all he can say. In the past we always used to say "very nice," but not anymore. Now, you are in my country and you will speak my language. I don't refuse to speak yours, but you speak mine.

Félicienne: Toronto is where I had the shock of my life. In Canada I learned that there was a difference between English and French Canadians. I had never been brought up with that idea in mind. To me, in Canada there weren't two races; we were Canadians and that was it. I never identified myself as a Quebecker. When I was a student in the United States, I was always a Canadian. But when I arrived in Toronto I was a Quebecker, a frog, I was the different one, the one who was not accepted at parties or anything else. Things didn't work out at all.

My two sisters were at the University of Toronto and my brother was at St. Michael's College. They had the same experience as me. All our friends were foreigners; I mean people from other countries. Any French friends we had were franco-Ontarians. My sisters and brother and I were made to feel like foreign students. I lived entirely apart from reality in Toronto because I never entered a home in Toronto. Never. Nor anywhere else in Ontario. In a year and a half that we spent there, none of us was ever invited into a family home in Toronto, or Ontario, except once a friend of my sister, who was a franco-Ontarian, invited her to her home in northern Ontario.

Why were we not accepted? Possibly we gave them a feeling of insecurity since as francophones we were something they didn't understand. The Englishman is used to travelling far and wide in his own language, but when he faces something unknown, it scares him.

Alain: The English in the Gaspé are very aggressive because they are scared. I can recall after the elections, on November 16, English people saying, jokingly perhaps, we would take the English and put them into reservations like the Indians. That's ridiculous! But the English here are afraid—afraid.

Félicienne: I think that's it. And another barrier back then was that nobody knew anything about Quebec. There was not an Ontarian with whom I went to school who had visited Quebec. They knew nothing about nothing.

Alain: Our independence will be just as advantageous to anglophones as to francophones. Let's not forget that independence for Quebec — our economy, all our wealth that has been going to the United States for a long time — is just as favourable to the English as to the French.

Félicienne: For the new Quebec I would like to see a country different from the other provinces. Free of all traces of Americanism and large-scale capitalism. I would like to see Quebec smaller, more picturesque, more honest, closer to the earth, less industrialized. That is the total antithesis of the present century, but this is what I would like to see.

Chapter 5

Saguenay, Lac St.-Jean, North Shore

The *Saguenay, Lac St.-Jean area is one of the unexpected surprises of Quebec. The road north from Quebec City passes through Laurentides Provincial Park, climbing 800 meters through tall stands of spruce and pine, passing hydro pylons carrying power south from the massive northern hydro developments. Two hundred and twenty km. from Quebec City, Chicoutimi comes into view, flanked by suburban shopping centres and the regional campus of the University of Quebec. This area of unexpectedly rich farmland, excellent hunting and fishing, and spirited, industrious people is known to few visitors.*

This region was first opened to settlement in the 1830s, and pioneers continued to homestead this region well into the 1900s. The first part of this century saw the rapid development of hydro-electric power, which in turn promoted the pulp and paper and aluminum-processing industries, resulting in stable wages and steady employment. This part of Quebec is widely known as militant union territory and a PQ stronghold, a reputation borne out in the provincial election results which sent six Péquistes and a lone Liberal south to Quebec City.

The road west from Chicoutimi leads through 66 km. of lush dairyland to Lac St.-Jean and the Pointe Bleue Indian Reserve. Here some 1,700 Montagnais Indians live, descendants of hunters and fishermen who have occupied these lands for the past 6,000 years. The rest of us are the newcomers. The native people here are a minority within a minority and have serious misgivings about the Quebec independence movement.

The final leg of this journey led me north again from the Saguenay, Lac

St.-Jean area to the more rugged North Shore of Quebec, a region of still unexplored wilderness bordered by a 1,300-km. Atlantic coastline. Apart from James Bay, this is the least populated area in the province but one that is very wealthy, thanks to the massive hydro developments, iron deposits, and forest resources. This is an area of busy restaurants and bars, luxury car dealers, excellent schools and recreational facilities. Statistics Canada shows that the boom town of Sept Îles (population 30,617; 89 percent French) had the highest 1975 average salary level in Canada at $12,592 as compared with Ottawa as $11,699 and Montreal's $10,872. Twenty-five years ago the population of this city was 1,500.

Saguenay, Lac St.-Jean, North Shore is almost completely French and several people I met wondered aloud why more English Canadians didn't visit their region. If the experience of this writer is any indication of the hospitality afforded the visitor, I can only recommend that more travellers head north. This part of Quebec and its people deserve to be better known.

Suzie Fortin
Family-planning worker, Chicoutimi
(F)

"There are five million of us surrounded by English everywhere — in the United States, the Maritimes, and the other English provinces ... I am a little afraid."

The sense of cultural and linguistic isolation felt by most Quebeckers, save that very small completely bilingual, bicultural group, is extremely difficult for an English Canadian to understand. The anglophone takes his international mobility and ease of access to things and places American for granted, and it rarely occurs to him that one-quarter of his fellow-countrymen might feel ill at ease outside Quebec, let alone Canada. Suzie Fortin is one of the many Quebeckers who feel like strangers in their own land.

I was born here in Chicoutimi in 1943. I work at the regional birth-planning association as a coordinator and have been here for about four years. This association deals with contraception, sexuality. I love the work, we cover the entire region and I go as far as Chibougamou.

I am married and have two children. Our family life is very rich and rewarding and we have frequent meetings, especially when my husband can come home for lunch. This is a very important moment in our lives. And then everyone returns to his own particular activities until we meet again in the evening and we spend the evening together as a family.

Family life here is intense. People of my generation generally come from rather large families, but that has all changed now. Now the average number of children per family here in the Saguenay, if I just look on my own street for instance, would be three or four. Contraception is used much more here in Quebec now; five years ago it was used in secret and with a great deal of difficulty. I participated in the founding of the association, and in 1968 when we founded the association the Archbishop's Palace did not accept us for a year because we were doing work that was condemned. We could talk only about the rhythm method. It was difficult for me during that period because people in the Bishop's Palace know me personally, and also my family. In 1970 we left and when we came back four years later things had changed. The Church no longer intervened directly.

Even today this job is still not the best thing to be doing at times — we were talked about in the press this year when the bishop attacked the association and denounced the work that we were doing. He said the little notebook that we use in order to give out information — it's called *The Little Guide to Family Planning* — is immoral and perverse. So we are still denounced from time to time in public. However, what the Church thinks does not influence people in their daily choices, so it poses very little problem, at least from what I have been able to see and judge. It is just as if people have said "Well, it's not the Church's business; it is our business." Of course, in some areas which are a little bit more conservative — from a moral point of view — it might be different but the population as a whole doesn't think this way. People don't consider themselves as being banned by their Church because of their birth-control practices. They remain practicing Catholics. This is a big change.

In general, I find people here are independent-minded — I think it is because of the geographic situation. We are isolated here. Chicoutimi is a beautiful city. Life isn't too fast, and nature is always close at hand. You still hear birds here; there are trees, and the forest isn't far. If you want to go off in the bush you can. It is like being a small country within a larger country here. There is a mentality of innovation, of creativity, which is really interesting. Of course it has disadvantages because any new fad really takes on quickly here. Social Credit was very popular here before elsewhere—all kinds of things like this. People love new fads: they don't want to be behind the times. They are very warm, warm-hearted, too. More tourists from the rest of Canada should visit us. A few come now, but not really very many. We'd like to see more.

No, I am not bilingual, but I can read English—I learned it at school. I live my life completely in French, but I can practice my English during my holidays because we always go to the Maritimes.

To be honest, I think that I have a mental block when it comes to English in the sense that I react negatively to it. I want to remain French; it is just as if I was to tell myself I must not speak English because otherwise I will become English. There are five million of us surrounded by English everywhere—in the United States, the Maritimes, and the other English provinces. Geographically, there is a danger, I am a little afraid. If we are not careful and if we really don't insist on it, I think that the natural trend then would be outright assimilation.

What is the Quebec identity? Well, I haven't really thought a lot about this, but I will give you the ideas that come to mind. What makes me a little different is perhaps my way of looking at the world. What seems to distinguish me is my way of looking at things—a certain sense of humour, a certain way of not taking oneself too serious, not being too sensitive. Perhaps being more able to see the pleasant side of life.

The English are more serious, more established, and stereotyped in their way of thinking and their way of doing things. The first few days after I arrive in an English environment I look for Quebeckers, and I recognize them by their smile. They laugh, they sing, whereas the English are always more pragmatic and serious. That's how you can spot them. My first day outside of Quebec is always rather sad. My first feeling is always one of being ill at ease. I am no longer at home. I am not quite sure that I am going to understand people. I am not sure that I am going to be on equal terms. It takes me a few days to adjust and to acquire confidence. I know it is due to myself as much as to others, but this is how I feel. Then after two or three days it is okay and then there is no problem.

I appreciate the fact that you did not call me a separatist. Yes, I am an *indépendantiste*. For a while I was very, very active in the PQ Party. I think that independence is essential. Whether it happens exactly as provided for by the party is not important. There might be other ways to reach real independence and we might find it. Political independence is not the only way. But the idea of independence is basic. Just like I would be fantastically disappointed if my son would stay always on his mother's apron strings. I want him to become a man and become independent. The same applies to Quebec. I want Quebec to be independent. Because we are different.

To be independent, for me, means able to do what you feel you want to do. You ask, "Is it necessary to have a new country for that?" No, not necessarily. In my opinion, what is important is for us to be able to fulfill our aspirations as a people within the political framework which will allow it. If Confederation will allow it, fine! Excellent! Bravo! If Confederation does not allow it and the only thing left is separation and disassociation—okay! What is dangerous is people who are not sure of themselves. When people are proud and affirm themselves, then life together, personally or politically, is possible.

In Canada today I think there is lack of understanding—a deep one—on both sides. I think we know the English very little and that the English know the French very little. I don't know if it is possible to get a well-rounded view of English Canadians through the media here in Chicoutimi. What I do see is that we get very little information on the rest of Canada. Oh, we get news of an airplane crash for instance in Manitoba, or things like that, but that doesn't help to understand a country.

We need to know what are people out there doing every day. What are they like? What makes them vibrate? What are they working on at the present time? What do people do for recreation? What are the volunteer organizations? That's what helps in understanding a country and that's what we don't know. We get nothing. I would say not only not very much but nothing at all. I don't think I could even name the provincial premiers. But what would really interest me if we had it on TV would be people, not politicians.

Of course there are extremists here—well, I don't want to name any names, but people who say, "We shall speak only French in Quebec. No one is ever going to speak English again in Quebec." But we are surrounded by an environment which is exclusively English, so it is idiotic to say that because people won't come here, or if they do come here they are no longer going to speak English. And when we want to go to other provinces the same would be true. I'd find it very unfortunate if Quebec became a kind of ghetto. But outside of that worry, I am optimistic.

Bertrand Tremblay
Newspaper editor, Chicoutimi
(F)

**"I think that Quebeckers are far more
hospitable than the French."**

*It is a long way from Chicoutimi to Paris; and after the Conquest of 1759
Quebec's ties with France were severed. It can be fascinating for an
anglophone to view through Québécois eyes some of the cultural differences
that today distinguish a Quebecker from a Frenchman. The well-travelled
editor of Chicoutimi's daily newspaper,* Le Quotidien, *Bertrand Tremblay, is
in a position to offer that perspective.*

I was born in this region. My parents came from here—they are still
living. My father has just celebrated his 80th birthday. On his side, the
Tremblay side, we are descended from Pierre Tremblay, who came here
to establish himself at Ste.-Anne de Beaupré about 300 years ago. All the
Tremblays are supposed to go back to this original Pierre Tremblay. My
mother came from just south of Chicoutimi.

Yes, I am a real Quebecker. To my mind, to be a Quebecker is to
belong to a people who are different from the whole of North America.
We are! Our culture has been maintained and preserved for three
centuries, a culture which is different and which is French. If we were
ever going to lose this culture, which we hold very dear, we would have
lost it after the Conquest of 1759. All the leaders, all the well-educated
people, left Quebec after the Conquest and headed back to France. What
was left in the way of educated people? Just the missionaries. There
would not be this Quebec culture if the missionaries had not stayed and
worked among the people. They alone remained with the 60,000
Canadiens who were descendants of France, who were poor, who had no
education but who had a great deal of heart, good judgement, and
immense determination. So to be a Quebecker for me is to be proud to
belong to this race. I am a descendant of Normans, of French rural
people—truly France at its best, its good, basic side.

I hope, personally, that we will be able to preserve Confederation but
with a respect for our culture. As a Quebecker, I have always been
Canadian, which is to say I belong to this community of Canadians. But
one thing I deplore is that, in my opinion, there has not really been any
respect for our Quebec culture on the part of other Canadians. It was

ignored by saying, "Oh well, Quebeckers will sooner or later assimilate."

We haven't assimilated, but we've adopted some English customs along the way that set us apart from France—things like the English breakfast. I hate the French breakfast—*le croissant*, that famous *croissant*. Even the coffee! It is undrinkable! And as far as sports are concerned, of course we are North Americans. We like football, baseball, hockey, whereas soccer is more popular in Europe. The way we take our holidays, going camping, is the American way, not the French way. And we travel like Americans do. We like long trips. We like to travel, whereas the Frenchman stays home. When he travels it is because he was invited to go but otherwise he stays put on the Mediterranean.

Another basic difference I would say between the metropolitan Frenchman and the Quebecker is that the Quebecker tries to get to know people before judging them. The Frenchman from Paris judges them before getting to know them. I should make a distinction here—a very clear distinction—between the Frenchman from Paris and the Frenchman from outside Paris. This second type is closer to our mentality, our way of looking at things, more so than the Frenchman from Paris.

I think that Quebeckers are open and frank. But the Parisian is a city person, similar in many ways to the Londoner, the New Yorker, or whoever. Parisians are open to the universe but it takes a tremendous effort for them to meet their neighbour. A tremendous effort. I think that Quebeckers are far more hospitable than the French.

The PQ seemed to be the only alternative to the government in power in November, so I voted PQ but I did not vote separatist. A desire to give Quebec a better government certainly helped the PQ in the Saguenay–Lac St.-Jean area. There were also several local factors which did not help the Liberal Party; for instance the strike which lasted five and a half months at Arvida. There was a great deal of social unrest; the situation was depressing; people were also angry at the government's extravagance and weakness.

I am a federalist because I think that we have a country which is the envy of the world. I think that we have in this Canada all the resources, all the possibilities, to be able to develop, maintain, and improve our situation in this world symphony. I am also a federalist because I am aware that we live in America. I am conscious that political formulas don't change reality and I am a federalist because we, here in Saguenay–Lac St.-Jean, live by trade with the outside: 95 percent of our production is sold outside Quebec, mainly to the United States and to Europe. Pulp, paper, aluminum, these industries are located here partly because of the cheap hydro-electric power.

I wouldn't really want us to be isolated. I wouldn't want any artificial boundaries to be set up around Quebec. I don't believe in a bilingual Canada from one end of the country to the other, but I do think that there is a francophone community outside Quebec which deserves to survive and which the anglophone majority can respect. With regard to the West, well, I don't have too much confidence there — they are too far away, much too removed and the mentality will probably never be really receptive to us. The West has never really understood the justification for the presence of the francophones and has always done everything possible to destroy us. The region is still new — it was opened up just 100 years ago and they don't understand us yet. But I do think that Ontario is sincere when it sees that finally the francophone presence can be enriching and rewarding.

Richard Lavoie
Factory worker, Chicoutimi
(F)

"One day somebody called my buddy a "gorf" — you know, "frog" spelled backward."

A 32-year-old native of Chicoutimi, Richard Lavoie joined the navy at the age of 17 and was stationed at the Cornwallis and Shearwater naval bases in Nova Scotia during his training in 1963. He left the navy three years later and returned to Chicoutimi, where he now lives with his wife and daughter.

After I joined the Canadian navy I had to spend four months in Montreal learning English. Then I was sent to the Cornwallis Naval Base. The first day on the parade square they started explaining things to us, and myself and the five other French guys who were there, we just didn't understand anything. It took us 15 days to get used to their accent in Nova Scotia. And I was bilingual at that point!

When we arrived, there were fellows from all over Canada. It was like a circus. They looked at us French Canadians like we were different people because we have a heavy accent. We were accepted by the people from Ontario, New Brunswick, and Prince Edward Island but the guys from

Vancouver and the West did not accept us at all. I'll tell you a story about that.

A French Canadian friend and myself were very friendly with an English guy from Calgary, I believe it was. Good buddies, we were—one would defend the other, that sort of thing. And then one day somebody called my buddy a "gorf"—you know, "frog" spelled backward. So he got angry and there was a fight with an English guy—a different one, I forget where he was from. We let them go ahead at first but the fellow from Calgary, who was friends with us, he ended up jumping my friend to defend the Englishman who had insulted him. Not good.

Another thing I remember very clearly. My buddy and I used to speak French together in the evening, after hours when we were in our bunks. Well, at one point one of the chiefs forbade us to speak French. He said, "If you are caught speaking French again, you are going to run around the parade square." They even forbid us speaking French after hours. I had a lot of difficulty getting used to that sort of thing. We didn't understand much of what they were talking about because most of the time they spoke fast with a local accent. And sometimes when I wanted to speak, I didn't have the exact words come to mind immediately, so I couldn't say it. It got awkward. All this was before Trudeau, of course.

Later, when I was based at Shearwater, we would go off the base, to Halifax, to go dancing or partying, in restaurants and so on. There, we were accepted because they are used to seeing people from all over. In fact, we were better liked than the English Canadians who went there.

For a while I went out with a local girl from Halifax. I never had any problem with her parents—I went to her house and I was received like a member of the family. Never had any problem with them on that account. I told them I was from Quebec and they accepted me. But people in Halifax I found accept other people very well because it is a fairly cosmopolitan city. But I tell you very frankly, Canada is not a bilingual country.

I am in favour of change, in favour of our language not being scoffed at by the rest of Canada. Let it be known that here we speak French. If somebody comes from outside, they should speak French to us. I am very proud of being a Quebecker, but separatism—I have mixed feelings about that. I am not a separatist with regard to finances and that sort of thing, or with regard to government. But we have to keep our language . . .

English Canadians must get it through their skulls that we are a people who have a different language and a different culture. We don't think like Englishmen; we think in our own way. If English Canadians can get it through their skulls that in Quebec you speak French and everything is done in French, I don't see any point in separation.

Philippe Laforest
Pioneer, St.-Nazaire
(F)

"Keep in mind that when I arrived here there were no roads; I was in the forest."

Approximately 66 km. east of Chicoutimi at the end of an unpaved road several miles from the small town of St.-Nazaire lives a remarkable pioneer. Philippe Laforest, born June 7, 1895, lives in a comfortable log cabin with his wife, near the original farm he homesteaded in the early part of the century. Mr. Laforest's experience is that of the earliest settlers on the land of New France, repeated since the days of Champlain, and still recurring in the remoter regions of the country. He speaks of the land with an intense pride and an almost mystical passion that is common only to those who have cleared, cultivated, and improved it with their own hands.

When somebody wants to write a book he has to find legendary characters or fictitious persons. The story I'm going to tell you is absolutely true. The main character is an interesting person and you are looking at that person now.

It was on June 20, 1910, and the sun was shining beautifully. It was extremely warm — must have been around 100 degrees Fahrenheit. The ground was dry and the brush crackled under the feet. I arrived on the shore of the river near where St.-Nazaire stands today around 10 in the morning.

The first thing I did was strike a match and set fire to the brush. In a few minutes flames were shooting 100 feet in the air. It was grand — rather beautiful and sinister at the same time. That evening, when the fire had burned itself out, I looked at the work I had done. The fight had begun between the settler and the virgin forest. The following morning I got down to work. I had a stout heart and strong muscles. I was armed with an axe and a saw and I chopped down and piled up those giant fire-blackened trees to finish burning all that wood. And that evening, after a hard day's work, the earth and myself were very similar. We were both black as crows.

The following spring I seeded that land and oats grew to a height of six feet. I did not need much grassland for my mare and two cows. A few years passed and I got married. Children were born, grew up, and left me as their turn came to found homes of their own. Every time one left, it was like a dagger in my heart. It lasted a week or two and life became normal again. Twenty-eight years passed, then one day adversity hit like lightning. Several fires in a row destroyed my property and I lost several members of my family, including my wife. A few years later I was married again. And again the children grew and like the first time began leaving me in turn to found homes of their own. And like the first time, every time one left it was like a dagger in my heart. It lasted for a while and life became normal again.

I can recall one day Harry, my eldest son who was deathly ill, came to spend two days at my house before dying. We were sitting under a shade tree because it was quite warm, having a drink and talking quietly, when suddenly he said, "Father, did you sell that palomino? If not, I would like you to drive me over to see it again." We arrived at his old farm, he got off the buggy, he opened the gate, and he walked a short distance into the field. That was 31 years ago, and I can still see him in my mind. He started talking. He was saying farewell to his land. I will not tell you his exact words, but when he came back to the buggy to return to my place I can't tell the one who was crying the more. Two months later we buried him in the family plot. It was unfortunate because I think he would have been a very good farmer.

Then the years passed. One evening toward the end of July I was coming back from work through a field of grain — the hay and oats that had grown to a height of six feet. There was a slight breeze and the ears of oats and barley brushed my face as I went by. So I stopped to simply look and smell. And that farm that I loved as much as my wife and more than myself, I found it beautiful, large, and prosperous. That land I had loved so much, that I had cleared myself, I was the undisputed master of, and I was proud of my accomplishment.

Sometime later, when the years began to feel heavy upon my shoulders, I decided to bid farewell to my land. One lovely evening in September as I was coming back from the city, where I had gone in to sign the final papers, as I got out of the car, I again looked at the land of mine, which I had loved so much. It seemed to be opening its arms to me and saying, "Stay with me . . . don't go away. I only have you and the last of your sons. For 60 years I have been feeding you well, along with your wife and children. Stay with me." I entered the house heavy-hearted and with my head bowed. Needless to say, it took me a long time to go to sleep that evening. It was the first time in 60 years that I spent the night in a house that was no longer mine.

That is the end of my story, and of my farm, which like so many others was abandoned by its owner. The land requires many sacrifices on the part of its owners, but it also gives those most precious of goods — fresh air, space, and freedom, magical words that stir people in all countries of the world. It is for all those reasons that I left the land to my son to take over after me. It is up to him to continue the work which was started by his ancestors. I hope, in fact I am convinced, that someday he will pass it on in turn to his own sons.

I remember how we used to celebrate St.-Jean Baptiste Day; even my wife here used to take part in the celebrations. I would pull up a stump and mount it on a wagon drawn by two horses and she would make bread on it as we drove through the village streets. Others depicted our ancestors' way of life in different ways. Some showed hunting; some showed fishing; some showed land clearing; some showed cattle raising. The parade would last a good part of the day, and in the evening there was a large bonfire and people danced around it and had a drink of scotch or brandy. We had a lot of fun, and we all felt like brothers. Of course, you had the visit of the authorities, such as the provincial member, the mayor, the federal member—they would come and share a meal with us.

Oh, and we had a band, a violin and an accordion and a mouth organ. Then there were the cadets who used to parade and had their own band playing a march. That was entertainment to us at that time. There were horse races, even dog races, and we had a tug-of-war.

Those celebrations, well, they are meant to commemorate our ancestors because they did something good right here in this region. They knew hardship, real hardship. I knew hardship myself! Keep in mind that when I arrived here there were no roads; I was in the forest. I wrestled my land from the forest without any real planning. When I arrived here I was 17 years old and I was alone. Do you know what I had for a companion? Only my books. I had left school at the age of 11 because then I had to go to work. It was time to start helping my parents because they could not afford to keep me in school any longer. There were too many of us for one farm, so we had to leave.

I'll never forget that forest. The trees were big; there was birch and spruce and of course that wood was not salable, so I had to burn it. Every evening there was nobody around, so I would be alone. The nearest neighbour was three miles away. I had a small oil lamp, just like the one you can see over there, hanging on the tree. Of course, I had to sit close to the lamp to be able to read. Times were hard when I was a young man. Today you won't find a really poor person around here. I consider myself rich compared to the early days. I raised 18 sons and six daughters— that's 24 in all. So I don't need to tell you that my wife worked quite a lot also. Look at her hands. That's not from spending time on the beach or at a hotel. She worked.

You see, I lost my first wife 36 years ago. I was a widower for five years. When I married this woman here, 31 years ago, I had 11 children. Do you know how many she had? She had 13! Ten sons and three daughters and I had eight sons and three daughters. We brought them all up together. It was a lot of people around the table — 24. We had to feed them, clothe them, house them, send them away to school.

If I tell you that I am the happiest man in the world and I had 24 children, that is just right. I don't have too many! I have a lot of affection for each and every one of them. They show me consideration, a lot of it. If you have only one or two, you never know what will happen, but if you have 24 and one goes wrong, it is not too serious. When none of them goes wrong, it is even better, and none of my children have gone wrong.

All my children and their families join us once a year. The tradition is that January 1 they all come here, all of them. Normally they get here about two days ahead of time. Last winter we served breakfast for 125 persons and we had 125 for supper. I rent a hall and I buy gifts for them all and we have a party. This is the traditional Québécois New Year's celebration. My grandsons and granddaughters total about 80. They are all my descendants, even if I don't know all their names by heart. Great-grandsons in the fourth generation; there are eight on the father's side and eight on the female's side. Because we are all from two families.

Yes, I am a true Quebecker. I love my province and I love my country. I don't go to Florida; I don't go over to Europe. The province is large enough and there are lots of beautiful things to be seen right here. I like it here. Every fall in October when the leaves begin turning, it is absolutely beautiful.

What do I think of the future of Quebec now? It is very difficult to say. Even the authorities here and the members of the legislative assembly don't know where they are going. I voted for the Union Nationale. In the past I have voted for So-Cred or the Liberals; it depended upon the party and the men who were running. But I felt we had reached the point where the Liberal government didn't work anymore.

I can still remember meeting a candidate for the Liberal Party in Lac St.-Jean Riding; his name was Scott and he was the first *Anglais* I'd ever seen. That was in 1906 or 1907, and I must have been nine or 10 years old. The only *Anglais* we'd seen before were tourists. Hardly anyone spoke English in the region at that time. By the way, Mr. Scott lost that election. I remember meeting Prime Minister Maurice Duplessis. He was the savior of the people, a great man. The province of Quebec will never produce another man like him again. He once said, "Cooperation, yes, but assimilation, never." He wanted the province to be French, but united with the rest of Canada—that impressed me very much. And this is why I will vote against the referendum.

Denise Côté
Nurse's aide, Alma
(F)

"I have a son who is a pilot."

Over again and again the Péquistes I interviewed spontaneously brought up personal experiences and political events that radically influenced their own beliefs. The two most common events cited are the October Crisis and the air traffic controllers dispute. Denise Côté, a mother of one and a committed PQ activist, has been affected by both.

I think probably what pushed me to join up was the October Crisis. That made me see things differently and influenced me to change parties and to become very attentive to what was going on politically. I think Trudeau panicked. Here in the Alma region things went on during the October Crisis that were atrocious, inhuman. One local man, whose parents I knew, was taken away by the police, as a number of people here were. His father died while he was in custody and the police took him to view the body in the middle of the night—not when others were there. Now that's just plain inhuman.

I've been an active Péquiste ever since 1970. I'm a good PQ Quebecker! I worked for the PQ in the last election. The Catholic clergy here is 90 percent in favour of the PQ, I am absolutely sure of it. At any rate you had clergy who definitely and decidedly said that they were in favour of the PQ. The Church only asked us to do our duty as citizens and vote as we have always done. I always notice that on the eve of the elections we are asked to go and do our duty by going to vote, but vote as our conscience dictates. This year they did the same thing.

In the November 15 election campaign there were some things that really were repugnant to me—that's a big word but that's it: repugnant. I worked in a poll, you know as a supervisor, and it was really disappointing to see some of the things done by the other parties to try and win the election at all costs. They would have done anything—buy votes, that sort of thing—but we just wanted to win as the Parti Québécois. We wanted to win but honestly, without buying off people, without preventing others from voting. When we called people, we knew that some were Liberals but we called them and said, "Go and vote: that's all we were asking." Whereas in some polls, they tried to prevent some people from voting—I don't understand that, really. Often it's your own neighbours who act that way. I found that a lack of maturity and responsibility.

I voted for both the party and the candidate. Our own Member of the National Assembly is a teacher. He has an M.A. in history and is very well informed. It is rather unusual in politics here to see someone who is as well informed. He knows where he is going. When he doesn't know, he is honest enough to say, "Well, in this thing, I am not really too aware of it, but we will look it up." So I like that.

At the present time the PQ are much closer to the population than the other parties were, and their actions speak louder. They give grants for day-care centres because there are 25,000 people in Alma and there was still no day-care centre here before the election. Now there is going to be one and it will receive grants from the province of Quebec. I also find the PQ very democratic. They are ready to give people information and always survey the population as to what we want. As far as I am concerned, the referendum is evidence of this democracy in action.

Within two years we all will have had time to think over the referendum. I will vote for it, but if the referendum is not passed, of course I will go along with that decision. I speak only French but I don't think we want a unilingual country. I think we want to leave people free to learn English. You come to see me, and you are not forcing me to speak English. You are making the effort to speak French because you know that here we speak that language. But if I go to Ontario, I should then strive to speak English because I would respect you as anglophones. That's the way I see things.

I live here in an English section, and you are going to meet people who can't speak a word of French. That's absurd! Some of these people have been here for 20 years. Let them make the effort to respect us!

And let them make some accommodations in our behalf. I'm thinking now of the language problem for pilots and the air controllers. It is stupid! I have a son who is a pilot. In fact, he has just finished his training to be a bush pilot. And he is being forced to speak English, working out of Bagotville, which is French Canadian. If he gives his orders in French he doesn't get any answer. They just wait for him to communicate in English. Yes, he's bilingual—he has to be. He probably doesn't speak it fluently, but in his work as a pilot, he must use English. Why? Why? Pilots are not asking to speak only French, but for at least the dispatcher, the controller, to be bilingual and speak both languages. So when they talk French to him, he will answer in French, and the same with English.

I don't agree with the Canadian Airline Pilots Association, which says that the language of aviation is English. There could be some errors made because pilots are not all perfectly bilingual. For instance, you want to come into airports like Mirabel in Montreal, there could be a very small error due to language. That is what I fear the most: that there will be a mistake because a French Canadian, a Quebecker, knows only enough English to be able to get into the airport, but just a little thing goes wrong. Then there could be a fatal accident.

I think that this is a political problem. They are just saying, "We are going to hang on to the English language." The Parti Québécois, I think, would not deny that we be at least bilingual in those locations. I've heard that the victory of the PQ in November was the result of that fight with the air traffic controllers.

The PQ have only been in for a short time now but I am very optimistic about the future. Oh, within the next four years we've got nothing to lose. We've lost nothing so far and we have got nothing to lose—on the contrary, everything to gain. That's the way I look at it.

Juliette Bégin
Housewife, Pointe-Bleue
(F)
"We feel more like Montagnais than Québécois because first of all we are Indian."

There are 1,700 Montagnais Indians living on the Pointe-Bleue Reserve five km. from Roberval on the shores of Lac St.-Jean. Like approximately 60 percent of Quebec's native people, French is the second language for the Montagnais; but whether their second language is French or English, the government of daily contact for the Indians is located in Ottawa, not Quebec City.

Today in Pointe-Bleue fewer than 20 families make the annual journey into the bush to live the traditional life. Juliette Bégin's experiences, related in excellent French, represent a way of life the tribe is now attempting to preserve.

I was born here at Pointe-Bleue and I went to school for a while but in my day studies were not as long as they are today. I went to school till—oh, about grade seven. Afterward I worked in private homes until I got married. I had never been into the bush but my honeymoon was spent in the bush. We left eight days after our wedding. That was in 1931. We took the canoe here on the edge of the lake and we went up to our hunting ground. We camped 20 times before getting to our hunting ground. We reached our hunting grounds at the end of August or the beginning of September.

Yes, it is far; all along the trip we were tenting. We would throw out the net and we would eat fish and we would put out traps to catch hare, rabbits. If we had a chance to kill a moose, well, of course we did. And we would cook it to conserve it—in the summer it is very difficult to conserve it. We had to bring all our provisions for the year—flour, grain, tea, sugar, salt—all the essentials, and a rifle of course. You couldn't carry anything that freezes in the winter.

We would put out traps for the fur-bearing animals. When we needed meat we used to go for moose or caribou because at the time there was a bit of caribou, but now there is none left there. I don't know whether they deserted us or what. There are no more left. And we ate beaver and muskrat. Beaver is very good. It's a little richer than beef, and rather fatty. And we had rabbit fur blankets. It took about 100 rabbit skins to make one blanket and you could sleep outside with that very comfortably. You would not feel the cold.

I remember that first trip well because I found it very hard. When you have never been into the bush and, you know, you are sleeping on boughs, fir boughs—no mattresses—it's hard the first time. I also found it hard to portage, to go by canoe, into the rapids. There are very dangerous rapids. The current was very strong and we capsized. There was still ice on the lake, but this was in a river that we capsized. We lost all our baggage. The canoe was broken in two and my husband finally was able to grab a branch and we were able to get out.

I had my little sister-in-law with me. She was nine or 10 at the time. We got onto a big rock and stayed there. My husband came and got us, but I didn't want to get off that rock. He put his little sister on his back and got her off. We had nothing left, of course, but a little further there was another little canoe cached. It was very, very small, about 12 foot. I said I didn't want to get back into the canoe because I was afraid, but I had to.

It was a good life. I can't say that we had a great deal of hardship because my husband was a good trapper and always had good hunts, as they say, but we had to work, always work. That's what life in the bush is—hard work. No, he doesn't hunt anymore—he's 72 years old now, although he looks much younger.

We had 16 children. Yes, that's a lot. I had only my fifth baby in the bush; all the others were delivered here at Point-Bleue. We used to take them into the bush until they started to go to school. Then we had to stay here. In our day we would go to school maybe for a little while—my husband didn't go at all. Today school is mandatory. That is a good thing, but I think it would be good for the Indians to come back to the traditional ways. Our young people today don't know what it was like, and that's too bad.

Only our two oldest children speak Montagnais, for instance; the others don't. So they have trouble communicating with their father—he doesn't speak French very well. I always speak in Indian to him. When I meet somebody who speaks Indian I will speak in Indian. Montagnais is a beautiful language, but it's rather complicated. Some people are working now to prepare a Montagnais dictionary and book of grammar.

We must try to preserve our language and our culture. There are so many beautiful things to save. Our chief is working hard to do it; he would like the young people to learn Montagnais, but it is very difficult to find teachers. I think at the present time there are only two, but there are some Indians taking courses now, to be able to teach our language to the students. Some is being taught in kindergarten and grades one and two, but that is not enough.

I guess we feel more like Montagnais than Québécois because first of all we are Indian. We have always lived on our reserve. Today we're proud of it because it is improving all the time. It didn't used to be like that. There were a great many tents here at one time, but now almost all Indians live in houses.

I would not be for independence for Quebec. It seems to me that it couldn't work. I am afraid of it. We have more contact with Ottawa than Quebec City because we are under federal jurisdiction. When we need things we go to the representative of the federal government, and the grants that we receive for all things done here—we always call on the federal government, less often the provincial government. Indians say, "Quebec is not our government"—we always say that. Our government is in Ottawa. It is not the government of Quebec, although the old-age pensions come from Quebec. If we separate, we couldn't deal with the federal government anymore. Then we would be stuck with Quebec.

I don't know Mr. Lévesque personally but I don't think I would have voted for him because of his independence and the separation of Quebec. Pierre Elliot Trudeau, I think he is a great man. Some people don't like him—to each his own, but I think he is a great man. I would vote for him always, always.

Aurelien Gill

Indian chief, Montagnais tribe.
Pointe-Bleue
(F)

"Indians are not immigrants."

Quebec's native people occupy a unique position in the province's cultural geography for several reasons: (1) they consider both French and English second languages; (2) the point of daily contact with the white world is the federal, not the provincial, government; (3) native land claims are often considered more immediate issues than French-English language disputes. The small Pointe-Bleue Indian Reserve reflects the ambiguous position of Quebec's native people vis-à-vis the white world. Chief Aurelien Gill, an articulate spokesman and experienced negotiator, is singularly unimpressed by the results of November 15, 1976.

I was born on the reserve in 1933, and at that time it was far different from today. Twenty years ago the majority of the people lived in the traditional way, hunting and fishing. Today it is far more urbanized. There are a great many houses now on the reserve, but formerly there were tents because people were nomadic. And now there is a great deal of social assistance because there is not much work. We are trying to create jobs but it is becoming more and more seasonal.

I went to school outside the reserve, and graduated in teaching. I taught in a city for a while but I asked to come back here to teach.

I've been chief for about two years. The Indian Act allows for two ways for choosing a chief: the traditional manner and that outlined by the Indian Act. The traditional way is a hereditary one—it goes from father to son and so on. The other system is that the chief is elected by the majority as well as the counsellors, the majority of Indians on the reserve. This latter method we use here.

We have elections every two years. Formerly there were elections for one chief and 12 counsellors but now we have only six counsellors. All Indians on the band list vote. A band list is kept up to date by the Department of Indian Affairs.

I feel that first of all I am an Indian. Then afterward I am a Quebecker, then I am a Canadian. I am international. I have the impression that today, in fact, a people have to share the entire world with those who are richer, those who are poorer. I think that Mr. Lévesque is offering a middle road between those who are very radical and those who are less, but who are nationalistic. And I think that Mr. Lévesque is far more international than we think.

I have noticed a difference between the francophones and the anglophones. The francophones are more open, tempermental; the anglophones are a little more reserved, a little bit more mercenary—orthodox, conservative. I know it is a stereotype but there is a little bit of truth in it. Now I also know that in the eyes of non-Indians, the Indian is inferior to the others. He is the fellow who has to be told what to do because he doesn't even understand the values. You have to think for him—he doesn't have much of a head on his shoulders. You have to govern for him; administer for him; you have to send him to school to get him out of the bush; he is too primitive. This is what is thought.

But I think we have values which non-Indians do not have—spiritual values that are totally different. There is more sharing among the Indians. The feeling of ownership is entirely different. What belongs to one Indian belongs to all Indians. Non-Indians are more capitalistic although the French are less so than the English.

My reaction to the PQ victory was one of anxiety. As Indians we are divided into two groups. There are approximately 20-30,000 Indians in Quebec in addition to the Inuit—approximately 4,000 Inuit, which people sometimes designate as Eskimos. I would say there are 55 to 60 percent whose second language is English, and about 40 to 45 percent whose second language is French.

We are unique because we are a minority within another minority, so if there is one group that should be well treated in Canada it is the Indians in Quebec. But I think there is some work to be done by Quebeckers vis-à-vis the Indians. We have a tradition which has existed since the beginning—all Indian reserves come under federal jurisdiction and are administered by the Indian Act. This has been so since Confederation, and even before Confederation. I am not going to say that the federal government has always wanted to have the Indians—maybe no government wanted the responsibility for administering the Indians—but it did happen that it came under federal jurisdiction. And I don't think that the Indian group want to separate from the federal government. It is very clear that there is direct affinity with the federal government: the country, in fact "our country" as Indians, is not only Quebec or Canada—it is the entire continent. We have no boundaries. There were none at the beginning but now there are physically. But in our minds, in the minds of many Indians there are no boundaries.

I know that some non-Indian groups—both francophone and anglophone—want to take over Indian territories, but whether the referendum is passed or not, it will be the same for us because our territorial rights are not always recognized. For me, independence is hypothetical. Because I think before becoming independent one has to own the land on which one is, and I think that in Quebec at the present time a great portion of the land still belongs to the Indians. This will have to be settled one time or another, because jurisdictionally and legally we do have rights. Before Quebeckers can declare their independence, the rights of others will have to be taken care of, and I don't think that the rights of Indians will disappear tomorrow even if the majority wanted them to disappear. For 400 years they have been trying to eliminate the rights of Indians, and of course we will defend ourselves as much as ever if independence comes.

One of our major problems is to try as Indians, and as a group, to get away from the dependency which has always existed since the arrival of the first New Canadians on Canadian soil. We want to be able to administer ourselves, to govern ourselves. Perhaps, to be perfectly fair, it should be the Indians who elect the Minister for Indian Affairs. I believe in the mosaic of different colours. Mr. Trudeau talks about having various colours and I think that we can have a country like that. Those who are here should be well treated, even if the group is very small.

Often people try to draw a parallel between the position of Quebeckers and Indians as minorities, but that's false. The francophones have institutions, universities, things that are working, whereas we on the Indian side, we do not have things of this type. I think that it would be to the advantage of those in power to help us to get things like this. Let's not consider us as immigrants — Indians are not immigrants.

Claude Guitar
Hydro worker, Haute Rive
(F)

**"Maybe we'll get our arses kicked, but
we're going to manage our own
affairs at last."**

Haute Rive is some six km. from Baie-Comeau. Claude Guitar, a New Brunswick native in his mid-20s, is an electrician at a hydro-electric installation that provides cheap power to one of the many local paper mills.

The availability of cheap power and abundant timber has been central to the rapid economic development along Quebec's North Shore. Mr. Guitar is married with two children.

I moved here from the area around Campbelltown, New Brunswick, in 1955. The people here are a little different than in New Brunswick and I like it like that. People here mind their own business. You do your thing and I do mine! This is due to the fact that we come from all over the place—the South Shore, New Brunswick, Quebec City, Montreal, everywhere. This is an industrial city but the industries are seasonal and in the wintertime there is lots of unemployment—maybe up to 10 percent—but in the summertime there is a lot of work to be done and when people work they earn a lot of money. The minimum salary at the paper mill is $7 per hour.

What are my politics? I have voted PQ in the past three elections. I voted for the man and he was elected, but I can't say that I am *indépendantiste* . . . I am in favour of independence to the extent of saying we should take over our heritage. I agree with Bill 101. I like that very much. In fact, I think that we are possibly not going far enough in that regard. It may frustrate some people but I think we could go even a little further. Another thing I like is that Lévesque is negotiating directly with the other provinces on education rights: "Accommodate the French minority and we'll do the same for the English." It's tit for tat and very fair.

I think Quebeckers, who have been insulted long enough by the English—if you will pardon the expression—are now slowly beginning to fight for their rights. On November 15 I was proud. I said, "Finally we're doing something. Maybe we'll get our arses kicked, but we are going to manage our own affairs at last." Until now French Canadians themselves did not try to take over what really belonged to them. If we don't have the top jobs it's partly our own fault. We did not push ourselves enough. We were afraid of failure, I guess, or afraid that we might not have the training required. You know, the English have a leadership mentality. For years the French Canadian would say, "I will learn English and then I will go and get the job." But nowadays the French Canadian says, "I am not going to learn English and I will get the job anyway just because I can do the work."

Now my wife is English by background, but at home we speak French. When we don't want the children to understand, we speak English. We went to Ontario two years ago on vacation and spoke English for 15 days. It is not possible to speak French except in northern Ontario, from North Bay to Sault Ste. Marie. A couple of times I tried to use French but they don't understand a damn thing. Strictly nothing. Not even yes or no. And they don't want to understand anything. We came back by way of Toronto and it is very much the same thing, the same mentality. They seemed frustrated that we should dare to speak to them in French.

I'll tell you an experience we had in Montreal, in Eaton's. I was with my wife, who is English, remember. Okay, I spoke to the saleslady in French; she answered me in English. So I spoke to her in English to tell her what I wanted. My wife realized that the lady was French, but she didn't tell me at that time. After we had left the store she told me, "That is a French lady you were speaking to, she speaks English well but she's French." I didn't notice the accent but my wife did. Now that sort of thing makes me mad. To me, people like that are traitors. They refuse to recognize their origins. Why? Perhaps it is shame because they work at Eaton's and they work for English people most of the time. If my wife had told me in the store that the lady was French I would have given her hell. But it is the sort of thing that makes you more convinced than ever about affirming your personality as a French Canadian.

The rest of Canada is always saying, "What does Quebec want?" I'll tell you. Quebeckers want to be recognized as a people. That's all.

Sylvio Lebel
Taxi driver, Baie-Comeau
(F)
"Bourassa liked to ride around in his big Cadillac and practice the politics of camouflage."

It has been observed that political parties don't win elections — governments lose them. To the extent that there are many, many people with the sentiments of Sylvio Lebel, this aphorism applies to Quebec. Apart from agreeing with the Bourassa Liberals on the federalism issue, not a single person I met commended them for providing "good government." Time after time people brought up examples, at their local level, of alleged patronage, corruption, and bribery by politicians and public officials. This alleged corruption was not a major issue in the PQ campaign but it nonetheless affected the votes of many Quebeckers, including Sylvio Lebel.

For the last two elections I have been working for the Parti Québécois; before that I was a Union Nationale supporter. I turned my back on the Union Nationale and the Liberals because their policies didn't reach the man in the street, the ordinary worker. The Parti Québécois to me seems a much more human party, much more open. They are closer to the poor people. I believe that absolutely. I really admire the Parti Québécois for that. Seven or eight years ago it didn't take long to become rich in politics. The fellow who wanted to become rich had to go into politics— Liberal or Union Nationale. They worked for themselves, and the poor people who had elected them were no longer their concern until the next election.

Look, in this region the people who made money were helped by the Liberal Party. I will not name them but I know them very well. In this area if you wonder where the man has made his money, you find that he was helped by the party in power. How? With contracts, services in construction, transportation, land development, nice little road contracts. Some mayors of towns and cities became rich this way too. The PQ isn't involved in that sort of thing. They're not a corrupt party and the people know it. In the last election the unions, they beat Robert Bourassa. He used to attack unionized people directly; he said that they were destroying the province. Bourassa liked to ride around in his big Cadillac and practice the politics of camouflage. But the Parti Québécois told the unionized workers they would work hand in hand with them. That is what beat the Liberal Party.

Yes, I am for independence. English Canada has controlled our economy long enough. I want a Quebec that is free and independent, but associated with Canada. Quebec is surrounded by Canada. I'd rather not need a passport in order to travel outside Quebec. For instance, if I want to go to Ottawa, I would like to be able to just take my car and drive there. Today I am happy with politics here. But I want Lévesque to be very careful. I don't want him to get into things like we have seen in the past with other parties. I am sure it is very difficult to govern a province when everyone is after you for favours, little contracts—it is very difficult. I can see that. That's why I ask the PQ to stand on their own two feet and be careful.

Paul Poisson

School administrator, Sept-Îles

(F)

**"The true separatists are the English,
who have never accepted Quebec."**

In charge of administering the primary and secondary school system on Quebec's sprawling and isolated North Shore, Paul Poisson faces the daily problem of trying to attract qualified second language teachers to remote locations.

Last year the Quebec government asked me, because of the experience I had acquired here, to go and set up a school structure for the Quebec Hydro Project at James Bay. The workers are mainly French, but there are English Canadians and Americans there as well. And I'll tell you, the Americans are far more open to French than the anglo-Canadians.

Some Canadian management staff are from the West and possibly because of the frame of mind that they have in the West and in Vancouver, they don't know too much about Quebec. But the Americans travel so much throughout the world, they often adopt the language of the country, whether Italian, French, or whatever. At the James Bay project the Americans prefer French to English, and send their children to the French school.

Here on the North Shore we're still pioneers of sorts. There is not yet the separation between social classes that you find in Rimouski or Quebec City or other cities. We don't have that here. Everybody speaks to each other. There are no separate clubs for different social groups. At the curling club, for example, labourers and professional people mix. People earn good wages, the city is highly unionized, and there is very little unemployment. A few years ago, in fact, we had the highest wages in Canada.

I think there are 35 different nationalities in Sept-Îles. About 10 percent are English-speaking and the rest speak French. As an educator I would like to see our second language programs improved. First, I would like the second language taught by people using their own mother tongue — English by true Englishmen and French by Frenchmen. That's very important. I am aware of the French immersion system in the Protestant school board in Greater Montreal and we would like to be able to adopt that in our schools, but we haven't succeeded yet because our schools are too small and staff are hard to find, especially for the smaller villages along the coast. Many of them can be reached only by boat or seaplane. So even though we want to improve our English programs in the schools, it's not easy to attract qualified staff.

Personally, I deplore Bill 101's attempt to limit English education in Quebec, but I don't agree with the other provinces either because francophones there often can't study in French. And isn't it odd that Ottawa has never been concerned with the problem of minorities in the rest of Canada until now? Now that Quebec appears to be mistreating its English minority, Ottawa feels it has to intervene. If they didn't do it previously, why do it now? I find that deplorable.

Personally, I don't want total independence. I think that it is possible to have a greater degree of autonomy though. I would say that the true separatists are the English, who have never accepted Quebec. They are the ones who are creating separatism with their own attitudes, especially people in the West who have never had any contact with Quebec. But as I understand the English mentality, they are pragmatic and I think they will accept compromise, and I'd rather see that compromise come a little late rather than never. I was brought up in a village that was English and French and we always got along fine, so I think it is possible for us to live together.

Let me tell you something about René Lévesque—he is a very pragmatic man, he and Claude Morin. People should understand that they are not true separatists; they are autonomists, autonomists to the end, not separatists. And there is a difference. They want certain rights for Quebec and the day those rights are secured, separation won't be mentioned anymore. That's the way I see it. But if we don't acquire those rights then separation may happen. The real separatists in that government are men like Robert Burns, Louis O'Neil, and Camille Laurin.

Chapter 6

The Outouais

The capital of the Outouais *(pronounced oot-oo-ay) area is the city of Hull (population 61,000, 90% French), located immediately across the Ottawa River from the national capital. Connected to Ottawa by three bridges, until the 1970s Hull meant little more to Ottawa residents than a late-night and Sunday drinking spot, and the place that produced the sulphurous stink of the E. B. Eddy paper and match company. In the past eight years virtually everything but the drinking laws has changed in Hull.*

The city is now a part of the National Capital Region, the paper mill has been erased by the federal government, and Hull has a new federally constructed skyline consisting of massive office towers housing some 15,000 federal civil servants. The low-paid industrial work force of Hull is giving way to white-collar administrative-technocratic cadres stacked in well-paid layers along the Ottawa River. Though increased prosperity may be coming to Hull, this has not prevented the Parti Québécois from winning the city's National Assembly seat.

Other communities in the Outouais such as Shawville, Perkins, and Pointe-Gatineau are less directly affected by the presence of the federal government and are more concerned with the changes brought about by the PQ victory, including the affect this has had on property values. Being on the Quebec-Ontario border seems to have placed property owners here in a rather vulnerable economic position, in part because of the negative reaction from potential house buyers in Ontario.

After making excursions to Hull and surrounding communities from my home in Ottawa, I drove east and then north to the well-known resort town of

234

St.-Jovite, in the heart of the Laurentians resort and skiing country. In an area heavily dependent on outside tourist dollars, the economic uncertainties created by the possibility of separatism are particularly noticeable.

Louise Bergeron
Civil servant, Hull
(F)

"If you're an Indian, a francophone, and a woman in the civil service today, you've got it made!"

One of the most important conclusions of the Royal Commission on Bilingualism and Biculturalism was that Canada's federal civil service was largely controlled by and responsive to the needs of English Canada. In 1966 Prime Minister Pearson firmly committed the federal government to a policy of civil service bilingualism, and by the end of 1976, 52,960 enrolments were recorded in French language classes and 10,053 in English (see Appendix D, page 325), at a cost estimated at half a billion dollars.

The improved position of French-speaking civil servants, while generally welcomed in Quebec, has not been achieved without some internal bitterness, as Louise Bergeron explains. Ms Bergeron, 30, occupies a middle-management position with the Canadian International Development Agency (CIDA) in Ottawa.

When I finished my degree in public administration at Laval I got a job offer from the federal government. When I told my friends I was coming to Ottawa, they all told me, "Don't go there, you will die of boredom. There are no discothèques, no French-language cinema, no French radio. They speak only English—you don't speak any English, so you will be bored to death." Of course, there was that taste of adventure for something new and I was being offered a higher salary than I could get in Quebec City. And I could work in my field of specialization, so I came to Ottawa.

First I worked for the Department of Regional Economic Expansion in the financial branch. I was the only woman at my level and the only unilingual francophone. All the bosses were English except my immediate superior, who spoke French. So the first thing they did was send me for three weeks on an English course and I came back to work in the office on financial figures. I quickly made a good anglophone friend who did not speak any French and she used to speak slowly, so I could improve my English.

In the first two years I had 18 weeks of English courses, and after a year and a half, I ended up chief of fiscal accounting, which meant I had to supervise five employees, five clerks who were English-speaking only. So conversations were very short! One of the men was about 50 and he was against female bosses. He was also anti-French and against university graduates who take over positions from older employees. I had no experience, I was a woman, a francophone, *and* a graduate! So it was cold war. I simply ignored his prejudice entirely and all I asked of him was to do his work. Well, we communicated only through memos. He would put the memos on my desk when I was not there. But the work got done. He finally spoke to me for the first time in a friendly way the week he found out I was leaving the Ministry.

Up to now, I don't have anything to complain about as far as work is concerned. Quite the contrary. I have advanced a bit faster than the average. The fact that I am a woman may have helped a bit. If you're an Indian, a francophone, and a woman in the civil service today, you've got it made! All I need now is to be Indian!

Recently I changed positions and my present position is classified as bilingual. I had to go for the public service bilingualism test. If I had not reached a certain level I would have had to take a language course, but the test was relatively easy and we were given every possible chance of succeeding. So I am now officially bilingual! But I prefer, you will notice, to speak with you in French. At all meetings that take place in my branch, whenever I say something it's in French. The disadvantage is that some anglophones don't understand anything at all. Apart from me, everything is in English, and I am the only one to speak French. But it's a bilingual position, *n'est-ce pas?*

Frankly, for me, being a Canadian means being a Quebecker first. My homeland is Quebec. But when I go to Europe—I travel very often in my job—I feel like a Canadian as compared to an American; that difference is very important because I don't want to be an American. If I had to make a choice between being American or Canadian, I would prefer to be Canadian. But where people know something about Canada, I identify myself as a Quebecker. As a federal employee, I represent the Canadian government, and I have a job to do. I like what I do, and I don't give a damn whether it is for the provincial or federal government or for Quebec or for Canada. What counts is that I like what I am doing. No, it doesn't worry me at all that Hull may become English because of the presence of federal public servants. They are here from eight to five, and after five you don't see them on the streets at all. So there is nothing to worry about. A lot of anglophones think that Hull is nothing at all— dirty, boring, French, the lowest class of society, and the Ottawa civil servants don't want to get dirty by coming here. That's the opinion they have of Hull—no respect for the place. Anglophones don't care for francophones anyway, especially since the Official Languages Act made them feel threatened in their jobs, because now the francophones are coming up in the civil service. For them, we are just a lot of bother and nothing else; we are going to steal their jobs, we force them to learn French.

Quebeckers are happy that the PQ won because it represents more than a victory of separatism. It represents the fact that Quebeckers are not afraid of change, and we are proud of that. I have never hidden the fact at work or outside that I have a very strong attachment to Quebec and that I had a lot of admiration for René Lévesque and I would be quite astonished to be told, "Shut up, it'll do you harm." That is ridiculous. Even our anglophone bosses give their opinions very openly. At work it doesn't matter what party you support. At least where I work anyhow.

No, it wouldn't bother me to remain within Confederation as such, but I think it is extremely important that Quebec and the other provinces acquire more independence from the federal government. Now, if the provinces become more independent, possibly there will be less work for federal public servants, but at that point we will just move and go work for the province! It won't be any problem, no problem at all.

Alain Corre
Private language teacher, Hull
(F)

"The Québécois are every bit as intelligent and knowledgeable as the Frenchman, but the Frenchman looks down his nose at them without even getting to know them."

As a language teacher Alain Corre provides some very topical information on the relative difficulty of learning French and English as second languages. And as a recent (1972) immigrant to Canada from France, he has some insightful observations on the cool reception many French immigrants are accorded in Quebec.

In the Canadian context it's much more difficult for an anglophone to learn French than for a francophone to learn English. The courses that we offer are divided into two categories: continuous courses where the student takes six hours a day and part-time courses where the student comes two times a week for three hours at a time. A French-speaking person in the full-time course would take 20 to 25 weeks to really learn English well. Now the part-time student is going to take five times as long, so if he comes six hours a week, it's going to take him about two years to become perfectly bilingual.

The English Canadian who wants to learn French is going to need 850 to 900 hours of instruction. *You have to count on 33 to 40 percent more time for the English Canadian to learn French.* The greatest part of this difference is due to the fact that in Canada the English influence is very strong. The French Canadian just has more opportunities to use his second language—when he goes into the stores, on the street when someone asks him for information, when he is buying gas, all kinds of situations. The English Canadian has a lot more difficulty in finding chances to use his French on the street.

There is another reason why English is an easier language to learn. To carry on a street conversation, you need about 500 words in English. To carry on the same average conversation in French, you need 850-900 words. Now when you move beyond this basic level—let's say to a higher level of bilingualism like level two in the federal civil service, which is the level required for a bilingual position—you need about a 1,500-word vocabulary in French and English. So once you arrive at this intermediate level of bilingualism, the number of words required in both languages is really the same. Then at the third level of bilingualism, which we call perfect bilingualism, I would say you need about 3,000-3,500 words in English and maybe around 3,000 in French. So by the time you get to complete fluency, the English vocabulary is actually about 500 words larger than the French vocabulary.

The other factor in learning a language is the aptitude of the students. I had experience teaching 1,500 to 2,000 students and, in my experience, everyone has pretty much the same aptitude for a language at the beginning. There are a few exceptions—maybe 1 percent are due to physical problems, problems of hearing, difficulty understanding certain sounds. Attempts have been made to measure students' aptitude and these tests have shown that aptitude is influenced by political, social, educational factors more than anything else and this aptitude can change, can improve, if you use proper teaching methods. It is not something that's fixed at birth. Aptitude is really a function of motivation. If you motivate someone sufficiently with good teaching methods, then their aptitude will improve.

Another factor that we always take into account is the linguistic background of the student and I must say the background of the students that I have seen here is very, very poor. Those who have a good base in the second language usually pick it up in the family, not at school. I am afraid I don't have a very good impression of the Canadian second language program in the schools. [See Appendix F, page 329.] Many of the teachers my students had in school were actually unilingual.

I've been here about five years now. I come from Reims, a city about 100 miles northeast of Paris. Why did I decide to emigrate? I didn't know a lot about Canada but there were some things that I didn't like about France. The most important was the restrictive world that I was living in. Now this wasn't only a question of economics, not really. I felt as if I was caught in a vise, caught in a system where I had a lot of trouble expressing myself socially and professionally. It's a bit like that in every country of old Europe. You are part of a clear social class group, and with very rare exceptions, that's where you were born and that's where you will stay.

Now, when I arrived in Canada, I realized that I could do what I wanted to do. I wasn't always surrounded by a group of people who knew me and who would say, "Look, he did that. You shouldn't do that. You can't do that." I can say what I want to say, circulate wherever I want, take risks if I feel like it. I don't have my parents, my family, my friends to tell me what to do or what not to do.

In France I grew up in a bureaucratic environment. My father was a civil servant and for generations there had been civil servants in our family. For 20 years my parents pushed the values of security, a good retirement, and pushed me in the direction of the civil service. So after 20 years of hearing this sort of thing, you say, "Yes, right, okay, I'll be a civil servant—it sounds like the right thing to do." But when I came to the end of my studies, I realized that I was being trapped in a system that really didn't suit me and I couldn't get out of that system without creating a lot of problems around me so the solution for me was to leave the country.

While I was thinking of emigrating, there were two possibilities open to me: Australia and Canada. I wrote to both countries and got a lot of information. The thing that really tipped the balance in favour of Canada is that a large francophone population lives here. When I came I was unilingual French and so it seemed a better choice than Australia. Algeria was another possibility but I don't like the hot weather. That's one problem you don't have here! As a matter of fact, I really love the winters here.

I notice a lot of differences between the Québécois and the French people. Differences in favour of the Québécois. In general, people are more relaxed, more open here. In France, there isn't a great deal of contact between one class and the other. You feel blocked off—you can't really move around in the society. Now here if a simple worker for example is unhappy in his work and has a complaint to make, he can go and see his boss much more easily than he can in France and he can talk to him directly—face to face—without a lot of ceremony and undue courtesy that exist in Europe and France.

Not many Frenchmen leave France, but many of those who do come to Quebec aren't very well received by the Québécois. Why? Because they have this bad habit of saying, "You Québécois, you don't know how to speak the French language. You speak with a funny accent. Hold on, I'll show you how to speak properly." People don't appreciate that sort of thing. The Québécois are every bit as intelligent and knowledgeable as the Frenchman but the Frenchman looks down his nose at them without even getting to know them.

People here ask me what I think of De Gaulle and his *"Vive le Québec libre."* Well, General de Gaulle always liked to shock people. At that point in his life—age 65—I think perhaps he thought of himself as some sort of superman. Let's face it, he may have overestimated himself a little, and this vanity led him to make a few mistakes. But I still liked General de Gaulle and respect him for what he did throughout his life. Now, as for his famous *"Vive le Québec libre,"* I think he did that on purpose. That wasn't a mistake. He wanted to push the Québécois a little bit and to stir up the anglophones at the same time. He liked to shock people, as I said—which he certainly did.

What do I think of the November 15 election result? Well, let's say I think it's a victory for the Quebec people. It is really a chance for them to express themselves in a way that they weren't able to do before. But personally I can't see Canada without Quebec and I can't see Quebec without Canada. It is one of the charms of Canada that this is a bilingual country. Hence the anglophone is able to enrich his culture with contacts with the French people. And of course the same thing vice versa. I think the ideal would be to be able to live together in harmony in a perfectly bilingual country where everyone could communicate in the two languages. Now, that's a little utopian, okay! There will always be a large group of French people and a large group of English people who will be separate from each other, but I think there are ways for the two communities to live close to each other and interact without melting into one uniform mass.

André Fillion
Civil servant, Hull
(F)
**"Bagpipes will never get through
to a Québécois."**

There was a time, not long ago, when civil servants didn't publicly discuss politics. It simply wasn't done. It may still not be the "done" thing officially, but the impact of November 15, 1976, has proven more powerful than the restraints of custom and tradition. Among the public servants I spoke with, the immediate reaction to the request for an on-the-record interview was that the issues were too important not to be discussed. One of these people is André Fillion, a 31-year-old bureaucrat at the middle-management level in the Public Service Commission.

At the last election I voted for the Parti Québécois. I am proud of it. Now whether I am a federalist or for Quebec independence, you have to define independence. First, to me, independence—economic and social and political—is impossible in the North American context at the present time. I don't believe in it. I think what we can tend toward would be independence, socially speaking. In the field of health, education, language at work, Quebec will really be able to impose its ideas; but with regard now to economic independence, I don't believe in that at all. The simple fact is that 95 percent of companies belong either to English capital or American capital and that cannot be changed overnight. It is impossible.

Now I also don't believe at all in a bilingual country. That's impossible too. I have gone from Halifax to Vancouver and I don't believe in it at all. It is false and stupid and even the federal government is revising its position on that. There will be no more bilingual positions in Edmonton or Calgary or Vancouver. It was stupid for the anglophones to speak French once a year. All that can happen, and all I can wish for, is as many rights for francophones as anglophones in areas like Ottawa-Hull. The public service language training program [see Appendix D, page 325] is a monumental farce where unbelievable amounts of money are spent with pitiful results. No one in the system believes in it; everybody knows it is a farce. It is there to create employment, and to fool people. Did you know that 90 percent of the budget spent for languages goes for anglophones and not for francophones? Maybe 2 percent of these civil servants assimilated enough French to be able to discuss even simple matters, or just to have an intelligent conversation—the maximum is 2 percent.

I think I have the right to work in my own language. To me that is important, but the only way to do this is to limit your choice of ministries, and for a francophone that means about three ministries where you can work in French: the Secretary of State, Public Service Commission, and possibly the Post Office Department.

Where I work now there are three anglophones among 120 francophones, and if they want to mix with us, at lunch or coffee breaks, they have to do it in French. It is up to them to become integrated with us and not the other way around. The anglophones who cannot talk French do not come and eat with us.

The reaction of French public servants on the morning of November 16 was very clear: people were proud; they were smiling. Everybody was proud of speaking French in the elevators. You had small groups talking in the offices—it was extraordinary. And the reaction of anglophones was "What happened?" Nobody could understand what had taken place. It was as though there had been a military coup. They never understood and I think they will never understand what took place in Quebec. All they know is what they see in the newspapers. The *Citizen* and the *Journal* or the Toronto *Sun* and things like that...but they know nothing about Quebec. They have never lived there. They don't know what a Québécois is!

A Québécois is not only pea soup and tourtière and big parties. That is all that anglophones see! Francophones think differently than anglophones; they are less pragmatic perhaps. I think the francophone public servant, even though he has a different management approach, is just as good as any anglophone. We are different culturally, of course.

Francophones are more attracted to the arts, in my view. Personally, I feel at home in Quebec and it is nearly impossible to feel at home when I am in Ontario or in B.C. or in Alberta. I am in a foreign country, I am there as a tourist—I will never feel anything other than that. There is nothing at all that takes place in those provinces which really moves me. There is nothing there that I can identify with. Bagpipes will never get through to a Québécois.

People like to tell me it is impossible to be in favour of independence for Quebec and at the same time work for the federal government. They say it is like being a spy. Well, I don't buy that. I give the best performance I can in my job, and for this I get a salary every second week. They get my knowledge, my performance, and I get a salary. It is a fair exchange. I don't have to believe in the Liberal Party and Mr. Trudeau or in Joe Clark or Broadbent to work for the federal government —just like the man who works for Dow Chemicals didn't have to agree with the Vietnam war.

I'm not afraid of losing my job. Twenty years ago in the federal government a francophone who would dare to speak French would nearly lose his job—it was that stupid. There was extremely strong segregation against the French and people used to be afraid of being francophones in the federal government. Now we're not afraid.

I'll tell you a funny thing that happened to me. A while ago I went to Eaton's in Ottawa to look for a suit. I found one that I liked, I tried it on. It suited me beautifully and the price was right—everything. The salesman comes over, he asks me "Can I help you?" I asked him if he spoke French. He said no. So I continued: I tried the suit, I looked at it, but we are not talking to each other. At the end the suit is fine and he really thinks that he is making a sale and will put $125 in Eaton's pocket. But I tell him in my best English that it is too bad he can't speak French; I will buy the same suit but it will have to be in Montreal, where people do speak French. He thought I was nuts. I said I would drive 125 miles to go to Eaton's just to be served in French. But if 25 persons go to Eaton's and ask to be served in French, you can be sure all salesmen will speak French and then francophones will have those jobs.

I guess my point is that I will never feel at home in Canada. All that I hope is that francophones will be better accepted in other provinces, that they'll have a chance to live in areas like Ottawa, Cornwall, Berwick, or Sudbury and at least live in their own language, go to school in their own language. I remain a Québécois. I am willing to limit myself in my advancement just to be able to live in Quebec. If I were to be offered a promotion tomorrow morning with $5,000 or $10,000 added to go and live in Toronto, I would turn it down.

Two years ago I got a dog. The only place where I could have it trained was at the Ottawa Kennel Club. Out of 15 persons with dogs, there might have been three or four francophones, and I was the only one among that group who insisted on teaching his dog in French. All the other francophones were so assimilated in this area that they ordered their dogs around in English. It may sound funny but even the dogs are assimilated in Ottawa.

Rachel L'Arrivée
Secretary, Hull
(F)

"Lévesque is really aiming for complete political independence and he can't be allowed to camouflage this with talk of economic association."

Within six months of their stunning November 15 victory, PQ organizers saw their card-carrying membership swell to 146,000. The federalist forces, although significantly less united than the indépendantistes, have organized some half-dozen voluntary groups, including the Quebec-Canada Movement, which Rachel L'Arrivée decided to join. A secretary and assistant to a francophone Member of Parliament, every weekday morning Mrs. L'Arrivée makes the short journey from her comfortable home on the Quebec side in Hull, across the Ottawa River to her office at the foot of Parliament Hill.

I came to live here in Hull when I got married. My husband is an engineer from the Gaspé and we met in Montreal and decided to establish ourselves in Hull and I am very happy here now. I really feel a part of the city, but, when I say that I am a Hull resident, it also means I belong to Ottawa. They are two different cities, of course but, at the same time, they have very close links. Ottawa-Hull is bicultural. Ottawa has mainly the anglophone element and Hull and surrounding areas have mainly the francophone element, although the two linguistic groups are found on both sides of the river. You can really live in French or in English, according to your own wishes.

No, I am not perfectly bilingual. I understand English very well and I can speak it, but I am not perfectly bilingual, and frankly that is unfortunate for me. I would like to be able to express myself better because I find that sometimes you want to tell people something and you don't have the correct expressions—you don't have the little subtleties and refinements. My friends are mainly francophones, of course, and I know many anglophones who are very nice but scope for discussion with them is limited.

As assistant to a francophone Member of Parliament, I work mainly in French. Fortunately, there are a great many French MPs in the Confederation Building, where our office is, but my work does require that I communicate with other people in the ministries, or even in other offices and then, of course, I use English as well, and I get along fairly well. I draft a great deal of correspondence, which means that I have to contact the constituents and study their problems and try and find solutions to the problems.

What do I think of the PQ victory? Oo-la-la! There is a great deal to be said. What Quebeckers voted for was honest government. They had had enough of promises.

But I criticize the PQ government for acting just as if Quebec were already separated and I think that this disappoints a great many people. It was elected to provide honest administration, but it has been going too far, acting as if Quebec were already independent and not respecting the two official languages, which are already established. I think that is going to create a lot of enemies for the party.

And let's be very clear about one thing. Lévesque and the PQ do a lot of talking about sovereignty-association and economic ties with Canada. Well, remember that every country has economic ties of some kind with its neighbours. Every country! Lévesque is really aiming for complete political independence and he can't be allowed to try and camouflage this with talk of economic association. I think it's vital for people to see this and to know exactly what they're voting for or against when the day of the referendum arrives.

I am a federalist, of course, almost unreservedly. Canada is a great country, large, wealthy, multicultural, and it is a young country with a great many possibilities. I am a Quebecker and also a Canadian. The wealth that belongs to others also belongs to me, to a certain extent.

I do think though that there is a positive element in what happened on November 15. For once everyone—francophones and anglophones— whether they are residents of Quebec or other provinces, at least now realize that a problem exists. We've been two solitudes, and now I think we are aware of this and aware of the fact that the problem has to be settled now—not in 10 or 15 years. So in that sense I think that the events of November 15 are very good. It will allow us once and for all to finally resolve the questions that face us.

For instance, we have to allow the francophone minorities outside Quebec to educate their children in their own language and also give them some services in French. Even in Ontario there is a great deal of discrimination, and I find that intolerable. Even though I am a federalist, I think that the time has come for us to respect francophone citizens as equal citizens and not make them feel that they are always being given something. Look, the Americans have a melting-pot society and an English-speaking way of life. Well, we don't! We have two languages and two cultures which have very deep roots in the past. This could be a very good mix, a mix that could result in a unique country, a unique place to live.

Quebec must not separate and I still have confidence that it won't — a great deal of confidence. I am working in the Quebec-Canada Movement because we are determined that Quebec will not separate. We are also determined to try and make not only Quebeckers understand that we have to remain in Confederation, but we're also determined to ask the other provinces to support us and prove to us clearly that we can and must live in Canada. Have you heard the song that says, "It's your turn now to talk of love?" Well, I find that song beautiful, but I think that anglophones should sing it to us, but you can't change people's attitudes overnight, can you?

Take Leonard Jones, the MP from Moncton, for instance. I think he has a racist, very discriminatory attitude, but all the same people did elect him as an MP. Maybe he is representative of some segments of the population down there and this is what scares us. There is very little time left to make everyone understand that the times are serious and that in a year or two the country may be broken up.

Maurice Joly
Electrician, Hull

(F)

**"I've always spoken two languages,
but that never got me
one cent more."**

A convinced indépendantiste for the past 14 years, Maurice Joly describes his involvement in the independence movement that predated the founding of the Parti Québécois.

I was born in 1938 to a family of 11 children, of whom nine are still living —seven brothers, two girls. Father was a farmer. When we left the farm I was 14 years old and my father bought a fruit store in the neighbouring village. I went to a one-room school with one teacher who taught seven classes, from first to seventh grades. Then after that I did two years in Maniwaki and two years at the *école technique.* My younger sister and I were the only ones who went beyond seven years of schooling; my family didn't have much money to educate all those children.

People in those days spent a lot of evenings with friends and neighbours—the farmers from one concession would go and meet neighbours from the next one. There were shooting matches with shotguns and we'd win turkeys. Sometimes we'd play to win apples too. I don't remember the name of this game, but to amuse ourselves we'd play cards and instead of winning money we'd win apples. There were a number of games, but most important was euchre. Everybody played euchre. Even today we play it.

I think because of the Church, there was a strong community spirit, working bees, all kinds of things actually: to renovate the church, to paint, to give a hand to the priest. The farmers themselves used to help each other out. Communications were pretty difficult then, not as easy as today. You couldn't telephone; you had to go by horse to the neighbour's. The Church was very strong at that time, oh yes. You didn't contest the Church, as you do today. If the village priest said something in the pulpit, well, it was absolute truth and there was no discussion.

I remember one priest very well. When he mounted the pulpit, he would actually name the sinners! If he met people who had been drinking and had done something wrong, he would name them in church and tell them what they were doing wasn't right. But there was a way for one to redeem oneself—that was to give maybe $50 to the church.

I don't practice my religion today. Maybe half my family still practice the faith; the other half, no. The Church in Quebec has lost a lot of ground in the last 15 years; really the people just decided...well, they're better educated now. Before, there was only the priest, the lawyer, the doctor—these three people were the ones who dictated everything. My father had studied in school for only four years; my mother for three. So when they met people who had gone to university, well, they did what they said; they didn't oppose them. We were brainwashed from every point of view; that's well known in Quebec. It was said that the Church didn't play politics, but when the priest in his pulpit said that heaven was blue, and hell red, well, you knew one party was red and one was blue. So you voted for the Liberals or Duplessis and the Union Nationale. But today things have changed. Radio, television have really educated people.

When I was around 20 or 22, in the 1960s, with the rise of the Liberal Party, I became conscious of political affairs and thought I would get involved. I listened to a lot of television programs — to René Lévesque, for instance, on his program *Point de Mire*. He was very informative. Oh yes, I listened to all the public affairs programs, so it was then I really became conscious of politics.

But this political awareness had its roots way back. My father used to work for a company called the Gatineau Boom. It was a company that transported logs by river to Hull, or to Gatineau. My brother also wanted to work there and since my father was working there he wanted to get him a job. But there was an English-speaking family in the area and that father wanted to have *his* sons employed there. His sons were about the same age as we were. The company always went to that family but they never came to us. It was always the same thing — the English family got the work because it was the English who were employing. I found this a gross injustice. It was unfair to the Quebeckers, wouldn't you say? But that sort of thing was always happening.

I think Quebeckers have been exploited. I've always spoken two languages, but that never got me one cent more; but an anglophone, he always gets a better salary than I do. And he's unilingual. I have this diploma in electrical contracting and I had to pass tests and about 80 percent of the work was in English. So I had to adapt myself to that regulation for pretty well all the jobs. I had to learn English terms.

But getting back to politics, my first contact with the independence movement was back around 1964-65 when I went to hear Pierre Bourgault give a speech. They were a few professors from the University of Ottawa and some other people who were invited; there might have been 30 people. In 1966 I campaigned for Indépendantiste Marcel Chaput in the jurisdiction of the Papineau. We lost, of course, but picked up a good number of votes. I stayed with the RIN [Rassemblement pour l'Indépéndance Nationale] until its dissolution. In '66-67 we decided it wasn't smart politics to divide our forces, so the RIN was dissolved and we all got behind Lévesque and the PQ.

Every month from about 1966 I have been supporting this movement. We're called friends of independence and every month we write cheques to the PQ. I give a series of postdated cheques; of course, I can't provide $500 at one time, but over a period of time, yes, I can contribute to maintain the party. The PQ has just raised about $1,300,000 from its members. Remember that — $1,300,000 from average people like me!

I am convinced that independence is inevitable. The work has just begun. It is necessary to convince most Quebeckers—at least 65 or 70 percent. Every day we have to do something to convince them.

Lyse Daniels-Cesaratto
Housewife, Aylmer
(F)
"Perhaps Mr. Trudeau can make love in French or in English, but I couldn't do it in English."

Eight km. southwest of the nation's capital lies Aylmer, a pleasant city of 25,714 people, 58 percent francophone. The community prides itself on being bilingual, but as is so often the case in Quebec it is usually one-way bilingualism practiced by the French people. Lyse Daniels-Cesaratto and David Taylor, whose interview follows this one, have different political views but concur in many ways in their analysis of small-town bilingualism.

I was born of a very French mother, and I think she is the one who gave me this pride in being a Quebecker. Here in Aylmer, francophones are supposed to represent 50 percent of the population but in reality, possibly half the French have been assimilated. That is, they have chosen English as their everyday language at home, in the stores, everywhere, and I'd like to know why. There is this mentality of a colonized people. I will try to explain that. Many people here are public servants and think their English gives them a privileged status. A French Canadian is seen possibly as a second-class citizen, so French mothers speak to their children in English, send them to English schools, speak first in English to people in the street. I think they perceive French as a shameful language, something to be hidden, maybe spoken at home, otherwise forgotten.

I will give you a very clear example. I attended a French course at the composite high school, close to here. Right in the middle of the course I heard at least 10 pupils out of 25 speaking English among themselves. A lot of teachers at that school told me that, at recess, the kids speak English first. It is a real concern.

Now I systematically refuse to speak English, even though I can speak it fairly well. If I want to live in French, I won't do it by speaking English. You want more examples of assimilation? Look at the stores in Aylmer. The first thing you are asked is: "Cash or charge?" People still don't know any better here. I say *"Pardon?"* in French. So they repeat "Cash or charge?" Finally the cashier asks a colleague to state the amount in French. If I'm in a good mood that day I will let it go by; if not, I will tell them they shouldn't be employed, being unilingual. The other day at a shopping centre I saw a sign *Bilingual Waitress Wanted*. They have the nerve to advertise for a bilingual waitress in English only!

You want another one? I had my account at the Toronto-Dominion Bank for three years; then one day the teller I had spoke only English. So I said, "Get the manager." I closed my accounts. I wrote to the papers and made it public that I had closed my account to protest the hiring of a person who spoke only English. Now we are beginning to make people aware of things like that. It is unacceptable that in Quebec francophones should have to be bilingual but anglophones not. In Ontario if you're French only, you can't get a job.

There is a welcoming sign here: *Aylmer—the Town of the Bilingual Chicken*. I found that very funny. People brag all over the place that this is the most bilingual city in Canada. What kind of bilingualism is it when 80 percent of anglophones here only speak English? Bilingualism here means that francophones speak English. It is always one-way bilingualism. I think people should make an effort, an honest effort, to see us, to respect us, the way we are.

A while ago the Quebec government forced the amalgamation of Aylmer, Lucerne, and Deschenes and there was to be a referendum to select a name for the city. A group of us francophones didn't like the name Aylmer for all kinds of reasons, so we opted for Portage-du-Lac. Rightly or wrongly, we submitted the name to the population. Well, there were people who were so fanatical they didn't want to even hear about Portage-du-Lac. We had tomatoes thrown at our windows;

buckets of paint were thrown at our signs; we received crank telephone calls day and night. The calls, being in English, could have been from assimilated francophones as well as from anglophones. Even people from Ottawa were in favour of keeping the name of Aylmer. Their slogan was "Aylmer Forever," but we felt that we had a right also to suggest a new name. Our slogan was "A New City, A New Name," but it didn't work out for us. In the end they carried the vote, and we accepted that result. It was a democratic choice.

Personally, I favour independence and I have for a long time. I am 31 years old. Since I began voting, I have been voting for sovereignty-association. On November 15 I jumped about six feet in the air. My reaction was very childish and my husband was quite ashamed of me. I raised the blinds and started making faces at my neighbours! But it was the first time I had voted for the winning party. For me, independence is first of all political independence. It means ensuring the survival of the people of Quebec. This may be possible within Canada, provided territorial bilingualism is recognized; that is, a unilingual French Quebec and a unilingual English Canada. If Canadians were to realize that this condition is necessary for survival of Quebec, if they were intelligent enough to accept it, I would be able to say that we don't need political independence. We could have institutional bilingualism at the federal level throughout Canada but in each province, in daily life, it would be unilingual.

Outside Quebec there are 976,000 francophones. Their future would be in danger with independence. Well, that is too bad, but they are lost in any case. Just look at the statistics and see to what extent assimilation has already taken place among those people. Even in Ontario, already one franco-Ontarian out of four chooses English at home, although nobody is pushing him. The same is true in Aylmer. I know it is sad but I feel that that is the law of nature.

Moving tomorrow to Vancouver or anywhere but Quebec and Acadia, I would send my children to English schools because if I sent them to French school they would be second-class citizens. I say this very honestly. To me, living in French is very important. I am bilingual but English is not my language, it is not my way of thinking . . . it doesn't come naturally to me. Living in French is like breathing. It is that vital to me. It is not a matter of philosophy, it is not intellectual. It is a "gut" feeling. To speak French, to see French movies, to hear the radio in French, to speak to my friends in French — it is my daily life. It would hurt me too much to have to speak English in English Canada. I would rather immigrate to a francophone country if we had to leave Quebec.

Trudeau has always refused to accept the concept of two nations. He refuses to see reality. I know that he is perfectly bilingual, but people like him can almost be counted on the fingers of one hand. There is a difference between being bilingual—being able to express yourself in two languages—and living in a language. There is the difference. There are different levels of knowing a language. Perhaps Mr. Trudeau can make love in French or in English, but I couldn't do it in English.

Nowhere in this world will you find a people with two equal cultures. We often hear of Switzerland as an example of multilingualism. But the Swiss cantons are unilingual. They speak German, French, Italian or Schwyzer-dütsch in any one given area, and everything is in that one language. But that doesn't prevent federal institutions from possibly operating in the other languages. Perhaps that should be the formula in Canada.

I know that there are a lot of people in Ottawa who have no interest in seeing Quebec becoming independent, and who are ready to do everything possible to prevent it. Sometimes I am afraid that the army will intervene to prevent independence in Quebec. October 1970 all over again.

Speaking of the October Crisis, personally I feel sympathy for the imprisoned FLQ members because they did something that was very necessary for Quebec. And I can tell you something else: if November 15 had not taken place, there would have been another FLQ. Personally, I even thought of resorting to violence. I felt this election was our last chance. I thought, "If PQ doesn't come in, we will have to use violence to make things happen in Quebec." I don't know whether I would have done anything violent, but that is the way my thinking was heading. But fortunately there was this great deliverance on November 15: we gave the PQ a chance to prove what it could do.

David Taylor
Civil servant, Aylmer
(E)

**"We have not yet made that big step
which takes the French into the
English homes and the English into
the French homes in large numbers."**

A 40-year-old official with the federal Anti-Inflation Board in Ottawa,

David Taylor has chosen to live on the Quebec side of the Ottawa River. But rather than viewing Aylmer as a dormitory suburb of Ottawa, Mr. Taylor, who is bilingual, has become involved in the community through the local Heritage Association. A native Manitoban, he is particularly sensitive to the wide cultural gap between French and English in Aylmer and speaks with conviction about the need for family-to-family contact between the two races.

What attracted us to Aylmer first was the open space and the chance to have a house with a little more land only a few minutes from downtown Ottawa. It really had nothing to do with culture or interesting buildings or any of these things which we see now as the more important reasons why we would want to live there. Aylmer is an exciting town because of the history of the area and also because of the mixed culture and the fact that it is 50 percent English and French. It has been termed the most bilingual town in Canada.

If you require that everybody be able to speak and understand both languages, no, Aylmer is not bilingual. But if you go to a public meeting or into most stores, you can be served and you can speak in your own language and be understood in the other language. That I think is probably what bilingualism means in Canada today. The Canada of the future and the Aylmer of the future I think will probably be one where everybody can speak and be understood in his own language.

People in public positions and most people in associations here are increasingly bilingual. Our Heritage Association was started mainly by anglophones but now we are entirely bilingual. That isn't to say that everybody speaks both French and English but our publications and our public meetings are all in English and in French. At one meeting you might have 80 percent French and at another meeting it might be 80 percent English; it depends entirely on who is speaking at the time and who asks questions and that type of thing. Our Board of Directors and our membership, which is approximately 300, runs about 40 percent French-speaking right now and 60 percent English.

Our children have gone to an English school since they have been in Aylmer. In France they were in French schools, but when they came back for pre-university we put them back in English schools. We learned French overseas in Paris while I was posted there by the government, and in that respect we have an advantage over many Canadians who didn't grow up in a French Canadian atmosphere. I was born in Manitoba and raised in Brandon and Winnipeg, and my family had never had any contact with Quebec, with Eastern Canada, or with French-speaking Canadians. The only thing we ever saw in French really was on the Corn Flakes box. When there was a request from Quebec for more interest in their language and more opportunity to use their language and culture in Canada, it was usually greeted with questions about why that was necessary because, after all, this was Canada, an English-speaking country. In recent years that became a stronger reaction as Quebec began to assert itself. Albertans in particular, I think, started to take a stronger approach, to say they considered that English was very much the international language and the official language of Canada. This is a more common reaction in Western Canada than, say, in the East, where English Canadians have had the opportunity to interface with French Canadians.

There was a great shock following the November 15 election in Quebec and that has brought a lot more understanding—at least an attempt to find out some of the answers to the problems that brought about those election results. The red necks now are starting to say, "Yes, maybe there is more to the problem than we ever thought." We have relatives in Calgary and Edmonton and many friends in all of those provinces in the West, and we have noticed this increased open-mindedness amongst all of them.

I think one problem in Quebec is that the French have been made to feel inferior with their language, and to some extent their culture, probably over the centuries. I am not so certain that it was always brought on by the English; to some extent it was caused by being surrounded by the Americans and the Torontonians with a very high standard of living and great success in commerce and other fields. Anybody speaking French and not being able to speak English didn't achieve that success. I think they were also held down to some degree by the clergy. I can understand that people in that situation would want to regain some strength and pride in their culture and their language.

But even today there is not enough interchange between the races. We have not made the big step which really takes the French into the English homes and the English into the French homes in large numbers. The English still don't understand what St.-Jean Baptiste holiday is. They don't understand many other things in the French culture because they have never been exposed to them, and the same is true with French Canadians.

When I was posted in Paris, we English and French Canadians mingled and got to know each other very well, probably better than we could in Canada. In France I gained a respect for the French Canadian culture. I got to know what it was about on neutral territory, where a person doesn't have to defend or fight for his culture or language. We had a chance to discuss openly and see each of our own cultures interact and that was great for both groups.

For example, at Christmastime we had a couple up to our house to celebrate Christmas and partway through the dinner or when we were giving away presents the wife turned and said, "This is amazing. You celebrate Christmas exactly the same way we do. We didn't figure you did this sort of thing. We thought that you celebrated Christmas in a strange way." O course there are minor differences, such as the early-morning Mass or staying up late for the morning tourtière and so on, but aside from that we basically celebrate the same things.

The interesting things are the little differences between the two and I think when both sides get to know those things and maybe start to celebrate them together, then we will accomplish what we have been aiming for—understanding. That will come, I am sure. Bilingualism is the first step toward it, and bilingualism is coming; I honestly believe that. It is happening. I see that most of the schoolchildren of our English-speaking friends are either going to a French immersion program or they speak French very well. And most 20-year-olds nowadays in the government can speak French. But until mass bilingualism is a reality there is no use even hoping we will get good communication between French and English in this country.

The federal government is doing its part in the national capital area, but when you drive down Ontario highways and see only English signs on the Ottawa side of the river, then you can't help but say that it is not a bilingual country. The Ontario government has not been doing as much as it should, despite the large French populations in many areas. On the Quebec side, I think the municipal governments and the provincial governments were pulling their weight as far as seeing that the two languages were respected. That might be shifting in the other direction now though... Since my children are in Quebec, obviously I would like to see that the English school system is continued in Quebec. I think it would be a mistake for the Quebec government to try and do away with English culture for people who have lived there for years. That is cultural genocide and it would be unforgivable.

One of the hopes for having better understanding between the two cultures is to have children get to know each other well. No wonder there's so little mixing between adults: our children are so divided at a young age. I would vote for a single school system with a high degree of interrelationship between French and English students. It would be basically a French language system that offers maybe a stream of English or possibly alternating courses in French and English. Perhaps that's the practical way.

I notice every morning on my way to work that there are two sets of school buses. In fact, there are probably four when you get down to it— English Protestant, English Catholic, French Catholic, and French Protestant—but the two big differences, of course, are between the

English and the French. When the French students look across the street and see the English students standing in a different group, they can't help but grow up with the feeling of being divided.

I should say one other thing. Both my daughters have friends who are French-speaking. I have often found it surprising, but it shows that children can break down those barriers. That's probably one of the hopes for our community.

I must say, like many Canadians, I alternate between pessimism and optimism. This referendum or future ones will depend entirely on whether the people of Canada and the other provinces make an attempt to allow Quebeckers to build up their pride in their language and find true acceptance of their culture in the rest of Canada. I also think that depends greatly on whether everybody keeps their cool. We Quebec English people are going through a difficult period and hopefully it won't result in the total erasure of our community, because it is after all a big community. There will be small insults and other things of that type that people will take to heart, but if everybody can keep their cool over the next few years, I think that we have the hope of regaining a unified Canada.

Antonio Renaud
Retired printer, Pointe-Gatineau
(F)

"Last year I turned down $40,000 for my house ... and this year I couldn't get $25,000 for it."

Younger wage earners think of their own and their childrens' futures, while retired people like Mr. Renaud remember the tough times of the past and find little need for radical change in the greatly improved present.

I was born in Hull in June, 1908, and spent all but the last six years there. I went to school up to grade eight, and after that I went to work at the

Eddy Match factory. I was 14 years old. Hull was an industrial city, lots of factories in those days. Management was English but the greater percentage of workers were French.

Times were tough here during the depression, let me tell you. My father lost his house. Nobody worked for two years. Today Hull has changed so much that I have a lot of difficulty finding my way around. Yes, the changes are for the better. In the not-too-distant future there will be 25,000 persons working in Hull for the federal government, and that pays well now. We used to always say that industry pays better than the government, but now it is the other way around. Of course I'm a federalist. People always say they are Quebeckers—I am a Quebecker too. But before that I am a Canadian. And I want to remain one. That election has changed so many things. Last year I turned down $40,000 for my house—the basement is finished and all—and this year I couldn't get $25,000 for it.

I was a Liberal organizer for years. In the neighbourhood I always had 20 polls, but we knew each other so well in those days that I could have told you, you are a Conservative, you are a Liberal, you are a So-Cred, you are a New Democrat. I could have told you because I had people who went around working for me and they went around houses in twos to make a kind of survey. We won nearly all the elections except when Diefenbaker came in.

Why have the Liberals been so strong in Quebec? Well, they have more of a socialist tendency than the Conservatives, and the Conservatives have a very definite policy on the Queen. Diefenbaker always pushes this. What's the word for it? Oh yes, he's a firm monarchist and we aren't.

The man I really admired was Lester Pearson. My wife and I met Mr. and Mrs. Pearson because I was party organizer. I brought Mr. Pearson here to Hull and had a big reception at the Richard Stadium. I had that place full and after all expenses were paid, I had $500 left to put in the Liberal Association Treasury. Pearson was a very, very good man. He wasn't a man to make fiery speeches; he was a diplomat, always spoke evenly. And he made an effort to speak French, although I spoke with him in English. But have you noticed, since Trudeau has been in power the ministers that speak French? Have you noticed that? I think that is very good. Bilingualism is needed in Canada. If you want to earn a living, you have to have both languages.

My personal opinion of René Lévesque? He is a man who fights very hard for the French language. But he is a bit of a dictator. I would put him close to Hitler. I am afraid of him. Do you know why? When he won the election on November 15, he said he wanted to form a good government and not worry about independence. But since then independence is all he talks about. That is what is angering people. It may cost him the next election.

I will be among the first to vote in the referendum. And I will vote against it. I want to remain a Canadian. Look, my wife and I wanted to have our family grow up in a better position than what we had. My parents knew too much misery. I said when I got married, "What I want is that my children will be better off than me." So I have four children — two teachers, a bank manager, and one works for General Electric as a secretary. All have good jobs. I'm not interested in independence.

Danielle Richer
Lawyer, Pointe-Gatineau
(F and E)

"Almost every country around the world envies the Americans for their standard of living and I don't wish to live otherwise."

The majority of people I talked to, including a good number of Péquistes, expresed fears that Quebec's standard of living might fall with separation. Quebeckers may have different tastes, customs, and interests than English Canadians but few would suggest they are less materialistic. Danielle Richer, a lawyer in her mid-20s practicing in Point-Gatineau across the river from Ottawa, enjoys Caribbean vacations, good clothes, and other outward signs of success. The prospect of belt-tightening for political reasons is not one that attracts her.

I began my studies in law in 1969 at the University of Ottawa and finished in 1972. After my probation period in Hull I opened my lawyer's office here in 1974. I have a general practice and at the present time I am trying to specialize in matrimonial and municipal law. Of course they are not related, but let's say that these are two specialties which can easily be practiced here in the region. In Quebec you can always speak French, plead in French in the courts. I have also used English on many occasions when both clients were English-speaking. And in this area no judge ever refused to hear a case because it was in English. Maybe there were problems elsewhere in other districts but I never heard about them. I prefer the French language, naturally because I started speaking English later. The area that I come from is not bilingual at all. I learned English when I was living with people who spoke the language, not at school. It is a necessity in North America—throughout the world—if you want to travel. It is an international language.

I considered myself a Canadian since elementary school. I don't deny being a Quebecker, of course, but I always had the impression that first of all I belonged to Canada. I have always had that deep impression and really not many arguments will take that away from me. I have travelled outside Canada and I always describe myself as a Canadian, not a Québécois—and people always look at us as Canadians. Of course they notice we speak French with our accent. When you say you come from Quebec, people say "Oh, you're from Canada then."

I am very happy to be part of Confederation. A country for me is not necessarily a nation as such or a culture as such; a country is a strategic and economic whole; it is a power. A nation, well, is something a little more personal which identifies much more closely with our own personality, our culture, or language. It is important, too, but I separate that idea from the idea of country.

My first reaction on the morning after the November 15 election? It was one of great doom and gloom and despair. It was a surprise because I had not expected this result. I was for the Liberal Party and it was the greatest possible political disappointment for my short political life. It was the first time that I actively participated in an election campaign and to watch a rather strong party like the Liberals come apart as they did was a great disappointment.

From a political point of view I am disappointed that the PQ is in power. I have thought a lot about this because I have a great many more friends of my own age who are PQ than are Liberals. So, of course, I discuss politics a great deal with these people. What strikes me the most is that they have no regard whatsoever, no concern, for what is happening throughout the world economically. On the international level I say that more and more we have to reach international economic agreements. We can't just put a fence around ourselves, you know. We will definitely have to have international agreements and think along international lines more and more.

I think it's illogical to have a movement of disunity within Canada now where we live so well with one of the world's highest standards of living. You remember there was hardly any emphasis on separation before the elections, and yet the day after, that was the only thing Lévesque was talking about—separating Quebec from Canada. This created a great deal of discontent among people who were not separatists but who voted for him because they voted for a change in government. Of course I will vote in a referendum and of course I will vote against separation. I have already attended a great many meetings where strategies were discussed; we federalists are organizing too, you know!

The PQ say that Canada is a satellite of the United States. I don't think so; but if it *is* a satellite, this is good because economically it gives us what we need. It gives us a high standard of living. I do not say that we should have the same culture, the same way of thinking, that they do in the U.S., but materially I think it is good. Almost every country around the world envies the Americans for their standard of living and I do not wish to live otherwise. Even if I am Canadian, I live in North America and I like that type of life. I think the PQ is far too socialist and dangerous, extremely dangerous. I hope it doesn't stay in power long enough to spoil things too much.

As far as the language bill is concerned, I appreciate the fact that the PQ want to guarantee that French will remain in Quebec—this should have been done a long time ago. But a just or a fair law on this subject is something practically impossible. I think it is utopian to try to impose a point of view by a law, and you cannot force people to speak a language they do not want to speak.

I have some admiration for Mr. Lévesque because he was a man who believed in something and he persevered a great deal. I think that Mr. Trudeau's personality is far stronger than that of René Lévesque. Maybe it is a little bold to go this far, but I find Mr. Trudeau more intelligent than Mr. Lévesque. If you look at his strategies, his way of acting, I find him brilliant. Let's say that I find Trudeau superior and I have the impression that in the match which is being played between the two, Trudeau will win out.

Canada's future is bright, as far as I am concerned. Canada will remain united. There have always been little crises since the beginning of Confederation, but I don't think there will be any crises now strong enough to break up Confederation.

Rosaleen Dixon
Newspaper publisher, Shawville
(E)

**"I have never known a bilingual
person who wasn't happy that
he was bilingual."**

*The visitor to Shawville is greeted by the somewhat incongruous sight of the
union jack fluttering placidly above the local Oddfellows hall. An agricultural
town of 1,724 inhabitants, 83 km. northwest of Ottawa-Hull, Shawville is
an Anglo enclave in Quebec like Shannon, Westmount, and Rock Island.
Rosaleen Dixon, owner of Shawville's weekly newspaper,* The Equity, *is a
strong opponent both of separatism and of Quebec's so-called "confessional"
educational system, which separates students by both language and religion.*

My family has been in Canada for several hundred years. I was a Leslie
before I was a Dixon. The first Leslies came from Germany in the 1700s
to Lunenburg, Nova Scotia, and on the Scotch side they came on the
Hector to Pictou. My grandfather, Robert Jamison Leslie, was a member
of Parliament in Quebec, which is interesting because we are really Nova
Scotia people. That was around the turn of the century, so that is our
earliest connection with Quebec. In those days Parliament was
conducted in both English and French, so it was easy for a Scot like him
to be able to handle himself up in Quebec. My father is Kenneth Leslie,
the poet. Yes, he is one of Canada's greatest — if not the greatest — poets.
He had four or five books published; he was one of those people who won
an early Governor-General's award for poetry. He was a young man then,
of course; that was a long, long time ago. He lived and worked in Nova
Scotia and died in Halifax last year.

The people who came to this area came up by the Ottawa River and
settled where they saw farms, where they liked the look of the hills.
Settlement has kept on right through the 1900s and we still have settlers
coming in from all over the place, Germany, the States, Canada. The
language here is English. The people are Irish, Scottish, Polish,
Ukrainian, German, and French. Shawville is very typical of any
Canadian village you would see anywhere, I think.

I have raised six children here and you have to feel it is a wonderful
place to live. Our oldest son and his wife are back with us, having done
their thing all over the world. It is the place they have chosen after

everywhere else and it is what we chose after everywhere else. I have lived in the States and in Europe—in Paris and Switzerland, and in Washington, D.C., and spent a great deal of time in New York City. When I was young I did a lot of travelling.

I am a Québécois by adoption. When we came to Shawville 25 years ago, this was a very small community, hardly known. It still is hardly known by Quebec. You say, "Shawville" and a lot of people in Quebec say that's in Ontario somewhere.

We came here because there was a newspaper here and we looked at it and bought it the next day. We were living in Ottawa at the time—my husband was working for the civil service—and we were not enchanted with the way of life. I'll tell you precisely why we live in a small town. It is because you are somebody in a small town and you are totally responsible for everything you do. Your little child just can't walk down the street and be an anonymous vandal or an anonymous anything. Every single thing that child does, the whole town knows who he is and what it is he has done. And with that kind of an upbringing you learn to be responsible for your actions, and you also learn a little bit about community responsibility. Our children, every single one of them, have a very, very strong sense of community responsibility and we think it is because of their upbringing in a small town.

There is also a sense of family. I don't know whether that has anything to do with small towns; it might. I think if you go into a lot of homes in a small town—not just Shawville but any town—you will see the granddaddy there being looked after by the younger generation. And the children are there and the grandchildren if necessary—there is a sort of a continuation. You don't just have one man, one woman, and 2.2 children sitting in a box somewhere.

The election? Sure, I remember that night very clearly. We have television in the bedroom, which is very convenient because you can fall asleep when it gets boring. But that night no one fell asleep. We stayed up to see what the hell was going to happen and it happened! But I didn't feel as if we were not in Canada anymore. The next day people were coming around looking so sad and worried and wondering what it was going to mean and where they were going to go, as if they had to go somewhere. We were very busy; we had to get the paper out.

The day after, the CBC swarmed in here, the Toronto newspapers, the Montreal newspapers. They were all rushing up to Shawville, pushing microphones in our faces, asking, "What will you do?" And then of course it became obvious to all these terrified people that really Quebec was still here, the ground was still under us, we were still on planet earth. Canada was still surrounding us; if you turned the radio on, you could still hear Ottawa radio, so that hadn't been cut off. The trucks were still

running, the buses were still running, the river was still flowing. ...
Finally it all settled down.

I am just a Canadian, you know. I figure that my people have been here
for so long and have worked so hard to build a wonderful country—they
did it for me—and all I do is try and carry on the work. It has been that
way all my life and if that is being a federalist . . . I am just carrying on—
"Carry on, Canada," sounds like a motto—I never thought of it that way
before but, sure, I am just a Canadian, that's what I am.

I think the best thing is for people to feel that Canada is important to
them, and for each individual to do whatever they feel is necessary to
keep Canada together. And that means not going about putting down
other people of another race, saying things that are derogatory about the
French or the English. I have a lot of English-speaking friends and a lot
of French-speaking friends, and when I am with either one group or the
other, I find them putting the other ones down to a great extent. In Hull
you see it a lot; they are putting down the English. In Ottawa you see
them putting down the French. It really angers me and I sometimes get a
little serious when everyone else is joking and I sort of draw people
together and say, "Well, look, I don't think that is funny." So I come off
as a spoil-sport, but people should get their sport some other way than
looking for faults in the other race. That is a racial thing; it has got
nothing to do with language, it has got nothing to do with anything else—
it is purely racial. It is like the Pakistani thing in Toronto.

I find very well-educated people and important people in the French
community in Hull showing a great deal of concern because there is so
much English being spoken and their children are being involved with
too much English. They should stop worrying about that and just make
sure that the children are learning the French that they want them to
learn—you know, instead of being negative, they should be positive.
Now a lot of English-speaking people in this area are worried that their
children are going to be assimilated by the French. Well, there is no way
because no matter how much French you learn, it is only to your benefit.
I have never known a bilingual person who wasn't happy that he was
bilingual.

Yes, I'm bilingual because way back when I was a little girl, my father
said to my mother, "My children must be bilingual." He wasn't, so they
took us all to France and made us learn French just by popping us into a
French school where there was no English, and that is such an easy way
to learn. It is fun but you don't have to go to France to do it—you can do
it right here if you have a French school.

In Shawville we don't have much of a French program in our English
schools. If you are going to teach kids to swim, you have to put them in
the water. You just don't show them the water and let them put their foot

in it and say, "See, it is wet." Well, that is the way French is taught and has been taught historically in Quebec to English children. Finally this year after wishing and asking for it for a long, long, time, there is going to be a little bit of French immersion. They are going to teach two courses in grade five and two courses in grade six, like social studies and physical education in French, and in grade seven they are going to teach geography and math in French. A lot of parents don't want their children to have anything to do with that at all because they say they are afraid that the first thing you know they will all be French. That is such a very funny attitude.

Another thing bothers me about our school system in Quebec. I think it is foolish to have Catholic children on one side of the street and Protestant children on the other, learning the same thing separately when they could be learning them together. That is divisive. We have track meets here, and I can tell you who is the highest Catholic jumper in the county and who is the highest Protestant jumper in the county — but we never know who the highest jumper of them all is!

You're damn right I'll vote in the referendum! I will not only vote in the referendum, I will try to find out how the referendum is going to be held and try to explain to other people what it means, because I suspect that it will be worded in a weird way that will be very difficult for people to understand. But even if Quebec were to separate, it is still going to be here, you know. I keep saying the grass is here, I am standing on the ground; I am running the print shop; I publish a newspaper; I raise a family; I have a wonderful garden; I have a lovely home. I don't expect anything to take those things away from me. I am not doing any separating. If the laws of the government change, as far as I am concerned that doesn't change me. I am me.

Robert Young
Farmer, Shawville
(E)
**"I've been trying to bilingualize our
family now for eight years."**

*Robert Young's ancestors have been in Quebec for about seven generations. A
successful English Protestant dairy farmer with four school-age children, he is
intent on seeing his children become bilingual so they can remain in Quebec
comfortably. Unable to send them to a French school, as he would prefer, Mr.
Young has chosen an alternative cause of action.*

I took my high school here and went to Ontario to college, but during the
time I was going to school here, we got from our parents a feeling that it
was kind of worthless for us to learn French. I think the only exam I ever
failed in high school was French. In fact I very seldom passed it! But in
the last maybe 12 years I've become involved with French people in the
rest of the province and become partially bilingual. We exhibit cattle at
Lachute and Quebec City, so I've developed a French vocabulary that
covers agriculture. Of course, if you started talking about atomic bombs
or something I wouldn't be able to follow the conversation. But French
people here often would rather speak English to me rather than listen to
me trying to speak French.

We have four children and we would have sent them to French school
if there had been one in Shawville, but there is no French Protestant
school here. Our oldest one, Ricky, entered his last year in high school
last fall. When he started school, we felt there wasn't enough French, so
for parts of three summers we had him live with French families.
Although he doesn't write real good French, he can speak it well. It really
made a difference.

In the early '60s Jean Lesage wanted to amalgamate the schools but he
got kicked out on his ass. Our high school, the Pontiac Protestant High
School, was being built to accommodate all the children in this area, and
of course the Catholic teachers and priests and nuns, who were at that
time controlling the school system, the education system in Quebec,
didn't agree with amalgamation. The English Protestant Teachers
Association didn't agree either because their lobbyists were getting
$20,000 or $30,000 a year and would have automatically been out of a job
when they amalgamated.

I certainly would like amalgamation, providing it was done with an English part and a French part in the school. Workshops would be together. Children would play together and, if they tried at all, they would emerge bilingual. I think Lachute is the only one they got built before the elections. We have friends whose children attend there and it works perfect. That's exactly what I'd like. Now Lévesque might go for this sort of school system but I don't trust some of his cabinet ministers too much.

I don't think that there's any bigotry here in Shawville. These fellows come up from CBC and accuse us of being bigoted and so on, but I don't think that's true. Well, maybe if you look hard enough you can find some. Relations between English and French here were okay until the government started meddling in it. I think probably relations aren't as good right now as they were two years ago. When you start telling people that they've got to do something and you push them, you know . . . well, you can pull a rope a lot easier than you can push it.

For example, before they announced Bill 22, English people were taking French classes just about every night of the week. You had to have your application in six months ahead to get into it. After they announced Bill 22, there was no more classes. People just quit taking French because they were told they had to learn it. You see, before the bill, people were learning it because they realized that it was the common-sense thing to do if they were going to live here. But when someone told them they had to, they're Irishmen and they don't like being told what they have to do.

The feeling I have is it's our country and we love it. I mean when our great-great-grandfathers came here it wasn't easy and I think that we're going to stay here even though it may not be real easy for a little while. We'll get along. If Lévesque don't like us, that's his problem, not ours. We'll still be here and that's that.

Pontiac has expressed itself very clearly as being anti-separatist Canada. Both our Members have the exact same sentiments or they certainly wouldn't be in office. They're both Liberals and are taking part in our Quebec-Canada Movement and so on without any qualms. I am planning to stay here—not all, but 90 percent of my generation will stay here. I think that it is our duty to educate our children so that they have the choice whether or not to remain in Quebec; but if they are going to hold a good job, either with the government or as a salesman or as a businessman or anything, they are definitely going to have to be bilingual. I realized this long before René Lévesque was premier of Quebec. I've been trying to bilingualize our family now for eight years.

I don't think that Lévesque will take Quebec out of Confederation because a lot of the French people are not accepting what he is doing. We have a lot of French friends who do not accept what is going on. Probably if everyone in his cabinet was as smooth as René Lévesque is they might.

I just hope that our Quebec-Canada Movement does a better job—I have been very disappointed in their actions in the last two or three months. We attended the organizational meeting and appointed an executive for this area and that's the last we have heard of them. They certainly should be having meetings and getting everyone ready to act because one thing for sure is that people who are really strong separatists are all going to vote. If people only hear one side of the story, it is bound to look good, but somebody has to tell them the other side and that is what we have to do.

Personally, I am very disappointed with the attitude that the CBC has taken over the last number of years since this crisis has started to build. I feel that they are doing what they think will attract people to watch their programs rather than relating the facts, which is supposed to be their job. Helping keep Canada together definitely should be part of their job. You know, in my personal experience, I have been interviewed by CBC television two times and I was made to look like an English separatist, which I certainly am not. I don't feel bigoted toward anyone or any people in this country, and they most certainly made me look like that and have done it to more than one person in the area.

I think Canada is a great nation. It has treated every one of us here maybe too well, maybe spoiled us. I think that it is really ridiculous for the people of Quebec to feel that they are being discriminated against. They should stop and realize that although they may not be as well off as B.C. because of this or that, or Alberta because of its oil, they are certainly much better off then their relatives over in France, who in no way are in the position that the people living in Quebec are.

I consider myself a Canadian who happens to live in part of the country that is Quebec. I am proud of being a Quebecker. You know, if I am somewhere and they look at my Quebec licence and make a dirty sign or something, it certainly irritates me. You get that a lot. It's happened to us in Ottawa. And we know one lady who had a new car—brand new, about a week old—and she was visiting Arnprior, and somebody painted white stripes all over it. We have had no one do any damage to us but at a stoplight, quite often you know, someone would look at us and give us the finger. But I think that these are people of less mentality than some of René Lévesque's crowd — like they are the same type only living on the other side of the river. I don't lose any sleep over it, but it bothers you that it happens. That's all.

It seems funny when I think about it that maybe someday, I'll be talking to my grandchildren and I'll have to talk to them in French. That might happen! I hope that they will stay here and I hope that they will still talk English. If our English culture is worth keeping, it will be kept.

If there are French people in Quebec whose grandchildren can't speak French, it must be because they didn't really respect their parents, their culture. I hope and I know that my children, and I hope my future grandchildren, will be proud to be English Canadians, living in the province of Quebec.

Tony Mann
Teacher, Perkins
(E)

"I have already decided that if I still live in Quebec when it separates, I will not bring my car into Ontario because I expect the tires to be slashed and the windows to be smashed."

Canada is a country of immigrants, and Tony Mann is one of the more recent arrivals. Enrolling at Carlton University in the mid-'60s, he completed B.A. and M.A. degrees and settled on the Quebec side of the Ottawa River to raise a family while teaching English at a community college in Ottawa. He often sees Quebec politics through Irish eyes and finds the parallels disturbing.

I went to school in Dublin and lived in England for a while and came to Canada in 1959. I came here really for a better life actually and to go to university. I grew up in Ireland hearing about the New World and the opportunities it afforded immigrants, particularly from Ireland, and I decided this was where I was coming. When I came here first, I was very unhappy. I was lonely and it was a real culture shock for me. I arrived in Ottawa. I came there originally because it was the capital and I thought it would be similar to Dublin and to London, where one had zoos, botanical gardens, symphonies, good theatre, good cinema. But I was very disappointed.

I knew certain facts in Irish history, and when I came to Canada and read Canadian history, I was really struck by the similarities. For instance, Ireland is essentially an agricultural country and so is Quebec. There is great dominance by the clergy in Quebec; there certainly is in Ireland. There are also these aspirations to be master of one's own house, certainly in Ireland, where they are still fighting the English to get them out of Northern Ireland. But I think beyond that there is the language question, which in Ireland you are made aware of very early, say at the age of seven. The Irish people lost their language and we were learning it in school as a second language.

It is interesting to me right now to see the debate going on in Canada to learn French as a second language or as one that you can speak equally with English. My experience in Ireland was that Irish was very difficult to learn for most people and most people resisted learning it simply because they were being coerced into learning it. I think that in Quebec today the government is taking the wrong approach to say to people that they have to learn French. I think that it will be a similar experience in Quebec to the one we had in Ireland; that people will say, "No we are not going to learn it." Or they will learn it in school and promptly forget it.

It seems to me that I am living my childhood all over again with this situation in Quebec and I must admit that I feel sad about it, really. Why? If Quebec really separates, I can only say that the hatreds with which I was familiar when I grew up in Ireland—the hatred of England, the hatred of the Northern Ireland people — will come to Canada and it will be hatred between French and English. It is a phase of nationalism that I don't think Canadians are really aware of.

It just couldn't possibly be an amiable parting. What is happening in stark terms is, if Quebec separates, it will break up Canada. That is really what will happen and you cannot expect the English to say, "Okay, bye-bye, and it was nice knowing you." They will be very angry!

My feeling is that if we are going to live in a democracy, and if we are going to have a certain fairness about this, there should be only one referendum. There should be only one and that's it! If Quebec decides in the first referendum that it wants to separate, I am ambivalent about that. On the one hand, I see what has happened in Ireland, where our leaders in 1921 went over and negotiated a settlement and partitioned our country and it has been the bane of Irish life ever since. Now if the federal government says, "Okay, you politicians in Quebec, you can go!" it's going to unleash incredible forces in Canadian history and Canadian nationalism that I am not sure will in fact be settled for another 100 years.

Actually, I don't think that separation or the break-up of Canada should be negotiable. I think that there should be maybe a redefinition of Confederation with the agreed-upon premise that we are not going to break Canada. We will, maybe, loosen certain areas of jurisdiction; we will try and accommodate you. At the moment there is a bilingualism policy in Canada which is not working, but could be made to work more effectively. But, no, I think separation is nonnegotiable.

I have a son—he's 14 months old. I will send him to a bilingual school in Ottawa if I can find one. If not, I will send him to a French school there. Why Ottawa? Because, contrary to what people may think, Ireland is a democracy and I was brought up to believe in democracy and I do want the choice. I don't want the government to tell me that because I was not educated in English in Quebec then I must send my son to a French school. That, I will not allow any government to do. A democrat cannot give in to that kind of coercion.

It may seem silly and it would save me money to stay put but there is a principle involved, and that is something that I would like my son to understand when he grows up: that you do not give in to coercion. I am prepared to pay extra to defend this principle. After all, my son is going to grow up in a democratic country, I hope. And I hope that we will be able to talk and I can pass on to him some of my ideas about democracy.

I was thinking of selling my house before the PQ government came into power. I must also admit I generally feel that there are better schools in cities and that was one of my reasons for wanting to sell, but since the PQ election I am afraid my agitation has become greater and I have wanted to sell the house in a more urgent way. Has the value gone up? Oh no, not at all! As a matter of fact I spoke to my real estate agent recently. The house has been up for sale for over six months and I asked him why it hasn't been sold and he said the market is absolutely flat; he said if I brought the price down maybe $15,000 ... He said, "Anything over $50,000 is not selling in Quebec now." I am sorry but my house is worth more than $50,000 and I am not going to sell it cheaply. I'm not going to take a shit-kicking. I just hope that the referendum won't go through.

Lévesque? As an individual, he is an impressive man; he seems sincere. But, on the other hand, I also am aware that he is a man who is saying to Canada, "I am going to break up this country," and in the end I am afraid I am against him totally. And I don't trust his cabinet. Camille Laurin, I think, has a revengeful colonial mentality. That is how I would put it. If you look at or read the submissions to his language board on Bill 101, every submission that anglophones made was treated with spite and malice and criticized. There was even a submission by the St.-Jean Baptiste Society where Laurin said that they hadn't gone far enough and he praised them! It is just typical of a revengeful, spiteful attitude and this is what Canadians are in for in the next few years.

As for Trudeau, well, I remember once when I was at school I read an essay on Timothy Healy, who was an Irish politician, and he was characterized at the end of the essay as a "brilliant disaster." Well, I really cannot say that about our Prime Minister. I think Pierre Trudeau has been just a plain disaster for this country since 1968. Remember the Trudeaumania in 1968 and the great things that we all expected? Let's face it, here we are in 1977 and there is this talk of break-up. All of his policies were supposedly designed to bring Canadians together and here we are more divided than ever! One has to lay the blame somewhere and certainly he deserves a lot of it. That is my view of Pierre Trudeau. We hear a lot about his great intellect, his great philosophies, but I'm afraid I am not at all impressed.

He was elected to be the leader of this country and also, if my understanding is correct, to bring this country together. But take the October Crisis. I was really on his side in the initial weeks, but since then evidence has come to light that we didn't get all the truth. There is an interesting point to be made here about the October Crisis. The reaction of a French Canadian Prime Minister to his own was so swift and so arrogant and so draconic that it is only a reflection of what will happen in the country at large between Canadians—French and English—if the country ever breaks up. It will be savage. I have already decided that if I still live in Quebec when it separates, I will not bring my car into Ontario because I expect the tires to be slashed and the windows to be smashed. I expect to be spat upon, and if Canadians think that is fanciful, well, there are many instances—Ireland, the French in Algeria, the Basques in Spain.

Yes, I see a lack of statesmanship at the national level. It seems there is a one-note tune being played all the time: bilingualism. Well, bilingualism is not the only thing. There is something else to a culture: there is a spirit, there is an animation, there is a freedom to a culture. I know because I am very aware of the culture I grew up in. That aspect is not being addressed by our leaders and this is strange in fact because, let's face it, the leaders—the federal leaders, who are French Canadian, like the Prime Minister and Chrétien—they seem to be so stubborn. If anybody should understand French aspirations, what the survival of a culture means, it should be these men, but they don't seem to understand.

I think in the end, when it comes down to five minutes to midnight, Canadians are going to really take a hard look at Trudeau and at that moment realize that he is not the man to save us. I think in the end they will go on his past record and say, "No I am sorry, somebody else must be at the helm." If they don't, I am sorry but I figure that we are in for a lot of trouble. In the end it is going to be nasty.

I like Canada and have decided to stay here. I feel that Canadians are in the process of building their own history, their own nationalism, and while it is a very painful process, I want to be here and want to contribute. I have no intention of ever going back to Ireland or to England, except for a holiday. As a matter of fact, this is my home now. My son has been born here and he is a Canadian and I am going to stay here.

Diana Skrastins
Student, Two Mountains
(E)
**"Yes, I can speak French
but I'd rather not."**

*If Bill 101 had been in effect 15 years ago this interview would have been
conducted in French instead of English. The daughter of immigrant parents,
Diana Skrastins is now completing her Bachelor of Education degree at
McGill University and facing the unpleasant prospect of a practically
nonexistent job market for English-speaking teachers.*

My parents are from Latvia, which is now a republic or a province of
Russia. They left during the outbreak of World War Two and have been
in Quebec for about 25 years now. One brother was born in Latvia and
one in France; another brother and I were born here in Quebec. We
moved to Vancouver for three years and I came back to Quebec at the age
of 12. Until then I didn't consider myself anything but Latvian because
my parents are very patriotic toward Lativa still. In Vancouver I figured
I'm Canadian, but I never really thought of myself as belonging just
solely to a province.

I don't consider myself very politically minded, but it's always there,
in the background. I read about it, what comes up in major issues, and I
must say I'm more interested in politics now than I was before the
election. I don't really appreciate what the PQ are doing to the English.
They're like trying to make us non-existent; that's how I feel. I'm
resentful toward it. Okay, so 80 percent of Quebec, if not more, is
French, but there are still a million English. They can't disregard us.

Thinking about immigrants coming into Quebec, even though French
and English are the national languages of Canada, somehow English
seems to be more so, because the majority of Canadians do speak it. So I
figure, immigrants coming into Quebec would rather probably speak
English than French. And I guess they would resent the new regulations.
Personally, I'm for bilingualism myself; I think they should have a
choice, but they don't now. Quebec always has been bilingual. I saw no
problems with it. I think the PQ are creating the problems by making it
totally French. People in business, they have to deal with companies
outside of Quebec which are English, and that can cause problems unless
you can speak English as well as French. I don't think they can survive

solely in French, unless the other provinces speak French, and they aren't going to change for us.

Another thing, I think the international language is English, and air traffic controllers should use it, even if a pilot happens to be French. I think there will be less confusion that way. I think if you have one language, it creates less problems than if you have two. I don't think that issue really helped the PQ get into power, although it may have had something to do with it.

Basically, what the French people want, from what I hear, is to maintain their culture. But I can't see why they can't do it while staying as a province whithin Canada. Because, well, my parents, as I mentioned before, are very patriotic, and there is a small Latvian society in Quebec and they have maintained their culture. I don't see why the French can't do the same. I mean, we are further away from Latvia than we ever were but if we can maintain our culture, why can't the French? That's how I feel. So I'm not for separatism and I'll vote against it.

Yes, I can speak French, but I'd rather not. I try to avoid it for reasons of embarrassment. I've been told I speak it fairly well, but you know, you are always more comfortable with the language you speak better. I can get by okay with English in downtown Montreal. In stores, most of the store clerks and cashiers are English-speaking. They'll talk to me in English before they will say anything in French, even though they themselves are French. I read some French newspapers sometimes, occasionally, but I won't go out of my way to listen to French radio or television, and I find just as good movies in English.

I don't think French instruction is that good in English schools. We had barely 45 minutes a day in high school, not more than that, about two hours a week, with little oral emphasis, which is what you would be using most of the time anyway. The teacher in the French class always said, "If you don't understand, I'll say it in English." So I came out of school with very bad French. I learned my French mostly through working in summer jobs. Like one summer I worked in a store which was mostly, like 95 percent French and that's where I learned it.

McGill is totally English. We never use French at the university. It's only when it comes to dealing with the government offices, like this summer, dealing with Manpower, and things like that. If they find out that you're English, they will talk to you in English, but otherwise it would be all in French. I guess going about getting summer jobs, applying to companies, outside the Montreal area would be difficult with only English.

Actually I'm for bilingual schools, like the French immersion classes that they have now in English schools. They are very effective. And I think a good system would be having schools where they teach half and half; half the courses in French, half in English. It might be confusing until things got going, but if your aim is bilingualism in Quebec, that would be a good way to start.

It might be a little touchy to do that in the other provinces, where the French population is not so great. But then again, you're talking about the national languages of Canada being French and English. It's really hard to say. I guess it depends on the province, on how many French people there are. I don't know what good it would be to have a bilingual system in Vancouver where not many people speak it.

I feel somewhat threatened about my profession now, I worry what will happen if they close down the schools at the rate that they are. I hear they plan to abolish English schools by 1980. I guess I'll be forced to leave. I really don't want to; I think it isn't fair. Quebec has been my home for years, and my family is going to remain here. I see no reason why I should leave. As a teacher I wouldn't need French if English schools stayed open, so I'm not planning on taking a French immersion course. But I think if unilingualism sticks in Quebec I would probably eventually take courses or try to become perfectly bilingual. But until I find out more what is going to happen, I don't think I'll do anything.

Michel Ménard
Garage owner, St.-Jovite
(F)
"The people are afraid of the future."

An objection to the PQ often heard from the business community is against that party's social democratic economic policies. Michel Ménard's views are particularly interesting since he is a PQ voter who is at the same time highly critical of the party. Mr. Ménard does business every day with visitors to Quebec's most popular tourist area, and is clearly concerned that their goodwill should be maintained, as he explained in his service station in the Laurentian resort of St.-Jovite.

I have been in business for the last ten years in the Laurentians and have a lot of opportunities to meet people of all different nationalities—all sorts of characters. Maybe that's one of the advantages, one of the reasons why I have stayed in business. I like it. Here in this region, the PQ won the election on November 15 and I must say that they got my vote. It was a vote for political change and not a vote for independence. I think that a lot of other people who voted PQ felt the same way that I did. My wife has always been PQ to the death and today, even she is beginning to change her opinion slowly. Let's say that she is still for the Parti Québécois but not for going out and attaining independence.

We want to be recognized as a people though, we Quebeckers. In the past, maybe we were a little bit afraid to say what we thought and to actually go out and prove outselves. We were always a little bit timid. Sometimes it takes a kick in the arse to get you moving.

The trouble is, there is no clear proof mathematically of what independence, if it went through, is going to give us economically. We just don't know. And this economic question mark is the biggest point. As a businessman, this question is the most important one in my mind and I think that is normal, because I have invested a certain amount of money here. I am building for the future. I am building for my wife. I am building for my children. So I wouldn't want to see business fall off with this threat of independence because investors have become afraid. At that point I am just not interested in independence. Most people, I think, are facing the future with a great deal of uncertainty. Those who have saved and built up something over the years, are they going to wake up one day with a diminished purchasing power—keeping in mind that it's already going down? And what affect is all this going to have on our tourist business? Will the tourists be afraid to come here? Will the investors and new industries be afraid to continue investing in Quebec? Now these are the sort of questions that no one has yet been able to give us precise answers on. The government talks to us about companies who are not afraid to continue to invest, but this is what we are told—there is nothing really concrete to prove this.

I know that the majority of Quebeckers and certainly the business people in this region are very, very happy to see the same tourists coming back year after year. I don't think they will feel unwelcome here. I certainly hope they won't because we want them to know that they are welcome and we want to see them here.

Another thing we are told a lot by independence spokesmen is that if we are independent, we won't have to pay any more taxes to the federal government. We will pay them all to the same place: Quebec City. But who says we won't have to pay more than twice as much to the provincial government? Let's remember that the federal government has certain programs that we benefit from, like family allowances. Unemployment insurance is a federal program too. What's going to happen to those things once independence comes? The province of Quebec has now taken over health insurance, but it doesn't have enough money to pay for it. It is always in the hole and has been every year. Really, it's a question of administration. The Quebecker is not an administrator. When the day comes that the Quebecker is a more able administrator, when he can manage his own budget and live within his means, then the Canadian economy will be twice as strong as it is today. That's my opinion. It's a question of administration.

Another thing that makes me afraid about the PQ is their socialism. They want everyone to share equally. Now personally I associate socialism with communism—one for all and all for one. I am just not in favour of that formula. If somebody wants a little bit more for himself, let him work a little bit harder and not try to live on the work of someone else. Unfortunately, that's what's happening these days. The people are asking for more, more, more from the government—more from the federal government, more from the provincial government. But for the government to be able to give people more, naturally, they have to raise taxes to find the money for all these things. If people would only stop asking for more and live within their means, then the economy would pick up. Everyone would be better off, but today no one will tighten his belt. Just look at a lot of strikes that we have today. You see in the newspapers that the workers have rejected the latest offer of management and have voted 99.9 percent for strike action. But if you go and talk to those guys who are on the picket line, you will be surprised at how many of them are really against the strike; many thought they had a fairly decent salary but were pushed into it by their unions.

Has Bill 101 affected me personally? You bet it has. Now, all the advertising and publicity that I receive at the garage—and that we have to pay $100 a month for—is strictly in French. Up until now it had always been bilingual, but all of a sudden we get this advertising material directly from Toronto, in French. I am talking here about tire specials, battery specials, monthly specials on tune-ups, that sort of thing for our displays out in front of the garage. I've got some English-speaking customers and now they have to ask me for explanations about this advertising. I have to tell them how much this or that tire costs, whether this particular special includes labour or not. It is all written in French, so they are in the dark. Now, I think that it should be bilingual, half English and half French. You have to be fair so that everyone can understand, but this unilingual advertising creates misunderstandings. This even applies to the sign here on my service station. It now says *Imperial Oil* but in the next two days the letters are going to be changed— the sign is going to real *Impériale*. That's all happening because of Bill 101. English is a universal language and it's the language of business. We can't forget that, but I'm just afraid that Quebec is going to lose, is going to miss out on opportunities because of this desire to be unilingual French. The future will show whether we are right or wrong.

Education is another question. My kids are young, they are not yet in school but one thing for sure—if the educational system continues the way it's going, there is every chance that my children will never go to a public school, but will be sent instead to a private school. I say this because the quality of teaching, I think, leaves a lot to be desired and I have got some proof. One of my brothers who is 20 years old left his technical school and joined the navy to learn a trade because the quality of instruction was better and at his school here in Quebec he was losing valuable time because of strikes and other conflicts. The student was caught in a squeeze between his employer and the teachers and as a result he was missing courses and time and might even lose his year. In certain schools we are beginning to see an extremist element develop. And another thing, my children are definitely going to be bilingual. If the second language was Italian, they would learn Italian. If it were German, they would learn German. You can't just limit yourself to one culture these days. Here the principal culture is French and they will have that culture, but they must learn the second language too so they aren't limited in all sorts of things that will open up in the future.

How do I sum up my feelings about the next few years? I am afraid, really afraid. Nobody can give you the right answer. Everyone is making suppositions, making guesses, making promises, but the fact is that the economy today continues to go downhill. This has been happening for years and years but nobody has been prepared to take the responsibility to say, "We must put an end to inflation and work to improve the economy." People haven't stopped to take account of where we are. We are spending, spending, spending, and buying and buying—but at some point you have to pay for what you want. As far as the referendum goes, sure, I'm going to vote. It is everyone's duty to vote, and it's hard to predict what the outcome will be, but I wouldn't think that Quebec will separate. The people do not want separation. This is the opinion of practically everyone I meet. The people do not want separation because they haven't been given clear answers—precise, exact answers as to what will happen after separation. The people are afraid of the future.

Chapter 7

Abitibi-
Temiscaming

Virtually all of northern Quebec, from Sept-Îles in the east to
Rouyn-Noranda in the west, is twentieth-century pioneering country. This
was still hushed wilderness 300 years after merchants, soldiers, craftsmen, and
wigmakers were jostling each other in the narrow streets of Quebec City.

Many French Canadians were not prepared to join the migration to Western
Canada after the hanging of Louis Riel in 1885 and the anglicization of the
school systems of the West in the 1890s. Some chose instead to move south to
the nearer New England states while others opened up northern Quebec.
Settlement here received a tremendous boost during the depression when the
Quebec government in desperation sent 50,000 colonists, many of them
Montreal unemployed, north by train. When the rail lines ended, they carried
on by canoe.

Many of these colonists of the '20s and '30s went to the vast
Abitibi-Temiscaming area, where I met their descendants—the first-
generation white natives of the north. The discovery of copper led to the
establishment of a mine and smelter and the towns of Rouyn-Noranda
(population 27,000; 85 percent French) in 1927. Today the mine is depleted
but the smelter continues as the younger residents of Rouyn-Noranda,
Val-d'Or, and other centres here look north to James Bay for new
opportunities.

This recent period of twentieth-century settlement was neither easy nor
romantic; many of the original colonists endured terrible hardship in the
struggle against forest, cold, and mosquitoes. The Social Credit movement
soon developed as a political alternative. Rouyn is the home of long-time

278

Créditiste leader, Réal Caouette, and the Rouyn-Noranda riding returned the sole Créditiste deputy elected on November 15.

Leaving Rouyn-Noranda, I drove south through pleasant silver-steepled villages and rolling dairy country en route to Ville-Marie and Temiscaming. I chose Temiscaming (population 2,165) for this chapter because it has suffered some of the worst effects of English commercial and cultural domination in Quebec; but this town decided to fight back long before talk of a Parti Québécois government and a referendum. Today, with a population almost evenly split between French and English, the policies of the PQ government are having a further polarizing effect on Temiscaming.

But to understand the politics of the present in Abitibi-Temiscaming one should really begin with the hardships of the 1930s, as the first interview in this chapter does.

Charles Legault
Tire-shop owner, Rouyn
(F)

"I got to know Réal Caouette and started going door to door with him on weekends."

The reality of pioneer settlements is usually far removed from the "westward-ho" sense of adventure and excitement depicted in film and television, as Charles Legault explains. He joined the Social Credit Party and soon came to know Réal Caouette. A long-time party worker, Mr. Legault reminisces about the bad old days in the lumber camps of his youth and the hope of a better life that Social Credit offered.

At a very, very young age I lost both my father and mother and started to work in cafés as a dishwasher, then as apprentice cook, and later as a cook. We used to work from five in the morning to eight or nine o'clock at night. Of course there wasn't very much to spend and my brother and I —the two eldest of the family—were working to provide for six children. Yes, six. The oldest was my sister Lucille. She was 12. The baby was two years old. I can tell you that I thank God today we never did separate; we always stayed together as a united family.

I came up here to take a job in the bush as a cook's helper and dishwasher for 30 families working as wood cutters. We were near a small place called Praessac, just north of Amos, Quebec. Thirteen miles from town over a bush road where horses were up to their bellies in mud. We used a log sloop that floated on the mud and went along that way. The people were very, very poor; it was pitiful!

One woman, Mrs. Larochelle, was pregnant and was going to have a baby and we had to take her in an emergency situation to the hospital. So we hitched up two horses to the sloop and we left. It was midnight and, you know, it takes a little bit of time to go 13 miles on that kind of road. So we got her to the hospital in Amos where she had her child with a great deal of difficulty and then she came back, after all this, and two months later she died as a result of her delivery.

This is an example I am giving you of the extreme poverty that existed in those days. And Mr. Larochelle had a family of 13 children. Mr. Larochelle had sons 16 or 17 years of age, maybe 18, but they couldn't find work. He just had an axe and his bucksaw and he worked on the roads at a dollar a day, but no more than 15 days a month. So, you can imagine...Those children suffered from hunger and there were flies and mosquitoes in that place that you wouldn't believe. It was terrible.

They weren't far from our camp and I couldn't stand it, so I said to my big boss: "You're going to put some of this food aside. Don't ask how much it is going to cost—don't worry about it—because I am going to feed these families or I am leaving." So they sent me beef quarters, beef sides, sugar, flour—as much as I asked for. I had 60 men and 30 families that depended on us. When they came, they ate as much as they possibly could and I told them, "If you want to take some home, go ahead, take it home." And, boy, did they take it home! They went away with bags full. Of course the mosquitoes had eaten them alive—their eyes were all puffed up and they were ill-clothed—but they ate. It cost a lot to feed my men and those families but I used to tell my boss, "If you don't want me to do it, give me my time and I'm going."

Anyway, it came time for me to leave for better things, so the women, the day of my departure, I gave them all the food that was not opened up already. I think there were about 60 women from families there. I separated it into equal parts—the cases of butter, beans, potatoes, everything. I gave the whole thing to them. There were women who were crying when I left because they knew that they were going to be hungry again.

After living through that experience, I came down to Amos and began looking into the Social Credit movement. I went to meetings in private homes, listened to discussions, read some books, and thought about it all. That winter, I went back up into the bush with my books and really began to understand the Social Credit philosophy. Why was it that the banks always had big offices and buildings, but weren't very interested in lending money to the people? Why were the interest rates so high? When there were men and raw materials available, all you needed for prosperity was some capital to provide equipment and get things moving. We read and discussed Social Credit pamphlets and papers—like these ones in my scrapbook here—and then went out to try to convince others. There was nothing in it for me personally, understand. I just wanted to find some way of dealing with the misery and injustice that I saw around me, that's all.

I got to know Réal Caouette and started going door-to-door with him on weekends. After a week's full work, we spent the weekend walking from door to door. We used to get thrown out more often than not, but sometimes people would offer us a meal. Sometimes not. We had to spend money out of our own pockets, and then the following Sunday we'd start off again. Of course in the evening we'd go to our neighbours to try and get some more subscriptions to the party and to try and get into their heads what we believed, what we thought ourselves.

Réal Caouette was well loved here, you know. He had a sense of humour. A great wit. The first time he was elected was in 1946. I lived at Val-d'Or at the time and he did too. He came in with a 1,000-vote majority in a by-election. He was often ridiculed and made to look the fool, but in the end Mr. Caouette was loved in the north, whether it be by French, Jews, Poles, or English.

Yes, it's going to be very difficult to replace Réal Caouette because he was a wonderful speaker. He knew Social Credit very well; he lived politics. I have confidence in his son Gilles, but I don't believe that Gilles can give to Social Credit the same enthusiasm that Réal Caouette gave it. Réal Caouette was not an organizer; he was an orator, a born orator. He used to thrill thousands; masses of people.

We Créditistes were greatly disappointed by the results of November 15 but Mr. Lévesque was elected democratically. We are trying to give constructive criticism now. What we don't approve of is the socialistic and separatist policies. We are not socialist and we are not separatists. We are for private enterprise because if Canada has gotten as far as it has today, it is not government initiative that did it; it was private enterprise.

The more division there is, the weaker we get. I am a Canadian for Canada as a whole. I am not a financier but I know the strong man wins all the marbles. There are six million French Canadians in Quebec surrounded by approximately 220 million English in Canada and in the United States and we depend on the United States and the anglophones for investments. But I like the idea of the referendum. We live in a democratic country, after all. I don't think it could be carried right now because the vote wasn't for separation.

However, I approve of Mr. Lévesque's idea that other provinces should give the French Canadians the same right that we have always given English Canadians in Quebec. I approve of that. We have not enjoyed our rights. Like Réal Caouette used to say, "If we don't have what we want, it's just because we didn't work and we didn't kick. We didn't shout loud enough. We are going to shout louder and louder to defend our rights, and the more you shout, the more you'll get your rights." A few years ago, take Air Canada—you didn't even have one French-speaking stewardess or hostess, but because of yelling in Parliament Mr. Caouette did obtain, first of all, bilingual air hostesses and also bilingual conductors on trains. So let's continue shouting, but while remaining in Confederation. Let's not make any enemies. This is still the way, I think, that we will gain the most.

I am proud of being a Canadian, a French Canadian, first of all, born in Quebec. I love my province and I love my country. Canada is beautiful. It is beautiful in Quebec but Canada is beautiful too. The Rockies are incredible! Yes, I think it's possible for a French Canadian to feel at home outside Quebec. Certainly. I am right next to the Ontario border here, 23 miles away and I have a great many clients in Ontario—French Canadians, English Canadians, good customers. They are all friends and brothers as far as I am concerned.

I go there in August, to a certain hotel in Kirkland Lake, and I have never been able to pay for my hotel room because the owner is a customer of mine and he never lets me pay for it. The guy has managers and accountants running his hotel for him, but his background is driving a truck. He never feels better than when he's behind the wheel of a truck, and when he comes back to his hotel at night you can't buy a drink for the guy. That's the kind of people you meet there.

All my clients in Ontario—whether they speak English or French—I get along fine with all of them. And that is why I am saying I wouldn't want there to be any animosity between Quebeckers and the English in Ontario.

Roland Lapointe
Caisse Populaire manager, Rouyn
(F)

"The anglophones in Montreal have been almost like parasites on the Quebec economy."

Canadian chartered banks are less influential in Quebec than in the other provinces because of the Caisse Populaire movement. Virtually every city, town, and village in Quebec has at least one Caisse Populaire, which provides the normal savings and loan services of any bank. Its closest counterpart in English Canada, although on a much smaller scale, is the credit union. The first Caisse Populaire was started in Lévis in 1920 by former House of Commons debates reporter, Alphonse Desjardins, partly as an alternative to the hated English control of Quebec's financial institutions. Today Quebec's Caisses Populaires have combined assets in the billions of dollars. Roland Lapointe, a former Royal Bank of Canada employee and defeated Parti Québécois candidate, reflects on his experiences in the world of English capital and his reasons for leaving it.

My father was one of the first pioneers here because the city of Rouyn was founded in 1926 and he arrived in 1927, the year I was born. I did my B.A. at Laval University and then took a job with the Royal Bank and stayed with them for 15 years.

I liked the bank but there was a colonizing mentality. In other words, at the Royal Bank they liked me and I liked the anglophones with whom I worked, and I understood them—but they did not understand me. I read *Le Devoir* at the Royal Bank and they said, "Why do you read *Le Devoir?* Why don't you read the *Gazette?* There is nothing in *Le Devoir.*" They said, "If you want any kind of future, speak English. Be smart! There is no future for you in French. Come along with us where the opportunities are. Speak French at home—we have nothing against it—but send your children to McGill." They just couldn't understand that I, Roland Lapointe, whose ancestors have been here for 300 years, would want to live here in my own language. It was very frustrating, and in the end I quit and joined the Caisse Populaire Movement.

The Caisse Populaire, which started about 50 years ago, belongs to us because it's our money, whereas the chartered banks belong mostly to the anglophones. In the Caisse Populaire, you have three and a half million members of credit unions throughout the province of Quebec. It belongs to three and one half million people, in other words. Here at the Rouyn-Noranda Caisse Populaire there are 15,000 members, with assets of $25 million. Our Caisse is very profitable, but in view of the fact that it is a cooperative, there are no profits, strictly speaking. The surpluses are distributed back to the members—those who borrow and those who deposit.

We don't compete with the chartered banks. We think that it's the banks that compete with the Caisses Populaires! When I worked for the Royal Bank, banks weren't really lending to individual borrowers, particularly to francophones who were very poor and who didn't have any economic power. But if you don't lend to these people they are not going to get ahead in life at all, that's for sure! The finance companies lent to them, but not the banks, so the Caisses Populaires, or credit unions, started with mortgage loans for individuals. The credit unions also opened up the personal loan field because loans were almost non-existent in commercial banks. They just didn't bother with small personal loans, which is why I say that the banks are competing with us because they are entering a field that we opened up. We lend at competitive rates and sometimes we give a little bit more on deposits because we don't have any profits or dividends to distribute at the end of the fiscal year.

In principle, you have to be a member of a credit union for three months before you are entitled to borrow. There are some anglophones who do belong but here at Rouyn it's all French. All business is in French here, so an anglophone coming in here would have to try to learn French as much as possible. The money deposited in the credit union normally stays in Quebec and returns to the Quebec economy. But when money is deposited in companies that are anglophone-controlled, that money can just as easily be used to develop Vancouver and Toronto and any other province really.

The anglophones in Montreal have been almost like parasites on the Quebec economy. The people who worked in important positions in companies, industry, have been English. We were not important, we were the natives, the blueberry pickers. You can't blame us for seeing it that way. But that's not the way it is anymore. If I were an anglophone I would preach bilingualism and say, "Look, we are going to give you everything possible to be French in Toronto," because there is no more danger for the English. That is the point. Years and years ago the language balance was still up in the air; I don't blame the anglophones for having prevented francophones from being free because if they hadn't maybe today Canada would be a French country. If they had left Louis Riel alone, if they hadn't crushed the French schools out West and in Manitoba, if they hadn't discriminated against the Métis, maybe today Alberta, Saskatchewan, and Manitoba would be French provinces. So I can't blame the anglophones, who were colonizers, from preventing us from taking the country as a whole. They were probably afraid that since we were conquered by arms in 1759 we would try to rise up and assert ourselves again. The English just didn't want to lose the country another time.

But today, Quebec cannot be subjected to the other nine provinces and the federal government. And of course we can't negotiate anything other than independence now because if we don't ask for independence, we won't get anything. With an anglophone, you have to ask for independence. But the independence we want is relative. We don't want to be one against nine all the time. We want to be one on one. So, if things begin to change, then we won't have to go all the way! Everybody is talking about Quebec now and people are beginning to understand. The new Commissioner of Official Languages, Max Yalden, says that Quebec is right in asking the other provinces to do the same thing for the French that we have been doing for the English for centuries. But it is too late. I think it is too late now. Quebec is going to become independent. You would not like to be dependent on somebody else, and neither do we!

Look, the real problem in Canada today isn't French-English. It's not that at all. It is the relationship between those who have been colonized and those who have been doing the colonizing; inferior to superior. That's what it is. And that's the reason why the Caisses Populaires were founded—because there were no instruments for economic liberation. We felt oppressed because we were taken for granted and we had no possibility of being ourselves. I am not trying to scare you here but it is a little bit like the revolution in Rhodesia. How many anglophones—white anglophones—control six million blacks? Two hundred thousand? And for them, of course, that's normal. Well, it's something like that here.

I feel optimistic about the future because we Quebeckers are rather intelligent people. We are not belligerent, even if Trudeau tried in 1970 to make us out to be violent. But any anglophone here knows that Quebeckers are not violent. Sometimes we are just too soft, in fact. I think that Trudeau through his intransigence and his facism has helped clarify the problem. Even if we think that he is a modern fellow, in practice he is still out of the Middle Ages, as far as I am concerned. He is a fellow who doesn't keep pace with reality and events.

Matter of fact, we should be grateful to Trudeau: if we had a more moderate Prime Minister—someone like Pearson—the Quebec-Canada situation would have taken more time to clarify. It would have been compromise after compromise and in the end things would have been still up in the air. Today the English, after the events of October, 1970, and November, 1976, see Quebec as they have never seen it before. They weren't even interested in seeing it before because it posed no threat, but now they do see Quebec, thanks to Mr. Trudeau. But Trudeau can't take any credit for this because he is a fanatic. I think he is a fanatic. I think he is a man who never wants to admit a mistake.

Diane Gagné
Civil servant, Évain
(F)
"If Paul Rose is a fanatic, then we can say that Trudeau is a fanatic and Lévesque is a fanatic too."

Mrs. Gagné, at the same time a committed separatist and a federal civil servant, discusses an issue that may be largely ignored in English Canada but is still very much in the minds of many Quebeckers: the situation of the FLQ prisoners in federal penitentiaries. During our conversation she was entertaining French-speaking visitors from Senegal and was looking forward to the day when Quebec would take its place among the world's 23 francophone countries.

I know René Lévesque personally. He is a good friend of one of our friends, and we often receive him when he comes here. I have no idea whether he is religious or not, but he is certainly a man who is very sincere—very sincere and sympathetic, but rather shy. He is not really all that exuberant, very reserved, polite and a very sensitive person. He really surprised me because I didn't imagine that he was like that before I knew him. He will sit around the dinner table for the whole evening and talk politics. He likes to eat. I wouldn't say that he is a gourmet but he likes good food.

I saw him three days before the election. He was here in the region and I said to him, "I guess it wouldn't be such a good idea for us to get into government so early, would it?" And he said, "Well, if we don't, four years from now it is going to be too late. Because in four years the situation will still be worse than it is today. It is deteriorating every day." Lévesque seemed very confident that he was going to get into power at that time. People said Lévesque was surprised with the outcome but he wasn't surprised at all. It's just that he is a very reserved man and not the type to say: "It's in the bag, boys. We're going to win this time." But he knew.

I'm a federal civil servant, but I feel like a stranger when I go to Ottawa. If I go to France, I can feel at home, but in Ottawa it is very difficult to find people who can speak French to you. Bilingualism in the federal government really leaves something to be desired. People don't make any effort.

I work as a social development officer for the federal Secretary of State's Department, and when I do my work there is no question of politics. The only thing is I am paid by the federal government, but so long as I am paying taxes to the federal government, I don't really feel too unhappy about that. No, I am not a bit afraid of losing my job if Quebec becomes independent. Then I will be able to work for Quebec.

I think Quebec will become independent. More and more the idea is taking hold. Quebeckers are a people who have been scared for so long, but the FLQ advanced the Quebec Nationalist Movement. Some people would never have awakened without that. I don't think the FLQ people are dangerous. I've met Jacques Rose, for instance. He is a worker, a boy who was brought up with principles and who is very concerned with workers' problems and trade unionist problems. I would hope that my children, later on, will be a little bit like that. You know, devoted people. He is not a fanatic and his brother Paul isn't a fanatic either. He is just committed. Completely committed. If Paul Rose is a fanatic, then we can say that Trudeau is a fanatic, and Lévesque is a fanatic too.

Paul Rose, Jacques Rose, and the FLQ forced people to wake up and listen. Look, I have 32 aunts and uncles and they were all anti-FLQ and anti anyone who said that the FLQ was right in any way whatsoever. Well, today, seven years later, they have more reservations and say, "Well, maybe Paul Rose wasn't completely wrong in what he was saying." I hope that the FLQ will be released from prison because they certainly are not dangerous boys. They are political prisoners; they are not criminals.

I am a separatist, and I think that it's about time for all Quebeckers, for once in our lives, to make our own decisions. Ottawa decides for us; we still look like children whose parents make the decisions. Quebeckers have never really had any choice about belonging to Canada or not. Well, we don't want to; we want to be independent.

Personally, I favour the solution proposed by the PQ—associate-state status with economic ties with the rest of Canada. But if English Canada says no to that, it doesn't prevent Quebec from working out an economic association with the United States. I'm also for a republican system of government after independence, and of course we would have a seat at the United Nations. We would deal with the world as a francophone nation, be represented fully on international bodies, and put an end once and for all to this parent-child relationship we have with Ottawa.

Foreign people are already beginning to understand what is happening in Quebec. In fact, you see the visitors we have at our home today? They're on a federal exchange program from Senegal, and already they're referring to us as Quebeckers and not Canadians. They speak an African-accented French but we communicate with each other with no problem. It's funny, I thought the Africans would be really jolly, open people—but these Senegalese at least are actually quite quiet and reserved, but maybe it's just that they're so far away from home. Anyway, they are very sympathetic to our cause. I don't think they've been independent for so very long themselves. We've also had visitors here from France in the last few months and it really surprised me to see how closely the French followed our election.

This is a very exciting time for Quebec, for Quebeckers. It makes you enthusiastic. We were so individualistic before but now we are a society. The celebration of Canada Day on TV had absolutely nothing to do with us. It is not our type of life, not our type of music. We have our own singers, composers, writers, and we are no longer interested in the English Canada type of thing. That show looked like something coming from the U.S.A. We don't need that.

Alain Guimont
CEGEP student, Rouyn
(F)
"I would be much prouder if I had a Quebec passport."

A 19-year-old CEGEP student, miner's son, and PQ activist, Alain Guimont conducts tours of Noranda's obsolescent copper smelter during the summer months. I have gone on many walking tours, but it was necessary to visit this smelter to experience my first coughing tour. After explaining the history of the mine and smelter to the tour group, Alain Guimont agreed to be interviewed. Apart from his lively views on Quebec politics, his comments provide a fascinating and rather disturbing insight into the immense cultural gulf separating young people in French and English Canada.

There is no Canadian culture. The only culture that exists here, Quebec has. Who founded Canada in the first place anyway? The Quebeckers of course! And then who tried to get hold of it? The English. And now who's up against the wall? The Quebeckers. The English try to say they have a culture. Well, maybe they do but it is far less strong than the Quebec culture. Take, for instance, our artisans, our handicrafts. Quebeckers have a great deal of tradition in woodworking and handicrafts. And we have singers, folklore singers.

Do I know any English Canadian performers? Well . . . like who? Gordon Lightfoot? Sorry, that means absolutely nothing to me. Joanie Mitchell and Murray McLaughlin — are they singers? No, I've never heard of the Canadian Brass. Anne Murray? Yes, that name rings a bell. She's a singer, I think. The Group of Seven? What's that? An orchestra?

Look, let me tell you who I like. Robert Charlebois, Rélix Leclerc, Louise Forestier, Harmonium, Beau Dommage, and Edith Butler, although she's not really a Quebecker. Is she any relation to you?

Look, I am just a simple fellow who loves politics like any Quebecker. This is an important subject for us because we are surrounded by 220 million anglophones and we are just a small minority. I don't feel at all like a Canadian. I feel like a Quebecker. Canada — nope, it doesn't mean anything to me. I don't even want to hear about it. I get a headache when I speak about Canada because I happen to think of it as a foreign country. If I have to go abroad I need a passport, a Canadian passport. I would be much prouder if I had a Quebec passport. That's the difference.

My family are all good Quebeckers. We were Créditistes before the PQ existed but now we are all PQ 100 percent, and during the election campaign we worked for the PQ party. The Créditistes won here because Abitibi is a Créditiste area — the people who work around here have their money and they are content; they don't care, really. But next time there is going to be a PQ candidate who wins, for sure.

My father worked at Noranda for 25 years and he doesn't like the English at all. He doesn't even want to talk about the English. He has reached a certain age when people don't have 45 ideas in their head, they just have one. One fixed idea and that's it. He retired in March, and in the winter my mother goes down south, but he doesn't go. He doesn't want to give any money to the English — he doesn't want to help them out at all.

I guess I understand how he feels. Personally I consider that the Quebeckers constitute a people, and I find it very important to contribute and work toward them becoming an independent people. It's time we woke up. Already our language is full of anglicisms. When the men go to work they go on this or that "shift." We say "car" instead of *char* or *voiture*, things like that. And a lot of our street names—Churchill Street, Stevens Street—are English. And don't forget the billboards and advertising. Of course this advertising business is all changing now because of the PQ, and I'm all for it. One hundred percent. And I'm completely in favour of the PQ's education policies. If people want to move here, let them and their kids learn French. If I lived in Ontario I'd have to speak English, so what's the difference, eh?

I'm not too sure that Quebec will become independent in the referendum because the people haven't developed enough. They really don't know too much about it. Sure I was happy enough with the PQ win but I didn't get too excited about it because I know they can't do miracles, particularly with the capitalistic system we have. There is no way to have much progress. In the federal election I voted Communist and the reason wasn't because I was for the Communist Party but because there was a Conservative Party and a Liberal Party and a Créditiste Party and the NDP, and I am against all of them. They are for the Canadian bourgeoisie and no change will come from them.

As for Trudeau, he may be a smart man but as a politician he comes across to me like a real clown. A joker. Of course it all seems very serious but if you take a serious look at the man there's nothing there but a big joke. Remember when Trudeau addressed the U.S. Congress? Boy, did he ever come out with some good ones then! "Let's unite our two countries for the good of us all." He nearly sold us out to the U.S.A. right there on the spot! Very funny man, but as a politician he's just a bit out of date, don't you think?

At the CEGEP almost all the teachers are Communists. Oh yes. The teachers of poetry and linguistics and geography and philosophy, they are all Communists, at least in Rouyn. But that doesn't make them separatists, because, for them, the PQ party will not change anything. It is only a Social Democratic Party.

After I finish CEGEP next year, I certainly won't stay here. My intention is to go to university and then travel, maybe to South America or Africa. I don't want to follow in my father's footsteps. He didn't like working in the mine. The money may be good but the working conditions are bad, mainly because the place is so old. No, it's not for me.

Paul Dickey
Union official, Évain
(F)

**"There are anglophones who have
been here for 25, 30, or 40 years
and who still don't know a
single word of French."**

*More than any other province, Quebec is made up of people whose roots reach
back to a single European country. However, not all Quebeckers originally
came from France, as unilingual francophone Paul Dickey demonstrates.*

My ancestors were Scots; the first ones who came to Canada with a
regiment from Britain, around 1756, I think. One part of the family is
francophone, and another branch is anglophone—it just depends on
where they live. Personally, I don't speak English even though my name
certainly isn't French.

My father arrived here in northwest Quebec in 1935 when they were
pioneering and colonizing this part of the province. He was born in
Montreal; his father, who worked on the Canadian National Railways,
was transferred to the Saguenay–Lac St.-Jean area. During the
depression there was no work, so the colonizing plan was really a saving
grace. My father and his family came partway by train and the rest of the
way by canoe and raft like real pioneers!

Each family was given a plot of land free of charge. They built their
houses during the spring and summer. The men worked as lumberjacks,
farmers, as pioneers really: in the winter they worked in the bush and in
the summer they cleared the land. That's how things started, slow but
sure.

I can remember, as a small boy, in the winter there was a team of two or
four horses hitched to a sleigh. My father would take on a load of hay and
wood and go up to LaSalle and sell the hay. That was 25 miles. He'd sleep
over in LaSalle and then the next day he would take on essentials—oats
and flour, salt, sugar, tea—all kinds of things, you know, to be able to
feed the family. And sometimes he brought a load back for the general
store. And do you know, Dad is on the same land today—in his third
house? He retires this year, in fact.

People here in the north are really friendly. They open up and make
you feel open. You can go almost anywhere, to any family, and you will
be warmly received even if they never met you before. They will offer

you a coffee, a meal, and you'll be part of the family very easily and very quickly. Probably there are many reasons for this, perhaps the isolation has something to do with it. A second factor would be that people often worked in the bush on their own. Most of the lumberjacks here used to work all winter in the woods and when they came out at Easter they really needed to see people. Today it's not like that, but the mentality remains the same.

Yes, it's cold here in the winter—you have minus 40 degrees—but it is a cold that is easier to endure than in the southern parts of the province, where it's humid. But I don't just like it here; I love it.

And I am not going to hide it—I have a little bit of nationalism. I was pleased with November 15. Yes, pleased. Look at the mining industry here. The mining industry was almost totally administered by anglophones, and this was true in the forestry industry too. You know, whether it be Noranda Mines or Dominion or CIP in the forestry field, all those who had the important positions were anglophones. It is not quite as true today, but I can recall 15 or 20 years ago, we had to work in English. Even today the working language is still often English and the orders and reports are made out in English. There are anglophones, particularly in Noranda, who have been here for 25, 30, or 40 years and who still don't know one single word of French. They probably don't feel the need to speak French. It's frustrating, when you think that in the midst of 40,000 francophones there is this population of 5,000 anglophones. I am not in favour of assimilation for them but they should be better integrated. I would find it normal for the anglophone population to at least be able to communicate in French. So nationalism for me is something important.

I am not for complete independence, but I would like for Quebec as a people and as a government to be on an equal footing with the rest of Canada in the fields of culture, language, work, employment. We will have to change the rules of the game and, for me, it's the Parti Québécois that can contribute to this. Federally, I voted NDP, not because I thought that they would win but I felt unable to vote Liberal or Conservative and voting Créditiste was just a little better than nothing. I really don't believe in their theories. I think it is far more based on personalities in that party even if they did win here.

I knew Réal Caouette and I know his son, Gilles. Réal was fantastic. Even if it was 10 years since he met you, he'd call you by your first name. That is always something that people like. And he would take on all kinds of problems which didn't necessarily concern a Member of Parliament. In the past I voted for Caouette as a type of linguistic protest. Caouette and the Créditiste party, particularly at the beginning, played a rather important role in this regard; but the questions of language are now being transferred to the provincial government level and I think that the new rules of the game will be established through Quebec City and not Ottawa.

I am a Quebecker before being a Canadian, but I still think that we can be proud of our country, Canada, as well. I am not afraid of stating that I am a Canadian. We have a country we can be very proud of. We can go anywhere in the world and we are respected as Canadians. But I still think that when the referendum comes along, the population of Quebec should say "Yes" because for once they would give a mandate to the Quebec government to really affirm itself vis-à-vis the rest of Canada. Even if we were to say "Yes" to separation, it wouldn't be separation as a great many understand it. If we say "No" to the referendum, then in my opinion it will mean going back 10 to 15 years.

I think there should be more than one question on the ballot too— maybe four or five questions. I wouldn't want to have only one question which would say, "Is it separation or not separation?" That would be stupid.

Roger Guy
Professor, University of Quebec at Rouyn, Beaudry
(F)

"French Canadians have the feeling that the choice which was made in 1867 wasn't really agreed to by the people."

"Is René Lévesque a true separatist?" is a topic of frequent discussion in Quebec today. Roger Guy sees Lévesque's separatist objective as a bargaining tool for the shaping of the first popular constitutional consensus in Quebec's history.

I don't think René Lévesque is in favour of total separation. He is in favour of a Quebec which would establish privileged links with Canada. Canada could remain one country, but what he really wants is a good margin of political sovereignty, I think. That is to say, rather strong power on the part of the francophone community. Lévesque's independence position is a position of negotiation. He has no choice. He has to go to extremes.

French Canadians have the feeling that the choice which was made in 1867 wasn't really agreed to by the people. We don't have the feeling of having personally made the choice. So it's just as if we have to do it all over again. We have to be able to say, "Well, I am in full possession of myself, of all my powers and I can do what I want with them, including conceding some to others."

Lévesque is a tactician but he is realistic. The trick of the referendum is for him to be able to say at one point that the Quebec people are in favour of total recovery of political powers and from that point on, he will be able to give up or negotiate certain powers willingly, which we have never done before.

I think there will be problems, but not major problems. The strongly nationalistic fringe of his supporters is relatively small. The important leaders of the PQ are not ultra-nationalistic. For instance, Claude Morin. I know him; he was my teacher at university. He's a very pleasant person, very human, very easy-going, and amusing. He is the complete opposite of a fanatic.

I voted PQ first for good government. I felt ashamed to be represented by the Liberal Party. What I hope for, as a minimum, is a renegotiation of the Confederation agreement, giving Quebec far more power than she has at present. I would hope for a privileged link with Canada as a whole. I think that this is something very precious that we should have.

There are lots of good reasons for not going all the way and splitting up the country. We have shared 200 years of history with Canada. Our ties with France go back 300 or 400 years and we have their language, yes, but we have no common political experience. We have far more reasons to establish privileged links with English Canada than we do have with France or any other country.

I met some people from France this summer and I felt as if I were meeting a distant relative. I know that we do have ties, but they are very distant. We may speak the same language but, all the same, it is not easy to really reach one another. Now when I meet an English Canadian I meet someone who resembles me much more even though I have trouble talking to him because we don't speak the same language. Where the visitor from France is a distant relative, the English Canadian seems like a close cousin, if you will. With the Frenchman from France, relationships are always more formal. With an English Canadian, it's more spontaneous. But we have to be able to talk to one another. That is the whole thing.

I think that when the French Canadians stand up on their own two feet and demand respect, from that point on the English Canadians will be more interested in them. They will be curious and want to listen. When you are a majority, you can forget a minority — but a minority can never forget the majority. If Quebec defines itself as being a majority in its corner of the country, then others won't be able to forget Quebec. And from that point, we can start talking. It comes back to Lévesque's idea of sovereignty. For me, his idea of sovereignty is to make French Canadians a majority capable of being able to speak to another majority.

I am not sure of what is going to happen in the future but I am confident. I am not afraid. If English Canadians are worried, it is because they are facing a choice that they don't want to accept. Psychologically, I have accepted the idea of independence, just as I have accepted the idea that Canada could remain united with renegotiation. I accept both ideas but so long as one hasn't accepted the entire gamut of possibilities, one feels threatened.

Regardless of the constitutional future, I know Canada will never be the same as it was. Francophones will affirm themselves more and more and it will never be like it used to be where they wanted to be forgotten and left alone. Things may or may not lead to complete independence, but we are going to create our own secure position and this is what makes me feel confident.

Joanne Rannou
CEGEP student, Ville-Marie
(F)

"There is just not enough information on Canada in the Quebec media."

Among the Quebec stereotypes alive and well in English Canada is the idea that virtually all Quebec students are convinced separatists with a poster of René Lévesque in their bedrooms. While some students may fit this image, Joanne Rannou isn't one of them. The forthcoming referendum will be her first opportunity to vote, and presents a particularly challenging decision for reasons she explains in this interview.

I wasn't able to vote on November 15—I would have liked to but I couldn't. My name was on the voters' list in Ville-Marie, and at the time I was 500 miles away at the Sherbrooke CEGEP. But I would have voted for the Parti Québécois—not for separation, but to further Quebec's development because we are different from the rest of Canada and I would like to have our rights more respected.

We have our own language, our own customs—an entire culture—and I would like this to be recognized throughout Canada. It's starting though. Even in British Columbia they don't call us Canadians anymore, they say "Quebeckers." But I think that in view of the fact that the Parti Québécois came into power the federal government and Mr. Trudeau—this is my own opinion of course—have taken a good hard look at our rights vis-à-vis the Canadian people.

Here in Ville-Marie we are very close to the Ontario border—25 miles away, as a matter of fact. Being so close has affected our French, so much so that we don't even notice it anymore. We speak what we think is very good French but we use lots and lots of English words. Like, we listen to "underground" music, we go to the "outfitters" before a fishing trip, we go for "boat rides," and after all that activity we come back to the cottage for a "charcoal steak" or "hamburger."

Personally, I try to eliminate all that from my vocabulary. If we want to hold onto our French culture we simply must eliminate English terms and sentence structures from our language. If we speak like the English, we will think like the English. We won't think French. We will become Americanized, and personally I want to remain a Quebecker. That's why I approve of the PQ's language legislation. We speak French and you owe us that. You owe us French schools and we must make sure we have them. Now any English Canadians moving to Quebec have to send their children to French schools. That may be a little hard for you, but I think it's quite fair. Just as we learn English in order to become bilingual, you should learn French in order to become bilingual. All I want is justice.

Of course I am going to vote in the referendum. For a referendum you really have to know what is going on and exactly what the consequences of any decision will be. I do try to read the papers and watch television regularly to inform myself as much as possible. I am going to take some courses dealing with politics this year, and I am really interested in learning more because I don't know all that much, and I feel it is very dangerous to give an opinion if you are not completely aware. We love our culture, but politics are far more than just culture. It is also a question of economics, a question of the relationship between Canada and the entire world, and you can't have just a sentimental point of view when you vote.

And you know, I don't feel very well informed about the rest of

Canada. The Quebec media put a lot of stress on what is happening in Europe and other countries overseas far more than in Canada. I think there is a lack of enough information on Canada in the Quebec media. In view of the fact that we are Canadians, we should know more about how things are going in the other provinces, not only how things are going in Quebec. I read *Le Devoir*, the Sherbrooke paper *La Tribune*, and watch the TV news most nights, but I still don't know a lot about the rest of the country, I must admit.

I don't want to see people voting in the referendum from ignorance or sentiment. They should be more aware of the total situation in Canada as well as Quebec. This deserves to be a well-thought-out vote. As things stand now, the media aren't doing their part to keep us informed.

Ron Burbridge
Cinema owner, Temiscaming
(E)
"I think they are going to a Nazi-type system."

A very open and friendly individual, Ron Burbridge returned to Temiscaming in 1972, after a 20-year absence, to manage the town's only movie theatre. He found that the place was no longer a classic single-industry undemocratic company town, commercially and politically controlled by outside English interests. But it is the changes since November, 1976, that particularly upset Ron Burbridge.

I left Temiscaming when I was 17, in 1953. I joined the armed forces and travelled around and got married. We left the Yukon in 1972 and returned here and took over the local theatre.

When I was growing up in Temiscaming everything was controlled by the companies. Take my dad, for instance — he was looked after all the way. When he got his paycheck from his work everything was paid for: rent, garbage, water, everything was knocked off by the company. Entertainment, the arena, curling club, everything supplied by the company at a reasonable cost.

When I went to school, it was the Ontario Department of Education in the Public School, even though this is Quebec. I passed the departmental exams set by Ontario government. French and English, we all went to one high school—in English. Up to grade eight we were separated. There was the separate school and the public school, but the high school combined everyone. There were a few French students who moved in from up north who had real problems with English, but everyone managed to learn English.

Looking back, I am sure that if you didn't speak English you didn't last on the job—it was just that simple. I don't think anybody complained that much in town, mainly because they didn't know anything else at that time. The priests pretty well controlled Quebec; they controlled the size of the family; they told the people in church what movies they could go to, what ones they couldn't go to, and so on. You know, people were being dominated from all sides, not only by the English ... they were being dominated by the Church as well. I guess they kind of grew used to it.

When I came back in '72 I found quite a bit more French in town. They might talk to you in French first whereas before I left in '53 they would talk English. I noticed that difference right away. The school system has changed quite a bit too. There are French and English high schools now, and our kids had to do a bit of adjusting coming from the Yukon where they got maybe a half-hour a week in French. Well, now, it's a bit heavier for them.

The November election? It wasn't believable. It just wasn't believable, that's all. I didn't even vote. I didn't want Bourassa and I didn't want Lévesque, so that didn't leave very much choice, did it? Maybe I got what I deserve now ... they say if you don't vote then don't complain about the government. But I think they are going to a Nazi-type system. I really honestly believe that, coming back with censorship. Lévesque has already stated he wants to control the radio and TV. Now that leaves only one other outlet—the newspaper. Already they are talking about some sort of spy network spying on businesses: if they are speaking English rather than French, they are to be reported to the government. It sure doesn't look good to me. Probably in a year or two we will have to leave Quebec because I won't put up with that. Meanwhile I'll probably have to hire somebody bilingual to do my bookwork and everything because all the correspondence from the government comes in French. I wrote and asked for English forms but I don't know if I'll get them or not.

And the movies themselves, we may be forced to show so many French, I don't know. As of now we may show a French film once a month—the straight sex, pornographic films for over-18s.

They're often Italian or Swedish, with French dubbed in. You get roughly the same people coming on those nights—you won't see them from one sex movie to another, but they never miss one. Personally, I think after you have seen one there is nothing more you can see. I don't know why they come back. But it would hurt my business if they didn't. It would hurt. Personally though, I don't care if I ever see one. You know, I go there to be entertained, not to watch that stuff. But if people like it, fine, I will bring it in.

People in Temiscaming like English-language films. Nearly everyone French or English in Temiscaming speaks English. But a third or so of the population speak *only* English. So if I show a French-language film, I lose these customers. No way around it. That's why we don't bring in films from Quebec or France. No, the English minority is not dictating what is showing. I am in it strictly for the business and if the people come to the movies, I make money, and I stay in business. The people are happy with the movies they see. If they didn't want the English ones, they wouldn't come out. Nobody is out on the street with a stick chasing them into the theatre. They can drive 50 miles to North Bay and see French movies or they can watch the French TV. I have talked to French-speaking Canadians and they assure me that they enjoy the English versions better.

The way things are right now, I'm all right. But the minute the government were to stick its finger in and say, "You have to show three French-language shows a month," or something, then I would be gone because it's just not economical. Maybe a few years from now it would be, I don't know. But I don't want someone to tell me what I can sell and what I can't sell.

Tom McDonald
Millwright, Temiscaming
(E)

**"Relations between the French and
the English have changed, I'll
admit; you have to be a little
more careful now."**

*Tom McDonald was born and raised in Temiscaming and works at the town's
major employer, the TEMBEC pulp and paper mill. The town was severely
jolted by the closure of the mill in 1972. A year later it was reopened under a
unique tripartite ownership arrangement involving private shareholders, the
workers and townspeople who hold a one-third interest, and the government of
Quebec. Tom McDonald's experience sheds light on two important questions
for Temiscaming: the direct influence of the PQ government as seen in changed
safety procedures on the shop floor, and the very immediate uncertainty facing
this young anglophone family head who is undecided about leaving Quebec.*

Oh yeah, I've noticed things have changed since November 15. Last
summer the separatists weren't very loud, they were in the background,
and now they have come out into the foreground. They realize that they
are holding the ball right now.

A year ago we would ask at our union meetings what the language
preference was, and if 99 guys out of 100 said English, well, then they
would be held in English. Now, if there is one person who demands that
it be in French, it has to be in French. Actually we use both languages
then. The guy who insists on meetings in French is just doing it to be
pigheaded—there isn't anybody that can't speak and understand
English.

You notice changes in the office too. We deal quite a bit with
companies in Montreal. I was assigned to the office a few months back,
when most of the literature was in English. Then I noticed it changing to
French and then there were two memos put out by the general manager
insisting that any correspondence outside of the mill to other parts of
Quebec had to be in French. If it could be in both languages, well then,
fine, but the preference in Quebec was French. And there was another
memo put out shortly after that that any internal memos or memos of
instruction put out on bulletin boards for the workers had to be in both
languages—again French preferable. The only correspondence that was
allowed simply in English was among the top brass.

Once in a while we had to apply for licences for our trucks and write for information regarding fuel taxes and this kind of thing. Any of this correspondence had to be in French whereas I used to be able to write it in English. That means I had to get it translated: I wrote it in English for a bilingual secretary and she translated it for me.

Shortly after this I shifted jobs; I went over to the Maintenance Department because I wanted to get a little stronger in the union. The trend seemed that people there had maybe more time and were more available to be approached, and I thought maybe I could work myself up in the union that way. The union is big money and big business now. The national president is making about $48,000 a year, and here the president of the local is on the board of directors, with a vote. That's quite a position.

But back to the changes I've noticed since the PQ victory. One is in the area of work safety. The pulp and paper industry has a high accident rate. Some of the accidents we have had show—see this? I lost part of this finger in a paper cutter when I was working at E.B. Eddy's in Hull back in 1972. I still remember the day, May 25. It was through negligence on a co-worker's part. I was adjusting a knife and the safety tag on the machine musn't have been showing properly and he turned the machine on. Then we had an accident here, I believe it was about 35 days ago. One of the tour superintendents was helping a worker to unblock a pipe that was plugged up with spent liquor and acid after the pulp had been cooked. As he unblocked it, some of this liquor went all over his back and he was burned quite badly. He missed two weeks' work.

Well, since the PQ has been in power, safety inspectors from Quebec come up to the mill regularly. They are protecting our lives and they are strict. And they follow up: "You have 10 days to fix that. You have 45 days to fix your saws. You have to have an anti-kickback device on that saw. The band saw is ancient equipment"—that sort of thing. It means buying a whole new saw and if you don't want to buy a new saw, that's it. They came back in 45 days and put a lock and key on it.

And that is just one instance where it seems that they are closer to labour and the working class than the Liberals were. Under them, you rarely saw any safety inspectors at the mill. As president of the shop stewards Safety Committee here at the mill, I must say this new concern about safety pleases me greatly. I think everybody got the heck scared out of them awhile ago when an older guy, just about to retire, lost a number of fingers on both hands. You know, it can happen to anybody: this guy had worked here about 35 or 40 years and he was a supervisor.

I am not really politically minded, but I follow politics now because it is going to affect our lives. But how it's going to change Quebec as a province, I can't say. If Quebec becomes a country in itself, if separation does occur, I will not be living here. Ontario is a mile away and if I wanted to continue working at TEMBEC and if there was a future here, then I would simply move across the river and my children would go to school in North Bay. True, I was born and raised in Temiscaming and I would like to stay here, but I haven't tied myself down with a house or any real property yet. We're waiting. About a year ago we decided to just bank our house money and see what happens with this referendum.

Number one in our mind is this Quebec situation, but the other thing is the mill. It shut down once before and a lot of people, like my father, got stung. He took a tremendous loss. Now the mill is planning to build a recovery boiler worth $45 million, and once that starts to be constructed I will know whether this is to be a lasting venture or not. But even if we got the recovery boiler, I would not buy a house in Quebec until after the referendum. It's too bad, because I like this town. Life is very slow; there is no great rush to get anywhere and you know your neighbours. In fact, you know everybody in town. I guess that could be bad too because you know everybody's business and vice-versa. But I'd hate to see it get bigger. I don't think it will. You can be assured your children can be out in the yard playing and if you happen to go inside for an hour and they happen to wander off there is not too much danger of anything happening to them. I'd hate to see it change.

Relations between the French and the English have changed, I'll admit; you have to be a little more careful now. At one time there were the Newfie jokes and here in Temiscaming and a lot of places you just turned them into French jokes. There is not so much of that anymore. Where at one time you could call a guy a crazy Frenchman if he did something silly, like dent his car, you can't say that now. Hmm, maybe that's good. I went to Montreal on June 24 for St.-Jean Baptiste and that was quite an experience. You would never say "crazy Frenchmen" down there! Not with about 50,000 Frenchmen dancing in the streets! One thing I appreciated was the art and the French culture. Everybody was having a good time. Now if this is what the French are trying to protect, I don't blame them at all.

Adèle Belanger-Hay

Housewife, Temiscaming

(F)

"There were bombs at our university, which was just on the outskirts of Westmount."

While English Canadian university students in the early and mid-'60s were largely removed from politics in that pre-nationalist, pre-protest period, their Quebec counterparts were experiencing the first FLQ bombings and the Quiet Revolution. Adèle Belanger-Hay was one of the thousands of Quebec university students whose views were shaped by this early Quebec radicalism.

Formerly in Quebec you had families which had the same political affiliation, but families today are dividing more and more on political matters. Like in my own family, which was Liberal, I'm one of those who opted for separatism with René Lévesque. So there are subjects that are taboo when you have a family reunion.

My father and mother remain very federalist and very Canadian and for them Quebec separatism is just unthinkable. I parted company with them on this issue when I was a student in history at the University of Montreal in the early '60s. We studied original anglophone texts, like the Durham Report of 1837 and the anti-French letters-to-the-editor columns after the 1837 Rebellion. Francophones were seen by the English as a negliglble, uncultured minority, unable to act alone, unable to do anything whatsoever. I started to see things in another light, and asked myself whether the anglophones today have not maintained the attitude that the francophone is an inferior being who can be exploited.

Then when the first FLQ bombs went off, that affected me and everyone else in Montreal. There were bombs at our university, which was just on the outskirts of Westmount. I remember one went off in a letterbox in front of the university. We thought it was a joke! We didn't believe it was anything more until we saw all these policemen around. No, I was never afraid. In 1963 there was a whole series of bombs and some people were arrested, people we knew in the student milieu.

At one point we learned that one of the boys we knew had been arrested for planting bombs. He was a friend of one of the students at school. This young girl continued to see him after he went to prison. They got married and when he came out of prison he finished his studies in New York. Now they are raising a family. But he was in prison seven or eight years.

The young people who did it came from a bourgeois environment and often from the elite families. I often had the impression that they were children who did what their parents had not dared to do. We French like to talk a lot about what needs to be done, but it often just remains talk.

Well, these people took some action and did what their friends and families perhaps only talked about. They did kill people, but that was not their intention. That was a risk they took. Personally, I think that the people who are in jail today should be parolled. If you think of other types of criminals who do horrible things—perhaps to my mind at least, worse than that—and who are freed long before the end of their sentence...

Everyone here in Temiscaming knows that I am a separatist and that I lived in Montreal in an intellectual milieu. When I came here three years ago, I noticed that the French spoken in Temiscaming is clearly influenced by the English, especially the sentence structures. Here, most people form their French sentences like you would an English sentence. For instance, they will end with a preposition, which is not possible in French. You have to finish with a noun or an article in French. So, for me, it is a city which is already been ruined by the anglophone population.

Of course this was a closed English company town for years, so it's not surprising the language has deteriorated. The company controlled the municipality and controlled the school board, even the schools were English schools. The elementary schools were French and English, but the high school level was unilingual English, which meant that the francophones did not continue their studies because of the language barrier. They stopped in the middle of the school year because they were unable to follow the class work, and they became cheap labour for the pulp and paper mill. This went on from after the First World War to the mid-'60s, when the Lesage government opened up all the closed towns.

Personally, I will vote for independence. I think that independence will give people back some of the pride they have lost over these years of English domination.

Chapter **8**

Conclusion

The Quebec-Canada problem is as complex as the wide spectrum of feelings, grievances, and viewpoints voiced by the people in these pages. Preparing this book has been a profound learning experience for me as an English Canadian, and its greatest value has been in helping to identify the major irritants and aspirations of the average Québécois who have brought the PQ from oblivion to power in nine short years.

Towards the middle of my journey it became clear that the PQ's November 15 victory was neither an electoral fluke nor simply a vote for René Lévesque, nor a straight anti-Liberal backlash. It was a vote for cultural survival. A large majority of PQ supporters are motivated by a very real fear and concern for the survival of their language and culture and see the Parti Québécois as the most effective defenders of that cause. It is significant that Bill 101, the first major piece of legislation enacted by Quebec's new government, deals directly with this issue of cultural survival on educational, economic, and political levels. Despite what some public opinion polls have contended, it is a delusion to think that Bill 101 is unpopular or seen as an extremist measure by the majority in Quebec. Quite the opposite: I left Quebec convinced that Bill 101 enjoys the support of a substantial majority of the francophone population and that the Lévesque government would be returned with an increased popular vote if an election were held tomorrow. Of course Bill 101 and the Quebec government remain generally unpopular among non-francophone Quebeckers, but this does not seriously threaten the PQ's power base.

It is mistaken and superficial to conclude, as many have, that Bill 101 and Quebec's policy of official unilingualism mean a rejection of bilingualism and the English language. These measures are seen by most PQ supporters as possibly extreme but necessary tactics to reverse the progressive anglicization of Quebec and particularly Montreal, and to re-establish the primacy of French in Quebec's economic and cultural life. While many of the people I interviewed see cross-Canada bilingualism as an unrealistic goal of the federal government, this does not mean they are opposed to personal bilingualism. In fact, I failed to meet a single person, unilingual French or otherwise, opposed to bilingualism for themselves or their children. It should also be remembered that Quebec is still the only province in Canada where second-language school instruction is mandatory. When PQ supporters say their aim is to make Quebec as French as Ontario is English, they mean it in the non-discriminatory sense.

I found little evidence to support the criticism that the new Quebec nationalism is excessively isolationist, anti-English, or tribalistic. In the course of meeting hundreds of people — often on an impromptu basis — I was never on any occasion treated with anything less than courtesy. I repeat — never. A handshake, eye contact, a genuine smile, an invittion to stay for lunch — this was the personal reality I experienced. It may have been pure coincidence but I met no Russel Smiths (see Chapter 4) among the French. But unfortunately, as the reader will know by now, French people do not always fare so well in English Canada. Too many times francophone tourists return to Quebec with stories of unpleasant personal experiences in the other provinces arising from the attitude of superiority they encountered among certain English-speaking Canadians who view the French language and culture as a sort of folkloric decoration not to be taken seriously. Separatists are not born — they are converted, and for some the conversion began outside Quebec. The rednecks and know-nothings of this country, while fortunately an endangered species, are the best friends the separatist movement could have.

Two broad views of English Canada as seen through Québécois eyes began to come into focus after spending several months in Quebec. First, there is a widespread uneasiness in Quebec concerning Western Canada's view of the French language and Quebec's position in Confederation. Rightly or wrongly, many Québécois see the West as uncomprehending of Quebec and Canadian history and, at the gut level, anti-French. Quebeckers are perhaps particularly sensitive to anti-French sentiment in the West because they are aware that not so long ago (less than 100 years) present-day Alberta, Saskatchewan, and Manitoba were predominately French. The crushing of the Riel Rebellion and the systematic discrimination against French educational rights in the schools of the West ensured that these provinces would become English-speaking, helped confine the French fact to Quebec, and made French Canadian separatism a geographic possibility.

Secondly, Québécois tend to see English Canadians as a people at times still too rooted sentimentally in their colonial past, while increasingly beguiled by American popular culture. Canada waited 98 years before adopting its own flag, and many of those who objected to the Official Languages Act in 1969 or the use of French in aviation today think of CBS or NBC reception on cable television as almost a God-given right.

In addition to the recurring issues of language and culture, the interviews revealed other prevalent views. The Air Traffic Controllers dispute has been a pivotal issue in Quebec politics, working to the enormous advantage of the Parti Québécois. The unwillingness or inability of the federal Department of Transport to ensure the use of French in Canadian aviation is seen as evidence of the insensitivity and numerical tyranny of the English majority in this country, and became the most important single election issue favouring the PQ in 1976.

Similarly, the October Crisis of 1970 has worked to the advantage of the PQ by providing a dramatic example of federal "repression" and over-reaction and by isolating and ultimately destroying the violent fanatical fringe of Quebec nationalism and establishing the PQ as the moderate and legitimate spokesman for independence. The October Crisis also inflicted long-term damage on Prime Minister Trudeau's personal and political popularity in Quebec.

Quebeckers, like other Canadians, are an essentially nonviolent people who deplored the death of Pierre Laporte, but many still feel today that Ottawa's response to the crisis was overly severe. On the question of parole for the 14 FLQ prisoners currently in federal prisons in Quebec feelings are mixed. The overwhelming English sentiment favours continued imprisonment. Many French speakers, perhaps torn between their inherent nonviolence and their sympathy for the prisoners' ideals, were visibly uncomfortable when I asked this question. The younger and more highly educated were inclined to favour parole, while older middle-class individuals were often opposed.

Another clear impression I received is of the immense personal popularity of Prime Minister Lévesque, which seems to have grown in the past year. He is seen by many Quebeckers, French and English, as a corruption-free, personally candid, and politically moderate leader. The nationalist movement in Quebec includes many middle-class supporters who expressed great faith in René Lévesque while voicing concern that the PQ would take a more radical socialist direction without him in command.

Virtually all the people I talked to, regardless of racial background, consider themselves Quebeckers and are proud to live in Quebec. Emotionally and culturally, it would be no easy thing for an English-speaking Montrealer to decide on a move to Toronto, to Calgary or Vancouver.

Quebeckers also remember what other Canadians tend to forget: that the first people on this continent to consider themselves Canadian spoke French, not English, and francophones were still the majority in Canada until well into the 1800s. The first daily newspaper in Quebec was *Le Canadien*. One can still meet old Quebeckers who jokingly tell the visitor that they are the "true Canadians." At Confederation, Georges Etienne Cartier could say, *"Nous sommes Canadiens,"* while Sir John A. Macdonald was busily proclaiming, "A British subject I was born, a British subject I will die." Of course, France made the task of developing a distinct identity much easier by abandoning Quebec 218 years ago, and no number of medals or declarations of support from the Paris of today will produce a crop of latter-day colonials in Quebec. It is far too late for that. The Quebec culture is the unique self-assured expression of a people whose roots were firmly established here more than 200 years before Confederation. The question now is: Can that culture survive and flourish within the Canadian framework, or will Quebec separate?

It was widely predicted that the PQ would be defeated on November 15, 1976, just as it is being predicted today that the independence referendum will not pass. Of course if the referendum is rejected in 1979 and the Quebec government is dissatisfied with the constitutional changes offered by Ottawa, it can be expected to hold a second independence referendum and who but the foolhardy would attempt at this point to predict the outcome? With the advent of mass-based political parties, restrictions on campaign funding, and the use of the popular referendum, Quebec has entered the most democratic phase in its history where it appears that issues will be decided in the open through public debate and previously powerful special-interest groups, from the Church to the anglophone business community, will have lost their privileged positions. Partly as a result, Canada now faces the most immediate and real danger of any period in its 110-year history. However, I have not returned from Quebec a pessimist. I believe there is still time to reshape Confederation into a form that will endure, but the time available for discussion, negotiation and political change is decidedly limited — a matter of four to six years at the most.

There is a widespread desire in Quebec — cutting across the traditional political categories of age, social class, education, sex, urban-rural factors, and regional sentiment — for increased political and economic autonomy. Of course increased autonomy does not constitute outright independence. Many disparate political groups, from autonomists to radical *indépendantistes* to the occasionally reform-minded federalist, congregate comfortably beneath the Parti Québécois umbrella, while attaching very different meanings to the word "independence."

For many of the people I spoke with at length, being in favour of independence means wanting to attain greater independence as a people—ensuring that Quebec's unique historical and cultural position is clearly and officially recognized. They are seeking full rights to live, work, and prosper in French. It is more a pragmatic than a symbolic goal, which the majority of Quebeckers hope may be possible within a revised and more decentralized Canadian federalism. As just one Canadian, I am in basic agreement with these aspirations and objectives.

If English Canada can accept the fact that Quebec is unique and is entitled to special status within Confederation, then we will survive as a nation. The idea is hardly revolutionary. It goes back to the very beginning of this country, as Sir John A. Macdonald saw it:

"You must make friends of the French without sacrificing the status of your race or religion. You must respect their nationality. Treat them as a nation and they will act as free people generally do—call them a faction and they will become factious."

Quebec is waiting—waiting for English Canada's reaction to the prospect of a new federalism that recognizes Quebec as the home of one of this country's two founding peoples. Once the Canadian public and their federal and provincial politicians have accepted the need for serious constitutional revisions, leading to a transfer of power and jurisdiction to the provinces, we will be in a position to negotiate a new federalism and a new stability for Canada.

The BNA Act is not inscribed in stone: it has been amended in the past and is in need of extensive amendment today.

The federal-provincial distribution of powers is as follows:

Federal	Provincial	Shared
Foreign affairs and trade	Education	Civil rights
Money supply and currency	Sales tax	Income tax
Banking, interest rates	Hospitals and public health	Pensions
The military and R.C.M.P.	Liquor regulation	Social services and health care
The criminal code	Civil law	Agriculture
Postal service	Municipal affairs	The judicial system
Census and statistics		Regulation of corporations
Navigation and shipping		Maintenance of prisons
Coastal and inland fisheries		Economic development programs
Indian affairs		Labour relations
Unemployment insurance		Communications regulation
		Consumer affairs
		Resource management

In areas such as agriculture, resource management, social services, and broadcast regulation, Quebec's long-standing desire for increased provincial control already finds support among other provincial governments. Other areas for possible federal-provincial negotiation are patriation of the Constitution, guarantees of language and educational rights, immigration, fisheries regulation, assistance to the arts, civil rights, and personal taxation. The rights of the 789,185 anglophones in Quebec and the 926,400 francophones living in the other nine provinces must also be safeguarded. Quebec separation would mean the abandonment and eventual assimilation of these two substantial minorities. The federal-provincial constitutional discussions that lie ahead also offer an excellent opportunity to deal with the special problems of the Atlantic provinces, the Prairies, and the West in areas such as national transportation policy, fisheries management, and regional economic development. At the same time, there is nothing to prevent the nine English-speaking provinces from following Quebec's lead and introducing compulsory second-language instruction in their schools, while the nation's universities could phase in bilingualism as an entrance requirement by the mid-1980s.

Finally, I think the time is right for a confident and statesmanlike act on the part of the federal government: immediate consideration of parole for the FLQ prisoners who are eligible and who are judged nonviolent. Such an action would help heal some of the worst scars of the October Crisis and indicate Ottawa's confidence in the outcome of the Canada-Quebec dialogue.

Before real reform can begin though, anglophones must stop feeling defensive and personally threatened by Quebec's quest for greater autonomy. It does take some time and effort for a non-Quebecker (and many anglo-Quebeckers) to appreciate how culturally isolated and threatened the French people on this continent feel. I remember very well during the first weeks of my journey how defensive I felt every time someone argued for increased Quebec or provincial autonomy. I felt that they were trying to take something away from me or my country. Then slowly I began to see that their primary motivation was the very human and understandable desire to preserve a language, culture, and way of life that are a part of my heritage too. We will all—French and English—be richer culturally and intellectually, more socially adaptable, and more worldly in outlook for living in a bilingual, bicultural society. A return to official unilingualism is a return to a cultural and intellectual straitjacket that increasingly belongs to the past. Canada can mean much more to its people than a rewarding economic superstructure. If we lose our bicultural character, however imperfect and awkward at times, we will lose ourselves.

The French have endured on this continent for more than 350 years and have shown their determination to be much more than a folkloric remnant of a bygone age. French and English have coexisted in this land for 220 years. We are no longer a "young" country. This is an exciting time to be alive and participating in Canada's most important national debate since Confederation. We have come too far together as a people to just give up and allow ourselves to go our separate ways now—it would be too sad and in the end quite unnecessary.

There will always be some space between Canadians and *Canadiens*, but with understanding and compromise that space need not become a wall.

Appendix A

Bill 101:
Charter of the French Language

(The Official Summary)

EXPLANATORY NOTES

This bill, which is to replace the Official Language Act passed in 1974, declares in section 1 that French is the official language of Québec.

In Chapter II, the act will recognize certain fundamental language rights, namely,

— the right of every person to have the civil administration, semipublic agencies and business firms communicate with him in French, and to speak French in deliberative assembly;

— the right of workers to carry on their activities in French;

— the right of consumers to be informed and served in French;

— the right of persons eligible for instruction to receive that instruction in French.

In Chapter III, the act will declare French to be the language of the legislature and the courts.

The statutes and regulations will be drafted in French, and only the French text will be official. However, an English translation of the legislative bills, statutes and regulations is to be printed and published by the civil administration.

Artificial persons addressing themselves to the judicial or quasi-judicial bodies will do so in French, and will use the official language in pleading before them, unless all the parties to the action agree to plead in English.

Procedural documents issued by bodies discharging judicial or quasi-judicial functions or drafted and sent by the advocates will be drawn up in French. It will be permitted to draft them in another language if the natural person to whom they are addressed agrees.

Judgments rendered will be required to be drawn up in French or to be accompanied with a duly authenticated French version; only the French version of the judgment will be official.

In Chapter IV, the act will make French the language of the civil administration.

It will prescribe that the official language is to be used to the exclusion of any other in the following cases:

— in the designation of the Government, the government departments, the other agencies of the civil administration and the services thereof, subject to certain exceptions;

— in the written communications of the civil administration with other governments and with artificial persons established in Québec;

— in the written communications between the different agencies of the civil administration;

— in signs and posters erected by the civil administration, with certain exceptions;

— in traffic signs.

It will make the use of French obligatory, without, however, forbidding the use of another language, in the following cases:

— in the drafting of texts and documents of the civil administration;

— in written internal communications within the agencies of the civil administration;

— in contracts entered into by the civil administration in Québec.

The use of either French or another language will be optional, under the act, in the following cases in particular:

— in correspondence between the civil administration and natural persons who address it in a language other than French;

— in contracts between the civil administration and parties outside Québec;

— in internal communications in school bodies in which the majority of the persons administered speak a language other than French and in school departments that give instruction in a language other than French.

In order to be appointed, transferred or promoted to an office in the civil administration, an appropriate knowledge of the official language will be required.

Municipal and school bodies, the health services and the social services will be required to comply with sections 15 to 23 before the end of 1983 and, upon the coming into force of this act, to take the required measures to attain that objective.

In Chapter V, the act will require the public utility firms, the professional corporations and the members of the professional corporations to ensure that their services are available in the official language, and to use the official language in their texts and documents intended for the public, and in their communications with the public administration and with artificial persons.

The professional corporations

— are to be designated by their French names alone;

—will not be authorized to issue permits except to persons whose knowledge of the official language is appropriate to the practise of their profession;

— will be allowed, however, to issue temporary permits valid for one year, renewable, only twice, with the authorization of the Office de la langue française, to persons whose knowledge of the official language does not meet the requirements of the act;

— will be allowed, furthermore, with prior authorization of the Office, to issue a restricted permit to a person already authorized to practise his profession outside Québec, authorizing him to practise his profession for the account of a sole employer, in a position that does not involve his dealing with the public.

In Chapter VI, the act will require employers to draw up their written communications to their employees and their offers of employment of promotion in the official language.

Collective agreements, the schedules to them, and decisions rendered pursuant to them or under the Labour Code will be required to be drafted in French, on pain of nullity.

An employer will be prohibited from dismissing, demoting of transferring a member of his staff for the sole reason that he is exclusively French-speaking or that he has insufficient knowledge of a particular language other than the official language. Any contravention of this provision, in addition to being an offence against this act, will give an employee the same entitlement to vindicate his rights under the Labour Code as if he were dismissed for union activities.

An employer will also be prohibited from making the obtaining of an employment or office dependent upon the knowledge of a language other than the official language, unless the nature of the duties requires the knowledge of that other language.

Associations of employees will be required to communicate with their members in French.

The chapter on the language of labour relations will be deemed a part of every collective agreement.

Chapter VII deals with the language of commerce and business.

The inscriptions on a product or on its wrapping or on a leaflet, brochure or card supplied with it will be required to be in French. The same rule will apply to catalogues, brochures and folders, toys and games, contracts pre-determined by one party, job-application forms, order forms, invoices, receipts and quittances, signs and posters and firm names.

French alone will be permitted on signs and posters and in firm names, with certain exceptions.

The chapter provides for certain cases where one language other than French will be allowed:

— in the labelling of certain products;

— in contracts pre-determined by one party, for instance, if that is the express wish of the parties;

— advertising carried in news media that publish in another language;

—messages of a religious, humanitarian, political or ideological nature, if for a non-profit motive.

In Chapter VIII, the act will prescribe that the instruction given in the kindergarten classes and in the elementary and secondary schools must be in French.

In derogation of that prescription, the following children, at the request of their father and mother, will be able to receive their instruction in English:

(a) a child whose father or mother received his or her elementary instruction in English, in Québec;

(b) a child whose father or mother, domiciled in Québec on the date of the coming into force of this act, received his or her elementary instruction in English outside Québec;

(c) a child who, in his last year of school before the coming into force of this act, was lawfully receiving his instruction in English, in Québec, in a public kindergarten class or in an elementary or secondary school;

(d) the younger brothers and sisters of a child described in paragraph c.

The Minister of Education will be authorized to empower such persons as he may designate to verify and decide on children's eligibility for instruction in English, even if they are receiving their instruction in French.

A certificate of eligibility obtained fraudulently or on the basis of a false representation will be void. Furthermore, the Minister of Education will have authority to revoke a certificate of eligibility issued in error.

An appeal will lie to an appeals committee established for that purpose by the Government from the decisions of the school bodies and the persons designated by the Minister of Education, regarding eligibility for instruction in English, and from the decisions of the Minister of Education revoking certificates of eligibility issued in error.

School bodies not already giving instruction in English will not be required to introduce it.

To obtain a secondary school leaving certificate, it will be necessary to have a speaking and writing knowledge of French.

The Government will have authority to make regulations extending the scope of section 73 to include such persons as may be contemplated in any reciprocity agreement that may be concluded between the Government of Québec and another province.

Nothing in the proposed act will prevent the use of an Amerindic language in providing instruction to the Amerinds.

The act recognizes Cree and Inutitunt as the languages of instruction in the territories of the Cree School Board and the Kativik School Board, and the other languages in use in the Cree and Inuit communities of Québec on the date of the signing of the Agreement contemplated in section 1 of the Act approving the Agreement concerning James Bay and Northern Québec.

The provisions governing the languages of instruction in the Cree and Inuit communities will also apply, with the necessary changes, to the Naskapi of Schefferville.

Chapter IX contains provisions of a general nature; thus,

—the act will allow the use of a language other than French wherever it does not require the use of the official language exclusively;

—it will be lawful to draft or publish in French alone, anything that by law must be drafted or published in French and English;

—wherever publication in several languages is permitted, it will be required to display the French version at least as prominently as every other language;

— nothing will prevent the use of a language in derogation of where international usage requires it.

—the Crees, the Inuit and the Naskapi of Schefferville will have the right to use their respective languages and will be exempt from the application of most sections of the act in the territories they occupy, respectively, and in their administrative bodies. It will be an objective of these bodies, however, to gradually introduce French into their administration. The Indian reserves are not subject to this act.

Title II establishes the Office de la langue française, consisting of five members, defines powers and duties of the Office, sets up terminology committees, and attaches the Geographical Commission (to which it gives the new title of Commission de toponymie) to the Office.

Specific functions of the Office de la langue française will be to verify whether the agencies of the civil administration are taking the required measures to comply with the act and to see that business firms having fifty or more employees adopt and apply francization programmes and obtain francization certificates.

Each business firm employing one hundred or more employees will be required to form a francization committee before 30 November 1977, composed of at least six persons, at least one-third of whom are worker representatives. The function of this committee will be to analyse the language situation in the firm, and, where necessary, adopt and apply a francization programme.

The Office will have authority to suspend or revoke the francization certificate in the case of a contravention. The bill provides for an appeal from any decision of the Office to deny, suspend or revoke a francization certificate.

The office, with the approval of the minister responsible for the application of the act, will be authorized to demand that any firm employing less than fifty persons prepare and implement a francization programme.

Title III establishes a Commission de surveillance de la langue française, which will be responsible for inquiring into contraventions of the act and preparing the records for the Attorney-General, who will have power to institute proceedings under the act.

Title IV establishes the Conseil de la langue française.

Title V deals with offences and penalties.

Finally, the bill contains a number of transitional and miscellaneous provisions. The Schedule lists the various constituents of the civil administration and the parapublic agencies.

Appendix B

A Quebec – Canada Chronology

Quebec		Canada	
1534	Jacques Cartier lands on Gaspé Peninsula.		
1535	Cartier sails up St. Lawrence to site of Quebec City and Montreal.		
1608	Champlain establishes settlement at Quebec.		
1625	Arrival of the Jesuits.		
1629	Quebec captu..d by the British.		
1632	Quebec returned to France by treaty.		
1634	Trois-Rivières founded.		
1642	Montreal founded.		
1681	Quebec population: 9,677.		
1682	La Salle descends the Mississippi to the Gulf of Mexico.		
1737	Opening of road from Montreal to Quebec.		
		1745	French fortress of Louisburg, Nova Scotia, captured by British.
		1749	Halifax founded.

Quebec		Canada	
1759	Battle of Plains of Abraham. Quebec captured by General James Wolfe for England.		
1760	Montreal surrenders.	1760	Establishment of British military régime.
1763	Quebec population: 65,000.	1763	Treaty of Paris. New France granted to Britain.
		1774	Quebec Act guaranteeing French language and religious rights in Quebec passed by British Parliament.
1775 1776	Quebec invaded by American armies; repulsed by English and French defenders.		
		1783	Emigration of Loyalists from the United States.
		1791	Constitutional Act, dividing Canada into Upper Canada (Ontario) and Lower Canada (Quebec).
		1793	Settlement of York (Toronto) begins.
1806	Foundation of *Le Canadien*, Quebec's first newspaper.		
		1812 1814	War between Canada and the United States.
1822	Act of Union, uniting Upper and Lower Canada.		
1825	Quebec population: 479,288.	1825	Ontario population: 157, 923.
1837	Rebellion against British authorities led by Louis Joseph Papineau.		
1838	Declaration of Independence of Lower Canada. Rebellion defeated; 12 patriots hanged in Montreal.		
		1840	Act of Union, reuniting Upper and Lower Canada.

Quebec	Canada
1851 Quebec population: 890,261.	1851 Adoption of decimal currency by Canada; first Canadian postage stamps. Ontario population: 952,004.
1864 Quebec and Charlottetown conferences discuss possible Confederation.	
	1867 Confederation. Canada becomes independent with passage of the British North American Act; provinces: Quebec, Ontario, Nova Scotia, New Brunswick. Prime Minister: Sir John A. Macdonald.
	1870 Manitoba enters Confederation.
1871 Quebec population: 1,191,516	1871 British Columbia enters Confederation. Canada population: 3,689,256.
	1875 Supreme Court created.
1879 Quebec-Montreal-Ottawa Railway completed.	1879 Protective national tariff established by Macdonald.
1883 Colonization of Temiscaming started.	
1885 Demonstrations throughout	1885 Métis revolt. Louis Riel hanged.
1886 Quebec protesting Louis Riel's hanging.	1886 Inauguration of trans-Canadian railway.
	1890
	1897 Manitoba schools affair.
1901 Quebec population: 1,648,898.	1901 Canada population: 5,371,315.
	1905 Saskatchewan and Alberta enter Confederation.
1912 Quebec granted territory of Ungava by federal government.	
	1917 W.W.I. Conscription introduced by federal

Quebec		Canada	

<table>
<tr><td></td><td></td><td></td><td>government. Women given the vote in federal elections.</td></tr>
<tr><td></td><td></td><td>1931</td><td>Statute of Westminster: Britain relinquishes involvement in foreign affairs of Commonwealth countries.</td></tr>
<tr><td>1936</td><td>Union Nationale Government of Maurice Duplessis elected.</td><td></td><td></td></tr>
<tr><td>1940</td><td>Quebec women granted the right to vote in provincial elections.</td><td></td><td></td></tr>
<tr><td>1942</td><td>W.W.II. Conscription introduced. Anti-conscription Bloc Populaire Canadien party formed.</td><td>1942</td><td>Plebiscite on Conscription held (approved).</td></tr>
<tr><td>1948</td><td>Quebec flag adopted.</td><td></td><td></td></tr>
<tr><td></td><td></td><td>1949</td><td>Newfoundland enters Confederation after two referenda. (51% in favour)</td></tr>
<tr><td>1951</td><td>Quebec population: 4,055,681.</td><td>1951</td><td>Canada population: 14,009,42.</td></tr>
<tr><td>1957</td><td>l'Alliance Laurentienne, Quebec's first separatist party, formed.</td><td></td><td></td></tr>
<tr><td>1959</td><td>Premier Duplessis dies.</td><td>1959</td><td>St. Lawrence Seaway opened.</td></tr>
<tr><td>1960</td><td>Quiet Revolution begins with election of Liberal government of Jean Lesage. René Lévesque enters politics as successful Liberal candidate. Formation of Le Rassemblement pour l'Indépendance Nationale, most enduring pre-PQ separatist movement.</td><td></td><td></td></tr>
<tr><td>1962</td><td>Nationalization of Quebec's hydro companies, organized by the province's Minister of</td><td></td><td></td></tr>
</table>

Quebec	*Canada*
Natural Resources René Lévesque.	
1963 First wave of FLQ bombings in Montreal.	
1964 Ministry of Education established.	
	1965 University of Montreal law professor Pierre Elliot Trudeau enters federal politics as a successful Liberal candidate.
	Canadian flag adopted.
1966 Quebec Legislative Assembly renamed the National Assembly.	
1967 Montreal hosts World Fair, Expo 67.	1967 Peliminary report of Royal Commission on Bilingualism and Biculturalism.
General Charles de Gaulle exclaims "Vive le Québec Libre!" in Montreal address.	
René Lévesque quits the Quebec Liberal Party.	
1968 Parti Québécois founded, René Lévesque president of party.	1968 Pierre Trudeau elected Prime Minister of Canada.
	1969 Official Languages Act.
1970 PQ receives 23% of the vote in provincial election.	1970 Voting age lowered to 18.
	October Crisis: kidnapping of Cross and Laporte, War Measures Act, eventual exile and imprisonment for FLQ members involved
1971 Victoria Charter: federal attempt to repatriate Constitution. Rejected by Quebec.	1971 Federal-provincial constitutional conference at Victoria.
1973 Parti Québécois receives 30% of vote in provincial election.	1973 R.C.M.P. breaks into Parti Québécois headquarters in Montreal.
1976 Election of Parti Québécois government headed by	1976 Dispute over use of French in aviation. Ottawa

Quebec	*Canada*
Premier René Lévesque.	established committee to study the matter.
1977 Quebec population: 6,283,100.	1977 Canada population: 23,291,000.
Passage of Bill 101 by National Assembly.	Prime Minister Trudeau offers to renegotiate Canadian Constitution.
Appointment of Quebec Parliamentary Commission to supervise the conduct of referendum on independence for Quebec.	
René Lévesque makes official visit to France.	

Appendix C

Popular Vote by Party in Quebec Provincial Elections

(1956-76)

1956	Liberal 44.5		1970	Liberal 45.5
	Union Nationale 52.0			Union Nationale 20.0
1960	Liberal 51.3			Parti Québécois 23.5
	Union Nationale 46.6			Créditiste 11.0
1962	Liberal 56.9		1973	Liberal 54.6
	Union Nationale 42.1			Union Nationale 5.0
1966	Liberal 47.2			Parti Québécois 30.3
	Union Nationale 40.9			Créditiste 10.99
	RIN 5.6		1976	Liberal 33.7
				Union Nationale 18.2
				Parti Québécois 41.3
				Créditiste 4.6

*Standings in the National Assembly
as of Nov. 15, 1976:*

Parti Québécois	71
Liberal	26
Union Nationale	11
Conservative	1
Other	1
TOTAL	110

Some Quebec — Canada Statistics

1   Mother Tongue of Quebeckers   Mother Tongue of All Canadians
(1976)   (1976)
Total Population: 6,234,445   Total Population: 22,992,605

French	79.8%	English	61.1
English	12.8	French	25.5
Italian	2.0	German	2.1
German	.4	Italian	2.1
Ukrainian	.2	Ukrainian	1.2
Other	2.8	Other	5.6
Not stated	2.0	Not stated	1.9

2   First Official Language of Federal Civil Servants, 1977

	English	*French*
Executive	81.9	18.1
Scientific and Professional	79.9	20.1
Administration and Foreign Service	73.8	26.2
Technical	82.0	18.0
Secretarial/Clerical	69.7	30.3
Operational	73.3	26.7
TOTAL	73.9	26.1

Total Strength of Federal Civil Service by
First Official Language: (1977)
English   196,894
French   69,720

SOURCE: Statistics Canada

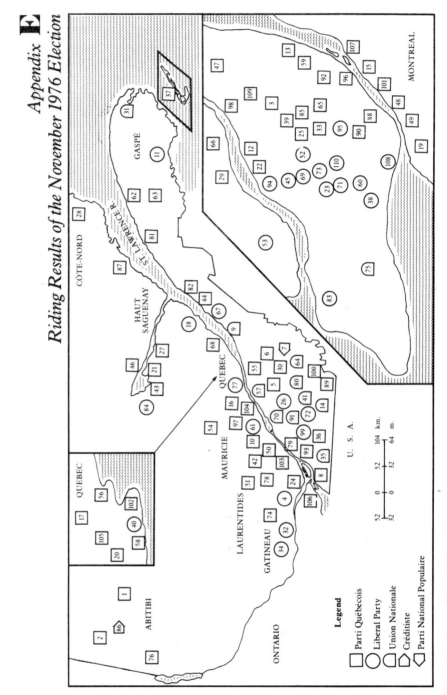

Appendix E

Riding Results of the November 1976 Election

1—Abitibi-Est, P.Q., Jean-Paul Bordeleau
2—Abitibi-Ouest, P.Q., François Gendron
3—Anjou, P.Q., Pierre-Marc Johnson
4—Argenteuil, P.L., Zoël Saindon (re-elec.)
5—Arthabaska, P.Q., Jacques Baril
6—Beauce-Nord, P.Q., Adrien Ouellette
7—Beauce-Sud, P.N.P., Fabien Roy, (re-elec.)
8—Beauharnois, P.Q., Laurent Lavigne
9—Bellechasse, U.N., Bertrand Goulet
10—Berthier, P.Q., Jean-Guy Mercier
11—Bonaventure, P.L., Gérard-D. Levesque (re-elec.)
12—Bourassa, P.Q., Patrice Laplante
13—Bourget, P.Q., Camille Laurin
14—Brome-Missisquoi, U.N., Armand Russell
15—Chambly, P.Q., Denis Lazure
16—Champlain, P.Q., Marcel Gagnon
17—Charlesbourg, P.Q., Denis de Belleval
18—Charlevoix, P.L., Raymond Mailloux (re-elec.)
19—Châteauguay, P.Q., Roland Dussault
20—Chauveau, P.Q., Louis O'Neill
21—Chicoutimi, P.Q., Marc-André Bédard (re-elec.)
22—Crémazie, P.Q., Guy Tardif
23—D'Arcy McGee, P.L., Victor Goldbloom (re-elec.)
24—Deux-Montagnes, P.Q., Pierre de Bellefeuille
25—Dorion, P.Q., Lise Payette
26—Drummond, P.Q., Michel Clair
27—Dubuc, P.Q., Hubert Desbiens
28—Duplessis, P.Q., Denis Perron
29—Fabre, P.Q., Bernard Landry
30—Frontenac, P.Q., Gilles Grégoire
31—Gaspé, U.N., Michel LeMoignan
32—Gatineau, P.L., Michel Gratton (re-elec.)

33—Gouin, P.Q., Rodrigue Tremblay
34—Hull, P.L., Oswald Parent (re-elec.)
35—Huntingdon, U.N., Claude Dubois
36—Iberville, P.Q., Jacques Beauséjour
37—Iles-de-la-Madeleine, P.Q., Denise Leblanc
38—Jacques-Cartier, P.L., Noël Saint-Germain (re-elec.)
39—Jeanne-Mance, P.Q., Henri Laberge
40—Jean-Talon, P.L., Raymond Garneau (re-elec.)
41—Johnson, U.N., Maurice Bellemare (re-elec.)
42—Joliette-Montcalm, P.Q., Guy Chevrette
43—Jonquière, P.Q., Claude Vaillancourt
44—Kamouraska-Témiscouata, P.Q., Léonard Lévesque
45—L'Acadie, P.L., Thérèse Lavoie-Roux
46—Lac-Saint-Jean, P.Q., Jacques Brassard
47—Lalontaine, P.Q., Marcel Léger (re-elec.)
48—Laporte, P.Q., Pierre Marois
49—Laprairie, P.Q., Gilles Michaud
50—L'Assomption, P.Q., Jacques Parizeau
51—Laurentides-Labelle, P.Q., Jacques Léonard
52—Laurier, P.L., André Marchand (re-elec.)
53—Laval, P.L., Jean-Noël Lavoie (re-elec.)
54—Laviolette, P.Q., Jean-Pierre Jolivet
55—Lévis, P.Q., Jean Garon
56—Limoilou, P.Q., Raymond Gravel
57—Lotbinière, U.N., Rodrigue Biron
58—Louis-Hébert, P.Q., Claude Morin
59—Maisonneuve, P.Q., Robert Burns (re-elec.)
60—Marguerite-Bourgeoys, P.L., Fernand Lalonde (re-elec.)
61—Maskinongé, P.L., Yvon Picotte (re-elec.)
62—Matane, P.Q., Yves Bérubé
63—Matapédia, P.Q., Léopold Marquis

64—Mégantic-Compton, U.N., Fernand Grenier
65—Mercier, P.Q., Gérald Godin
66—Mille-Iles, P.Q., Guy Joron
67—Montmagny-L'Islet, P.L., Julien Giasson (re-elec.)
68—Montmorency, P.Q., Clément Richard
69—Mont-Royal, P.L., J.B.J. Ciaccia (re-elec.)
70—Nicolet-Yamaska, U.N., Serge Fonfaine
71—Notre-Dame-de-Grâce, P.L., Bryce Mackasey
72—Orford, P.L., Georges Vaillancourt (re-elec.)
73—Outremont, P.L., André Raynauld
74—Papineau, P.Q., Jean Alfred
75—Pointe-Claire, U.N., William F. Shaw
76—Pontiac-Témiscamingue, P.L., Jean-Guy Larivière (re-elec.)
77—Portneuf, P.L., Michel Pagé (re-elec.)
78—Prévost, P.Q., Jean-Guy Cardinal
79—Richelieu, P.Q., Maurice Martel
80—Richmond, U.N., Yvon Brochu
81—Rimouski, P.Q., Alain Marcoux
82—Rivière-du-Loup, P.Q., Jules Boucher
83—Robert-Baldwin, P.L., John O'Gallagher
84—Roberval, P.L., Robert Lamontagne (re-elec.)
85—Rosemont, P.Q., Gilbert Paquette
86—Rouyn-Noranda, R.C., Camil Samson (re-elec.)
87—Saguenay, P.Q., Lucien Lessard (re-elec.)
88—Sainte-Anne, P.Q., Jean-Marc Lacoste
89—Saint-François, P.Q., Real Rancourt
90—Saint-Henri, P.Q., Jacques Couture
91—Saint-Hyacinthe, U.N., Fabien Cordeau
92—Saint-Jacques, P.Q., Claude Charron (re-elec.)
93—Saint-Jean, P.Q., Jérôme Proulx

94—Saint-Laurent, P.L., Claude E. Forget
  (re-elec.)
95—Saint-Louis, P.L., Harry Blank (re-elec.)
96—Sainte-Marie, P.Q., Guy Bisaillon
97—Saint-Maurice, P.Q., Yves Duhaime
98—Sauvé, P.Q., Jacques-Yvan Morin (re-elec.)
99—Shefford, P.L., Richard Verreault (re-elec.)
100—Sherbrooke, P.Q., Gérard Gosselin
101—Taillon, P.Q., René Lévesque
102—Taschereau, P.Q., Richard Guay
103—Terrebonne, P.Q., Élie Fallu
104—Trois-Rivières, P.Q., Denis Vaugeois
105—Vanier, P.Q., Jean-François Bertrand
106—Vaudreuil-Soulanges, P.Q., Louise Sauvé
  Cuerrier
107—Verchères, P.Q., Jean-Pierre Charbonneau
108—Verdun, P.L., Lucien Caron (re-elec.)
109—Viau, P.Q., Charles Lefebvre
110—Westmount, P.L., George Springate
  (re-elec.)

SOURCE: Rapports préliminaires des présidents d'élection — Élections générales 1976.
(Compilation du 30 novembre 1976).

*Provincial Second
Language Programs*

(1976-77)

	Total Enrolment	2nd Language Enrolment	% of Total	Minutes per wk.
Newfoundland	157,430	67,196	42.7	137
PEI	26,915	16,203	60.2	132
Nova Scotia	195,692	87,404	44.7	151
New Brunswick	107,068	70,926	66.2	149
Ontario	1,854,678	839,821	45.3	139
Manitoba	215,865	85,021	39.4	127
Saskatchewan	217,627	56,685	26.0	159
Alberta	435,741	115,945	26.6	126
British Columbia	535,375	152,989	28.6	134
TOTAL (9 provinces)	3,746,391	1,492,190	39.8	139
Quebec	1,108,615	719,337	64.9	137

SOURCE: Statistics Canada. Education in Canada is a provincial responsibility under the BNA Act. The 1977 Report of the Commissioner for Official Languages provides (pp. 188-189) the disturbing finding that second language enrolments at the high school level in *all* Canadian provinces except Quebec have dropped substantially between 1970-71 and 1976-77. Quebec is the only Canadian province in which minority language rights have been in full effect since Confederation. British Columbia, Prince Edward Island, Nova Scotia, and Newfoundland (as of 1976) do not even make mention of second language rights in their provincial education acts.

Glossary

Air Traffic Controllers Dispute   Disagreement over the status of the French language in Canadian aviation. (See also page 159.)

Bill 22   Quebec language law enacted by the Bourassa Liberal government in 1974.

Bill 101   Comprehensive PQ language bill replacing Bill 22 in August, 1977.

British North America Act (BNA)   Act of British Parliament in 1867 establishing Canadian independence and defining the federal-provincial sharing of powers.

CBC   Canadian Broadcasting Corporation, the state-financed ntional radio and television service, with English network headquarters in Toronto and the French ivision, *Radio-Canada*, in Montreal.

CEGEP   *Collège d'enseignement général et professionel*, part of Quebec's secondary educational system between high school and university, offering two- to three-year academic and non-academic programs.

Canadien   The original French word identifying a resident of North America.

Chansonniers   Quebec popular singers.

FLQ   *Front de Libération du Québec*, a Quebec-based terrorist organization active in the 1960s and early '70s, dedicated to the achievement of independence by violent means.

Federalism   A system of government based on the sharing of powers between the national and regional authorities.

Federalist   One who supports Canadian national unity.

Francization   Policy of establishing and extending the use of French in political, economic, and social life in Quebec.

330

Indépendantiste   One who favours independence for Quebec.

Jean Lesage   Liberal Prime Minister of Quebec, 1960-66, a progressive who reruited younger highly educated people to government. He wrested greater provincial autonomy from Ottawa and initiated the Quiet Revolution (see below), and changed the title of his office from Premier to Prime Minister.

Joual   French spoken with Quebec accent and slang. The term is derived from the Quebec pronunciation of *cheval*, the French word for "horse."

MNA   Member of the National Assembly, also referred to a "deputy."

Maurice Duplessis   Leader of the Union Nationale Party and Premier of Quebec, 1936-39, 1944-59. A friend of the Catholic Church and business interests, and a Quebec nationalist.

National Assembly   Quebec's legislature, located in Quebec City.

November 15, 1976   Date of the election that made the Parti Québécois the government of Quebec.

October Crisis   Confrontation between the FLQ and the federal government in 1970, precipitated by two FLQ political kidnappings and the imposition of the War Measures Act by Ottawa, suspending all civil liberties. (See also page 28.)

Péquiste   One who supports the Parti Québécois (PQ).

Quebec City   Capital of the prvince, often referred to simply as Quebec.

Québécois   A resident of Quebec.

Quiet Revolution   Also known as *La Révolution Tranquille*. The rapid and far-reaching process of social, economic, and political reform in Quebec from the early to the late '60s. Its main features: an end to Quebec's political isolation, weakening of the influence of the Church, modernization of the educational system, and enlargement of government's role in economic and social affairs.

Referendum   referring of political questions to the electorate for a direct decision, such as the planned Q referendum on Quebec independence.

Robert Bourassa   Liberal Premier of Quebec, 1970-76.

Séparatiste   One who supports Quebec independence. The term has been discarded by most supporters of the cause, who now prefer the word *indépendantiste*.

Bibliography

History and Politics:

Canada Year Book. Ottawa: Queen's Printer, annual publication.

CARELESS, J. M. S., and R. CRAIG BROWN (eds.). *The Canadians*. Toronto: Macmillan Company of Canada, 1968. 2 vols.

COOK, RAMSAY. *French-Canadian Nationalism*. Toronto: Macmillan Company of Canada, 1969.

CREIGHTON, DONALD. *The Road to Confederation*. Toronto: Macmillan Company of Canada, 1964.

DESBARATS, PETER. *René*. Toronto: McClelland and Stewart, 1976.

Encyclopedia Canadiana. Toronto: Grolier, 1975.

JAY, RICHARD. *Languages in Conflict*. Toronto: McClelland and Stewart, 1972.

LÉVESQUE, RENÉ. *An Option for Quebec*. Toronto: McClelland and Stewart, 1968.

LAVER, J. A. *Canada: An Outline History*. Toronto: McGraw-Hill Ryerson, 1973.

McNAUGHT, KENNETH. *The Pelican History of Canada*. Markham: Penguin Books of Canada, 1969.

Preliminary Report of the Royal Commission on Bilingualism and Biculturalism. Ottawa: Queen's Printer, 1967.

RIOUX, MARCEL. *Quebec in Question*. Toronto: James Lorimer & Co., 1971.

SIMION, RICHARD (ed.). *Must Canada Fail?* Montreal: McGill-Queen's University Press, 1977.

SMILEY, DONALD. *Canada in Question: Federalism in the 70's*. Toronto: McGraw-Hill Ryerson, 1976.

SMITH, DENIS. *Bleeding Hearts, Bleeding Country*. Edmonton: Hurtig Publishers, 1971.

TRUDEAU, P. E. *Federalism and the French Canadians*. Toronto: Macmillan Company of Canada, 1968.

VALLIÈRES, PIERRE. *White Niggers of America:* Toronto: McClelland and *Stewart, 1971.*

Quebec Literature:

Note: all books cited are English translations. Publication dates refer to the translated work.

AQUIN, HUBERT. *Prochaine Episode*. Toronto: McClelland and Stewart, 1972.

BLAIS, MARIE-CLAIRE. *A Season in the Life of Emmanuel*. New York: Farrar, Straus & Giroux, 1966.

CARRIER, ROCH. *La Guerre, Yes Sir!* Toronto: Anansi, 1970.

FERRON, JACQUES. *Tales from an Uncertain Country*. Toronto: Anansi, 1972.

GÉLINAS, GRATIEN. *Tit-coq*. Toronto: Clarke, Irwin & Company, 1967.

GLASSCO, JOHN (ed.), *The Poetry of French Canada in Translation*. Toronto: Oxford University Press, 1970.

GODBOUT, JACQUES. *Knife on the Table*. Toronto: McClelland and Stewart, 1976.

HÉMON, LOUIS. *Maria Chapdelaine*. Toronto: Macmillan Company of Canada, 1973.

LEMELIN, ROGER. *The Plouffe Family*. Toronto: McClelland and Stewart, 1975.

ROY, GABRIELLE. *The Tin Flute*. Toronto: McClelland and Stewart, 1958.

SAVARD, JEAN-GUY. *The Master of the River*. Montreal: Harvest House, 1976.

TREMBLAY, MICHEL. *Les Belles-Soeurs*. Vancouver: Talonbooks, 1974.

Place Index